Beginner's Guide to Kotlin Programming

John Hunt

Beginner's Guide to Kotlin Programming

 Springer

John Hunt
Midmarsh Technology Limited
Marshfield, Wiltshire, UK

ISBN 978-3-030-80892-1   ISBN 978-3-030-80893-8 (eBook)
https://doi.org/10.1007/978-3-030-80893-8

This Springer imprint is published by the registered company Springer Nature Switzerland AG
The registered company address is: Gewerbestrasse 11, 6330 Cham, Switzerland

For my son, Adam. I could not be more proud of you and the man you have grown up to be.

Preface

So you are interested in Kotlin; you are not alone! Kotlin is now the second most popular programming language on the Java Virtual Machine (JVM). Only Java is more popular, with Scala and Clojure now significantly behind Kotlin in popularity.

The aim of this book is to introduce Kotlin and Android development to those with limited programming experience via a set of examples developed as the book progresses.

As such this book is divided into five parts; Part I introduces the functional side of the Kotlin programming language, Part II develops the object-oriented features in the Kotlin language, and Part III considers collections or container data types in Kotlin. Part IV expands on this with some of the features in Kotlin that allow concurrent programs to be written. The final part of the book, Part V, introduces Android Development using Kotlin.

Some of the key aspects of this book are as follows:

1. It assumes very little knowledge or experience of Kotlin or programming.
2. It provides a basic introduction to Kotlin but expands on those to end on advanced topics such as generic types and co-routines.
3. Kotlin's support for functional programming is presented.
4. Following on from introducing the basic ideas behind functional programming, the book presents how advanced functional concepts such as closures, currying and higher-order functions work in Kotlin.
5. The book also provides extensive coverage of object orientation and the features in Kotlin supporting classes, inheritance and interfaces.
6. The book includes exercises at the end of most chapters with online solutions.
7. Android mobile application development using Kotlin is also introduced. The focus is on the core concepts used within Android development such as Activities, Fragments and Views.
8. All code examples (and exercise solutions) are provided online in a GitHub repository.

Chapter Organization

Each chapter has a brief introduction, the main body of the chapter, followed by a list of (typically) online references that can be used for further reading.

Following this, there is typically an *Exercises* section that lists one or more exercises that build on the skills you will have learnt in that chapter.

Sample solutions to the exercises are available in a GitHub online repository that supports this book.

What You Need

You can of course just read this book; however, following the examples in this book will ensure that you get as much as possible out of the content.

For this, you will need a computer.

Kotlin is a cross platform programming language and as such you can use Kotlin on a Windows PC, a Linux box or an Apple Mac, etc. So you are not tied to a particular type of operating system; you can use whatever you have available. However you will need to install some software on that computer. At a minimum, you will need Kotlin and editor to write your programs in.

You will also need some form of editor in which to write your programs. There are numerous generic programming editors available for different operating systems with VIM on Linux, Notepad++ on Windows and Sublime Text on Windows and Macs being popular choices.

Using an integrated development environment (IDE) editor such as IntelliJ IDEA, however, will make writing and running your programs much easier.

Using an IDE

A very widely used IDE for Kotlin is IntelliJ IDEA (and for Android development its cousin the Android Studio IDE); it is not the only IDE for Kotlin by any means, but it is the most popular.

Other IDEs available for Kotlin include

- Visual Studio Code: This is a very good free editor from Microsoft that has really useful features https://code.visualstudio.com.
- Sublime Text is more of a text editor that color codes Kotlin; however, for a simple project it may be all you need https://www.sublimetext.com.
- Eclipse with the Kotlin plugin see https://marketplace.eclipse.org/content/kotlin-plugin-eclipse.

Downloading the IntelliJ IDEA IDE

IntelliJ is provided by JetBrains who make tools for a variety of different languages. The IntelliJ IDEA IDE can be downloaded from their site—see https://www.jetbra ins.com/. Look for the menu heading 'Tools' and select that. You will see a long list of tools, which should include IntelliJ IDEA.

Select the IntelliJ IDEA option. The resulting page has a lot of information on it; however, you only need to select the 'DOWNLOAD' option. Make sure that you select the operating system you use (there are options for Windows, macOS and Linux).

There are then two download options available: Professional and Community. The Professional version is charged for option while the Community version is free. For most of the work I do in Kotlin, the Community version is more than adequate, and it is therefore the version we will download and install (note with the Professional version you do get a free trial but will need to either pay for the full version at the end of the trial or reinstall the Community version at that point).

Assuming you selected the Community edition, the installer will now download, and you will be prompted to run it. Note you can ignore the request to subscribe if you want.

You can now run the installer and follow the instructions provided.

Conventions

Throughout this book, you will find a number of conventions used for text styles. These text styles distinguish different kinds of information.

Code words, variables and Kotlin values, used within the main body of the text, are shown using a Courier font. For example:

This program creates a top-level activity (the MainActivity). This activity can be used to display Fragments (Fragment) that act as sub-windows displayed within the activity.

In the above paragraph, MainActivity and Fragment are classes available in a Kotlin Android library.

A block of Kotlin code is set out as shown here:

```
print("Enter an integer: ")
val input = Scanner(System.`in`)
val num = input.nextInt()
if (num > 0) {
    println("$num is positive")
    println("$num squared is ${num * num}")
}
```

Note that keywords and strings are shown in bold font.

Any command line or user input is shown in italics and colored purple:

```
> kotlinc hello.kt
```

Or
```
Hello, world
Enter your name: John
Hello John
```

Example Code and Sample Solutions

The examples used in this book (along with sample solutions for the exercises at the end of most chapters) are available in a GitHub repository. GitHub provides a web interface to, and a server environment hosting, Git.

Git is a version control system typically used to manage source code files (such as those used to create systems in programming languages such as Kotlin but also Python, Java, C#, C++ and Scala). Systems such as Git are very useful for collaborative development as they allow multiple people to work on an implementation and to merge their work together. They also provide a useful historical view of the code (which also allows developers to roll back changes if modifications prove to be unsuitable).

If you already have Git installed on your computer, then you can clone (obtain a copy of) the repository locally using:

```
git clone https://github.com/johnehunt/kotlin-book.git
```

If you do not have Git, then you can obtain a zip file of the examples using

```
https://github.com/johnehunt/kotlin-book/archive/mas
ter.zip
```

It is of course possible to install Git yourself if you wish. To do this, see https://git-scm.com/downloads. Versions of the Git client for macOS, Windows and Linux/Unix are available here.

However, many IDEs such as IntelliJ IDEA come with Git support and so offer another approach to obtaining a Git repository.

For more information on Git, see http://git-scm.com/doc. This Git guide provides a very good primer and is highly recommended.

If you have any questions regarding the examples, please contact john.hunt10@gmail.com.

Marshfield, UK   John Hunt

Contents

Chapter 1
Introduction

What is Kotlin?

Kotlin is a general-purpose programming language in a similar vein to other programming languages that you might have heard of such as Java, Python, C++, JavaScript or Microsoft's C# and VisualBasic.

It is a relatively new language with Kotlin 1.0 only being released in February 2016. It originated with the JetBrains company, which initially unveiled Project Kotlin back in July 2011. It was intended as a new language that targeted the Java Virtual Machine (or JVM). The JVM is a runtime environment that allows programs to be executed on any platform (operating system) that supports the JVM. Although the JVM was originally designed to run programs written in the programming language Java; multiple languages can now be compiled to run on the JVM including Kotlin, Scala and Clojure.

As a language Kotlin has been gaining interest over recent years, particularly since Google announced that Kotlin was now the preferred language for Android application development in May 2019. It is particularly well supported in this respect in the Android Studio application development IDE (which is incidentally built on top of the JetBrains IntelliJ IDEA IDE).

This increased interest in Kotlin is driven by several factors:

1. Its flexibility and simplicity which makes it easy to learn.
2. The concise nature of its syntax (at least when compared with languages such as Java and C#).
3. Its ability to run on (almost) any operating system, but particularly the big three operating systems Windows, macOS and Linux.
4. The availability of a wide range of libraries that can be used to extend the basic features of the language. This is partly due to its compatibility with Java - which allows it to exploit the libraries built for that language.
5. The availability of a version of Kotlin that uses the JavaScript runtime provided by Node.js which offers another alternative to where and how it is used.

© The Author(s), under exclusive license to Springer Nature Switzerland AG 2021
J. Hunt, *Beginner's Guide to Kotlin Programming*,
https://doi.org/10.1007/978-3-030-80893-8_1

6.   The ability to run Kotlin natively on the host operating system which has potential performance benefits.
7.   It is free!

Kotlin itself is now looked after by the Kotlin Foundation. Originally most of the development costs associated with maintaining and developing the language are borne by JetBrains although other organisations such as Google are increasingly becoming involved with the language and the Kotlin Foundation.

Kotlin Versions

There have been several major version of Kotlin over the years. A brief history of the releases of the Kotlin language is given below:

- July 2011 JetBrains unveils project Kotlin.

  - Feb 2012 JetBrains open source Kotlin under Apache 2 license.

- Kotlin v 1.0 released 15th Feb 2016.
- 2017 Google announced first-class support for Kotlin on Android.
- Kotlin v1.1 released 1st March 2017.

  - introduced support for JavaScript runtime.

- Kotlin v1.2 released 28th Nov 2017.
- Kotlin v1.3 released 29th Oct 2018.

  - introduced coroutines for asynchronous programming.

- 7th May 2019 Google makes Kotlin its preferred language for Android development.
- 17th Aug 2020 Kotlin 1.4.
- 5th May 2021 Kotlin 1.5.

This raises the question which version of Kotlin to use. In this book we are focussing on Kotlin 1.4/1.5 as those are the current releases of Kotlin at the time of writing.

Kotlin Programming

There are several different programming paradigms that a programming language may allow developers to code in, these include:

- **Procedural Programming** in which a program is represented as a sequence of instructions that tell the computer what it should do explicitly. Procedures and/or functions are used to provide structure to the program. Control structures such as if statements and loop constructs are used to manage which steps are executed and how many times. Languages typifying this approach include C and Pascal.

- **Declarative Programming** languages that allow developers to describe how a problem should be solved. The language/environment then determines how the solution should be implemented. SQL (a database query language) is one of the most common declarative languages that you are likely to encounter.
- **Object Oriented Programming** is an approach that represent a system in terms of the objects that form that system. Each object can hold its own data (also known as state) as well as implement behaviour that defines what the object can do. An object oriented program is formed from a set of these objects co-operating together. Languages such as Java and C# typify the object oriented approach.
- **Functional Programming** languages decompose a problem into a set of functions. Each function is independent of any external state operating only on the inputs they received to generate their outputs. The programming languages Haskell and Clojure are examples of a functional programming language.

Some programming languages are considered to be *hybrid* languages; that is they allow developers to utilise a combination of difference approaches within the same program. Kotlin is an example of a *hybrid* programming language as it allows the developer to write very procedural code, to use objects in an object oriented manner and to write functional programs. Elements of each of these programming styles are covered in this book.

Kotlin Libraries

As well as the core language, there are numerous libraries available for Kotlin. These libraries extend the functionality of the language and make it much easier to develop applications. These libraries cover.

- RESTful Web Service frameworks such as Ktor.
- Database access libraries.
- Concurrency libraries.
- Logging frameworks allowing you to record information during the execution of an application that allows for detailed analysis at a later date.
- Testing and mocking libraries.
- Machine Learning and Data Analysis libraries.
- Mobile application development libraries.
- Image compression libraries.
- Games libraries such as KTX.

A very useful resource to look at, which introduces many of these libraries is https://www.kotlinresources.com/.

Kotlin Execution Environment

Kotlin can be executed in several ways as shown by the following diagram:

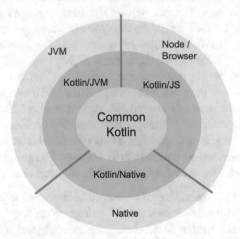

The core part of the language is Common Kotlin and this is the part of the language that is available on all platforms on which Kotlin executes.

However, Kotlin can be executed on JVM, JavaScript or Native runtimes. Each of these provides access to underlying facilities. For example, when running on the Kotlin/JVM platform it is possible to access any and all Java libraries. In turn when running on the Kotlin/JS platform it is possible to access underlying JavaScript libraries. These platforms are executed by an underlying runtime such as the JVM (Java Virtual Machine) or Node.js (a JavaScript runtime environment) or using the JavaScript runtime of a Web Browser.

Kotlin/Native is slightly different in that it is a technology used to compile Kotlin to native binaries that are run directly on the underlying operating system and do not need another runtime environment.

Where is Kotlin Used

Given that there are several different ways in which Kotlin can be executed, what platforms are commonly used? The answer is that the Kotlin/JVM platform is the most widely used platform by far, with minimal current uptake for Kotlin/JS and Kotlin/Native (at the time of writing). Ae Kotlin survey in 2020 rlooked at the platforms targeted by Kotlin developers. This found that 60% of the developers surveyed were using the JVM runtime and 60% were targeting Android. Only 7% were using the Kotlin Native runtime and only 6% were using the JavaScript runtime. This indicates that the majority of developers are using Kotlin on the JVM platform or on the Android mobile operating system.

However, this only illustrates part of the story, the same survey also found that Kotlin developers are nearly equally split between working on Android mobile applications (57%) and backend services (47% probably accessed from those mobile applications). Only 10% of Kotlin developers are developing desktop applications with just 6% developing Kotlin based web front ends.

Kotlin JVM Environment

When used on the Kotlin/JVM environment, Kotlin is similar to languages such as Java and C# in that it is compiled into an intermediate format known as byte codes. These byte codes are executed by a program known as a Virtual Machine. It is known as a Virtual Machine because it emulates a computer machine and allows the byte codes to be executed. Originally (back in the mid 1990s) the Virtual Machine interpreted the byte codes, however there have been several different approaches adopted to optimise the execution of byte codes within the JVM over the last 25 years. The current version adopts a hybrid strategy allowing some code to be interpreted but for commonly used code to be converted into native machine code.

The Java Virtual Machine (or JVM) is so called because it was designed and developed to execute byte codes generated by the Java compiler. However, there are currently several languages which can be compiled to byte codes including Kotlin, Scala and Clojure.

The following diagram illustrates the basic idea behind the JVM. A file containing Kotlin code will have a `kt` extension. This is compiled by the `kotlinc` compiler into a `class` file. The `class` file contains the byte code version of the Kotlin code. Indeed, all JVM languages compile to `class` files. A class file is then run by the Java Virtual Machine (aka JVM). The JVM then runs on the host platform (that is Windows, Unix, Linux or MacOS etc.):

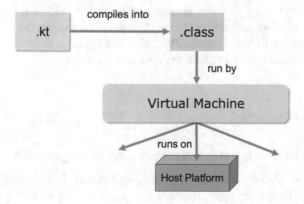

The above diagram is more complicated (and slightly different) for Kotlin Android application; however this will be discussed in Part 5 of this book which explores running Kotlin on Android devices.

Kotlin Documentation

As previously noted, there are versions of Kotlin that can run on the JVM, as JavaScript (or JS) using Node.js and natively on the underlying operating system. Each of these versions have some differences as well as Common aspects. This is reflected in the online documentation available for Kotlin. For example, the following image shows the type of buttons displayed across the top of the documentation web pages:

The meaning of each button is:

- Common provides documentation on the features of Kotlin that are available on all platforms.
- JVM presents the features that are available on the JVM platform.
- JS provides documentation for those features available when using the JavaScript runtime.
- Native indicates the facilities available when running Kotlin natively.

This can be seen if you look at the documentation for the listOf() function with the JVM button selected. See the following URL:

• https://kotlinlang.org/api/latest/jvm/stdlib/kotlin.collections/list-of.html

The above web page provides information on how to create a list of things in Kotlin. However, there are buttons to indicate what platform you are interested in. In this book we will be focussing on the JVM platform as that is both the most common platform used and the platform with the richest feature set.

Running Kotlin Programs

There are several ways in which you can run a Kotlin program, including

- Interactively using the Kotlin REPL (or Read Evaluate Print Loop) interpreter.
- Compiled to a class file and run using the *java* command with appropriate Kotlin libraries.
- Compiled into a class file and run using the *kotlin* command.

- Run a script file using the `kotlin -script` option.
- Run *as a* script file specifying the Kotlin interpreter to use within the script file.
- From within a Kotlin IDE (Integrated Development Environment) such as IntelliJ IDEA.

Interactively Using the Kotlin REPL Interpreter

It is possible to use Kotlin in interactive mode. This uses the Kotlin REPL (named after **R**ead **E**valuate **P**rint **L**oop style of operation).

Using the REPL, Kotlin statements and expressions can be typed into the Kotlin prompt and will then be executed directly. The values of variables will be remembered and may be used later in the session.

To run the Kotlin REPL, Kotlin must have been installed onto the computer system you are using. Depending on your platform this can be done in several ways, for example on an Apple Mac you can use Homebrew:

$ *brew install kotlin*

While on a Window machine you can download the kotlin-compiler zip from GitHub and add the bin directory to the system PATH.

Once installed you can open a Command Prompt window (Windows) or a Terminal window (MacOS) and type `kotlinc-jvm` into the prompt. This is shown for an Apple Mac computer below:

```
● ● ●                        ⌂ jeh — -zsh — 79×18
Last login: Tue Aug 18 09:28:41 on ttys000
[jeh@Johns-iMac ~ % kotlinc-jvm
Java HotSpot(TM) 64-Bit Server VM warning: Options -Xverify:none and -noverify
were deprecated in JDK 13 and will likely be removed in a future release.
Welcome to Kotlin version 1.4.0 (JRE 14.0.1+7)
Type :help for help, :quit for quit
>>> println("Hello World!")
Hello World!
>>> 5 + 4
res1: kotlin.Int = 9
>>> val name = "John"
>>> println(name)
John
>>> :quit
jeh@Johns-iMac ~ % █
```

In the above example, we interactively typed in several Kotlin commands and the Kotlin interpreter 'Read' what we have typed in, 'Evaluated 'it (worked out what it should do), 'Printed' the result and then 'Looped' back ready for further input. In this case we

- Printed out the string 'Hello World'.
- Added 5 and 4 together and got the result 9.
- Stored the string 'John' in a variable called name.
- Printed out the contents of the variable name using the builtin println() function.

To leave the interactive shell (the REPL) and go back to the console (the system shell), type in: quit.

Running a Kotlin File

We can of course store the Kotlin commands into a file. This creates a program file that can then be run as an argument to the java or kotlin command.

For example, the following file (called hello.kt) contains the 4 commands/statements defined within a special function called main(). Don't worry about this for the moment; it is only needed to indicate to the runtime JVM environment where the *main* entry point to your program is.

To run the hello.kt program you must first compile it into the byte code format understood by the JVM. This is done using either the javac command (with the appropriate Kotlin libraries) or by using the kotlinc compiler command directly. For example:

```
● ● ●                    kotlin-book — -zsh — 80×9
[jeh@Johns-iMac kotlin-book % kotlinc hello.kt -include-runtime -d hello.jar
[jeh@Johns-iMac kotlin-book % ls -la
total 2672
drwxr-xr-x   4 jeh  staff      128 12 Aug 10:16 .
drwxr-xr-x  29 jeh  staff      928 12 Aug 10:07 ..
-rw-r--r--   1 jeh  staff  1363308 12 Aug 10:16 hello.jar
-rw-r--r--@  1 jeh  staff       98 12 Aug 10:08 hello.kt
jeh@Johns-iMac kotlin-book %
```

In this case we are compiling the `hello.kt` file and including the `-include-runtime` and `-d` options. The `-include-runtime` option ensures that the output of the compiler includes all Kotlin dependencies required to run the file. The `-d` option provides the destination for the compiled code; which in this case is the `hello.jar` file. This is a file that contains one or more `class` files wrapped up in a format that the JVM understands. Jar files are just a convenient way to group together all the `class` files needed to run our hello world application.

We can now run the program contained within the `hello.jar` file using the JVM. The JVM is represented by the command `java`:

```
● ● ●                    kotlin-book — -zsh — 60×9
jeh@Johns-iMac kotlin-book % java -jar hello.jar

Hello World!
9
John
jeh@Johns-iMac kotlin-book % ▌
```

As the JVM (`java` command) is available on a wide range of different platform, this makes it very easy to create Kotlin programs that can be stored in files and run when needed on whatever platform is required (Windows, Linux or Mac). This illustrates the cross platform nature of Kotlin applications.

Executing a Kotlin Script

It is also possible to execute a file containing a stored Kotlin program as a Script. A script is a stand-alone file that can be run directly without the need to (explicitly) compile the Kotlin code. The script file only needs to contain Kotlin statements; there is no need to define function called main as we did earlier. A file containing the command for a Kotlin script has a `kts` extension. For example, we can create a file as shown below called hello.kts:

We can now run this Kotlin script using the `kotlinc` command with the `-script` option:

$$\$ \; kotlinc \; -script \; hello.kts$$

This is shown below:

```
● ● ●                kotlin-book — -zsh — 66×10

jeh@Johns-iMac kotlin-book % kotlinc -script hello.kts
Java HotSpot(TM) 64-Bit Server VM warning: Options -Xverify:none a
nd -noverify were deprecated in JDK 13 and will likely be removed
in a future release.
Hello World!
9
John
jeh@Johns-iMac kotlin-book % ▊
```

Another scripting option is to explicitly define the Kotlin file as a Script file (this option has been available since 2016). This requires that a special line to be added to the start of the Kotlin file that indicates the Kotlin command (or interpreter) to use with the rest of the file. This line must start with '#!' (also known as a shebang or sha-bang and even hashing) and must come at the start of the file.

To convert the previous sections file into a Script we would need to add a reference to the Kotlin script interpreter. For example:

However, we cannot just run the file as it stands. If we tried to run the file without any changes then we will get an error indicating that the permission to execute the file has been denied:

```
$ ./hello.kts
-bash: ./hello.kts: Permission denied
$
```

This is because by default you can't just run a file. We need to mark it as executable. There are several ways to do this, however one of the easiest on a Mac or Linux box is to use the chmod command (which can be used to modify the permissions associated with the file). To make the file executable we can change the file permissions to include making it executable by using the following command from a terminal window when we are in the same directory as the hello.kts file:

```
$ chmod +x hello.kts
```

Where +x indicates that we want to add the executable permission to the file.

Now if we try to run the file directly it executes and the results of the commands within the file are printed out:

```
                    kotlin-book — -zsh — 56×6
[-rwxr-xr-x@  1 jeh   staff    95 12 Aug 12:27 hello.kts   ]
jeh@Johns-iMac kotlin-book % ./hello.kts
Hello World!
9
John
jeh@Johns-iMac kotlin-book %
```

Note the use of the '. /' preceding the file name in the above; this is used on Linux/Unix computers to tell the operating system to look in the current directory for the file to execute.

Using Kotlin in an IDE

We can also use an IDE such as IntelliJ IDEA to write and execute our Kotlin programs. A simple program is shown using IntelliJ below:

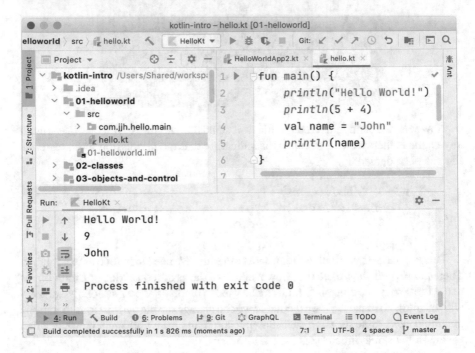

In the above figure the same set of commands are again listed in a file called `hello.py`. However, the program has been run from within the IDE and the output is shown in an output console at the bottom of the display.

Useful Resources

There are a wide range of resources on the web for Kotlin; we will highlight a few here that you should bookmark. We will not keep referring to these to avoid repetition, but you can refer back to this section whenever you need to:

- https://kotlinlang.org/ The main Kotlin home page.
- https://kotlinlang.org/foundation/kotlin-foundation.html Kotlin Foundation.
- https://kotlinlang.org/docs/reference/ The main Kotlin documentation site. It contains tutorials, library references, set up and installation guides as well as Kotlin how-tos.
- https://kotlinlang.org/user-groups/user-group-list.html List of Kotlin User Groups world wide.

Part I
Kotlin Programming

Chapter 2
A First Kotlin Program

Introduction

In this chapter we will look at a simple Kotlin program and understand what it is doing. We will also modify it to become more interactive and will explore the concept of Kotlin variables (specifically *vals* and *vars*).

Hello World

It is traditional to get started in a new programming language by writing a *Hello World* style program. This is very useful as it ensures that your environment, that is the compiler, the JVM runtime, the editor or IDE, any environmental settings, etc. are all set up appropriately and can process (or compile) and execute (or run) your program. As the 'Hello World' program is about the simplest program in any language, you are doing this without the complexities of the actual language being used.

In Kotlin the simplest version of the *Hello World* program merely prints out a string with a welcome message. This program is shown below:

```
fun main() {
    println("Hello World!")
}
```

This defines the *main* function; that is the entry point to the application. The main function is defined using the keyword fun which precedes the name of the function; in this case main.

© The Author(s), under exclusive license to Springer Nature Switzerland AG 2021
J. Hunt, *Beginner's Guide to Kotlin Programming*,
https://doi.org/10.1007/978-3-030-80893-8_2

The body of the function (what the function does) is defined between the opening and closing curly brackets ({ }). In this case all this does is call the println() function passing in the string "Hello World!". This function is used to generate a line of output from the program.

You can use any text editor or IDE (Integrated Development Editor) to create a Kotlin file. Examples of editors commonly used with Kotlin include Emacs, Vim, Notepad++, Sublime Text or Visual Studio Code; examples of IDEs for Kotlin include IntelliJ IDEA and Eclipse. Using any of these tools we can create file with a .kt extension. Such a file can contain one or more Kotlin statements that represent a Kotlin program. Note that any file containing Kotlin code must always have a .kt extension.

For example, we can create a file called hello.kt containing the above main() function in it.

Setting up Your Program

To write our hello world program we will create a new Kotlin file within the IntelliJ IDE. Of course, you don't have to use IntelliJ for this, but we will assume you are; if you are using a different editor or IDE then you may have to look up the equivalent steps.

Starting up Kotlin

The first thing to do is to start up your IntelliJ IDE if it is not already running. When you do this it will ask you whether you want to create a new project, open an existing project or obtain a project from VCS (Version Control System), for example:

In this case select the 'New project' option.

On the new Project dialog, select the 'Kotlin' option in the left hand panel and then fill out the project details as required. The panel is shown below. Give the project a suitable name such as helloworld or app, select the location you ant to save the project into and you may also need to select he Project JDK (this indicates the version to be used for the Java runtime and libraries that underpin Kotlin):

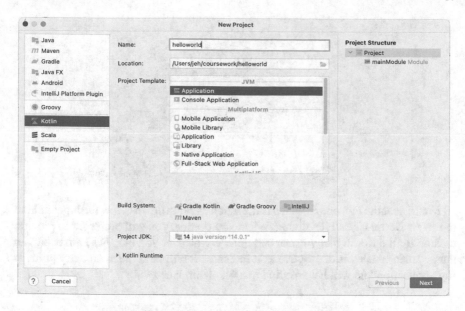

Now click 'Next'. You will now see information on the main module. A Kotlin application can be comprised of one or more modules. A module is a group of associated features that might be built and distributed together. We will be using a single module for our application, you can therefore just click 'Finish'.

You should now see an empty editor window displayed to you.

Create a New Kotlin File

We will now create a new Kotlin file to hold your program. To do this open the src node in the left-hand Project view by clicking on the arrow next to the src label. Then continue to expand the tree of nodes down to the directory shown in blue called kotlin. This is where we will define our application. Once you have selected the kotlin node use the *right mouse button* menu. On this menu select 'New' followed by 'Kotlin Class/File', see below:

First select the File option which is the second option down below the input field in the 'New Kotlin Class/File' dialog. When you do this, you will prompted to provide a name for the Kotlin file; you can call the file whatever you like, but I am using the name 'main' as that is descriptive as it indicates it will hold the main entry point to my application and will help me find this file again later:

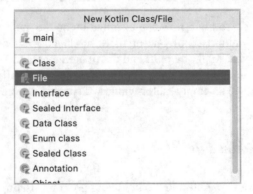

Now click OK. Notice I did not need to add `.kt` to the end of the filename; IntelliJ will do that for me (if you did add `.kt` then don't worry IntelliJ will be fine with that as well).

Create the Main Function

The first thing we will do is create the main function for our hello world application. This is shown below:

```kotlin
fun main() {
    println("Hello World!")
}
```

And in the editor window of the IDE:

```
main.kt ×
1 ▶  ⊝fun main() {
2          println("Hello World!")
3      ⊝}
```

One question this raises is where does the `println()` function come from? In fact, `println()` is a predefined function that can be used to *print things out* followed by a carriage return/newline (there is also a `print()` function that merely prints things out—it does not include the carriage return/newline). On the JVM runtime it actually maps to the underlying JVM `System.out.println()` operation.

The output is actually printed to what is known as the standard output stream. This handles a stream (sequence) of data such as letters and numbers. This output stream of data can be sent to an output window such as the Terminal on a Mac or Command window on a Windows PC. In this case we are printing the string "`Hello World`".

By predefined here we mean that it is built into the Kotlin environment and is understood by the JVM runtime system This means that the JVM knows where to find the definition of the `println()` function which tells it what to do when it encounters that function.

You can of course write your own functions and we will be looking at how to do that later in this book.

The `println()` function actually tries to print whatever you give it,

- when it is given a string it will print a string,
- if it is given an integer such as `42` it will print 42,
- if it is a given a real number such as `23.56` then it will print 23.56,
- If a boolean value (true or false) is given that it will print out true or false.

Also note that the text forming the Hello World string is wrapped within two double quote characters; these characters delimit the start and end of the string; if you miss one of them out then there will be an error.

To run the program, if you are using an IDE such as IntelliJ, then you can select the green arrow next to the line with fun main() {on it as this will run your application for you. Alternatively you can select the file in the left hand tree and from the right mouse button menu where you can select Run. If you want to run this program again you can merely click on the green arrow in the tool bar at the top of the IDE.

The result of running this very simple *hello world* program is given below:

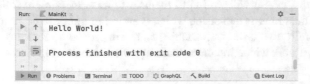

Interactive Hello World

Let us make our program a little more interesting; lets get it to ask us our name and say hello to us personally.

The updated program is:

```kotlin
fun main() {
    println("Hello World!")
    print("Please Enter your Name: ")
    val name = readLine()
    println("Hello $name")
}
```

Now after printing the original 'Hello World' string, the program then has three additional statements. One prompts the user to enter their name, the next actually reads in the user input (this is the readLine() function) and the final statement prints out a welcome message to the user.

The result of running this program is:

```
Hello, World!
Please Enter Your Name: John
Hello John
```

We will look at each of the new statements separately.

The first statement is:

```
print("Please Enter your Name: ")
```

Notice that were have used a different print style function here—print(). This function prints out the value passed to it without a carriage return/new line. This means that the cursor is left on the same line as the prompt allowing the user to type in their name after the prompt string.

The next statement is:

```
val name = readLine()
```

This statement does several things. It first executes another function called readLine(). This function, is again a *built-in* function that is part of the Kotlin language. In this case it will wait until the user types something in followed by the return key. It then returns that string which is stored in the variable name. In Kotlin there are actually two types of variable; there are *vals* and there are *vars*. In this case we used a val which indicates that once the value is set in name it cannot be changed. That is, it is only possible to write a value into name once. In contrast a var can have a new value assigned to it any number of times. We will return to *vals* and *vars* in a later section.

The end result of the above statement is that whatever the user types in is then returned as a String as the result of executing the readLine() function. In this case that result is then stored in the *variable* name (which will be of type String).

The final statement we added to this program is shown below:

```
println("Hello $name")
```

The last statement again uses the built-in println() function, but this time it uses a facility within Kotlin known as *string templates*. A *string template* is a very useful feature that allows Kotlin values or expression to be embedded within a String. That is a programmer can embed variable names within a string as long as they are preceded by a dollar sign ($). When Kotlin processes this string it replaces the variable (in this case $name) with the value of that variable. In fact any Kotlin code can be embedded in a string if you enclose it within a ${...} block within a string. This this feature will be used extensively in the examples presented in this book.

Variables

Kotlin is a *statically* typed language. The word *static* is used here to indicate that the type of data that a variable can hold will be determined when the program is compiled (aka at compile time). Later on it will not be possible to change the type of data that the variable can hold; thus if a variable is to hold an Integer it cannot later on hold a String. This is the approach adopted by languages such as Kotlin, Java and C#.

Although this may seem like an obvious approach, it is not the only way in which programming languages handle typing. For example, Python and JavaScript are what might be called dynamically typed languages. That is, the type of a variable is determined by the type of data it holds. In this case if a variable holds a number then its type is numeric, but if it holds a string then its type might be String. In languages such as Python and JavaScript the type of a variable can therefore change over time. For example, a variable might hold the number 42 at one point in the program and the string "John" at another.

This can add flexibility to the program but can also lead to unexpected issues at other times. Both approaches have their pros and cons; but for many people the flexibility of a dynamic language is outweighed by the security afforded by a static typed language.

In many traditional programming languages, it is the developer who must specify the type of a variable. This can lead to quiet verbose code with a lot of apparently redundant statements, such as:

```
Person p = new Person();
```

Kotlin takes a different approach; it allows the programmer to decide if they wish to specify the type or rely on the compiler to infer the type of the variable at compile time. In both cases the type is fixed at that point before the program is actually run.

The ability of the Kotlin compiler to determine the type of the variable statically at compile time for the developer is known as *type inference* and is a concept that is becoming increasingly common with the more recent versions of Java starting to adopt it to some extent.

For example, in Kotlin the above code can be written as:

```
val p = new Person()
```

In this case the type of p is still Person but this has been *inferred* by the Kotlin compiler for the developer.

It is of course still possible to explicitly state the type of the val p in Kotlin (and for a public API this is considered good style) but it is optional. If we did want to specify the type of the val p we can do so by following the declaration of p with a colon and the type that p can hold, for example:

```
val p: Person  = new Person()
```

Vals and Vars

Another aspect that is different between a language such as Java and Kotlin is that it has the concept of *val* and *var*. Both keywords are used to declare a new variable. However, once a val has been set it is not possible to change its value; where as a var can have its value changed as many times as required.

For example, in the following simple variation on the Hello World application, the val message is declared to hold the string "Hello Kotlin World!". This is the value that it will hold for the lifetime of the program; it is not possible to change it:

```
fun main() {
    val message = "Hello Kotlin World!"
    println(message)
}
```

In contrast if we had used the keyword var to declare the variable; then its value can change during the lifetime of the program, for example:

```kotlin
fun main() {
    var message = "Hello Kotlin World!"
    println(message)

    // because message is a var can reassign
    message = "Goodbye - End of the World!"
    println(message)
}
```

This is a fundamental difference between older style languages and languages such as Kotlin. A val is an *immutable* value; that is it cannot be changed and this idea of immutability has been gaining in popularity over the last decade.

This is because in general the benefits of immutability include:

- Immutable data is often easier to use.
- Immutable data reduces the number of possible interactions between different parts of a program.
- Immutable data can be safely shared between multiple concurrent threads of execution.
- Working with immutable data is often easier, as there is less that can go wrong, and the design space is *smaller*.
- Immutable objects support pure functions with *Referential Transparency*. That is when you call a function (such as add/+) with the same parameters (for example 5 + 4) it will always return the same result (in this case 9). Which makes it easier to reason about the behaviour of a program.
- When we add the values 5 and 4 tougher the result 9 does not affect 5 or 4 (which is what you would expect in maths but may not be so obvious in a computer program).

In the remainder of this book we will try to always use *vals* in preference to *vars* unless we need to be able to change a value as a program executes (for example a count value would be a var).

String Formatting

As well as the use of String Templates in Kotlin, it is possible to use special control characters to help layout the output produced by a string. An control control character is a character precede by a back slash (''\). It indicates to the print or println functions that it should treat that following character as special and that it will be used to help manage the output of the string.

The control characters supported in Kotlin are:

- \t—Inserts tab
- \b—Inserts backspace
- \n—Inserts newline
- \r—Inserts carriage return
- \'—Inserts single quote character
- \"—Inserts double quote character
- \\—Inserts backslash
- \$—Inserts dollar character.

For example running the following code:

```
println("\tHello")
```

Will print out a tab followed by the String Hello.

Naming Conventions

You may have noticed something about some of the variable names we have introduced above such as message and name. Both these variable names are formed of a set of lower case characters. However in many cases a variable name needs to be more descriptive such as userName or courseTitle with the second 'words' in the variable name capitalised. This is known as modified Camel Case (as it looks a bit like a camels hump). Standard Camel Case is illustrated by a variable such as CourseList where each word is capitalised. This format is usually reserved for classes in Kotlin.

All these examples highlight a very widely used naming convention in Kotlin, which is that variable names should:

- be all lowercase except when starting a *new* word within a variable name,
- be more descriptive than variable names such as *a* or *b* (although there are some exceptions such as the use of variables *i* and *j* in looping constructs),
- with individual words separated by capital letters as necessary to improve readability.

This last point is very important as in Kotlin (and most computer programming languages) spaces are treated as separators which can be used to indicate where one thing ends and another starts. Thus it is not possible to define a variable name such as:

- user name

As the space is treated by Kotlin as a separator and thus the compiler thinks you are defining two things 'user' and 'name'.

When you create your own variables, you should try to name them following the Kotlin accepted style thus name such as:

- `myName, yourName, userName, accountName`
- `count, totalNumberOfUsers, percentagePassed, passRate`
- `whereWeLive, houseNumber,`
- `isOkay, isCorrect, statusFlag`

are all acceptable but

- `A, aaaaa, aaAAAaa`
- `My_name, my_Name, My_Name or my_name`
- WHEREWELIVE

Do not meet the accepted conventions.

However, it is worth mentioning that these are merely commonly adhered to *conventions*. Thus if you define a variable name that does not conform to the convention Kotlin will not complain (although the analysis tools within the IDE might highlight what you are doing as being a contravention of the standard).

Assignment Operator

One final aspect of the statement shown below has yet to be considered.

```
val name = readLine()
```

What exactly is this ' = ' between `name` variable and the readLine() function?

It is called the *assignment* operator. It is used to assign the value returned by the function `readLine()` to the variable `name`. It is probably the most widely used operator in Kotlin. Of course, it is not just used to assign values from functions as the earlier examples illustrated. For example, we can also use to store a string into a variable directly:

```
val myVariable = 'Jasmine'
```

Kotlin Statements and Expressions

Throughout this chapter we have used the phrase statement to describe a portion of a Kotlin program, for example the following line of code is a statement that prints out a string 'Hello' and the value held in `name`.

```
println("Hello $name")
```

So what do we mean by a statement? In Kotlin a statement is an instruction that the JVM runtime can execute.

Such a statement may be formed of a number of elements such as a call to a function and an assignment of a value to a variable. In many cases a statement is a single line in your program but it is also possible for a statement to extend over several lines particularly if this helps the readability or layout of the code. For example, the following is a single statement but it is laid out over 5 lines of code to make it easier to read:

```kotlin
println("The total population of " +
        city +
        " was " +
        numberOfPeopleInCity +
        " in " + year)
```

As well as statements there are also expressions. An *expression* is essentially a computation that generates a value, for example:

4 + 5.

This is an expression that adds 4 and 5 together and generates the value 9.

Comments in Code

It is common practice (although not universally so) to add comments to code to help anyone reading the code to understand what the code does, what its intent was, any design decisions the programmer made etc.

Comments are sections of a program that are ignored by the Kotlin compiler—they are not executable code.

A single line comment is indicated by the // characters in Kotlin. Anything following those characters to the end of the line will be ignored by the compiler as it will be assumed to be a comment, for example:

```kotlin
// This is a comment
print("Please Enter your Name: ")
val name = readLine()
// This is another comment
println("Hello $name") // comment to the end of the line
```

In the above, the two lines starting with a // are comments—they are for our human eyes only. Interestingly the line containing the println() function also has a comment—that is fine as the comment starts with the // and runs to the end of the line, anything *before* the // characters is not part of the comment.

Kotlin also supports multiple line comments. These are comments that span multiple lines and usually provide extended descriptions for the benefit of developers reading the code at a later date. An example of a multiple line comment provided for the main function is given below:

```
/*
 * The main Function used to start
 * this simple Hello World
 * application.
 */
fun main() {

    val message = "Hello Kotlin World!"
    println(message)

}
```

A multiple line comment starts with /* and ends with */. Everything between /* and */ is part of the comment and will be ignored by the compiler.

Multi-line comments may be used to explain a complex or non obvious algorithm, allowing clarity to be brought to such code.

In many cases multi-line comments are used to explain the purpose or role of a function or a class of things. Such multi-line comments typically start with /** and end with */. These can be picked up by a Kotlin comment processing tool such as Dokka. These comments often embed Markdown code as well as special elements prefixed with an '@' symbol used to describe parameters to functions (@param), the author of the code, cross references (@see) and versions (@since). These @ symbols are collectively known as KDoc. Some of these are shown below:

```
/**
 * The *main* Function used to start
 * this simple Hello World
 * application.
 * @author John Hunt
 * @since 1.0
 * @see Main
 */
fun main() {
    val message = "Hello Kotlin World!"
    println(message)
}
```

In the above the word main is emphasised and information on the author, which version introduced this function and a cross reference are provided. For more information see https://kotlinlang.org/docs/kotlin-doc.html.

Basic Types

In Kotlin there are a set of built-in data types that you can use. For example, `Int` is a built in data type used to represent integer numbers. `String` is a built in type used to represent an ordered sequence of characters. In turn `Double` is a built in type used to represent real or floating point numbers.

The following tables summarise these types. Notice that for both integers and real numbers you can choose the level of range of values that are supported by different integer or real number types. This is because a `Byte` takes up less memory than an `Int`. If all your numbers can fit within the range of values that can be represented by a `Byte` then this will use less memory than if you used the same number if Ints. If you are hold a million integer values all in the range 1 to 10 then this can make a significant difference in the memory footprint of your application.

Integer types

Type	Size (bits)	Min value	Max value
Byte	8	-128	127
Short	16	$-32{,}768$	$32{,}767$
Int	32	$-2{,}147{,}483{,}648$ (-2^{31})	$2{,}147{,}483{,}647$ $(2^{31}-1)$
Long	64	$-9{,}223{,}372{,}036{,}854{,}775{,}808$ (-2^{63})	$9{,}223{,}372{,}036{,}854{,}775{,}807$ $(2^{63}-1)$

Some examples are given below:

```kotlin
val count = 1 // Int (the default)
val small: Byte = 1
val large = 3000000000L // Long
```

Note that if you do not specify the type of the val or var holding an integer, then the type defaults to Int. In the above we have used the letter L to explicitly indicate that the literal 3,000,000,000 is of type long (although Kotlin can infer this itself).

Floating point types

Type	Size (bits)	Description
Float	32	Represents a single-precision 32-bit IEEE 754 floating point number
Double	64	Represents a double-precision 64-bit IEEE 754 floating point number

Some example are given below:

```kotlin
val temperature = 45.23 // Double
val price = 2.78F // Float as indicated by 'F' at end of number
```

Note that to explicitly specify the `Float` type for a value, add the suffix f or F. If such a value contains a value that cannot be held within a Float then it will be truncated.

Boolean types

Type	Values	Description
Boolean	True/false	Used to represent the truth (or not) of something

Some examples are given below.

```
val flag = true
val isOkay = false
```

Unsigned Integer Types

The standard Kotlin library has included unsigned integers since Kotlin 1.5 (they were in Beta between Kotlin 1.3 and 1.4 which means that they were still experimental up until Kotlin 1.5). This library includes unsigned integer types `UInt`, `ULong`, `UByte` and `UShort`. It also includes a set of related functions such as conversion operations. Unsigned integers are integers that can only contain zero or positive integers (they cannot hold negative numbers). This is because they do not use any memory to store the sign (+ or −) with the number (as they can only be non negative numbers). This means that they can hold an integer you know to only be positive in an unsigned type more efficiently than in a regular *signed* integer type.

For example, if we are counting the number of players in a game there will be zero or more players; there will never be a negative number of players. We could there for use a `UByte` to hold such a number which is (slightly) more efficient than using a regular `Byte`.

Some examples of using unsigned integer types are given below:

```
// Can indicate Unsigned using 'U' after an integer literal
val zero 0U // defines unsigned literal Zero
val ten = 10.toUInt()          // Converting int to UInt
// Illegal can't have a negative unsigned int
// val minusOne: Uint = -1U
```

However, as of Kotlin 1.5 arrays of unsigned integers remain in Beta; this is likely to change in subsequent versions.

Numeric Conversions

Unlike many languages Kotlin does not automatically convert from one numeric type to another. Instead explicit conversion operators/methods must be used. All numeric types support conversions to other types using the following methods:

- toByte(): Byte
- toShort(): Short
- toInt(): Int
- toLong(): Long or use the latter L after an integer literal, e.g,. 34L
- toFloat(): Float or use the letter F after ta numeric literal e.g. 34.5F
- toDouble(): Double
- toChar(): Char

For example, a Double to an Int you can use:

```
val d = 45.3
val i: Int = d.toInt()
```

It is also possible to convert Strings to numeric values (assuming the string hold a number, for example:

```
val s = "42"
val I: Int = s.toInt()
```

Online Resources

See the Kotlin Standard Library documentation for:

- https://kotlinlang.org/docs/reference/basic-syntax.html for a basic introduction to the syntax of Kotlin.

Exercises

At this point you should try to write your own Kotlin program. It is probably easiest to start by modifying the *Hello World* program we have already been studying. The following steps take you through this:

1. If you have not yet run the *Hello World* program, then do so now. To run your program you have several options. If you have set up an IDE such as IntelliJ IDEA, then the easiest thing is to use the 'run' menu option. Otherwise if you have set up the Kotlin compiler and runtime on your computer, you can run it from a Command prompt (on Windows) or a Terminal window (on a Mac/Linux box).

2. Now ensure that you are comfortable with what the program actually does. Try commenting out some lines—what happens; is that the behaviour you expected? Check that you are happy with what it does.

3. Once you have done that, modify the program with your own prompts to the user (the string argument given to the `print()` function before the `readLine()` function). Make sure that each string is surrounded by the double quote characters (".."); remember these denote the start and end of a string.

4. Try creating your own `val` and `var` variables and storing values into those instead of the `val` variable `name`.

5. Add a `print()` or `println()` statement to the program with your own prompt.

6. Include an assignment that will add two numbers together (for example 4+ 5) and then assign the result to a `val` variable called `total`.

7. Now print out that variables value once it has been assigned a value.

Make sure you can run the program after each of the above changes. If there is an error reported attempt to fix that issue before moving on.

You must also be careful with the case of the letters in your program—Kotlin is *very* case sensitive; therefore the function `print()` is not the same as Print()—so be careful.

Chapter 3
Flow of Control

Introduction

In this chapter we are going to look at the flow of control statements in Kotlin. These statement are used to control the flow of execution within a program based on some condition. These conditions represent some choice point that will be evaluated too *true* or *false*. To perform this evaluation it is common to use a comparison operator (for example to check to see if a temperature is greater than some threshold or while some boolean flag is true then repeat a set of instructions). In many cases these comparisons need to take into account several values and in these situations logical operators can be used to combine two or more comparison expressions together.

This chapter first introduces comparison and logical operators before discussing the null and condition operators. It then considers if statements, when expressions, while and do-while loops, for loops and repeat loops. It concludes by introducing a simple application that uses both a while loop and an if statement.

Operators

Comparison Operators

Before exploring `if` statements and various types of looping mechanism we need to discuss *comparison operators*. These are operators that return *Boolean* values. They are key to the conditional elements of flow of control statements such as `if`.

A comparison operator is an operator that performs some form of test and returns `true` of `false`.

These are operators that we use in everyday life all the time. For example, do I have enough money to buy lunch, or is this shoe in my size etc.

In Kotlin there are a range of comparison operators represented by typically one or two characters. These are:

© The Author(s), under exclusive license to Springer Nature Switzerland AG 2021
J. Hunt, *Beginner's Guide to Kotlin Programming*,
https://doi.org/10.1007/978-3-030-80893-8_3

Operator	Name	Description	Examples
==	Equals	Tests if two values are equal	3 == 3
!=	Not equals	Tests that two values are *not* equal to each other	2! = 3
<	Less than	Tests to see if the left-hand value is less than the right-hand value	2 < 3
>	Greater than	Tests if the left-hand value is greater than the right-hand value	3 > 2
<=	Less than or equal to	Tests if the left-hand value is less than *or* equal to the right-hand value	3 <= 4
>=	Greater than or equal to	Tests if the left-hand value is greater than or equal to the right-hand value	5 >= 4

Logical Operators

In addition to comparison operators, Kotlin also has logical operators.

Logical operators can be used to combined Boolean expressions together. Typically, they are used with comparison operators to create more complex conditions. Again, we use these every day for example we might consider whether we can afford an ice cream *and* whether we will be having our dinner soon etc.

There are five logical operators in Kotlin these are listed below:

Operator	Name	Description	Examples
&	And	Returns true if both left and right are true	(3 < 4) & (5 > 4)
&&	Short cut and	Short cut version of the and operator; the right hand operand is only evaluated if the left hand operand is true	(3 < 4) && (5 > 4)
I	Or	Returns true if either the left or the right is true	(3 < 4) I (3 > 5)
II	Short cut or	Short cut version of the or operator; the right hand operand is only evaluated if the left hand operand is false	(3 < 4) II (3 > 5)
ˆ	Exclusive or	Indicates XOR or exclusive OR; it will only evaluate to true if only one of the operands is true; if both operands are true then the XOR test evaluates to false	(2 < 3) ˆ (5 < 2)
!	Not	Returns true if the value being tested is false	!flag

Numeric Operators

Kotlin has several numeric operators such as the + operator used for addition. These numeric operators are listed below:

Operator	Description	Examples
+	Performs numeric addition if the left hand operand is a number. If the left hand operand is a strings then performs string concatenation	println(1 + 2) println(2.2 + 3.4) println("Hello " + "World") println("Hello" + 2)
−	Subtract the second operand from the first	println(2 - 1) println(2.1 - 1) println(3 - 1.5)
*	Multiples operands together	println(2 * 3) println(2.5 * 3.4) println(3 * 2.5)
/	Divides first operand by second operand. If both the operands are integers then performs integer division; if at least one of the operands is a floating point number then performs pointing point division	println(6/3) println(5/2) println(5/2.3) println(3.4/1.2)
%	The Modulus (or Remainder) operator. It returns the remainder from a division, for example 5% 2 will return 1 as 2 goers into 5 twice remainder 1	println(6%3) println(5%2) println(5%2.3) println(3.4%1.2)
++	Increment operator that adds one to a value held in a var	count++
−	Decrement operator used to subtract one for a value held in a var	count−

Assignment Operators

As well as the basic + , −numeric operators there are also a set of assignment operators. These act as short cut operators that provide a concise way of performing common arithmetic operations.

Operator	Description	Examples
+=	Equivalent of x = x + y	x + = y
-=	Equivalent of x = x − y	x − = y
*=	Equivalent of x = x * y	x * = y
/=	Equivalent of x = x / y	x / = y
%=	Equivalent of x = x % y	x % = y

The if Statement

An if statement is used as a form of conditional programming; something you probably do every day in the real world. That is, you need to decide whether you are going to have tea or coffee or to decide if you will have toast or a muffin for breakfast etc. In each of these cases you are making a choice, usually based on some information such as I had coffee yesterday, so I will have tea today.

In Kotlin such choices are represented programmatically by the `if` condition statement.

In this construct if some condition is *true* some action is performed, optionally if it is *not true* some other action may be performed instead.

Working with an if Statement

In its most basic from, the if statement is

```
if (<condition-evaluating-to-boolean>)
    statement
```

Note that the condition must evaluate to `true` or `false`. If the condition is `true` then we will execute the statement or block of statements. If you want to group a block of statements together to be run if the condition is true then you can use curly brackets to create a code block. For example,

```
if (<condition-evaluating-to-boolean>) {
    statement
    statement
    statement
}
```

Note that it is a common convention to use the curly brackets with an if statement even if there is only a single statement as this helps to make it clear which statements are associated with the if block. Indentation is not significant in Kotlin and is only used as an aid to the reader. However, if code is mis-aligned it can give a false impression to the that reader and therefore curly bracket code blocks are considered good style as it always makes it explicit what is part of the conditional statement and what is not.

Let us look at a simple example of an if statement in Kotlin:

```
val i = 5
val j = 10
if (i < j) {
    println(i)
}
```

In this example, a test is made to see if i is less than j; if the result of this condition is true then the value of i will be printed out. If the condition is not true; then nothing will be output.

For example, the above code outputs:

5

If we wish to execute multiple statements when our condition is true we can group several lines together into a code block using the curly brackets. For example;

```kotlin
fun main() {

    println("Starting")

    print("Enter a number: ")
    val inputString = readLine()
    val number = inputString!!.toInt()

    if (number > 0) {
        // Multiple lines grouped together for the if statement
        println("$number is positive")
        println("$number squared is ${number *number}")
    }

    println("Bye")

}
```

If we now run this program and input 2 then we will see:

```
Starting
Enter a number: 2
2 is positive
2 squared is 4
Bye
```

However, if we enter the value -1 then we get

```
Starting
Enter a number: -1
Bye
```

Note that neither of the statements within the if condition block were executed.

This is because the two statements are associated with the if statement and will only be executed if the Boolean condition evaluates (returns) true. However, the statement println("Bye") is not part of the if statement; it is merely the next statement to executed after the if statement (and its associated println() statements) have finished.

Else in an if Statement

We can also define an *else* part of an `if` statement; this is an optional element that can be run if the conditional part of the `if` statement returns `false`. For example:

```
fun main() {
    println("Starting")

    print("Enter a number: ")
    val inputString = readLine()
    val number = inputString!!.toInt()
    if (number > 0) {
        println("$number is positive")
        println("$number squared is ${number *number}")
    } else {
        println("$number Its negative")
    }

    println("Bye")

}
```

Now when this code is executed, if the number entered is less than zero then the else condition will be run. However, we are *guaranteed* that at least one (and at most one) of the two blocks of code associated with the `if` statement will execute.

For example, in the first run of the program, if we enter the value 1 then the output will be:

```
Starting
Enter a number: 1
1 is positive
1 squared is 1
Bye
```

In the second run of the program, if we enter the value -1, then the block of code associated with the else element of the if statement will be run:

```
Starting
Enter a number: -1
-1 Its negative
Bye
```

The Use of Else If

In some cases there may be several conditions you want to test, with each condition being tested if the previous one failed. This *else-if* scenario is supported in Kotlin by the `else if` elements.

The `else if` elements of an if statement follows the if part and comes before any (optional) else part. For example

```kotlin
fun main() {

    println("Starting")

    print("Enter a number: ")
    val inputString = readLine()
    val number = inputString!!.toInt()

    if (number > 0) {
        println("$number is positive")
        println("$number squared is: ${number *number}")
    } else if (number == 0) {
        println("$number Its Zero")
    } else {
        println("$number Its negative")
    }

    println("Bye")

}
```

If we run this version of the program and enter 0, we will see:

```
Starting
Enter a number: 0
0 Its Zero
Bye
```

Here we can see that the first if condition failed (as the number is not greater than Zero). However, the next `else if` must have returned `true` as the number is equal to Zero and then the message `0 Its Zero` was printed out. Having executed this statement the if statement then terminated (the remaining `else` part was ignored).

Kotlin if Expression

In Kotlin if statements are actually expressions. In all of the previous examples, the if statement actually returned the value `Unit` (represented by `()`) which represents no value. However, it is possible for an if expression to return something other than Unit.

For example, it is quite common to want to assign a specific value to a variable dependent on some condition. For example, if we wish to decide if someone is a teenager or not then we might check to see if they are over 12 and under 20. We could write this as:

```
fun main() {
    val age = 18
    var status = ""

    if (age > 12 && age < 20)
        status = "teenager"
    else
        status = "not a teenager"

    println("$age - you are $status")

}
```

If we run this, we get the string 18- you are teenager printed out.

However, this is quite long and it may not be obvious that the real intent of this code was to assign an appropriate value to status.

An alternative in Kotlin is to use the if statement as an *if expression*. The format of an if expression is

```
<result> = if <condition> <result1> else <result2>
```

That is the result returned from the *if expression* is the first value unless the condition fails in which case the result returned will be the value after the else. It may seem confusing at first, but it becomes easier when you see an example.

For example, using the *if expression* we can perform a test to determine the value to assign to status and return it as the result of the if expression. For example:

```
fun main() {
    val age = 18

    val status = if (age > 12 && age < 20)
        "A teenager"
    else
        "not a teenager"

    println("$age - you are $status")

}
```

Again, the result printed out is 18- you are a teenager, however now the code is much more concise, and it is clear that the purpose of the test is to determine the result to assign to status. We can also make status a val rather than a var now; which is considered much better Kotlin style (often referred to as idiomatic Kotlin).

Nesting if Statements

It is possible to *nest* one if statement inside another. This term *nesting* indicates that one if statement is located within part of another if statement and can be used to refine the conditional behaviour of the program.

An example is given below. Note that it allows some behaviour to be performed before and after the nested if statement is executed/run.

```kotlin
fun main() {
    val snowing = true
    val temp = -1

    if (temp < 0) {
        println("It is freezing")
        if (snowing) {
            println("Put on boots")
        }
        println("Time for Hot Chocolate")
    }

    println("Bye")
}
```

In this example, if the temperature if less than Zero then we will enter the outer if block of code. If it is not less than zero we will skip the whole if statement and jump to the println("Bye") statement which is after both if statements.

In this case the temperature is set to -1 and so we will enter the if statement. We will then print out the 'It is freezing' string. At this point another if statement is *nested* within the first if statement. A check will now be made to see if it is snowing. Notice that snowing is already a Boolean value and so will be either true or false and illustrates that a Boolean value on its own can be used here.

As it is snowing, we will print out "Put on boots".

However, the statement printing out "Time for Hot Chocolate" is not part of the nested if. It is part of the outer if. Thus we print out this string whether it is snowing or not.

Null and Conditional Statements

Null is a special value that is used to representing *nothingness*, that is an absence of a value. In programming languages such as Java a variable that can hold a reference type (such as an object or instance of a class) can have the value null. However, if an attempt is made to perform some operation on a null value then this can result in an error being generated. For example, in Java this error is the NullPointerException error. In Java the ability to set a variable to null and then have a NullPointerException generated is generally considered a weakness in the language design.

By default Kotlin does not allow vals or vars to be set to null. Only certain vals or vars, marked as allowing the value null, can be set to null. These are called *nullable* types. Thus it is the programmer who decides which variables can be nullable (that is can hold the value null). By default variables are not nullable (or are non-null types).

For example, the following code snippet illustrates a non-nullable variable:

```
// Standard variable - cannot be set to null
var nonNullableVar = "abc"
println("nonNullableVar: $nonNullableVar")
// nonNullableVar = null // Compilation error
```

In the above code snippet the commented out line will not compile as it will generate a compiler error stating that 'Null can not be a value of a non-null type String'.

To specify a nullable type we need to explicitly specify the type with a trailing '?', for example:

```
// Nullable variable - can be set to null
var nullableVar: String? = "abc"
println("nullableVar: $nullableVar")
nullableVar = null
println("nullableVar now: $nullableVar")
```

When we run this code snippet the output is:

```
nullableVar: abc
nullableVar now: null
```

Note that the type of the variable nullableVar is String? not String; this indicates that it is a *nullable* type that can hold a reference to a String or the value null.

The benefit of non-null and nullable types in Kotlin is that for standard/normal variables they can never be null and thus calling a property such as length on a variable of type String will never generate a NullPointerException (as a standard String variable can never have the value null).

However, a *nullable* variable can have the value `null`, thus `nullable Var.length` may work or may result in a `NullPointer Exception` being generated depending upon whether it holds the value `null` or not.

Because of this it is not legal to write the following code:

```
println(nullableVar.length)
```

The compiler will provide a warning indicating that the variable `nullableVar` can be `null` and therefore this operation is not *safe*.

To overcome this you have several options:

1. explicitly check for null conditions,
2. use the *safe call* operator which is written as ?.,
3. use the elvis operator that is written as ?:,
4. Apply the *not-null assertion* operator which is written as !!,
5. Perform a *safe cast* to covert the variable type into a non null type.

Each of these approaches is described below.

Explicitly Checking for Null Conditions

It is possible to explicitly check whether a *nullable* variable is `null` or not and take appropriate action. For example:

```
// Nullable variable - can be set to null
var nullableVar: String? = "abc"
val result = if (nullableVar == null) -1 else nullableVar.length
println("result: $result")
```

In this example, if the value of `nullableVar` is `null` then `result` is set to `-1` otherwise it is set to the length of the string held in `nullableVar`. This is determined to be *safe* by the compiler because it can analyse the code and knows that it is impossible to get to the `else` part of the `if` when the value of `nullableVar` is `null`.

The Safe Call Operator

Another option is to use a Safe Call. This is an invocation of some behaviour on a *nullable* variable in which the safe call operator is used. The safe call operator is written as ? .; that is it is the combination of the '?' and '.' Characters. This operator is essentially a shorthand version of the above code, that is if the variable holds a *non null* value then that value is used, if not the ? . operator returns `null`. For example:

```
// Nullable variable - can be set to null
var nullableVar: String? = "John"
println(nullableVar?.length)

nullableVar = null
println(nullableVar?.length)
```

The above code snippet uses the ?. safe call operator to invoke the length property on the string held in nullableVar. In the first example this is the string "John". However, in the second example the variable has been set to null. This does not however, result in a NullPointerException being raised. Instead the value null is returned as the result of the call to length. The output from this code example is shown below:

```
4
Null
```

It is also possible to chain the safe call operator such that the result returned by an operation is used to call a subsequent member function for example:

```
company?.department?.head?.name
```

In this case if company is null or the property department or head are null the overall result of this call chain will be null.

It is also possible to use the ?. safe call operator on the left hand side of an assignment, for example:

```
company?.department?.head?.name ="John"
```

In this case if a null value is returned by any of the elements on the left hand side, then the assignment is not evaluated (performed) at all.

Thus the safe call operator ensures that you will never get an error generated from the operation being invoked.

The Elvis Operator

The so called elvis operator is also formed of two characters. These characters are the "?" and ":" characters as in ?:. It is called the elvis operator as the question mark looks a little like the quiff Elvis wore.

The purpose of the Elvis operator is to allow a default value other than null to be returned when calling a function or property on a nullable variable. For example it is the equivalent of writing the following in a shorthand form:

```
val l1 = if (nullableVar == null) -1 else nullableVar.length
```

In this example, if nullableVar currently holds the value null then the result of the if expression is -1 rather than null.

Using the Elvis operator we can write:

```
val l2 = nullableVar?.length ?: -1
```

In this case if the result of the safe call operator is null then the elvis operator will return -1 otherwise it will just return the value returned from length. For example:

```
nullableVar = "John"
val l2 = nullableVar?.length ?: -1
println(l2)

nullableVar = null
val l3 = nullableVar?.length ?: -1
println(l3)
```

The output generated by this code snippet is:

```
4
-1
```

The Not-Null Assertion Operator

The *not-null assertion* operator is formed of two exclamation marks i.e. !!. This operator is used to treat a nullable variable as a non-null type. If the current value of the *nullable* type is null when the operator is applied then a NullPointerException error will be generated. Otherwise it will be treated as a normal *non-null* type. For example:

```
nullableVar = "John"
val l4 = nullableVar!!.length
println(l2)
nullableVar = null
val l5 = nullableVar!!.length
println(l3)
```

However, the compiler will analyse the code and see that the nullableVar is set to null the line before the not-null assertion operator is applied; in this case it will not even compile the code as it knows that it will always result in a NullPointerException error being generated.

Smart Compilation

The Kotlin compiler is smart enough to work out whether a value is null or not in many situations. This is illustrated below.

```
var total: Int? = null
// total++ // won't compile as total may be null
if (total != null) {
    total++
}
```

The first line of this code declares a new var called total of type Int? (that is it is a *nullable* integer). However, it currently holds the value null. This means that if we attempt to increment total using the increment (++) operator (which is the same as saying total = total + 1) then we would be trying to add 1 to null which is illegal. Thus the second line in the example has to be commented out as it would generate a compile time error. We could of course use one of the nullable operators to handle this such as the safe dot operator (? .). However, in this case we are using an explicit if statement that will check to see if total is null. If it is not null then we can safely increment total. The compiler is smart enough to understand this and allow the increment of total within the if block.

Safe Casting to Non Null Type

The final option related to nullable values is to cast them to a *non-null* type explicitly. This is done using the as? operator known as the *safe cast* operator. This type of cast is safe because it will either convert a value in a type to a non-null type or return the value null (if the value to be cast is null). For example:

```
val total: Int? = null
println(total as? Int)
```

The output from this code example is:

```
null
```

When Expression

Kotlin's when expression allows for a selection to be made between a number of alternative tests and as such is similar in nature to the case statement in Pascal and

C or the `switch` statement in Java. However, compared to the `switch` statement in Java it allows much wider matching capabilities both in the types that can be compared and in the test clause of the expression. This allows for greater flexible in the language construct. Also note that the when expression is an expression (and not just a statement) thus it returns a value and can be used as part of an assignment clause.

The conditional element in the when expression is much more flexible than in languages such as C and Java and can be:

- A numeric literal such as `42` or `3.14`,
- A boolean value such as `true` or `false`,
- A String,
- A test for the type of value being considered,
- A value in a range,
- An instance,
- An object.

The syntax for a when expression is:

```
when (<value to test> {
    condition -> statement or statement block
    // Further conditions
    else -> statement or statements (optional)
}
```

A simple example of a when expression is given below. This expression merely tests an integer against a set of values, note that a comma can be used to separate a number of values to be compared that have the same associated behaviour:

```
val value = 1
when (value) {
    0 -> println("It is a 0")
    1, 2 -> println("It is a 1 or 2")
    3 -> println("It is to high")
    else -> println("Default")
}
```

This means that

- if `value` is 0 then the message "It is a 0" will be printed out.
- If `value` is 1 or 2 then the message "It is a 1 or 2" will be printed out
- If `value` is 3 then the message "It is to high" will be printed out.
- otherwise if it is any other value then the default `else` clause will be run and the message "Default" will be printed out.

Note that it is not required to have an `else` clause. That is, the `else` clause is an optional element of a when expression and can be included or not as required by the programmer.

The output from the above example code is:

```
It is a 1 or 2
```

In this case we have not used the fact that the when expression is an expression, however this usage is illustrated below:

```
val value = 1
val message = when(value) {
    0 -> "Invalid number"
    1, 2 -> "Number too low"
    3 -> "Number correct"
    4 -> "Number too high, but acceptable"
    in 5..10 -> "Number too high, might be acceptable"
    !in 10..20 -> "What are you on"
    else -> "Bad number"
}
println("message: $message")
```

In the above example the result of the when expression is saved into the message val. This example also illustrates a few other when *condition* examples:

- in 5...10 indicates that if the value is in the range 5 up to and including 10 then use the associated string.
- !in 10...20 indicates that if the value is not in the range 10 to 20 use the associated string.

Note that only one of the conditions will be triggered and that each condition is tested in turn and thus the first one that matches will be used and only the first one. The output from this example is therefore:

```
message: Number too low
```

We are not restricted to just using numbers in a when *condition* (as is the case in some other languages). For example, the following example uses a String as the type to be tested:

```
val value2 = "John"
when (value2) {
    "John" -> println("Dad")
    "Denise" -> println("Mum")
    else -> println("Not mum or dad")
}
```

In this case if `value2` holds a reference to the String "John" we will print out "Dad", if holds reference to the String "Denise" it will print out "Mum" otherwise it will print out the message "Not mum or dad". The actual output from this code is:

```
Dad
```

We can in fact use any type with a when expression, if we have a custom type `Person` then we can use such a type with the when expression and test for equality between instances of the type, for example:

```
val person = Person()
val person1 = person
when (person1) {
    person -> println("its me")
    else -> println("its not me")
}
```

In the above example `Person()` is what is known as a class in Kotlin. We will look at classes in several later chapters. The output from this code snippet is:

```
its me
```

We can even use a when expression to determine what type of thing we have. This can be done using the `is` operator. Thus allows us to check whether a `val` or `var` holds something that is an `Int`, or a `String`, or a `Double` etc. This is illustrated below (note `Any` means that the val x is any type of thing):

```
val x: Any = 32
when (x) {
    is Int -> println("Its a Int")
    is Double -> println("Its a Double")
    is Boolean -> println("Its a Boolean")
    is String -> println("Its a String")
    is Person -> println("Its a Person")
    else -> println("its something else")
}
```

The result of running this code snippet is:

```
Its a Int
```

If you need to have more than one statement associated with each condition within a when expression, you can use curly brackets to group them together. For example:

```
val total = 34
when (total) {
    0 -> {
        print("Its Zero")
        println("Never mind")
    }
    in 1..5 -> println("Not Bad")
    else -> println("Excellent")
}
```

While Loop

The while loop exists in almost all programming languages and is used to iterate (or repeat) one or more code statements as long as the test condition (expression) is true. This iteration construct is usually used when the number of times we need to repeat the block of code to execute is not know. For example, it may need to repeat until some solution is found or the user enters a particular value.

A while loop is known as a *conditional loop* as the number of times the loop will be repeated is not known at the start. Instead the loop is repeated while some *condition* is true.

The behaviour of the while loop is illustrated in below.

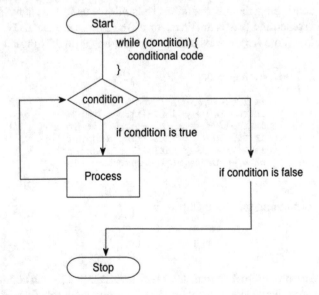

The Kotlin while loop is a statment (rather than an expression) and has the basic form:

```
while (<test-condition-is-true>) {
    statement or statements
}
```

As shown both in the diagram and can be inferred from the code; *while* the test condition/expression is `true` then the statement or block of statements in the while loop will be executed. Note that if a single statement is present then the curly brackets are optional (but their use is considered good style).

Note that the test is performed *before* each iteration, including the first iteration; therefore, if the condition fails before the first iteration of the loop statement or block of statements, then the code contained in the loop may never be executed at all.

The following illustrates an example `while` loop in Kotlin:

```
fun main() {
    var count = 0
    println("Starting")
    while (count < 10) {
        print("$count, ")
        count++
    }
    println()
    println("Done")
}
```

In this example while some variable `count` is less than the value 10 the `while` loop will continue to iterate (will be repeated). The `while` loop itself contains two statements; one prints out the value of the `count` variable while the other increments `count` (remember `count++` is equivalent to count = count + 1).

Note we have used the version of `print()` that does not print a carriage return when it prints out a value.

The result of running this example is:

```
Starting
0, 1, 2, 3, 4, 5, 6, 7, 8, 9,
Done
```

As you can see the statements printing the "Starting" and "Done" messages are only run once. However, the statement printing out the `count` variable is run 10 times (printing out the values 0 to 9).

Once the value of count is equal to 10 then the loop finishes (or terminates).

Note that we needed to initialise the count variable before the loop. This is because it needs to have a value for the first iteration of the while loop. That is before the while loop does anything the program needs to already know the first value of count so that it can perform that very first test. This is a feature of the while loops behaviour.

Do Loop

In some cases, we want to execute the body of statements at least once; you can accomplish this with the do loop construct:

```
do
    statement
while (test expression)
```

This loop is guaranteed to execute at least once, as the test is only performed after the statement has been evaluated. As with the while loop, the do loop repeats until the condition is false. You can repeat more than one statement by bracketing a series of statements into a block using curly brackets { }, for example:

```
fun main() {
    var count = 0
    println("Starting")
    do {
        print("$count, ")
        count++
    } while (count < 10)
    println()
    println("Done")
}
```

The above do loop prints the numbers from 1 up to 9 and terminates when count equals 10.

```
Starting
0, 1, 2, 3, 4, 5, 6, 7, 8, 9,
Done
```

The logic of the while loop is illustrated in below.

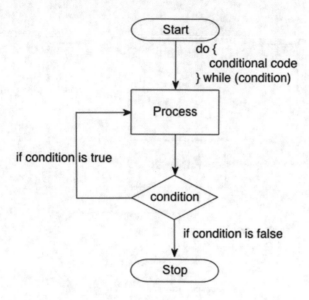

For Loop

In many cases we know how many times we want to iterative over one or more statements (as indeed we did in the previous section). Although the `while` loop can be used for such situations, the `for` loop is a far more concise way to do this. It is also typically clearer to another programmer that the loop must iterate for a specific number of iterations.

The `for` loop is used to step a *variable* through a series of values until a given test is met. It is also known as a *counted loop* as the number of times the loop will be repeated is known at the start of the loop.

The behaviour of the `for` loop is illustrated in below.

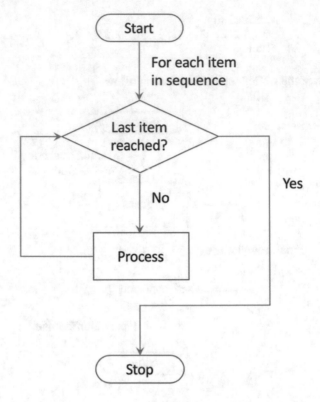

This flow chart shows that some sequence of values (for example all integer values between 0 and 9) will be used to iterate over a block of code to process. When the last item in the sequence has been reached, the loop will terminate.

Many languages have a for loop of the form:

```
for (i in iterable) {
    statement or statements
}
```

Where iterable can be an integer range, an integer progression or some object that is iterable such as a String or some from of data collection or container. If you are familiar with for loops in languages such as C or C++ this may seem strange as a for loop in those languages only loops over a series of integer values. However the for loop construct in Kotlin is very flexible and can loop over not only a range of integer values but also a set of values held in data structures such as a list of integers or Strings. We will return to this feature of the for loop when we look at collections/containers of data in a later chapter.

The simplest format of the Kotlin for loop when using a range of values is

```
for (<variable-name> in <startvalue>..<endvalue>) {
    statement
    statement
}
```

An example is shown below which equates to the while loop we looked at earlier:

```
println("Print out values in a range")
for (i in 0..9) {
    print("$i, ")
}
println()
println("Done")
```

When we run this code, the output is:

```
Print out values in a range
0, 1, 2, 3, 4, 5, 6, 7, 8, 9,
Done
```

As can be seen from the above; the end result is that we have generated a for loop that produces the same set of values as the earlier while loop. However,

- the code is more concise,
- it is clear we are processing a range of values from 0 to 9 (note that it is up to and including the final value) and
- we did not need to define the loop variable first.

For these reasons *for* loops are more common in programs in general than *while* loops.

One thing you might notice though is that in the while loop we are not constrained to incrementing the count variable by one (we just happened to do this). For example, we could have decided to increment count by 2 each time round the loop (a very common idea). In fact, the Kotlin for loop allows us to do exactly this; a third element that can be provided to the for loop is the *step* value to increment the loop variable by each time round the loop, for example:

```
// Now use values in a range but increment by 2
println("Print out values in a range with an increment of 2")
for (i in 0..9 step 2) {
    print("$i, ")
}
println()
println("Done")
```

When we run this code, the output is.

```
Print out values in a range with an increment of 2
0, 2, 4, 6, 8,
Done
```

Thus the value of the loop variable has jumped by 2 starting at 0. Once its value was 10 or more then the loop terminates. Of course, it is not only the value 2 we could use; we could *step* (increment) by any meaningful integer, 3, 4 or 5 etc.

Above we noted that the `for` loop included the values in the range 0 to 9; however if you wish to loop up until the maximum value (that is not to include the maximum value) then you can use the `until` operator:

```
println("Print out values in a range to but not including 9")
for (x in 0 until 9)
    print("$x, ")
println()
println("Done")
```

This will loop from the value 0 up to the value 8 but not the value 9:

```
Print out values in a range to but not including 9

0, 1, 2, 3, 4, 5, 6, 7, 8,
Done
```

Also notice that in the above example we did not use the curly brackets as the for loop only contained a single statement. This is legal but is not considered best practice.

We can also loop using `until` with a *step* value other than 1:

```
println("Print out values in a range to but not including 9 with
step 2")
for (x in 0 until 9 step 2) {
    print("$x, ")
}
println()
println("Done")
```

The output from this code snippet is:

```
Print out values in a range to but not including 9 with step 2
0, 2, 4, 6, 8,
Done
```

It is also possible to loop from a higher integer value down to a lower value using the `downTo` operator:

```
println("Iterate down from one value to a lower value")
for (i in 5 downTo 0) {
    print("$i * $i = ${i*i}; ")
}
println()
println("Done")
```

This generates:

```
Iterate down from one value to a lower value
5 * 5 = 25; 4 * 4 = 16; 3 * 3 = 9; 2 * 2 = 4; 1 * 1 = 1; 0 * 0 =
0;
Done
```

Repeat Loops

Kotlin includes another loop statement called the `repeat` statement. This is similar to a for loop in that it is a counted loop. That is the number of times the loop will be repeated is known at the start. However, it differs from a for loop in that the loop variable is not made explicit. This is useful in situations where you know you want to loop a certain number of times, but you do not need to reference the loop index.

The repeat loop has the following syntax:

```
repeat (number-of-times-to-loop) statement or block of statements
```

This is illustrated below:

```
fun main() {

    repeat(3) {
        print("Hello, ")
    }
    println()

}
```

The output from this program is:

```
Hello, Hello, Hello,
```

Loop Control Statements

Break Loop Statement

Kotlin allows programmers to decide whether they want to break out of a loop early or not (whether we are using a `for`, `while` or `do-while` loop). This is done using the `break` statement.

The `break` statement allows a developer to alter the normal cycle of the loop based on some criteria which may not be predictable in advance (for example it may be based on some user input).

The `break` statement, when executed, will terminate the current loop and jump the program to the first line after the loop. The following diagram shows how this works for a for loop:

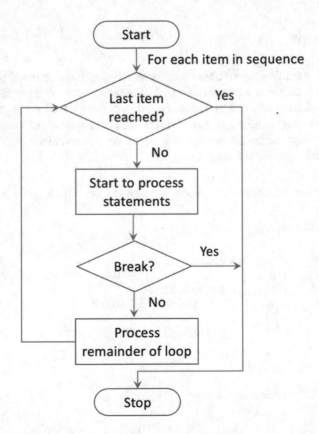

Typically, a guard statement (`if` statement) is placed on the break so that the `break` statement is conditionally applied when appropriate.

This is shown below for a simple `for` loop that is set up to loop from 0 up until 10. However within the `for` loop an `if` statement is used such that when the value of i is 5 the break statement will be executed. This will cause the program to break out of the loop. This means the values of i from 6 to 9 will never be executed:

```
val y = 10
val x = 5

for (i in 0 until y) {
    if (i == x) {
        break
    }
    print("i: $i, ")
}
println()
```

If we run this code snippet the loop should print out:

```
i: 0, i: 1, i: 2, i: 3, i: 4,
```

The break statement can come anywhere within the block of code associated with the loop construct (whether that is a for loop, a while loop or a do-while loop). This means that there can be statements before it and after it.

It is also possible to label an outer loop construct. If this label is then used with the break statement, the break statement will break out of the labelled loop rather than the loop it is directly defined within. For example, in the following nested loop example, the outer most for loop is labeled with loop@. Note that the format of the label is < label-name>@ when used on the looping construct which we will break out of. Within the inner for loop there is a condition, that if i equal 3 then the program will break out of the loop with the label loop. Note the syntax is now break@ <label-name>:

```
loop@ for (i in 0 until 4) {
    for (j in 0 until 2) {
        if (i == 3) {
            break@loop
        }
        println("$i - $j, ")
    }
}
```

When this program is run the output generated is:

```
0 - 0,
0 - 1,
1 - 0,
1 - 1,
2 - 0,
2 - 1,
```

   As can be seen the outer loop is terminated when i is 3 (which also terminates
the inner loop). This allows for fine grained control when breaking out of a loop.

Continue Loop Statement

The continue statement also affects the flow of control within the looping
constructs for, while anddo-while. However, it does not terminate the whole
loop; rather it only terminates the current iteration round the loop. This allows you
to skip over part of a loop's iteration for a particular value, but then to continue with
the remaining values in the sequence.

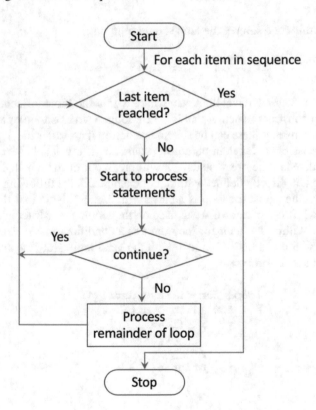

   A guard (if statement) can be used to determine when the continue statement
should be executed.

As with the break statement, the continue can come anywhere within the body of the looping construct. This means that you can have some statements that will be executed for every value in the sequence and some that are only executed when the continue statement is not run.

This is shown below. In this program the continue statement is executed only for odd numbers and thus the two println() statements are only run if the value of i is even:

```kotlin
fun main() {
    for (i in 0 until 10) {
        print("$i ")
        if ((i % 2) == 1) {
            continue
        }
        println("hey its an even number")
        println("we love even numbers")
    }
    println("Done")
}
```

When we run this code we get

```
0  hey its an even number
we love even numbers
1  2  hey its an even number
we love even numbers
3  4  hey its an even number

we love even numbers
5  6  hey its an even number
we love even numbers
7  8  hey its an even number
we love even numbers
9  Done
```

As you can see, we only print out the messages about a number being even when the values are 0, 2, 4, 6 and 8.

It is also possible to label a loop construct for use with the continue statement. In this case a labelled continue statement will cause the program to jump out of any loops within the labelled loop and then to continue with the next iteration of the labelled loop. This is illustrated by the following program:

```
fun main() {
    outer@ for (i in 1..4) {
        println("i = $i")
        for (j in 1..4) {
            val result = i + j
            if (result == 5) continue@outer
            println("\t$i + $j = $result ")
        }
    }
}
```

When we run this program the output obtained is:

```
i = 1
    1 + 1 = 2
    1 + 2 = 3
    1 + 3 = 4
i = 2
    2 + 1 = 3
    2 + 2 = 4
i = 3
    3 + 1 = 4
i = 4
```

As can be seen from this the inner loop is terminated each time the value of result is 5 at which point the next iteration of the outer loop is then triggered.

When with Continue and Break

Prior to Kotlin 1.4 it was not possible to use an unlabelled continue or break with an iteration construct inside a when expression. That is you could not use unlabelled continue and breakstatements within a when expression to determine if the program should continue or break out of a loop. This was because continue and break were reserved with respect to the when expression for future use. It was thus necessary to explicitly label a loop and then use the loop with continue and break.

In Kotlin 1.4 it was decided that continue and break would not be used specifically by the when@ expression and thus from this version on it is possible to use these special control operations without labels. This is illustrated below for Kotlin 1.4 and 1.5:

```
fun main() {
    for (i in 0..10) {
        when (i) {
            2 -> continue
            4 -> break
            else -> println(i)
        }
    }
}
```

A Note on Loop Variable Naming

Earlier in the book we said that variable names should be meaningful and that names such as 'a' and 'b' were not in general a good idea. The one exception to this rule relates to loop variable names used with for loops. It is very common to find that these loop variables are called 'i', 'j' etc.

It is such a common convention that if a variable is called 'i' or 'j' people expect it to be a loop variable. As such.

* you should consider using these variable names in looping constructs,
* and avoid using them elsewhere.

But this does raise the question why 'i' and 'j'; the answer is that it all goes back to a programming language called Fortran which was first developed in the 1950s. In this programming language loop variables had to be called 'i' and 'j' etc. Fortran was so ubiquitous for mathematical and scientific programming, where loops are almost *di rigour*, that this has become the convention in other languages which do not have this restriction.

Dice Roll Game

The following short program illustrates how a while loop can be used to control the execution of the main body of code. In this program we will continue to roll a pair of dice until the user indicates that they do not want to roll again. When this occurs the while loop will terminate:

```kotlin
import kotlin.random.Random

fun main() {

    val MIN = 1
    val MAX = 6

    var rollAgain: String? = "y"

    while (rollAgain == "y") {
        println("Rolling the dices...")
        println("The values are....")

    val dice1 = Random.nextInt(MIN, MAX)
    println(dice1)
    val dice2 = Random.nextInt(MIN, MAX)
    println(dice2)
    print("Roll the dices again? (y / n): ")
    rollAgain = readLine()
    }

}
```

When we run this program the results of rolling two dice are shown. The program will keep looping and printing out the two dice values until the user indicates that they no longer want to roll the dice:

```
Rolling the dices...
The values are....
2
6
Roll the dices again? (y / n): y
Rolling the dices...
The values are....
4
1
Roll the dices again? (y / n): y
Rolling the dices...
The values are....
3
6
Roll the dices again? (y / n): n
```

There are two things to note about this program; the first is that we have used the readLine() function to obtain input from the user. This function returns a string or a null value and thus the rollAgain variable must be *nullable*.

The other thing to note is that we are using the Random type from the kotlin.random library. As this is not one of the default libraries loaded when

Kotlin starts up we must indicate to the program that it should load the Random type from this library by adding the following import statement to the start of the program file:

```
import kotlin.random.Random
```

Online Resources

See the Kotlin Standard Library documentation for:

- https://kotlinlang.org/docs/reference/null-safety.html Considers nullability in Kotlin.
- https://kotlinlang.org/docs/reference/control-flow.html documentation on flow of control in Kotlin.
- https://kotlinlang.org/docs/reference/returns.html documentation on continue and break.

Exercises

There are five different exercises in this section, you can select which you are interested in or do all five.

Check Input is Positive or Negative

The aim of this exercise is to write a small program to test if an integer is positive or negative.

Your program should:

1. Prompt the user to input a number (use the `readLine()` function). You can assume that the input will be some sort of number.
2. Convert the string into an integer using the toInt() method available to convert Strings to Ints. We will assume that the user either enters nothing or they enter a valid integer.
3. You can check whether they entered something by testing for a null value.
4. Now check whether the integer is a positive number or a negative number.
5. You could also add a test to see if the number is Zero using an else block.

The output from such a program might be:

```
Please input a number: 5
Number is positive
```

Or

```
Please input a number: -1
Number is negative
```

Or indeed:

```
Please input a number: 0
Number is zero
```

Test if a Number is Odd or Even

This exercise requires you to write a program to take input from the user and determine if the number is odd or even. Again you can assume that the user will enter a valid integer number.

Print out a message to the user to let them know the result.

To test if a number is even you can use

```
(number % 2) == 0
```

Which will return true if the number is even.

The output from this program is illustrated below:

```
Please input a number: 2
Number is even
```

Or

```
Please input a number: 3
Number is odd
```

Kilometres to Miles Converter

The aim of this exercise is to write a program to convert a distance in Kilometres into a distance in miles.

1. Take input from the user for a given distance in Kilometres. This can be done using the `readLine()` function.
2. Convert the value returned by the `readLine()` function from a string into an integer using the `toInt()` method.
3. Now convert this value into miles—this can be done by multiplying the kilometres by `0.621371`
4. Print out a message telling the user what the kilometres are in miles.

Once you have done this you can add a few further features to vitrify the input entered by the user:

1. Modify your program such that it verifies that the user has entered a positive distance (i.e. they cannot enter a negative number).

An example of the output from the conversion program is given below:

```
Please input a distance in kilometers: 10
10 km as 6.21371 miles
```

Calculate the Factorial of a Number

Write a program that can find the factorial of any given number. For example, find the factorial of the number 5 (often written as `5!`) which is `1 * 2 * 3 * 4 * 5` and equals `120`.

The factorial is not defined for negative numbers and the factorial of Zero is 1; that is `0 != 1`.

Your program should take as input an integer from the user.
You should:

1. Determine if the number is less than Zero, in which case you should print out an error message.
2. Check to see if the number is Zero—if it is then the answer is 1—print this out.
3. Otherwise use a loop to generate the result and print it out.

For example:

```
Please input a number: 5
5 ! factorial is 120
```

Or

```
Please input a number: 0
1 ! factorial is 1
```

And

```
Please input a number: -1
Factorial is not defined for negative numbers
```

Chapter 4
Number Guessing Game

Introduction

In this chapter we are going to bring everything we have learned so far together to create a simple number guessing game.

This will involve creating a new Kotlin program, handling user input, using the if statement as well as using looping constructs.

We will also use an additional library or package, that is not by default available to your program; this will be the random number generator library.

Setting Up the Program

We want to make sure that we don't overwrite whatever you have done so far, and we would like this Kotlin program to be separate from your other work. As such we will create a new Kotlin file to hold this program in the intelliJ IDE.

We will create a new Kotlin file to hold your program. To do this select the src node in the left-hand Project view. Once you have selected this use the *right mouse button* menu. On this menu select 'New' followed by 'Kotlin Class/File', see below:

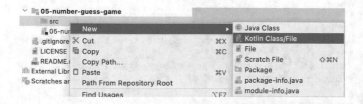

First select the File option which is the second option down below the input field in the 'New Kotlin Class/File' dialog. When you do this, you will prompted to provide a name for the Kotlin file; you can call the file whatever you like, but I am using the

© The Author(s), under exclusive license to Springer Nature Switzerland AG 2021
J. Hunt, *Beginner's Guide to Kotlin Programming*,
https://doi.org/10.1007/978-3-030-80893-8_4

name 'NumberGuessGame' as that is descriptive and will help me find this file again
later:

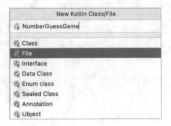

Now click OK.

The next thing we will do is create the main function for our number guess game
with a simple welcome message that can be used at the start of the game:

```
NumberGuessGame.kt ×
1
2 ▶  ⊙fun main() {
3          println("Welcome to the number guess game")
4     ⊙}
```

We can now run our embryonic program. To do this we can select the green arrow
next to the fun main() line in the editor window. Notice that the generated code
that sits behind our `main()` function is called `NumberGuessGameKt` (which is
derived from the name of the file that the function is defined in).

When we do this the Run console will be opened at the bottom of the IDE and
the output displayed:

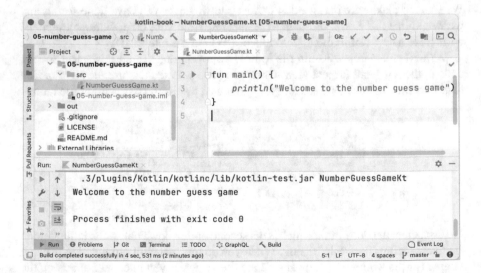

From now on you can rerun the `NumberGuessGameKt` program merely by clicking on the little green arrow at the top right-hand side of IntelliJ (it allows you to rerun the last program that IntelliJ executed).

What Will the Program Do?

The aim of our number guess game is to guess the number that the program has come up with.

The main flow of the program is shown in the following diagram:

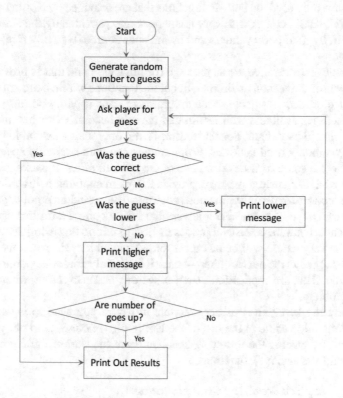

Essentially the program logic is

- The program randomly selects a number between 1 and 10.
- It will then ask the player to enter their guess.
- It will then check to see if that number is the same as the one the computer randomly generated; if it is then the player has won.
- If the player's guess is not the same, then it will check to see if the number is higher or lower than the guess and tell the player.

- The player will have 4 goes to guess the number correctly; if they don't guess the number within this number of attempts, then they will be informed that they have lost the game and will be told what the actual number was.

Creating the Game

Generate the Random Number

We will start off by looking at how we can generate a random number. Up to this point we have only used the built-in functions that are provided by Kotlin by default. In actual fact Kotlin comes with very many *packages* provided by the Kotlin Foundation itself, by third party vendors and by the open source (typically free) software community.

The Kotlin `kotlin.random` package (or library) is one that is provided with Kotlin as part of the default environment; but the functions within it are not automatically loaded or made available to the programmer. This is partly because there are so many facilities available with Kotlin that it could become overwhelming if they were all included by default. For this reason Kotlin only makes available by default the most commonly used facilities. Programmers can then explicitly specify when they want to use some facilities from one of the other libraries or packages.

The `kotlin.random` package provides implementations of pseudo-random number generators for use in application programs. These random number generators are referred to as *pseudo* because it is very hard for a computer to truly generate a series of random numbers; instead it does its best to mimic this using an algorithm; which by its very nature will be based on some logic which will mean that it is not impossible to predict the next number—hence it is not truly random. For our purposes this is fine but there are applications, such as security and encryption, where this can be a real problem.

To access the `kotlin.random` module in Kotlin you need to *import* it; this makes the module visible in the rest of the Kotlin file (in our case to our program). This is done by placing the following statements are the start of the file before the declaration of the `main()` function.

```
import kotlin.random.Random

val numberToGuess = Random.nextInt(1, 11)
```

Once we have imported it, we can use the functions within this package, such as `Random.nextInt()`. This function returns a random integer between the first and (up to but not including) the second parameter's value. In the above example it means that the random number generated will be between 1 and 10.

The val `numberToGuess` will now hold an integer which the player of the game must guess.

Obtain an Input from the User

We now need to obtain input from the user representing their guess. We have already seen how to do this in previous chapters; we can use the readLine() function which returns a String (or null if there is no input) and then the toInt() function that will convert that String into an integer (we will ignore error checking to make sure they have typed in a number at this point). Kotlin however, does not allow an operation to be invoked when a value might be null; it is therefore necessary to specify what value should be used if the call to readLine() returned null. To do this we use the Elvis operator ? :. This operator was introduced int he last chapter and indicates that the left hand value should be returned unless it is null, in which case the right hand value will be used instead. Thus the following statement says "take the users input unless its null in which case use the empty string":

```
print("Please guess a number between 1 and 10: ")
val guess:String = readLine() ?: ""
var intGuess = guess.toInt()
```

The string is then turned into an Int value using toInt() and stored in the var intGuess.

Check to See if the Player Has Guessed the Number

We now need to check to see whether the player has guessed the correct number.

We could use an if statement for this, however we are going to want to repeat this test until the user has guessed correctly.

We will therefore use a while loop and check to see if their guess equals the number to be guessed:

```
print("Please guess a number between 1 and 10: ")
val guess:String = readLine() ?: ""
var intGuess = guess.toInt()

while (numberToGuess != intGuess) {

}
```

The loop above will be repeated if the number they entered did not match the number to be guessed.

We can therefore print a message telling the player that their guess was wrong:

```
print("Please guess a number between 1 and 10: ")
val guess:String = readLine() ?: ""
var intGuess = guess.toInt()

while (numberToGuess != intGuess) {
    println("Sorry wrong number")

}
```

Now we need the player to make another guess otherwise the program will never terminate, so we can again prompt them to enter a number:

```
print("Please guess a number between 1 and 10: ")
val guess:String = readLine() ?: ""
var intGuess = guess.toInt()

while (numberToGuess != intGuess) {
    println("Sorry wrong number")
    // TBD ...
    print("Please guess again between 1 and 10: ")
    val guess = readLine() ?: ""
    intGuess = guess.toInt()
}
```

Check They Haven't Exceeded Their Maximum Number of Guess

We also said above that the player can't play forever; they have to guess the correct number within 4 goes. We therefore need to add some logic which will stop the game once they exceed this number.

We will therefore need a variable (var) to keep track of the number of attempts they have made.

We should call this variable something meaningful so that we know what it represents, for example we could call it countNumberOfTries and initialise it with the value 1:

```
var countNumberOfTries = 1
```

This needs to happen before we enter the while loop.
Inside the while loop we need to do two things:

- check to see if the number of tries has been exceeded,
- increment the number of tries if they are still allowed to play the game.

We will use an if statement to check to see if the number of tries has been met; if it has we want to terminate the loop; the easiest way to this is via a break statement.

```
if (countNumberOfTries == 4) {
    break
}
```

If we don't break out of the loop we can increment the count using the '+ + ' increment operator. We thus now have:

```
print("Please guess a number between 1 and 10: ")
val guess:String = readLine() ?: ""
var intGuess = guess.toInt()
var countNumberOfTries = 1


while (numberToGuess != intGuess) {
    println("Sorry wrong number")

    if (countNumberOfTries == 4) {
        break
    }

    print("Please guess again between 1 and 10: ")
    val guess = readLine() ?: ""
    intGuess = guess.toInt()
    countNumberOfTries++
}
```

Notify the Player Whether Higher or Lower

We also said at the beginning that to make it easier for the player to guess the number; we should indicate whether their guess was higher or lower than the actual number. To do this we can again use the if statement; if the guess is lower we print one message but if it was higher we print another.

At this point we have a choice regarding whether to have a separate if statement to that used to decide if the maximum goes has been reached or to extend that one with an else if. Each approach can work but the latter indicates that these conditions are all related so that is the one we will use.

The while loop now looks like:

```
print("Please guess a number between 1 and 10: ")
val guess:String = readLine() ?: ""
var intGuess = guess.toInt()

var countNumberOfTries = 1
while (numberToGuess != intGuess) {
    println("Sorry wrong number")

    if (countNumberOfTries == 4) {
        break
    } else if (intGuess < numberToGuess) {
        println("Your guess was lower than the number")
    } else {
        println("Your guess was higher than the number")
    }

    print("Please guess again between 1 and 10: ")
    val guess = readLine() ?: ""
    intGuess = guess.toInt()
    countNumberOfTries++
}
```

Notice that the if statement has a final else which indicates that the guess was higher; this is fine as by this point it is the only option left.

End of Game Status

We have now covered all the situations that can occur while the game is being played; all that is left for us to do is to handle the end of game messages.

If the player has guessed the number correctly, we want to congratulate them; if they did not guess the number, we want to let them know what the actual number was. We will do this using another if statement which checks to see if the player guessed the number or not. After this we will print an end of game message:

```
if (numberToGuess == intGuess) {
    println("Well Done You Won!")
    println("You took $countNumberOfTries goes to complete the
game")
} else {
    println("Sorry - You Loose")
    println("The number you needed to guess was $numberToGuess")
}

println("Game Over")
```

Note that we are using String templates so that the output generated will include information such as the number of tries made or the number to be guessed. This is done using the '$' notation which indicates that the current value of the following val or var should be inserted into the string.

The Complete Listing

For ease of reference the complete listing is provided below:

```
import kotlin.random.Random
val numberToGuess = Random.nextInt(0, 11)

fun main() {

    println("Welcome to the number guess game")

    print("Please guess a number between 1 and 10: ")
    val guess:String = readLine() ?: ""
    var intGuess = guess.toInt()

    var countNumberOfTries = 1
    while (numberToGuess != intGuess) {
        println("Sorry wrong number")

        if (countNumberOfTries == 4) {
            break
        } else if (intGuess < numberToGuess) {
            println("Your guess was lower than the number")
        } else {
            println("Your guess was higher than the number")
        }
```

```kotlin
        print("Please guess again between 1 and 10: ")
        val guess = readLine() ?: ""
        intGuess = guess.toInt()
        countNumberOfTries++
    }

    if (numberToGuess == intGuess) {
        println("Well Done You Won!")
        println("You took $countNumberOfTries goes to complete
the game")
    } else {
        println("Sorry - You Loose")
        println("The number you needed to guess was
$numberToGuess")
    }

    println("Game Over")

}
```

And a sample run of the program is shown here:

```
Welcome to the number guess game
Please guess a number between 1 and 10: 5
Sorry wrong number
Your guess was higher than the number
Please guess again between 1 and 10: 3
Sorry wrong number
Your guess was lower than the number
Please guess again between 1 and 10: 4
Well Done You Won!
You took 3 goes to complete the game
Game Over
```

Hints

Blank Lines Within a Block of Code

You may have noticed that we have used blank lines to group together certain lines of code in this example. This is intended to make it easier to read the code and are perfectly allowable in Kotlin. Indeed, the Kotlin layout guidelines encourage it.

Exercises

For this chapter the exercises all relate to adding additional features to the game:

1. Provide a cheat mode, for example if the user enters -1 print out the number they need to guess and then loop again. This does not count as one of their goes.
2. If their guess is within 1 of the actual number tell the player this.
3. At the end of the game, before printing 'Game Over', modify your program so that it asks the user if they want to play again; if they say yes then restart the whole game.

Chapter 5
Functions in Kotlin

Introduction

When you build an application of any size you will want to break it down into more manageable units; these units can then be worked on separately, tested and maintained separately. One way in which these units can be defined is as Kotlin functions.

This chapter will introduce functions, how they are defined, how they can be referenced and executed. It will also introduce the use of parameters to functions and values being returned from functions. It also introduces anonymous functions and lambdas. It concludes by considering function closures and recursion.

What Are Functions?

In Kotlin functions are groups of related statements that can be called together, that typically perform a specific task. Such functions may or may not take a set of parameters or return a value.

Functions can be defined in one place and called or invoked in another. This helps to make code more modular and easier to understand.

It also means that the same function can be called multiple times or in multiple locations. This help to ensure that although a piece of functionality is used in multiple places; it is only defined once and only needs to be maintained and tested in one location.

Functions are also part of the type system in Kotlin. Thus a function that takes an Int and returns an Int has the type (Int) - > Int (which can be read as a function(Int) returns Int).

© The Author(s), under exclusive license to Springer Nature Switzerland AG 2021   81
J. Hunt, *Beginner's Guide to Kotlin Programming*,
https://doi.org/10.1007/978-3-030-80893-8_5

Defining Functions

The basic syntax of a named function is illustrated below:

```
fun functionName(parameter list): return-type {
    statement
    statement(s)
    return <value>
}
```

This illustrates several things:

1. All named functions are defined using the *keyword* fun; this indicates the start of a *function definition*.
2. A function can have a name which uniquely identifies it; you can also have *anonymous* and *lambda* functions.
3. The naming conventions that we have been adopting for variables also apply to functions. That is, the names of function are by default all lower case, with the different elements of the function name separated by a capital letter for example increment() and getNextPlayer().
4. A function can (optionally) have a list of parameters. These parameters allow data to be passed into the function. These are optional as not all functions need to be supplied with parameters. However the round brackets () are always required when defining a function and when invoking that function.
5. A colon after the function parameter list is used to specify the optional return type. If no return type is specified then Unit is assumed. Unit indicates that no value is returned from a function. If you wish to return a value then you must specify the type of the value being returned.
6. The curly brackets indicate the end of the *function header* and the start of the *function body*. The function header defines the signature of the function (what its called and the parameters it takes). The function body defines what the function does.
7. The scope of the function body is from the opening curly bracket until the closing curly bracket.
8. One or more Kotin statements make up the function body.
9. The function may optionally return a result; this is indicated by the return keyword.

An Example Named Function

The following is one of the simplest functions you can write; the function takes no parameters and has only a single statement that prints out the message "Hello World":

```
fun printMessage() {
    println("Hello World!")
}
```

This function is called `printMessage` and when called (also known as invoked) it will run the body of the function which will print out the String, for example:

```
fun main() {
    printMessage()
}
```

Note that the case is significant here; in Kotlin printMessage() and printmessage() are two completely different functions.

The output generated by the function is:

```
Hello World!
```

Be careful to include the round brackets () when you call the function. This is because if you just use the functions' name then you are merely referring to the location in memory where the function is stored, and you are not invoking it.

Function Parameters

A function can have zero or more parameters. That is, data can be supplied to a function when it is invoked, and this data is made available via a set of function parameters. At this point it is worth clarifying some terminology that relates to the parameters defined as part of the function header and the data passed into the function via these parameters:

- A *parameter* is a variable defined as part of the function header and is used to make data available within the function itself.
- An *argument* is the actual value or data passed into the function when it is called. The data will be held within the parameters.

Unfortunately many developers use these terms interchangeably but it is worth being clear on the distinction.

A Function with Parameters

We could modify the function to make it a little more general and reusable by providing a parameter. This parameter could be used to supply the message to be printed out, for example:

```
fun printMessage2(msg: String) {
    println(msg)
}
```

Now the `printMessage2` function takes a single parameter. We have to define the type that the parameter can hold; in this case we have indicated that the parameter `msg` is of type `String`. The parameter becomes a `val` which is available within the body of the function. However, this parameter only exists within the body of the function; it is not available outside of the function. In addition as it is a `val` it is not possible to reassign a value to it within the function.

This now means that we can call the `printMessage2()` function with a variety of different messages:

```
fun main() {
    printMessage2("Hello World")
    printMessage2("Good day")
    printMessage2("Welcome")
    printMessage2("Ola")
}
```

The output from calling this function with each of these strings being supplied as the argument value is:

```
Hello World
Good day
Welcome
Ola
```

Multiple Parameter Functions

So far the functions we have defined have only had zero or one parameters; however that was just a choice. We could easily have defined a function which defined two or more parameters. In these situations, the parameter list contains a list of parameter names separated by a comma.

For example.

```kotlin
fun greeter(name: String, message: String) {
    println("Welcome $name - $message")
}

fun main() {
    greeter("Jasmine", "Have a Nice Day!")
}
```

Here the greeter() function defines two parameters; name and message both of type String. These parameters (which are local to the function and cannot be seen outside of the function) are then used within the body of the function.

The output is.

```
Welcome Jasmine - Have a Nice Day!
```

You can have any number of parameters defined in a function. However each parameter is separated from the next parameter by a comma ', '. In addition each parameter must include the type of the parameter (even if all the parameters have the same type).

Default Parameter Values

Once you have one or more parameters you may want to provide *default* values for some or all of those parameters; particular for ones which might only be required in some situations.

This can be done very easily in Kotlin; all that is required is that the default value must be declared in the function header along with the parameter name and type. The default value comes after the type and is preceded by an equals sign '= '. Note that the type of the default value must match the type of the parameter.

If a value is supplied for the parameter, then it will override the default. If no value is supplied when the function is called, then the default will be used.

For example, we can modify the greeter() function from the previous section to provide a default message such as "Live Long and Prosper".

```kotlin
fun greeter2(name: String,
             message: String = "Live Long and Proper") {
    println("Welcome $name - $message")
}

fun main() {
    greeter2("Theeban")
    greeter2("Jasmine", "Have a Nice Day!")
}
```

Now we can call the `greeter2()` function with one or two arguments.
When we run this example, we will get:

```
Welcome Theeban - Live Long and Proper
Welcome Jasmine - Have a Nice Day!
```

As you can see from this in the first example (where only one argument was provided) the default message was used. However, in the second example where a message was provided, along with the name, then that message was used instead of the default.

Note we can use the terms *mandatory* and *optional* for the parameters in `greeter2()`. In this case.

- `name` is a *mandatory* field/parameter,
- `message` is an *optional* field/parameter as it has a default value.

Named Arguments

So far we have relied on the position of a value to be used to determine which parameter that value is assigned to. In many cases this is the simplest and cleanest option.

However, if a function has several parameters, some of which have default values, it may become impossible to rely on using the position of a value to ensure it is given to the correct parameter (because we may want to use some of the default values instead).

For example, let us assume we have a function with four parameters.

```
fun greeter3(name: String,
             title: String = "Dr",
             prompt: String = "Welcome",
             message: String = "Live Long and Proper") {
    println("$prompt $title $name - $message")
}
```

This now raises the question how do we provide the `name` and the `message` arguments when we would like to use the default values for `title` and `prompt`?

The answer is to use *named* parameter passing. In this approach we provide the name of the parameter we want an argument/value to be assigned to; position is no longer relevant. For example:

```
greeter3(name = "Jasmine", message="Have a Nice Day!")
```

In this example we are using the default values for `title` and `prompt`. This produces the following output:

```
Welcome Dr Jasmine - Have a Nice Day!
```

Now that we are using named parameters, we do not need to worry about the order of those parameters. We can thus change the order of the parameters, for example:

```
greeter3(message="Have a Nice Day!", name="Jasmine")
```

This is completely legal and results in the same output as the previous example:

```
Welcome Dr Jasmine - Have a Nice Day!
```

We can actually mix *positional* and *named* arguments in Kotlin, for example:

```
greeter3("Jasmine", message="Have a Nice Day!")
```

Here "Jasmine" is bound to the `name` parameter as it is the first parameter, but "Have a Nice Day!" is bound to `message` parameter as it is a named argument. We can of course have any number of positional parameters, followed by any number of named parameters, for example:

```
greeter3("Jasmine",
         title = "Ms",
         message="Have a Nice Day!")
```

Prior to Kotlin 1.4 you could not have *named* parmeters followed by *positional* parameters. That is the following example would not work prior to Kotlin 1.4:

```
greeter3(message="Have a Nice Day!", "Jasmine")
```

As this would result in the compiler generating an error.

However, since Kotlin 1.4 this has been allowed. For example give a function `max()` that calculates the maximum of two values:

```
fun max(x: Int, y: Int): Int  = if (x > y) { x } else { y }
```

Then we can write:

```
println("max(x=3, 4): " + max(x=3, 4))
```

Which will generate the output:

$$max(x=3,4):\ 4$$

However, the position parameter and the named parameters must make sense. It if not possible to write:

```
println("max(4, x=3): " + max(4, x=3))
```

This is because the positional argument is assumed to be for the parameter x and thus there are two values being bound to x. This will generate a compile time error.

Arbitrary Number of Arguments

In some cases, you do not know how many arguments will be supplied when a function is called. Kotlin allows you to pass an arbitrary number of arguments into a function and then process those arguments inside the function.

To define a parameter list as being of arbitrary length, a parameter is marked with the keyword `vararg`. For example:

```
fun greeter4(vararg params: String) {
    params.forEach { print("$it , ") }
    println()
}

fun main() {
    greeter4("John")
    greeter4("John", "Denise")
    greeter4("John", "Denise", "Phoebe", "Adam")
    greeter4("John", "Denise", "Phoebe",
             "Adam", "Jasmine", "Gryff")
}
```

The `vararg` keyword can only be applied to one parameter in a given function. In addition, if a `vararg` parameter is not the last parameter in the list, then the values for the following parameters must be passed in using the *named* argument syntax.

The above code snippet generates.

```
John ,
John , Denise ,
John , Denise , Phoebe , Adam ,
John , Denise , Phoebe , Adam , Jasmine , Gryff ,
```

Also note that this version of the greeter function uses a forEach operation to iterate over the parameter values passed into the function. We will look at this operation in more detail later in the book. For now, accept that the value of the special variable it is bound to each of the parameter values passed into the function in turn.

Parameters Are Vals

In Kotlin all parameters to functions are *vals*. This means that once the function has been invoked it is not possible to reassign a value to that parameter (this is not the case for example in Java). This means that it is not possible to write the following;

```
fun add(i: Int) {
    i = i + 1      // won't compile i is a val
}
```

The aim is to protect the programmer against accidentally assigning a value to a parameter and then using that new value later in the function while expecting that the parameter still holds the value passed in!

Returning Values from Functions

It is very common to want to return a value from a function. In Kotlin this can be done using the return statement. Whenever a return statement is encountered within a function then that function will terminate and return any values following the return keyword. Note that the function declaration or header must indicate that a value will be returned and what the type of that value will be. Within the function body, the type of the actual value returned must match that in the function declaration.

For example, the following defines a simple function that squares whatever integer values have been passed to it:

```
fun square(num: Int): Int {
    return num * num
}
```

Note if you forget to declare the return type for a function then the compiler will default the return type to be Unit. This indicates that nothing is returned. This would result in a compile time error indicating a mismatch between the declaration of the function header which indicates that the function returns Unit and the function body which attempts to return something such as a String or an Int. This is shown below for the situation where we have explicitly declared the function as returning Unit:

```
fun square(num: Int): Unit {                          1  2  ^  v
    return num * num

}
                    Type mismatch.
                    Required: Unit
                    Found:    Int
                    Change return type of enclosing function 'square' to 'Int'

                    value-parameter num: Int
```

Note that the IDE has tried to help the developer here by suggesting that a fix could be to change the return type to Int.

The square() function defined earlier will multiply whatever it is given by itself and then return that value. The returned value can then be used at the point that the function was invoked, for example:

```
fun square(num: Int): Int {
    return num * num
}

fun main() {
    // Store result from square in a variable
    val result = square(4)
    println("result: $result")
    // Send the result from square immediately to
    // another    function
    println("square(5): ${square(5)}")
    // Use the result returned from square in a
    // conditional expression
    if (square(3) < 15) {
        println("square(3) is less than 15")
    }
}
```

When this code is run, we get:

```
result: 16
square(5): 25
square(3) is less than 15
```

Anonymous Functions

So far in this chapter we have focussed on *named* functions; that is functions defined with an explicit name.

Kotlin also possesses another type of function known as an *anonymous* function. This is a type of function that does not have a specific name provided for it when it is defined.

The format used to define an *anonymous* function is:

```
fun(parameter list):return-type { func body}
```

As before the `:return-type` is optional, however if your function returns a value, then the return type must be specified.

An *anonymous* function can be useful in situations where you need to define some behaviour on the fly and use it in that specific situation. As such functions are *anonymous* they do not pollute the namespace of functions associated with your program. However, they can only be invoked at the point of declaration unless a reference to the anonymous function is stored into a variable.

The following statement declares an anonymous function and then stores it into a `val` called `func`:

```
val func = fun(i: Int): Int { return i + 1 }

fun main() {
    println(func(5))
}
```

When the val `func`, along with the round brackets () is used above, it accesses the *anonymous* function and executes it. This causes the value 5 to be passed into the anonymous function and to have its value incremented by one. This value is returned by the function which is then printed out, for example:

6

Single Expression Functions

Kotlin provades a shorthand form syntax for functions where the body of the function is a single expression and that expression generates the result for the function. This shorthand form is available in both the named function and anonymous function formats.

Using the shorthand form to define a named function we can write:

```
fun name(parameter list) = single expression
```

Where as if we are defining an anonymous function we can write:

```
fun(parameter list) = single-expression
```

In both cases the return type is automatically inferred by the compiler from the result of the single expression that forms the body of the function.

An example of using this shorthand function definition form for a named function is given below:

```
fun incrementer(x: Int) = x + 1
```

Here the function `incrementer(Int)` has a return type of `Int` while the body of the function is comprised of the single expression x+ 1. It is of course possible to define a return type explicitly and this can be considered good practice as it is useful documentation to any developer reading the function definition. For example:

```
fun incrementer(x: Int): Int = x * 3
```

An example of using this shorthand function definition form for an anonymous function is given below:

```
val adder = fun(i: Int) = i + 1
```

Again the return type is inferred from the result of adding one to the integer i. We can use these function in the normal way:

```
fun main() {
    println(incrementer(5))
    println(adder(5))
}
```

The output of this application is:

```
15
6
```

Lambdas

A lambda expression is a *function literal* definition that is simpler than an *anonymous* function. Compared to lambdas, anonymous functions allow the programmer to specify the return type and to have larger more complex function bodies with potentially multiple return statements. However, in many cases an anonymous function is just a single expression and this can be simplified using the lambda syntax.

Lambda functions do not declare an explicit return type (it is inferred by the Kotlin compiler). The lambda expression is always surrounded by curly brackets and may be assigned to a val, var or passed as a parameter to a function etc.

The syntax used to define a lambda is:

```
{ (parmater list) -> expression }
```

Lambdas can have any number of arguments but only one expression (that is a statement that returns a value) as their body. When the expression is executed, and the value generated from it is returned as the result of the function.

As an example, let us define a couple of lambdas:

```
val increment: (Int) -> Int = { x -> x + 1 }
val increase = { x: Int -> x + 1 }

fun main() {
    println(increment(5))
    println(increase(5))
}
```

In both these examples, the lambda only takes one parameter. In both cases the lambda is stored in a val. In the first example we explicitly state that type of the val; in this case (Int) - > Int. This indicates that we expect the val to hold a reference to a function that takes an Int as a parameter and returns an Int as a result.

In the second example the Kotlin compiler is used to infer the type of the val increase. In both cases the result of the lambda is generated by the expression x + 1 which returns an Int. Note that for the second lambda we had to specify the type of the variable x as it could not be inferred by the compiler as the val increase does not specify the type of function it will reference.

To invoke the lambdas, we can access the reference to the function held in the vals and then use the round brackets to cause the function to be executed, passing in any values to be used for the parameters:

```kotlin
fun main() {
    println(increment(5))
    println(increase(5))
}
```

When this program is executed the value 6 is printed out twice.

```
6
6
```

Other examples of lambda functions are given below (illustrating that a lambda function can take any number of arguments from zero upwards):

```kotlin
val func0: () -> Unit = { println("no args") }
val func1 = { print("no args") }
val func2: (Int, Int) -> Int = { x, y -> x * y }
val func3 = { x: Int, y: Int -> x * y }
```

These can be used as shown below:

```kotlin
fun main() {
    println(increment(5))
    println(increase(5))

    func0()
    func1()
    println(func2(3, 4))
    println(func3(2, 3))

}
```

The output from this code snippet is:

```
no args
no args
12
6
```

Lambdas Versus Anonymous Functions

You may be wondering why Kotlin has both *anonymous* functions and *lambda* functions as they seem to play a similar role. The short answer is that anonymous functions are more flexible than lambda functions and have one particular feature which is significantly different to lambdas—they can have multiple return statements.

An anonymous function is more flexible than a lambda function because:

- It can have any level of complexity to the body of the function where as a lambda has a body comprised of a single expression.
- There can be multiple return statements in the body of the anonymous function where as a lambda has a single implied returned value for the single expression that makes up the lambda body.
- It is possible to explicitly specify the return type of an anonymous function, where as it is determined by the compiler for a lambda.

Recursive Functions

A recursive solution in a programming language such as Kotlin is one in which a function calls itself one or more times in order to solve a particular problem. In many cases the result of calling itself is combined with the functions current state to return a result.

In most cases the recursive call involves calling the function but with a smaller problem to solve. For example, a function to traverse a tree data structure might call itself passing in a sub-tree to process. Alternatively a function to generate a factorial number might call itself passing in a smaller number to process etc.

The key here is that an overall problem can be solved by breaking it down into smaller examples of the same problem.

Functions that solve problems by calling themselves are referred to as *recursive* functions.

If such a function does not have a termination point then the function will go on calling itself to infinity (at least in theory). In most languages such a situation will (eventually) result in an error being generated.

For a recursive function to be useful it must therefore have a *termination* condition. That is a condition under which the recursive function does not call itself and instead just returns (often with some result). The termination condition may be because:

- A solution has been found (some data of interest in a tree structure).
- The problem has become so small that it cannot be solved with further recursion. This is often referred to as a base case. That is, a base case is a problem that cannot be solved with further decomposition of the problem.
- Some maximum level of recursion has been reached, possibly without a result being found/generated.

We can therefore say that a *recursive* function is a function defined in terms of itself via *self-referential* expressions. The function will continue to call itself with smaller variations of the overall problem until some termination condition is met to stop the recursion. All recursive functions thus share a common format; they have a recursive part and a termination point which represents the base case part.

The key benefit of recursion is that some algorithms are expressed far more elegantly and with a great deal less code when implemented recursively than when using an iterative approach. This means that the resulting code can be easier to write and easier to read.

Calculating Factorial Recursively

As an example we will write a recursive function to calculate the factorial for an given integer. The factorial of a number is the result of multiplying that number by each of the integer values up to that number, for example, to find the factorial of the number 5 (written as 5!) we can multiple 1 * 2 * 3 * 4 *5 which will generate the number 120.

```
fun factorial(n: Int): Int {
    return if (n == 1)
        1 // Base case
    else
        n * factorial(n - 1) // Recursive call
}
```

This function will return the value 1 if the number passed in is 1—this is the base case. Otherwise it will multiply the value passed in to it with the result of calling itself (the `factorial()` function) with n − 1 which is the recursive part.

The key to understanding this function is that it has:

1. A termination condition that is guaranteed to execute when the value of n is 1. This is the base case; we cannot reduce the problem down any further as the factorial of 1 is 1!
2. A recursive part. In this part, the function recursively calls itself but with n − 1 as the argument; this means each time it calls itself the value of n is *smaller*. Thus the value returned from this call is the result of a smaller computation.

To clarify how this works we can add some print statements (and a depth indicator) to the function to indicate its behaviour:

```
fun spacer(str: String, times: Int) {
    for (i in 0..times) {
        print(str)
    }
}

fun factorial(n: Int, depth: Int = 1): Int {
    return if (n == 1) {
        spacer("\t", depth)
        println("Returning 1")
        1 // Base case
    } else {
        spacer("\t", depth)
        println("Recursively calling factorial(${n-1})")
        // Recursive call
        val result = n * factorial(n - 1, depth + 1)
        spacer("\t", depth)
        println("Returning: $result")
        result
    }
}

fun main() {
    println("Calling factorial(5)")
    println(factorial2(5))
}
```

When we run this version of the program then the output is:

```
Calling factorial(5)
        Recursively calling factorial(4)
            Recursively calling factorial(3)
                Recursively calling factorial(2)
                    Recursively calling factorial(1)
                        Returning 1
                    Returning: 2
                Returning: 6
            Returning: 24
        Returning: 120
120
```

Note that the depth parameter is used merely to provide some indentation to the print statements.

From the output we can see that each call to the `factorial()` function results in a simpler calculation until the point where we are asking for the value of 1! which is 1. This is returned as the result of calling `factorial(1)`. This result is multiplied with the value of n prior to that; which was 2. The causes `factorial(2)` to return the value 2 and so on.

Tail Recursion Optimisation

Although Recursion can be a very expressive way to define how a problem can be solved, it is not as efficient as iteration using a loop based operation such as a for or while loop. This is because a function call is more expensive for the JVM runtime to process that a `for` loop. In part this is because of the infrastructure that goes along with a function call; for example it is necessary to set up an internal stack with values stored for each separate function invocation so that all local variables are independent of any other call to that function. It is also related to associated unwinding of the stack when a function returns. However, it is also affected by the increasing amount of memory each recursive call must use to store all the data on that stack.

In some languages optimisations are possible to improve the performance of a recursive solution. One typical example relates to a type of recursion known as *tail recursion*. A tail recursive solution is one in which the calculation is performed before the recursive call. The result is then passed to the recursive step, which results in the last statement in the function just calling the recursive function.

In such situations the recursive solution can be expressed (internally to the computer system) as an iterative problem. That is the programmer is able to write the solution as a recursive algorithm but the interpreter or compiler converts it into an iterative solution. This allows programmers to benefit from the expressive nature of recursion while also benefiting from the performance of an iterative solution. Kotlin is one of the languages that allows for this optimisation.

You might think that the `factorial` function presented earlier is tail recursive; however it is not because the last statement in the function performs a calculation that multiples n by the result of the recursive call.

However, we can refactor the `factorial` function to be tail recursive. This version of the `factorial` function passes the evolving result along with each recursive call, via the `accumulator` parameter. We can then mark the function with the keyword `tailrec` which tells the Kotlin compiler that it should try to perform the tail recursion optimisation on this function. The resulting function is given below:

```
tailrec fun factorialTailRec(acc: Int = 1, n: Int): Int {
    // Termination condition
    return if (n == 1)
        acc // Base case
    else
        factorialTailRec(acc * n, n - 1) // Tail Recursive call
}
```

The difference between a tailrec recursive function and a non tailrec recursive function in Kotlin can be seen using the following two recursive functions. The initial bang() function will fail when the RuntimeException is thrown (a type of error condition that causes the program to terminate). This causes the program to print the error stack trace which will show what functions were called and when:

```
fun bang(x: Int): Int {
    return if (x == 0) throw RuntimeException("Bang!")
    else bang(x - 1) + 1
}
```

The output from this function is given below:

```
Exception in thread "main" java.lang.RuntimeException: Bang!
    at TailRecursiveAppKt.bang(TailRecursiveApp.kt:39)
    at TailRecursiveAppKt.bang(TailRecursiveApp.kt:40)
    at TailRecursiveAppKt.bang(TailRecursiveApp.kt:40)
    at TailRecursiveAppKt.bang(TailRecursiveApp.kt:40)
    at TailRecursiveAppKt.bang(TailRecursiveApp.kt:40)
    at TailRecursiveAppKt.main(TailRecursiveApp.kt:65)
    at TailRecursiveAppKt.main(TailRecursiveApp.kt)
```

From this it is clear that the bang() function has been called once from the main() function, but a further 4 times due to recursion (I.e. The bang() function has called the function bang() 4 times).

If we now modify this function to be a tail recursive version and mark it with tailrec as shown below:

```
tailrec fun bangTailRec(x: Int): Int {
    return if (x == 0) throw Exception("Bang!")
    else bangTailRec(x - 1)
}
```

When we run this version of the function we now get the following output:

```
Exception in thread "main" java.lang.Exception: Bang!
   at TailRecursiveAppKt.bangTailRec(TailRecursiveApp.kt:45)
   at TailRecursiveAppKt.main(TailRecursiveApp.kt:66)
   at TailRecursiveAppKt.main(TailRecursiveApp.kt)
```

Which shows that the bangTailRec() function has been invoked only once. This is because the recursive algorithm described in our code has been converted into a loop by the compiler which results in a more efficient runtime version of the function.

Inline Functions

One issue with all of the above is that a function will be invoked with all the inherit overheads of this. If all our function does is add one to a number that could be quiet expensive. To get around this overhead, whilst still allowing the expressiveness of a function, Kotlin provides the keyword inline. This allows the compiler to try to inline the function. That is the compiler can try and replace the function call with the actual expression represented by the function. For example:

```
inline fun calculate(): Int = 2 + 3
```

Online Resources

See the online Kotlin documentation for:

- https://kotlinlang.org/docs/reference/functions.html for how to use functions in Kotlin.

Exercises

Calculate Prime Numbers

The aim of this exercise is to write a function that can identify (print out) all the prime numbers in a given range.

A Prime Number is a positive whole number, greater than 1, that has no other divisors except the number 1 and the number itself.

That is, it can only be divided by itself and the number 1, for example the numbers 2, 3, 5 and 7 are prime numbers as they cannot be divided by any other whole number.

However, the numbers 4 and 6 are not prime numbers because they can both be divided by the number 2. In addition the number 6 can also be divided by the numbers 2 and 3.

You should write a function to calculate prime number starting from 1 up to the value passed into the function. In the `main()` function ask the user for the maximum number to calculate prime numbers up to and then invoke your `prime()` function passing in this number.

If the user inputs a number below 2, print an error message.

For any number greater than 2 the `prime()` function should loop for each integer from 2 to that number and determine if it can be divided by another number (you will probably need two for loops for this; one nested inside the other).

For each number that cannot be divided by any other number (that is its a prime number) print it out.

For example:

```
Please input a number: 5
Prime number 3
Prime number 5
```

Adding Functions to the Number Guess Game

You can go further with the number guess game presented in the last chapter.

Take the number guess game and break it up into a number of functions. There is not necessarily a right or wrong way to do this; look for functions that are meaningful to you within the code, for example:

1. You could create a function to obtain input from the user.
2. You could create another function that will implement the main game playing loop.
3. You could also provide a function that will print out a message indicating if the player won or not.
4. You could create a function to print a welcome message when the game starts up.

Chapter 6
Higher Order Functions

Introduction

In this chapter we will explore the concept of high-order functions. These are functions that take as a parameter, or return (or both), a function. To do this we will first look into how Kotlin represents functions in memory and explore what actually happens when we execute a Kotlin function.

Recap on Functions in Kotlin

Let us first recap a few things regarding functions in Kotlin:

Functions (mostly) have a name and when invoked (or executed) the body of code associated with the function is run.

There are some important ideas to remember when considering named functions:

- functions can be viewed as named blocks of code and are one of the main ways in which we can organise our programs in Kotlin,
- functions are defined using the keyword fun and constitute a function header (the function name and the parameters, if any, defined for that function) and the function body (what is executed when the function is run),
- functions are invoked or executed using their name followed by round brackets '()' with or without parameters depending on how the function has been defined.

This means we can write a function such as the following getMessage() function:

```kotlin
fun getMessage(): String {
    return "Hello Kotlin World!"
}
```

© The Author(s), under exclusive license to Springer Nature Switzerland AG 2021
J. Hunt, *Beginner's Guide to Kotlin Programming*,
https://doi.org/10.1007/978-3-030-80893-8_6

We can then call it by specifying its name and the round brackets:

```
fun main() {
    val message = getMessage()
    println(message)
}
```

This of course prints out the string "Hello Kotlin World!" which is what you should expect by now.

Functions as Entities

A few chapters back we threw in something stating that if you forgot to include the round brackets then you were referencing the function itself rather than trying to execute it!

What exactly does that mean? Let's see what happens if we forgot to include the round brackets but included the box operator :: which allows us to reference the function:

```
fun main() {
    val message2 = ::getMessage
    println(message2)
}
```

The output generated now is:

```
function getMessage (Kotlin reflection is not available)
```

which might look very confusing at first sight.

What this is actually telling you is that you have referenced a function called getMessage and that the additional reflection tooling is not part of the current project runtime.

This probably still does not help much. So what does it actually mean? It means is that message2 is actually a reference to the function getMessage() rather than holding the *result* of the function getMessage(). If you like it has become an alias referencing the same getMessage() function. This is illustrated by the following diagram:

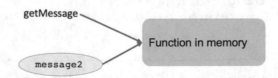

This means that when we run either getMessage() or message2() what actually happens is we go to the area in memory that holds the body of the function and then because we have the round brackets we run that function.

This has two implications:

1. we can create aliases to functions,
2. we can pass the reference to a function around.

In the above code we do this using a named function, however it is much more common to do this with an *anonymous* or even more typically a *lambda* function. For example:

```kotlin
fun main() {
    val func: () -> Unit = { println("Hello World") }
    val func1 = func
    func()
    func1()
}
```

This illustrates how we might define a *lambda* function and store a reference to it into a variable func. Notice that the type of this variable is () - > Unit in other words it references a function that takes no parameters and return Unit. We then assign this reference to the val func1. This means they both reference the same *lambda* function and both func and func1 are of the same type.

Box Operator

The box operator (::) can be used to obtain a reference to a *named* function. By default when you access a named function it must be invoked, it is not possible to merely reference the function, thus in Kotlin it is not possible to write:

```kotlin
fun increase(i: Int) = i + 1

fun main() {
    println(increase(5))
    val inc = increase
}
```

If you try this you will get a compilation error telling you.

```
Function invocation 'increase(...)' expected
```

However, you can use the box operator (: :) to obtain a reference to the *named* function that allows you to reference it without invoking it.

We can now modify the above program as shown below:

```
fun increase(i: Int) = i + 1

fun main() {
    println(increase(5))
    val inc = ::increase // obtain reference to function
    println(inc)
    println(inc(5))
}
```

In this program we obtain a callable reference to the named function increase() and store that reference into the val inc. This means that both the name increase and the val inc reference the *same* functionality. As such inc is essentially an *alias* to the increase function. Calling either increase(5) or inc(5) will execute *exactly* the same block of code and will generate the same result 6.

The output from this program is therefore:

```
6
fun increase(kotlin.Int): kotlin.Int
6
```

Note that the reference held in inc is to the increase function that takes and Int and returns an Int. This the type of the val inc is (Int) - > Int.

Higher Order Function Concepts

Given that we can assign a reference to a function into a val or var; then this might imply that we can also use the same approach to pass a reference to a function as an argument to another function.

This means that one function can take another function as a parameter. Such functions are known as *Higher Order Functions* and are one of the key constructs in *Functional Programming*.

In fact in Kotlin, Higher-Order Functions are functions that do at least one of the following (and may do both):

- take one or more functions as a parameter,
- return as a result a function.

All other functions in Kotlin are *first-order* functions.

Many of the functions found in the Kotlin libraries are *higher order functions*. It is a common enough pattern that once you are aware of it you will recognise it in many different libraries.

Higher Order Function Example

As an example, consider the following higher order function `processor()`. This function takes an integer and a function as parameters. Within the body of `processor()`, the function passed in as a parameter is applied to the integer parameter. The result of the function being executed is then returned:

```
// Takes a function and an int
fun processor(x: Int, func: (Int) -> Int): Int {
    return func(x)
}
```

The function `processor` is a *higher order function* because its behaviour (and its result) will depend on the behaviour defined by another function—the one passed into it.

We could now define a function to increment a value by 1 or a function to multiple an integer by itself. These functions could then be used with the `processor()` function to obtain a result. For example:

```
fun main() {
    // Anonymous function
    val increment = fun(i: Int)= i + 1
    println(processor(5, increment))

    // Lambda function
    val mult: (Int) -> Int = { x -> x * x }
    println(processor(5, mult))
}
```

Note that we have used both an *anonymous* function and a *lambda* function in this example. Now we can use the functions `increment` and `mult` as parameters to `processor()`.

The output from the above program is:

6
25

Higher Order Functions and Lambdas

It is common to define the *lambda* to be used with a Higher Order Function at the point at which the Hight Order Function is being invoked.

```
// Lambda declared inline
println(processor(5, { x -> x - 1 }))
```

This generates:

4

This is such a common pattern in Kotlin that it even provides a special syntax to make it easy to create *lambda* functions at the point of invocation. This syntax allows the lambda to be defined after the function parameters as long as the function is the last parameter in the higher order functions parameter list. It is referred to as *Trailing Lambda Syntax* and is the preferred Kotlin style.

This is illustrated below:

```
// Idiomatic Kotlin form
println(processor(5) { x -> x - 1 })
```

Kotlin even allows for an even shorter form of this syntax using an implicit it parameter (if there is just one parameter specified):

```
// Short hand form - only available if just one parameter
println(processor(5) { it - 1 } )
```

Using Higher Order Functions

Looking at the previous section you may be wondering why you would want to use a higher-order function or indeed why define one at all. After all could you not have called one of the functions (increment, mult) directly by passing in the integer to used? The answer is of course, we could have done:

```
multi(10)
```

And this would have exactly the same effect as calling:

```
processor(10, mult)
```

The first approach would seem to be both simpler and more efficient.

The key to why higher-order functions are so powerful is to consider what would happen if we know that some function should be applied to the value 10 but we do not yet know what it is. The actual function will be provided at some point in the future. Now we are creating a reusable piece of code that will be able to apply an appropriate function to the data we have, when that function is known.

For example, let us assume that we want to calculate the amount of tax someone should pay based on their salary. However, we do not know how to calculate the tax that this person must pay as it is dependent on external factors. The calculateTax() function could take an appropriate function that performs that calculation and provides the appropriate tax value.

The following listing implements this approach. The function calculateTax() does not know how to calculate the actual tax to be paid, instead a function must be provided as a parameter to the calculateTax() function. The function passed in takes a number and returns the result of performing the calculation. It is used with the salary parameter also passed into the calculateTax() function.

```
fun simpleTaxCalculator(amount: Double) = amount * 0.3

fun calculateTax(salary: Double,
                 func: (Double) -> Double): Double {
    return func(salary)
}

fun main() {
    val tax = calculateTax(45000.0, ::simpleTaxCalculator)
    println("Tax payable: $tax")
}
```

The simpleTaxCalculator function defines a function that takes a number and multiplies it by 0.3.

The calculateTax() function is a named function that takes a Double and a function to invoke.

Within the main function a call is then made to the calculateTax() function passing in the Double 45,000.0 as the salary and a *callable reference* to the simpleTaxCalculator function. This is defined using the box operator (::) that creates a reference to the function that can be passed into the calctlateTax() function without being invoked. We need to do this as simeplTaxCaculator() is a named function.

Finally, it prints out the tax calculated. The result of running this program is:

```
Tax payable: 13500.0
```

Of course we could have used an *anonymous* function or a *lambda* function to define the tax calculation behaviour, for example:

```
fun main() {
    val tax = calculateTax(45000.0) {amount -> amount * 0.25}
    println("Tax payable: $tax")
}
```

In this case the *trailing lambda* syntax is used and the *lambda* function calculates the tax as 25% of the amount. This generates:

```
                    Tax payable: 11250.0
```

Thus the function `calculateTax()` is a reusable function that can have different tax calculation strategies defined for it.

Functions Returning Functions

In Kotlin as well as passing a function into another function; functions can be returned from a function. This can be used to select amongst a number of different options or to create a new function based on the parameters.

For example, the following code creates a *lambda* function that can be used to check whether a number is even, odd or negative based on the string passed into it. It also provides a default *lambda* function that always returns `true`. Notice that the syntax used allows the body of the function to be defined using a single when expression, thus the when expression defines the complete body of the function and returns a value given any input. The returned value is of course a lambda function:

```
fun makeChecker(s: String): (Int) -> Boolean =
    when (s) {
        "even" -> { n: Int -> n % 2 == 0 }
        "positive" -> { n: Int -> n >= 0 }
        "negative" -> { n: Int -> n < 0 }
        else -> { n: Int -> true }
    }
```

Note the use of the `else` clause to handle input to the function that is not "even", "negative" or "positive".

This function is a *function factory* for lambda functions that can be created to perform specific operations. It is used below to create four functions that can be used to validate what type a number is:

```
fun main() {
    val isEven = makeChecker("even")
    val isPositive = makeChecker("positive")
    val isNegative = makeChecker("negative")
    val isInteger = makeChecker("")

    println("isEven(3): ${isEven(3)}")
    println("isPositive(3): ${isPositive(3)}")
    println("isNegative(3): ${isNegative(3)}")
    println("isInteger(3): ${isInteger(3)}")
}
```

This generates the following output:

```
isEven(3): false
isPositive(3): true
isNegative(3): false
isInteger(3): true
```

Of course, it is not only *lambda* functions that can be returned from a function; it is also possible to return *anonymous* functions. As with a lambda function, an *anonymous* function can be returned directly from a function as long as the return type matches the function type:

```
fun makeAnonFunction(): (Int, Int) -> Int {
    return fun(x: Int, y: Int) = x + y
}
```

It is also possible to returned a *named* function (which can also be defined within the scope of the function) from a function. However, it is then necessary to return the *callable reference* to the named function using the box operator:

```
fun makeNamedFunction(): (Int, Int) -> Int {
    fun adder(x: Int, y: Int): Int {
        return x + y
    }
    return ::adder
}
```

We can then use these factory functions as shown below:

```
fun main() {
    val func1 = makeAnonFunction()
    println("func1(3, 2): ${func1(3, 2)}")
    println("func1(3, 3): ${func1(3, 3)}")
    println("func1(3, 1): ${func1(3, 1)}")

    println("-------------")

    val func2 = makeNamedFunction()
    println("func2(3, 2): ${func2(3, 2)}")
    println("func2(3, 3): ${func2(3, 3)]")
    println("func2(3, 1): ${func2(3, 1)}")
}
```

Which produces the output

```
func1(3, 2): 5
func1(3, 3): 6
func1(3, 1): 4
-------------
func2(3, 2): 5
func2(3, 3): 6
func2(3, 1): 4
```

Online Resources

Further information on *higher order functions* in Kotlin can be found using the following online resources:

- https://en.wikipedia.org/wiki/Higher-order_function Wikipedia page on Higher Order functions.
- https://kotlinlang.org/docs/reference/lambdas.html Higher Order Functions and Lambdas in Kotlin.
- https://www.tutorialspoint.com/functional_programming/functional_program ming_higher_order_functions.htm A tutorial on higher order functions.

Exercises

The aim of this exercise is to explore *higher order functions*.

You should write a higher order function with the signature:

```
fun myHigherOrderFunction(I: Int, func: (Int) -> Int): Int
```

This function takes an integer parameter and a second function to apply to the parameter. The second function takes an `Int` and returns an `Int`.

Now you should write a simple program that uses the higher order function you just created to execute a function passed to it.

An example of the sort of thing you might implement is given below:

```
fun doubler(i: Int) = i * 2
fun tripler(i: Int) = i * 3

fun main() {
    println(myHigherOrderFunction(5) { it + 1 })
    println(myHigherOrderFunction(5) { it - 1 })
    println(myHigherOrderFunction(5) { it * 2 })

    println(myHigherOrderFunction(5, fun (i: Int): Int {
        return i + 2
    }))
    println(myHigherOrderFunction(5, ::doubler))
    println(myHigherOrderFunction(5, ::tripler))
}
```

Sample output from this code snippet is:

```
6
4
10
7
10
15
```

Chapter 7
Curried Functions

Introduction

Currying is a technique which allows new functions to be created from existing functions by *binding* one or more parameters to a specific value. It is a source of reuse of functions in Kotlin which means that functionality can be written once, in one place and then reused in multiple other situations.

The name Currying may seem obscure, but the technique is named after Haskell Curry (for whom the Haskell programming language is also named).

This chapter introduces the core ideas behind currying and explores how currying can be implemented in Kotlin. The chapter also introduces the concept of closures and how they affect curried functions.

Currying Concepts

At an abstract level, consider having a function that takes two parameters. These two parameters, x and y are used within the function body with the multiply operator in the form x * y. For example, we might have:

```kotlin
fun operation(x, y) = x * y
```

This function `operation()` might then be used as follows.

```kotlin
val total = operation(2, 5)
```

Which would result in 5 being multiplied by 2 to give 10. Or it could be used:

```kotlin
val total = operation(2, 10)
```

© The Author(s), under exclusive license to Springer Nature Switzerland AG 2021
J. Hunt, *Beginner's Guide to Kotlin Programming*,
https://doi.org/10.1007/978-3-030-80893-8_7

Which would result in 10 being multiplied by 2 to give 20.

If we needed to double a number, we could thus reuse the `operation()` function many times, for example:

```
operation(2, 5)
operation(2, 10)
operation(2, 6)
operation(2, 151)
```

All of the above would double the second number. However, we have had to remember to provide the value 2 so that the number can be doubled. Of course the number 2 has not changed between any of the invocations of the `operation()` function. What if we fixed the first parameter to always be 2, this would mean that we could create a new function that apparently only takes one parameter (the number to double). For example, let us say that in pseudo code we could write something like:

```
val double = operation(2, *)
```

Such that the '*' acts as a wild card for the missing parameter. We could now write:

```
double(5)
double(151)
```

In essence `double()` is an alias for `operation()`, but an alias that provides the *value 2* for the first parameter and leaves the second parameter to be filled in by the future invocation of the double function.

Note that the above is an imaginary syntax; it is *not* part of Kotlin.

Kotlin and Curried Functions

A curried function in Kotlin is a function where one or more of its parameters have been *applied or bound* to a value, resulting in the creation of a new function with one or more fewer parameters than the original. For example, let us create a named function that multiplies two numbers together:

```
fun multiply(x: Int, y: Int) = x * y
```

This is a general function that does exactly what it says; it multiplies any two numbers together. These numbers could be any two integers etc.

We can thus invoke it in the normal manner:

```
fun main() {
    println("multiply(2, 5): ${multiply(2, 5)}")
}
```

The result of executing this program is:

```
multiply(2, 5): 10
```

We could now define a new function that takes a function and a number and returns a new (anonymous) function that takes one *new* parameter and calls the function passed in, with the number also passed in, and the new parameter:

```
fun multyBy(num: Int, func: (Int, Int) -> Int): (Int) -> Int {
    return fun(y: Int) = func(num, y)
}
```

Look carefully at this function; it has used or *bound* the number passed into the multBy() function to the invocation of the function passed in, but it has also defined a new variable 'y' that will have to be provided when this new anonymous function is invoked. It then returns a reference to the anonymous function as the result of multBy().

The multBy() function can now be used to bind the first parameter of the multiply() function to anything we want. For example, we could bind it to 2 so that it will always double the second parameter and store the resulting function reference into a val double:

```
val double = multBy(2, ::multiply)
```

We could also bind the value 3 to the first parameter of multiple to make a function that will triple any value:

```
val triple = multBy(3, ::multiply)
```

Which means we can now write:

```
println("double(5): ${double(5)}")
println("triple(5): ${triple(5)}")
```

which produces the output:

```
double(5): 7
triple(5): 8
```

You are not limited to just binding one parameter; you can bind any number of parameters in this way.

We could of course have also used an *anonymous* function or a *lambda* with the `multBy()` factory function, for example:

```
val doubler = multBy(2) {i, j -> i * j}
val tripler = multBy(3) {i, j -> i * j}

println("doubler(5): ${doubler(5)}")
println("tripler(5): ${tripler(5)}")
```

The output from this is:

```
doubler(5): 10
tripler(5): 1
```

Curried functions are therefore very useful for creating new functions from existing functions.

Closure

One question to consider is what happens when an *anonymous* function or *lambda* references some data that is in scope where it is defined but is no longer available when it is evaluated? This question is answered by the implementation of a concept known as *closure*.

Within Computer Science (and programming languages in particular) a *closure* (or a *lexical closure* or *function closure*) is a function (or more strictly a reference to a function) together with a referencing environment.

The *referencing environment* records the context within which the function was originally defined and if necessary a reference to each of the *non-local* variables of that function. These non-local or *free variables* allow the function body to reference variables that are external to the function but which are utilised by that function. This referencing environment is one of the distinguishing features between a functional language and a language that supports function pointers (such as C).

The general concept of a lexical closure was first developed during the 1960s but was first fully implemented in the language Scheme in the 1970s. It has since been used within many functional programming languages including LISP, ML, Scala and now Kotlin.

At the conceptual level, *closure* allows a function to reference a variable available in the scope where the function was originally defined, but not available by default in the scope where it is executed.

For example, in the following simple program, the variable `more` is defined outside the body of the function referenced by the val `increase`. This is permissible as the variable is defined within the body of the main() function. Thus the variable more is *within scope* at the point of definition.

```
fun main() {
    var more = 100
    val increase: (Int) -> Int = { i -> i + more }

    println(increase(10))
    more = 50
    println(increase(10))
}
```

Within the *main()* function we then invoke the *increase* function by passing in the value 10. This is done twice with the variable more being reset to 50 between the two. The output from this program is shown below:

```
110
60
```

Note that it is the *current* value of more that is being used when the function executes, and not the value of more present at the point that the function was defined. Hence the output is 110 and 60 that is 100 + 10 and then 50 + 10.

This might seem obvious as the variable more is still in scope within the main() function. Thus when the lambda function is invoked it can reference the var more. However, consider the following example:

```
var increment: (Int) -> Int = { x -> x + 1 }

fun main() {
    println(increment(5))
    resetFunc()
    println(increment(5))
}

fun resetFunc() {
    // Local val is bound and stored in function
    // as it is used within the function body
    val addition = 50
    increment = { a -> a + addition }
}
```

In the above listing a val increment holds a reference to a lambda function. Initially the function adds 1 to whatever value has been passed to it. In the main function this function is called with the value 5 and the result returned by the function is printed. This will be the value 6.

However, after this a second function, resetFunc(), is invoked. This function has a variable that is *local* to the function. That is, *normally* it would only be available within the function resetFunc(). This variable is called addition and has the value 50.

The variable addition is used within the function body of a new *lambda* function definition. This lambda takes an integer and adds the value of addition to that integer and returns this as the result of the function. This new function is then assigned to the property increment.

Now when the second invocation of increment occurs back in the main() function, the resetFunc() method has terminated and *normally* the variable addition would no longer even be in existence. However when this program runs the value 55 is printed out from the second invocation of increment. That is the function being referenced by increment when it is called the second time in the main() function is the one defined within resetFunc(); which uses the variable addition. This is an example of *closure* as the *lambda* defined within the resetFunc() has *closed around* the local variable addition.

Online Resources

Further information on currying see:

- https://en.wikipedia.org/wiki/Currying Wikipedia page on currying.
- https://wiki.haskell.org/Currying A page introducing currying (based on the Haskell language but still a useful reference).

Exercises

This exercise is about creating a set of functions to perform currency conversions based on specified rates using currying to create those functions.

Write a function that will curry another function and a parameter in a similar manner to multBy in this chapter—call this function curry().

Now define a function that can be used to convert an amount into another amount based on a rate. The definition of this conversion function is very straight forward and just involves multiplying the number by the rate.

Now create a set of functions that can be used to convert a value in one currency into another currency based on a specific rate. We do not want to have to remember the rate, only the name of the function.

For example:

```
fun convert(amount: Double, rate: Double) = amount * rate

fun main() {
    val dollarsToSterling = curry(0.77, ::convert)
    println(dollarsToSterling(5.0))

    val euroToSterling = curry(0.88, ::convert)
    println(euroToSterling(15.0))

    val sterlingToDollars = curry(1.3, ::convert)
    println(sterlingToDollars(7.0))

    val sterlingToEuro = curry(1.14, ::convert)
    println(sterlingToEuro(9.0))
}
```

If the above code is run the output would be:

```
3.85
13.2
9.1
10.26
```

Part II
Object-Oriented Kotlin

Chapter 8
Kotlin Classes

Introduction

A class is one of the basic building blocks of Kotlin. It is also a core concept in a style of programming known as Object Oriented Programming (or OOP). OOP provides an approach to structuring programs/applications so that the data held, and the operations performed on that data, are bundled together into classes and accessed via instances (or examples) of those classes.

This chapter considers the core constructs in Kotlin used to define classes.

Classes

Classes act as *templates* which are used to construct instances. Classes allow programmers to specify the *structure* of an instance (i.e. its member properties) and the behaviour of an instance (i.e. its member functions) separately from the instance itself. This is important, as it would be extremely time-consuming (as well as inefficient) for programmers to define each instance individually. Instead, they define classes and create *instances* of those classes.

As an example, in an OOP style program, employees might be represented by a class `Employee` where each employee has an `id`, a `name`, a `department` and a `deskNumber` etc. They might also have operations associated with them such as `takeAHoliday()` or `getPaid()`.

A particular employee *instance* would then have their own values to represent their name, employee id, desk number etc. An instance is therefore an example of a class. All instances of a class possess the same data properties and behaviour but contain their own data values. Each instance of a class has the same programmer interface.

© The Author(s), under exclusive license to Springer Nature Switzerland AG 2021
J. Hunt, *Beginner's Guide to Kotlin Programming*,
https://doi.org/10.1007/978-3-030-80893-8_8

In many cases classes are used to represent real world entities (such as employees, bank accounts, orders, players in a game etc.) but they do not need to, they can also represent more abstract concepts such as a transaction between one person and another (for example an agreement to buy a meal).

What are Classes for?

We might represent any type of data item using a combination of properties (or fields) and behaviours. These properties will use existing data types such as Ints, Doubles, Booleans and String or other classes.

For example, when defining the class Person we might give it:

- a property for the person's name of type String,
- a property for their age of type Int,
- a property for their email of type Email,
- some behaviour to give them a birthday (which will increment their age),
- some behaviour to allow us to send them a message via their email,
- etc.

In Kotlin classes are thus used:

- as a template to create instances of that class,
- define *member functions* for common behaviours for a class of things,
- define *member properties* to hold data within the instances.

Instances of a class, on the other hand, can:

- be created from a class,
- hold their own values for properties,
- execute member functions within the context of the instance,
- may have many copies in the system (all with their own data).

What Should a Class Do?

A class should accomplish one specific purpose; it should capture only one idea. This is know as the *Single Responsibility Principle*. If more than one idea is encapsulated in a class, you may reduce the chances for reuse, as well as contravene the laws of encapsulation in object-oriented systems. For example, you may have merged two concepts together so that one can directly access the data of another. This is rarely desirable.

Class Terminology

The following terms are used in Kotlin (and other languages that support object orientation):

- *Class* A class defines a combination of data and behaviour that operates on that data. A class acts as a template when creating new instances.
- *Instance* An instance is an example of a class. All instances of a class possess the same data fields/attributes but contain their own data values. Each instance of a class responds to the same set of requests.
- *Property* The data held by an object is represented by its properties (also sometimes known as an attribute, field or an instance variable). The "state" of an object at any particular moment relates to the current values held by its properties.
- *Member Function* A member function (referred to in several other Object Oriented languages as a method) is a function defined within a class.
- *Message* A message is sent to an instance requesting some operation to be performed or some property to be accessed. It is a request to the object to do something or return something. However, it is up to the instance to determine how to execute that request. A message may be considered akin to a function call for object oriented programming. A message call is typically represented using the *dot notation* in object oriented languages. Thus the receiver of the message is to the left of the 'dot' and the requested behaviour or property to the right.

Note many Object Oriented Programming Languages use the terms instance and object interchangeable (such languages include Java, C#, Python etc.). However in Kotlin an `object` is a different concept to an instance. Objects will be discussed in the next chapter.

Classes Versus Instances

An instance is an example of a class. All instances of a class possess the same data variables but contain their own data. Each instance of a class has the same set of properties as all instances, but each property can have its own values. This is illustrated below:

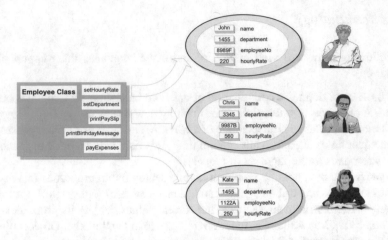

Property is the special name in Kotlin given to the data which is held by an instance. The "state" of an instance at any particular moment relates to the current values held by its properties.

Class Definitions

In Kotlin, a class definition has the following format

```
class nameOfClass constructor(<constructor parameter / property
list>) {
    init {} // initialisation block
    member properties
    member functions
}
```

Although you should note that you can mix the order of the definition of the init{} blocks, properties and member functions as required within a single class. The following code is an example of a class definition:

```
        class Person constructor(val name: String,
                                 var age: Int ) { }
```

Although this is not a hard and fast rule in Kotlin, it is common to define a class in a file named after that class. For example, the above code would be stored in a file called Person.kt; this makes it easier to find the code associated with a class. This is shown below using the IntelliJ IDE:

This very simple class definition actually captures several things, these are:

- It defines a new *public* class called Person.
- The class Person has two *properties*, name and age.
- The name property is a *public read-only* property (referred to as a val property).
- The age property is a *public read–write* property (referred to as a var property).
- The class defines a constructor that takes two parameters, one of type String that will be used to initialise the name property; and one of type Int that will be used to initialise the age property.
- The keyword constructor is *optional* but is used here to explicitly state that the contents of the brackets will define the constructor. Strictly speaking this is the primary constructor (there can be secondary constructors known as *auxiliary* constructors which we will look at later in this chapter).
- The {} for the class body is optional here as there is no class body.

Working with the Class Person

New instances (examples) of the class Person can be created by using the name of the class and passing in the values to be used for the parameters required by the constructor.

For example, the following creates two instances of the class Person:

```
fun main() {
    val p1 = Person("John", 36)
    val p2 = Person("Phoebe", 21)
}
```

The val p1 holds a reference to the *instance* of the class Person whose properties hold the values "John" (for the name) and 36 (for the age). In turn the val p2 references an instance of the class Person whose name and age properties hold the values "Phoebe" and 21. Thus in memory we have:

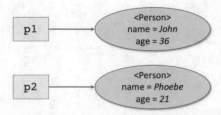

The two vals reference separate *instances* or examples of the class `Person`. They therefore respond to the same set of operations or member functions and have the same set of properties (such as `name` and `age`); however, they have their own values for those attributes (such as "John" and "Phoebe").

Each instance also has its own unique identifier—that shows that even if the attribute values happen to be the same between two objects (for example there happen to be two people called John who are both 36); they are still separate instances of the given class. This identifier or hashcode can be seen when the instances are printed, for example:

```
fun main() {
    val p1 = Person("John", 36)
    val p2 = Person("Phoebe", 21)

    println(p1)
    println(p2)
}
```

When this code is run `p1` and `p2` will generate different identifiers as hexadecimal numbers along with the type of instance being printed, for example:

```
Person@1b28cdfa
Person@eed1f14
```

Note that actual number generated may vary from that above but should still be unique (within your program).

Be Careful with Assignment

Given that in the above example, `p1` and `p2` reference different instances of the class `Person`; what happens when `p1` or `p2` are assigned to another variable? That is, what happens in this case:

```
val p1 = Person("John", 36)
val px = p1
```

What does the val px reference? Actually, it makes a complete copy of the value held by p1; however, p1 does not hold the instance of the class Person; it holds the address of the instance. It thus copies the address held in p1 into the variable px. This means that both p1 and px now reference (point at) the same instance in memory; we therefore have this:

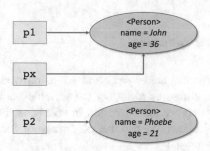

Of course, if p1 was a var and was subsequently assigned a different object (for example if we ran p1 = p2) then this would have no effect on the value held in px; indeed, we would now have:

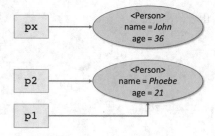

Working with Properties

When we used the println() function to print the instances held by p1 and p2, we got what might at first glance appear to be a slightly odd result:

```
val p1 = Person("John", 36)
val p2 = Person("Phoebe", 21)
println(p1)
println(p2)
```

The output generated was

```
Person@1b28cdfa
Person@eed1f14
```

What this is showing is the name of the class (in this case Person) and a hexadecimal number indicating a unique value for each instance held in memory. Neither of
which is particularly useful as it certainly doesn't help us in knowing what information p1 and p2 are holding. The only thing it does it indicate that they are separate
instances in memory.

Accessing Member Properties

We can access the properties held by p1 and p2 using what is known as the *dot*
notation. This notation allows us to follow the variable holding the instance with
a dot ('.') and the *property* we are interested in accessing. For example, to access
the name of a Person instance we can use p1.name or for their age we can use
p1.age:

```
val p1 = Person("John", 36)
println(p1.name)
println(p1.age)
```

The result of this is that we output

```
John
36
```

Which is rather more meaningful.

Using String Templates

We can combine these properties together in a *String template*. A String template
allows a string to bee constructed from String literal elements and the values of vals
or vars currently in scope, for example:

```
println("${p1.name} is ${p1.age}")
println("${p2.name} is ${p2.age}")
```

In this case we are accessing the name and age properties of the instances held by
p1 and p2 and so these expressions will both be wrapped in curly brackets (${...})
within the String template. If we run this code we now get:

```
John is 36
Phoebe is 21
```

Updating Properties

We can also update the attributes of an object directly, for example we can write:

```
p1.age = 57
```

This will update the `age` property of the instance being referenced by the val `p1`. If we now run

```
println("${p1.name} is ${p1.age}")
```

then we will get:

```
John is 57
```

However, we cannot modify the `name` property as this was defined as a `val`. A val is a *read-only* property and thus any attempt to reset the `name` once the class has been instantiated will result in a compile time error.

We will see in a later chapter that we can refine how properties are accessed, stored and where they are visible.

Classes and Constructors

Simplifying the Class Person

We can now return to the definition of the class Person we presented earlier:

```
class Person constructor(val name: String,
                         var age: Int ) { }
```

We can simplify this definition because the `constructor` keyword is *optional* and the class body, in this case, is also optional as it is empty.

The minimum definition of this class is therefore:

```
class Person(val name: String, val age: Int)
```

Kotlin will infer the constructor keyword between the name of the class and the round brackets (). In fact the presence of a constructor at all is optional. If we are creating a class with no properties and no behaviour, then the minimal class definition in Kotlin is illustrated by the class Bag below:

```
class Bag
```

This is a complete Kotlin class, albeit one that does not do very much. It defines a new class, with a default zero parameter constructor (provided by the compiler) and no additional behaviour over the vary basic default behaviour available for all instances. That is, it can be printed etc. We can therefore write:

```
class Bag

fun main() {
    val b = Bag()
    println(b)
}
```

When this program is run the output generated is:

```
Bag@1fb3ebeb
```

Primary Constructors

Every class has a single primary constructor. It is up to the programmer to decide if this is a zero parameter constructor or one that takes a set of parameters. If the class has a zero parameter constructor then that is provided automatically by the compiler if a primary constructor is not defined.

If you want to create a constructor that will allow data to be provided when the class is instantiated then it is defined following the class name (with the optional constructor keyword) in the class definition.

Defining Default Constructor Parameters

It is possible to provide default values for the parameters to a constructor. This makes any parameters with a default value an *optional* parameter. To define a default value for a parameter all you need to add is an assignment operator (=) followed by the value to use if that parameter is not provided. This is shown for the class `Person2` below:

```
class Person2(val name: String = "", val age: Int = 0)
```

In class `Person2` both name and age are now optional constructor params; as name defaults to "" and `age` to 0.

If all params have default values then the compiler generates a zero parameter constructor which can be useful for Java inter-operability.

Given the definition of the `Person2` class all of the following are now valid ways to create an `Person2` instance:

```
fun main() {
    val p1 = Person2("John", 36)
    val p2 = Person2("Denise")
    val p3 = Person2()
}
```

The example creates an instance of the class `Person2` with the `String` "John" and the `Int` 36. The second creates an instant of the class `Person2` with the `String` "Denise" and default value for the `age` parameter (the `Int` 0). The final example creates an instance of the class `Person2` with the empty `String` "" and the `Int` 0.

Named Constructor Parameters

Using the class `Person2` we can go further as we can use *named parameter passing* rather than positional parameter passing. This is a similar idea to that used with Kotlin functions.

Using named parameter passing the position that a parameter is placed is no longer significant. Thus we can also create instances of the `Person2` class using:

```
val p4 = Person2("Adam", age=42)
val p5 = Person2(age=23, name="Jasmine")
val p6 = Person2(age=21)
```

In this code snippet, the first `Person2` instance uses *positional parameter* passing for the first parameter name (which obtains the value "Adam") and named parameter passing for the `age` parameter.

In the second example, named parameter passing is used for both the `age` and the `name` parameters and thus the position of these parameters is not significant.

In the final example only the `age` parameter is passed in and thus the `name` parameter will use the default value "".

Private Properties

It is also possible to define a constructor property that is marked as `private`. Such a property:

- requires that a value is provided when the instance is created,
- provides a property that is accessible through the internals of the class,
- but which is not accessible from outside the class.

For example, the following class `Person3`, defines an additional constructor property `id`. However the `id` property is `private` to the class and thus is only accessible within the body of the class:

```
class Person3(private val id: String,
              val name: String = "",
              val age: Int = 0) {
}
```

This means that when an instance of the `Person3` class is created a value for the `id` must be provided although `name` and `age` are *optional* parameters to the constructor. In turn `name` and `age` are public *read-only* properties, however `id` is a *private* property and thus not accessible from outside the class. This is shown by the following simple application:

```
fun main() {
    val p1 = Person3("id1", "John", 50)
    println("${p1.name} is ${p1.age}")
    // compile time error id is a private property
    // println("${p1.id}")
}
```

The output from this program is:

```
John is 50
```

Auxiliary Constructors

Every class in Kotlin has a primary constructor, however *optionally* any class in Kotlin can also have one or more *auxiliary constructors*. Auxiliary constructors are defined:

- within the body of the class,
- using the `constructor` keyword,
- do not have an explicit name,
- must call another constructor (either another auxiliary constructor or the primary constructor). This ensures that the primary constructor is the sole point of entry to the class. This is done by specifying the constructor to invoke by postfixing the constructor signature with ':' followed by `this()` and the parameter list used to select the constructor to invoke.

To illustrate the use of an auxiliary constructor, if we wanted to allow a Person to be instantiated with just an `age`, then one way to do it would be to define an auxiliary constructor. This is illustrated in the following example. It defines an auxiliary constructor for the `Person4` class that takes an integer to use for a Persons age without the need to define the person's name:

```kotlin
class Person4(val name: String, var age: Int) {
    // Auxiliary constructor
    constructor(age: Int) : this("unnamed", age) {
        println("In auxiliary constructor")
    }
}
```

This example illustrates the syntax used with an auxiliary constructor. It uses the constructor keyword to define the auxiliary constructor and then it uses the `:this()` syntax to invoke another constructor (in this case the primary constructor) that takes a String and an Int.

Note that the only thing this auxiliary constructor does is to call the primary constructor providing a default name for all *unnamed* person. There is therefore no need to define a constructor body and thus we could have written the class as follows:

```kotlin
class Person4(val name: String, var age: Int) {
    // Auxiliary constructor
    constructor(age: Int) : this("unnamed", age)
}
```

This is a very common idiom or pattern for auxiliary constructors to use.

We can now use this constructor to construct a new instance of the `Person4` class using only an `age` (but where the `name` property will be set to "unnamed"):

```
fun main() {
    val p1 = Person4(21)
    println("${p1.name} is ${p1.age}")
}
```

The result of executing this program is:

```
In auxiliary constructor
unnamed is 21
```

It should be noted that thanks to the availability of default values for parameters in the primary constructor, it is far less common to need to define auxiliary constructors than might be the case in other languages. Indeed the example used for the class Person4 would be much simpler to define using default parameter values.

Initialisation Behaviour

One issue with the approach taken to defining constructors in Kotlin is how do you define any behaviour you want to run when an instance of a class is created? The answer is that you can define one or more initialisation blocks.

An initialisation block is a block of code that is run after the instance of the class is created and just after the *primary* constructor is executed (which will initialise all the constructor parameters) but before any *auxiliary* constructors are executed. The initialisation behaviour is guaranteed to execute before any client code has access to the instance.

An initialisation block is defined using the keyword init followed by a block of code, for example:

```
class Person5(val name: String = "", var age: Int = 0) {

    /**
     * Defines initialisation behaviour that is run just
     * after the class is instantiated.
     * Has access to all constructor parameters whether they
     * are properties or not
     */
    init {
        println("In Init")
    }
}
```

Now when an instance of the class Person5 is created the init{} block will be executed and the String "In Init" will be printed out. This is illustrated by the following code:

```
fun main() {
    println("Creating instance")
    val p1 = Person5("Jasmine", 23)
    println(p1)
    println("Done")
}
```

The output from this short program is given below:

```
Creating instance
In Init
Person5@1b28cdfa
Done
```

As you can see between the String "Creating instance" being printed out and printing out the instance the "In Init" string has been printed.

Actually it is possible to have multiple init{} blocks in a class. If there are multiple init blocks then each is run in turn in the order that they are defined in the class. For example:

```
class Person5(val name: String = "", var age: Int = 0) {
    init {
        println("In Init")
    }

    init {
        println("In Init 2")
    }

    init {
        println("In Init 3")
    }
}
```

When an instance of Person5 is now created the output is:

```
Creating instance
In Init
In Init 2
In Init 3
Person5@1b28cdfa
Done
```

This does raise the question why would you have multiple initialisation blocks. There are several justifications for the presence of multiple init blocks in Kotlin:

- *Modularisation of your initialisation behaviour.* Each block could be used to initialise a specific part of the class, thus separating out different initialisation concerns.
- *Stepped initialisation behaviour.* A property needs to be defined based on behaviour in one init{} block which is then used by another init{} block. For example:

```kotlin
class Foo() {
    val x = Bar.getValue()

    init {
        // check the validity of x and abort if invalid
    }

    val y = Bar.getDerivedValue(x)   // requires x to be valid

    init {
        // Check validity of y and
        // continue with initialisation if all ok
    }
}
```

In this case the first init block checks that the value provided is valid and if it is not then the initialisation process will abort (for example it could throw an exception which is discussed in a later chapter). If the value of x is valid then the property y is set based on the value in the property x. This is then checked in the second init block and if all is ok then the remainder of the initialisation process is completed.

Defining Instance Behaviour

Writing Member Functions

Classes do not only hold data; they can also hold behaviour. This behaviour is defined within member functions. That is functionality that is a member (part of) a classes definition. Or to put it another way member functions represent functionality that is tied to an instance of the class. Note that in several other Object Oriented Programming languages member functions are referred to as *methods* and many developers still colloquially use the term with reference to Kotlin.

Member functions are defined:

- within the body of a class,
- are declared using the keyword fun,
- followed by the name of the member function,
- will have a parameter list which may be empty defined using round brackets,
- have a return type that will either be Unit or a specific type such as Int or String,
- have a body which defines the behaviour of the member function,
- have access to all other member functions and member level or constructor properties.

An example of a simple member function is given by the following class that has a member function called birthday(). This member function takes no parameters and increments the age property by 1:

```kotlin
class Person6(val name: String = "",
              var age: Int = 0) {

    fun birthday() {
        println("Happy birthday you were $age")
        age++
        println("You are now $age")
    }

}
```

If we now create an instance of the class Person6 and call the birthday() member function on it using the *dot* notation, then the age will be incremented by 1, for example:

```kotlin
fun main() {
    val p1 = Person6("Adam", 21)
    println("${p1.name} is ${p1.age}")
    p1.birthday()
    println("${p1.name} is now ${p1.age}")
}
```

When we run this code, we get.

```
Adam is 21
Happy birthday you were 21
You are now 22
Adam is now 22
```

As you can see Adam is initially 21; but after his birthday he is now 22.

Member Functions with Parameters

Member functions (like standard functions) can be given parameters. Thes are defined within the member functions round brackets and there can be zero or more parameters. Each parameter has its own type specified using the format:

```
<parameter name> : Type
```

If there is more than one parameter then each parameter declaration is separate by a comma, for example:

```kotlin
class MathUtils {
    fun add(x: Int, y: Int) {
        println(x + y)
    }
}
```

In this example, the member function add() prints out the result of adding two parameters together. The parameters are declared within the round brackets of the member function declaration. In this case both parameters are of type Int and their declarations are separated by a comma.

Member Functions Returning Values

Member functions also have a return type specified; the default if a type is not explicitly specified is Unit. Unit indicates that the member function returns nothing. However, any valid type can be returned from a member function. This is specified by:

```
: <Type>
```

After the member function name and parameter list, for example:

```kotlin
class MathUtils {
    fun add(x: Int, y: Int): Int {
        return x + y
    }
}
```

In the above example, the add() member function function returns a value of type Int. The actual value to return is indicated using the keyword return. Thus in this case the value returned is the result of adding x and y together.

Parameters Are Vals

In Kotlin all parameters to member functions are vals (which is the same as is the case for functions). This means that once the member function has been invoked it is not possible to reassign a value to that parameter. This means that it is not possible to write the following;

```
class MathUtils {
    fun add(i: Int) {
        i = i + 1      // won't compile i is a val
    }
}
```

The aim is to protect the programmer against accidentally assigning a value to parameter and then using that new value later in the member function.

Named Member Function Parameters

As is the case with both functions and constructor parameters, values can be passed to member functions using either *positional parameter passing* or *named parameter passing*. It is also possible to mix positional and named parameter passing in the same member function invocation. Some examples of the options available when invoking a member function are given below:

```
class Math {

    fun max(x: Int, y: Int): Int {
        return if (x > y) {
            x
        } else {
            y
        }
    }
}

fun main() {
    val math = Math()

    println("math.max(3, 4): "      + math.max(3, 4))
    println("math.max(3, y=4): "    + math.max(3, y = 4))
    println("math.max(x=3, y=4): " + math.max(x = 3, y = 4))
    println("math.max(y=3, x=4): " + math.max(y = 3, x = 4))

    // illegal as 4 will bind to x and so will 3
    // println("math.max(4, x=3): " + math.max(4, x=3))
}
```

As you can see from this there is a lot of flexibility in how parameters are passed in. Also note that once you are using named parameter passing then the order in which the parameters are presented is no longer significant.

Prior to Kotlin 1.4 it was possible to mix positional and named parameter passing. Instead it was necessary to list all the positional parameters first and then all the named parameters; that it was not possible to use named parameter passant then position in the same member function invocation. However, since Kotlin 1.4 this has been allowed. The is illustrated below:

```
fun main() {
    val math = Math()

    // Can now use positional after named if sequence is correct
    println("math.max(x=3, 4): " + math.max(x=3, 4))

    // Still invalid as positional param is assumed to be x
    // println("math.max(4, x=3): " + math.max(4, x=3))
}
```

However, it should be noted that if you do this you need to make sure that the *named* parameters do not clash with the *positional* parameters, for example math.max(y= 3, 4) would be illegal and will not compile as the *named* parameter is y and the *positional* parameter is also bound to y.

Default Parameter Values

As with both functions and constructors member function parameters can be provided with a default value. This means that they become optional parameters. For example:

```kotlin
class Math {
  fun add(x: Int, y: Int = 1): Int = x + y
}

fun main() {
    val math = Math()

    println("math.add(5, 3): ${math.add(5, 3)}")
    println("math.add(5): ${math.add(5)}")
}
```

In this example the second parameter y is an *optional* parameter. If a value is not provided then the default value 1 will be used; if a value is provided then the default value will be ignored. The output from this program is presented below:

```
math.add(5, 3): 8
math.add(5): 6
```

Variable Parameter Lists

Kotlin allows a member function to have a maximum of one variable argument parameter.

A variable argument parameter can have any number of values supplied to it and within the function those values will be made available inside the function as an array (arrays are discussed in more detail later in the book). However, Kotlin restricts the last parameter in a parameter list to being defined as a variable argument list using the keyword varargs.

An example of a member function that can take a variable argument list is give below:

```kotlin
class Printer {
    fun echo(vararg args: String) {
        for (arg in args) println(arg)
    }
}
```

The echo member function can be given zero or more strings; these strings can be comma separated and can be processed within the echo member function. In this case we use the for loop structure to loop over each of the values in the args String array in turn, printing out each value.

Examples of using the echo() member function are given below:

```kotlin
fun main() {
    val printer = Printer()
    printer.echo()
    println("--------")
    printer.echo("John")
    println("--------")
    printer.echo("John", "was", "here")
}
```

The output from this program is shown below:

```
--------
John
--------
John
was
here
```

The This Reference

Let us look for a moment at the special variable *this*. It is used to represent the instance within which a member function is executing. This provides the context within which the member function runs and allows the member function to access the data held by the object. Thus *this* is the instance itself.

All member properties and member functions can be explicitly referenced using the *this* self reference. It can be useful to do this when a local val or var has the same name as a member level property. By default Kotlin looks locally within a member function for a specific named local val or var before looking in the instance for a member property. Thus if a local val or var has the same name as a member level property then it is necessary to prefix the member level property with the this keyword.

An example of this is shown below:

```
class Person6(val name: String = "",
              var age: Int = 0) {

    fun birthday() {
        val age = this.age
        println("Happy birthday you were $age")
        this.age++
        println("You are now ${this.age}")
    }

}
```

Referencing Member Functions

It is also possible to create a callable reference to a member function. This allows a reference to a member function to be created at one point in your program but invoked at another point. This is done using the box operator (::). The callable reference can either be with reference to a whole class of things (such as Strings) or to a particular instance (such as the specific string "42").

The following illustrates a callable reference to the member function toInt() on the class String. In this example we are defining a new val func3 which will hold a callable reference to the String.toInt member function using the box operator::

```
// A callable reference to a method on class String
val func3: (String) -> Int = String::toInt
```

This can be used by calling func3() and passing in a string:

```
println("funcs('3'): ${func3("3")}")
```

If we want to apply this operation to a specific string we can use a *bound* callable reference:

```
// A bound callable reference
val func4: () -> Int = "4"::toInt
```

This can be invoked just by calling the function (as no parameter is required):

```
println("func4(): ${func4()}")
```

Single Expression Member Functions

Kotlin actually provides two ways in which a member function can be defined; as well as the approach presented so far there is the *single expression* member function definition. This form of member function definition is intended as a convenient shorthand form that can be used if:

- a member function body is formed on just a single expression,
- the return value for the function can be directly inferred from the single expression.

In this case there is no need to use curly brackets to define the body of the member function nor is there a need to use the `return` keyword to explicitly return the value.

In addition the return type can be inferred by Kotlin based on the result of the single expression.

The general format of a single line member function is

```
fun member-function-name(parameter-list) = single-expression
```

For example, the following class `Author`, all of the member functions provide the same behaviour with the same signature. However, each definition uses a different syntax form:

```
class Author(val name: String) {
    fun printMe1(): Unit {
        println("Author - $name")
    }
    fun printMe2(): Unit = println("Author - $name")
    fun printMe3() = println("Author - $name")
}
```

Each version of the `printMe()` member function does the same thing; the first version `printMe1()`, uses the traditional long hand form of a member function declaration.

The second form uses the shorthand form but explicitly specifies the return type as `Unit`. However, this could have been inferred by Kotlin and thus the third version is the most concise and most common shorthand form.

Any code that uses the class `Author` however will not see a difference between any of these member functions, for example:

```
fun main() {
    val author = Author("John")
    author.printMe1()
    author.printMe2()
    author.printMe3()
}
```

The output from this program is:

```
Author - John
Author - John
Author - John
```

Defining a Default String Representation

In a previous section we printed out information from the instances of class Person by accessing the properties name and age.

However, to do this we needed to know the internal structure of the class Person. That is, we need to know that there are properties called name and age available in this class.

It would be much more convenient if the instance itself knew how to convert itself into a String to be printed out!

In fact we can make the class Person do this by defining a member function that can be used to convert an instance into a String for printing purposes. This member function is the toString(): String member function. It is expected to return a String which can be used to represent appropriate information about a class.

The signature of the member function is:

```
fun toString(): String
```

This is to some extent a special member function as all things in Kotlin know how to convert themselves to a String to be printed or logged etc. In fact our class Person already knows how to print itself as a String, its just that the default behaviour provided isn't very useful to us, it merely prints the name of the class and a unique hashcode generated for the instance.

However, we can override this default behaviour with our own definition of the toString() member function defined within the class Person.

To do this we must define a new member function but mark it with the keyword override (the exact meaning of override will be explained in the chapter on class inheritance).

We can add this member function to our class Person and see how that affects the output generated when using the println() function.

We will return a String from the toString() member function that provides and the name and age of the Person instance:

```
class Person(val name: String = "", var age: Int = 0) {
    override fun toString() = "Person($name, $age)"
}
```

Note that in the `toString()` member function we format the returned string using a String template that references the `name` and `age` properties. If we now run the following code:

```kotlin
fun main() {
    val p1 = Person("John", 56)
    val p2 = Person("Denise", 53)
    val p3 = Person("Phoebe", 23)
    val p4 = Person("Adam", 21)
    println(p1)
    println(p2)
    println(p3)
    println(p4)
}
```

The output generated is:

```
Person(John, 56)
Person(Denise, 53)
Person(Phoebe, 23)
Person(Adam, 21)
```

Which is much more useful.

Providing KDoc

It is common to provide a comment for a class, a property or a member function explaining what they do, their purpose and any important points to note about them.

This can be done by providing a comment containing KDoc and block tags that can be used to explain the specific meaning of various elements of your code.

The KDoc syntax is that the documentation must be contained within a comment that starts with /** and ends with */. Every line of the comment may begin with an asterisk, which is not considered part of the contents of the comment.

By convention, the first paragraph of the documentation text (the block of text until the first blank line) is the summary description of the element, and the following text is the detailed description. This summary can be picked up by IntelliJ and used to provide a popup window with more information on the type.

Every block tag begins on a new line and starts with the @ character.

The following illustrates some of these ideas for the class Person:

```
/**
 * This is a simple class representing information
 * about a person.
 *
 * @property name the name of this person.
 * @property age the age of this person
 * @constructor Creates a new person.
 *
 * @author John Hunt
 * @since 1.0
 */
class Person(val name: String = "", var age: Int = 0) {
    override fun toString() = "Person($name, $age)"
}
```

Equality Between Instances

Equality between instances is represented by two operators in Kotlin == and ===
(and their not versions != and !==). They have different meanings of equality:

- == Represents structural or value equality. For example, two instances of the type
  Person may be considered equal if the data they hold is the same, for example
  "John" aged 32 is equal to another "John" aged 32.
- != is the inverse of ==.
- === Represents referential equality that is the data involved must be literally the
  same instance rather than just equivalent.
- !== is the inverse of ===.

This is illustrated for the following version of the class Person. This class overrides the default version of the equals() member function. This member function
can be called explicitly or *implicitly* via the == and != operators. That is these
operators use the equals() member function under the hood.

```
class Person(val name: String, val age: Int) {
    override fun equals(other: Any?): Boolean {
        return when (other) {
            null -> false
            is Person ->
                ((other.name == name) && (other.age == age))
            else -> false
        }
    }
}
```

We can now use this class and its implementation of the `equals(Any?)` member function in the following program:

```kotlin
fun main() {
    val p1 = Person("John", 21)
    val p2 = Person("John", 21)
    val p3 = p1
    // checks for reference equality
    println("p1 === p2: ${p1 === p2}")
    // checks for structural equality
    println("p1 == p2: ${p1 == p2}")
    // again structural equality
    println("p1.equals(p2): ${p1.equals(p2)}")
    println("p1 !== p2: ${p1 !== p2}")
    println("p1 === p3: ${p1 === p3}")
    println("p1 !== p3: ${p1 !== p3}")
}
```

The output from this program is given below:

```
p1 === p2: false
p1 == p2: true
p1.equals(p2): true
p1 !== p2: true
p1 === p3: true
p1 !== p3: false
```

As can be seen from this `p1` and `p2` are structurally equal but not referentially equal (that is they contain the same data but are not the same reference). In contrast `p1` and `p3` both reference the same instance of the class `Person` and are therefore referentially equal.

Automatic Memory Management

The creation and deletion of objects (and their associated memory) is managed by the Kotlin Memory Manager. Indeed, the provision of a memory manager (also known as automatic memory management) is one of Kotlin's advantages when compared to languages such as C and C++. It is not uncommon to hear C++ programmers complaining about spending many hours attempting to track down a particularly awkward bug only to find it was a problem associated with memory allocation or pointer manipulation. Similarly, a regular problem for C++ developers is that of memory creep, which occurs when memory is allocated but is not freed up. The application either uses all available memory or runs out of space and produces a run time error.

Most of the problems associated with memory allocation in languages such as C++ occur because programmers must not only concentrate on the (often complex) application logic but also on memory management. They must ensure that they allocate only the memory which is required and deallocate it when it is no longer required. This may sound simple, but it is no mean feat in a large complex application.

An interesting question to ask is "why do programmers have to manage memory allocation?". There are few programmers today who would expect to have to manage the registers being used by their programs, although 30 or 40 years ago the situation was very different. One answer to the memory management question, often cited by those who like to manage their own memory, is that "it is more efficient, you have more control, it is faster and leads to more compact code". Of course, if you wish to take these comments to their extreme, then we should all be programming in assembler. This would enable us all to produce faster, more efficient and more compact code than that produced by Kotlin or languages such as Java.

The point about high level languages, however, is that they are more productive, introduce fewer errors, are more expressive and are efficient enough (given modern computers and compiler technology). The memory management issue is somewhat similar. If the system automatically handles the allocation and deallocation of memory, then the programmer can concentrate on the application logic. This makes the programmer more productive, removes problems due to poor memory management and, when implemented efficiently, can still provide acceptable performance.

Kotlin therefore provides automatic memory management. Essentially, it allocates a portion of memory as and when required. When memory is short, it looks for areas which are no longer used. These areas of memory are then freed up (deallocated) so that they can be reallocated. This process is often referred to as *Garbage Collection*.

Class Design Considerations

The following guidelines may help you to decide whether to split the class with which you are working. Look at how you describe the class. Consider the following points:

- Is the description of the class short and clear? If not, is this a reflection on the class? Consider how the comment can be broken down into a series of short clear comments. Base the new classes around those comments.
- If the comment is short and clear, do the class and instance variables make sense within the context of the comment? If they do not, then the class needs to be re-evaluated. It may be that the comment is inappropriate, or the class and instance variables inappropriate.

- Look at how and where the attributes of the class are used. Is their use in line with the class comment? If not, then you should take appropriate action.

Online Resources

If you want to explore some of the ideas presented in this chapter in more detail here are some online references:

- https://en.wikipedia.org/wiki/Object-oriented_programming This is the wikipedia entry for Object Oriented Programming and thus provides a quick reference to much of the terminology and history of the subject and acts as a jumping off point for other references.
- https://dev.to/charanrajgolla/beginners-guide---object-oriented-programming which provides a light hearted look at the four concepts within object orientations namely abstraction, inheritance, polymorphism and Encapsulation.
- https://www.tutorialspoint.com/kotlin/kotlin_class_and_object.htm A Tutorials Point course on Object Oriented Programming and Kotlin.
- https://kotlinlang.org/docs/reference/equality.html discusses equality in Kotlin.

See the following for further information on Kotlin classes:

- https://kotlinlang.org/docs/reference/classes.html the Kotlin Standard library Class tutorial.
- https://kotlinlang.org/docs/reference/kotlin-doc.html documentation on KDoc documentation tags.

Exercises

The aim of this exercise is to create a new class called `Account`.

1. Define a new class to represent a type of bank account.
2. When the class is instantiated you should provide the account number, the name of the account holder, an opening balance and the type of account (which can be a string representing 'current', 'deposit' or 'investment' etc.). This means that there must be a constructor to initialise these constructor properties.
3. Provide three instance member functions for the `Account`; `deposit(Double)`, `withdraw(Double)` and `getBalance()`. The behaviour of these member functions should be as expected, `deposit(Double)` will increase the balance, `withdraw(Double)` will decrease the balance and `getBalance()` returns the current balance.
4. Define a simple test application to verify the behaviour of your `Account` class.

It can be helpful to see how your class `Account` is expected to be used. For this reason a simple test application for the `Account` is given below:

```
fun main() {
    val acc1 = Account("123", "John", 10.05, "current")
    val acc2 = Account("345", "Denise", 23.55, "savings")
    val acc3 = Account("567", "Phoebe", 12.45, "investment")

    println(acc1)
    println(acc2)
    println(acc3)

    acc1.deposit(23.45)
    acc1.withdraw(12.33)
    println("balance: ${acc1.balance}")
}
```

The following output illustrates what the result of running this code might look like:

```
Account('123', 'John', 10.05, type='current')
Account('345', 'Denise', 23.55, type='savings')
Account('567', 'Phoebe', 12.45, type='investment')
balance: 21.17
```

Chapter 9
Objects and Companion Objects

Introduction

This chapter will discuss the difference between *objects* in Kotlin and instance of a class. This is important as many other object-oriented languages use these terms interchangeably. However, in Kotlin they are significantly different concepts, defined with different language constructs and used in different ways.

Singleton Objects

Kotlin provides another type that can sit along side the class type. It is directly supported by the language construct `object`. A Kotlin *object* is a singleton object that is accessible to any Kotlin code that has visibility of that object definition. The term *singleton* here refers to the fact that there is a single example of the object definition within the Virtual Machine (JVM) executing the Kotlin program. This is guaranteed by the language itself and does not require any additional programmer intervention.

If you have never come across the concept of a *Singleton* object before it may appear an odd idea. However, it is very widely and commonly used within the object oriented programming world. Examples of the singleton concept can be found in Java, C#, Smalltalk, C++ etc. and have been documented in various ways since it was first popularised in the so-called Gang of Four patterns book. The four authors of this book are Erich Gamma, Richard Helm, Ralph Johnson and John Vlissides (collectively known as the "Gang of Four", or GoF for short). They popularised the patterns concepts and ideals (see the online and book resources sections at the end of this chapter for links and references).

So what are *design patterns*? They are essentially useful recurring solutions to problems within software design. For example, "I want to loosely couple a set of objects, how can I do this?", might be a question facing a software designer. The

© The Author(s), under exclusive license to Springer Nature Switzerland AG 2021
J. Hunt, *Beginner's Guide to Kotlin Programming*,
https://doi.org/10.1007/978-3-030-80893-8_9

Mediator design pattern is one solution to this. If you are familiar with design patterns you can use them to solve problems in your designs with well established solutions. Typically early in the design process, the problems are more architectural/structural in nature, while later in the design process they may be more behavioural. Design patterns actually provide different types of patterns some of which are at the architectural/structural level and some of which are more behavioural. They can thus help every stage of the design process.

The *Singleton* design pattern describes a type that can only have one instance constructed for it. That is, unlike other types it should not be possible to obtain more than one instance within the same program. Thus the Singleton design pattern ensures that only one instance of a type is created. All elements that use an instance of that type; use the same instance.

The motivation behind this pattern is that some classes, such as those classes that involve the central management of a resource, should have exactly one instance. For example, an object that manages the reuse of database connections (i.e. a connection pool) could be a singleton.

However, implementing a singleton in some language can be more complex than initially thought, as it is necessary to ensure that it is not possible to have multiple instances of the singleton concept, to ensure thread safely in a concurrent environment etc. Kotlin solves this problem by making the singleton concept part of the language.

Singleton Objects in Kotlin

As mentioned above Kotlin supports the concept of a singleton object using the keyword `object`. An object can have .

- one or more `init{}` blocks,
- zero or more member functions,
- zero or more member properties,
- its own override of `toString()`.

The member functions and properties can be public or private etc.
Note, however that an object *cannot* have a constructor.
An example of the definition of a simple object `MathsUtils` is given below:

```kotlin
object MathUtils {

    // Specifying useful member properties
    val ZERO = 0
    val MIN: Int = -100

    // Member property to be initialised in init block
    val MAX: Int

    // Initialisation block
    init {
        MAX = 100
    }

    // Providing utility member functions
    fun add(x: Int, y: Int) = x + y
    fun sub(x: Int, y: Int) = x - y
    fun isLessThanMax(x: Int) = x < MAX

}
```

This `MathsUtil` object has three public member level properties `ZERO`, `MIN` and `MAX`.

- `ZERO` and `MIN` are initialised at the point of declaration.
- The `MAX` property is initialised within the `init{}` block that is run when the singleton object is created.

The object also provides three member functions that can be used to add two numbers together, subtract two numbers and check whether a number is less than the `MAX` number allowed.

It is now possible to directly access the member functions and member properties of the object in a program. For example:

```kotlin
fun main() {
    // Now uses singleton object to access member functions
    println("MathUtils.ZERO: ${MathUtils.ZERO}")
    println("MathUtils.MIN: ${MathUtils.MIN}")
    println("MathUtils.MAX: ${MathUtils.MAX}")

    println("MathUtils.add(2, 3): ${MathUtils.add(2, 3)}")
    println("MathUtils.sub(6, 2): ${MathUtils.sub(6, 2)}")
}
```

Note that there will only ever be a single instance of the `MathsUtil` object in a single running program.

The output from this program is given below:

```
MathUtils.ZERO: 0
MathUtils.MIN: -100
MathUtils.MAX: 100
MathUtils.add(2, 3): 5
MathUtils.sub(6, 2): 4
```

It should also be noted that objects are also part of the Kotlin type system and that defining a new object defines a new type that can be used in your application.

For example, if we create an object `Session` then we can create vals and vars of type `Session` and we can assign the singleton object to a `val` or `var` of that type. This is illustrated below:

```
object Session {
    val id: Int = 5

    override fun toString(): String {
        return "Session($id)"
    }
}

fun main() {
    println(Session)

    val s: Session = Session
    println(s)
}
```

In the above code, the `Session` object has a public val `id` property and its own implementation of `toString()`. The `main()` function then prints out the `Session` singleton object before assigning it to the val s. The val s references the same instance of the `Session` object as the name `Session` does. In fact when we define an object the name of the object is both its type (i.e., `Session`) and the name used to reference the single instance of that type (i.e. `Session` again). The end result is that in effect s becomes an alias for the `Session` object.

Anonymous Objects

It is also possible to create *anonymous* objects that are defined at the point that they are used. As they are anonymous they do not have a name and cannot be referenced elsewhere within a program. They can have all the features of a named object such as member properties, member functions, init{} blocks and a `toString()` member function etc. However, they do not have a name and do not explicitly add a new type to the type system.

An example of an *anonymous* object is given below:

```
fun main() {

    // Defines a new object which is anonymous
    val obj = object {
        var x: Int = 0
        val y = 42

        val MAX: Int

        init {
            MAX = 100
        }

        fun printMe() {
            println("Print Me")
        }
    }

    // Use single instance of anonymous object
    println(obj)
    println(obj.MAX)
    println("obj.x = ${obj.x}, obj.y = ${obj.y}")
    obj.x = 50
    println("obj.x = ${obj.x}, obj.y = ${obj.y}")
    obj.printMe()
}
```

In the above program an anonymous object is created and stored into a val `obj`. This object has three properties x, y and MAX. MAX is initialised in an `init{}` block. It also possesses a member function `printMe()`. The output from this program is given below:

```
AnonymousObjectAppKt$main$obj$1@1fb3ebeb
100
obj.x = 0, obj.y = 42
obj.x = 50, obj.y = 42
Print Me
```

Note that the name of the anonymous object is comprised of $ and a sequence number—that is it has a name but not one you are expected to use.

Companion Objects

Companion objects are singleton objects' for a class—they can be used to provide utility functions such as factory member functions that will support the concept being modelled by the class (they therefore play a similar role to static content within Java or C# classes).

As a companion object is an object, it is a singleton instance that sits alongside the class. To define a companion object it must.

- be defined within the body of the class,
- be marked as a companion object,
- must not have a name.

When used in this way companion objects are useful placeholders for house keeping behaviour, for factory operations, for data shared across all instances of a class etc.

From the point of view of the user of the class; the companion object and the class appear to be a single concept. For example, consider the following definition of a `UserSession` class and a companion object.

```kotlin
class UserSession private constructor(val id: Int) {

    // Companion (singleton) object
    companion object {
        private val MAX = 100
        private var count = 0
        private fun next() = count++
        fun create(): UserSession {
            next()
            return UserSession(count)
        }
    }

    fun printData() {
        println("Id is $id and MAX is $MAX")
    }

    override fun toString(): String {
        return "UserSession($id)"
    }

}

fun main() {
    val session1 = UserSession.create()
    println(session1)
    val session2 = UserSession.create()
    println(session2)
}
```

Notice that the companion object for the UserSession class has a private val MAX, a private var count (initialised to zero) and a private member function next().

By default all member functions and properties are public (accessible anywhere); here we are making the property MAX and count properties and the member function next() visible only within the UserSession type. That is they are available to the *companion* object and also to the code defined within the class UserSession. However, they are not available to anything external to the UserSession.

The companion object also has a *factory* member function create(). This member function uses the companion object member function next() to increment the count property before it creates a new UserSession instance.

Also as a reminder note that the next() member function uses the single line member function declaration format where as the create(), printData() and toString() are using the long hand member function declaration form.

A final point to note is that the *constructor* for the UserSession class has been defined using the long hand form; that is using the constructor keyword. This is so that we can mark the constructor as being private. This indicates that the constructor can only be accessed from within the scope of the class UserSession or its *companion* object.

It is therefore no longer possible to directly create an instance of the class UserSession externally to the class. The only way to obtain a new instance of the class is via the create() companion object factory member function. This means that full control of how UserSessions are created is given over to the companion object—this is a common factory pattern (another Gang of Four or GoF pattern) and provides controlled access to the instance creation process.

From a client of the UserSession concepts' point of view, they can now only create a new session using the create() factory member function. This is illustrated below:

```kotlin
fun main() {
    val session1 = UserSession.create()
    println(session1)
    val session2 = UserSession.create()
    println(session2)
    session1.printData()
}
```

The two UserSession instances above are created using the UserSession objects' create() member function. Their ids are automatically allocated via this member function (which also increments the count property). The output from the program is given below:

```
UserSession(1)
UserSession(2)
Id is 1 and MAX is 100
```

Note that the toString() member function is used to print the formatted String version of the instances and printData() printed the id and the value of the MAX property.

Companion Object Behaviour

It may at first seem unclear what should normally go in a member function defined in the class as opposed to what should go in a member function defined in a companion object. After all, they are both defined with the class as a whole and relate to the same overall concept.

However, it is important to remember that one defines the behaviour which will be part of an instance and the other the behaviour which can be shared across all instances of the class being implemented.

In order to maintain clarity companion object member functions should only perform one of the following roles:

- *Application Entry Point* It is common to see main() function but sometimes it is useful to define an *object* with a main() member function. This object acts as an *entry point* for your application and the main() member function as the behaviour to be executed. Although note the member function must be marked with @JvmStatic for compatibility with the JVM runtime environment. For example:

```kotlin
object HelloWorldApp {

    /**
     * Defines entry point for a Kotlin application.
     * Need to indicates that the compiler should generate
     * byte codes that are compatible with the Java definition
     * of a static member function that it expects to find
     * to run a program
     */
    @JvmStatic
    fun main(args: Array<String>) {
        println("Hello World!")
    }

}
```

- *Answering enquiries about the class* This role can provide generally useful information, frequently derived from companion object properties. For example, it may be possible to obtain data on the number of instances of the class that have been created.
- *Instance management* In this role companion object member functions control the number of instances created. For example, a class may only a certain number of instances to be created (for example a database connection pool manager object that may only allow 10 database connections to be created).

- *Examples* Occasionally, companion object member functions are used to provide helpful examples which explain the operation of a class.
- *Testing* companion object member functions can be used to support the testing of an instance of a class. You can use them to create an instance, perform an operation and compare the result with a known value. If the values are different, the member function can report an error. However, test frameworks are generally a better approach.
- *Support for one of the above roles.*

Any other tasks should be performed by an instance level member function.

An Object or An Instance

In some situations you may only need to create a single instance of a class and reference it wherever it is required. A continuing debate ponders whether it is worth creating such an instance or whether it is better to define the required behaviour in an object. The answer to this is not straight forward as there are several factors that should be taken into account including:

- The use of an object in Kotlin guarantees you a singleton instance within the current JVM. This means that it also limits you to a single instance in the current JVM and over time this may be a problem.
- The creation of an instance has a very low overhead. This is a key feature in Kotlin and it has received extensive attention.
- You may be tempted to treat the object as a global reference. This suggests that the implementation has been poorly thought out.
- It is not possible to extend objects using a concept known as inheritance (which will be discussed later in this book). However, it is possible to extend a class via inheritance. Since inheritance is one of the ways in which the reuse of data and behaviour can be achieved, this limits the future development of objects within your application.

In deciding whether to use a Kotlin *object* or a Kotlin *class* to hold data and/or behaviour you need to consider the context in which it will be used, how you expect to develop the concept and whether there will ever be a need for more than one instance of that concept.

Online Resources

There are many online references to design patterns available including:

- http://www.oodesign.com Quick reference list of design patterns.
- https://sourcemaking.com/design_patterns Introductory descriptions and examples of patterns.
- https://hillside.net/patterns/patterns-catalog List of patterns based sites.

Book References

1. *Design Patterns: Elements of Reusable Object-Oriented Software* (Gang of Four Design Patterns Book), E. Gamma, R. Helm, R. Johnson and J. Vlissades, 0201633612, Addison-Wesley, 1994.
2. Hands on Design Patterns with Kotlin, Alexey Soshin, Packt Publishing, 1788998014, 2018.

Exercises

The aim of this exercise is to add housekeeping style member functions to the Account class.

You should follow these steps:

1. We want to allow the Account class from the last chapter to keep track of the number of instances of the class that have been created.
2. Print out a message each time a new instance of the Account class is created indicating the account holder name and the type of account created.
3. Print out the number of accounts created at the end of the previous test program.
4. An example of the type of output generated might be:

```
New Account created for John of current
New Account created for Denise of savings
New Account created for Phoebe of investment
Account('123', 'John', 10.05, type='current')
Account('345', 'John', 23.55, type='savings')
Account('567', 'Phoebe', 12.45, type='investment')
balance: 21.17
3 instances of Account class created
```

Chapter 10
Further Kotlin Properties

Introduction

Many object-oriented languages have the explicit concept of encapsulation; that is the ability to hide data within an object and only to provide specific gateways into that data. These gateways are functions defined to *get* or *set* the value of an attribute (often referred to as getters and setters). This allows more control over access to the data; for example, it is possible to check that only a positive integer above zero, but below 120, is used for a person's age etc.

In many languages such as Java attributes can be hidden from external access using specific keywords (such as private) that indicate the data should be made private to the object.

Kotlin provides a higher level of abstraction than languages such as Java by explicitly supporting the concept of a Property. These properties can also have explicit setters and getters defined for them.

In this chapter we will explore the idea of a property further including how to implement custom getters and setters.

Property Declarations

Properties can be defined in several locations within a program, for example they can be defined within the body of an object, within the constructor of a class or the body of a class, within a companion object or indeed at the top level of a program. The section will discuss some of these aspects of properties in more detail.

© The Author(s), under exclusive license to Springer Nature Switzerland AG 2021   169
J. Hunt, *Beginner's Guide to Kotlin Programming*,
https://doi.org/10.1007/978-3-030-80893-8_10

Types Held by a Property

Properties can hold values of any valid Kotlin type including:

- Byte, Short, Int, Long etc.,
- Float and Double,
- Booleans,
- instances of any class,
- built-in classes,
- third party library classes and custom classes,
- objects,
- enumerated values.

Top Level Properties

Properties can be defined at the top level of a program.

That is a property does not need to defined within a class, an object or defined locally to a function or member function. A free standing property defined within a file can be accessed in the remainder of that file.

For example, if a file contained the following declarations outside of any class, object or function this would be valid and would declare properties that can be accessed through out the rest of that file:

```kotlin
val MIN = 1
val MAX = 100
val calculator = Calculator()

var count = 0
```

These statements declare three top level vals MIN, MAX and calculator. They also defines a top level var count.

The top level properties are now accessible anywhere within the rest of the file.

For example we could now write the following main() function within the same file:

```
fun main() {
    println(MIN)
    println(MAX)
    println(count)
    count++
    println(count)
    println(calculator)
}
```

Here the properties MIN, MAX, calculator and count can be accessed directly.

The output from this program is:

```
1
100
0
1
Calculator@548c4f57
```

Constructor Parameters

Properties can be defined within the *constructor* of a class, however they are not the only element that can be defined within the constructor. It is also possible to have plain *constructor parameters*.

Constructor parameters are parameters that must be provided when a class is instantiated but which are not properties (and thus do not have an associated keyword val or var). Such constructor parameters are only available within the init{} block of the class (and when invoking superclass constructors as discussed in a later chapter on class inheritance).

There are therefore two types of parameter to a constructor:

- Constructor parameters with a very limited scope (i.e. The init{} block).
- Constructor properties which have at least a scope for the whole body of the class and by default are publicly accessible from outside the class.

The following class illustrates the differences between a *constructor parameter* and a *constructor property*.

```kotlin
class GamePlayer(firstName: String,         // constructor param
                 surname: String,           // constructor param
                 var age: Int,              // read-write property
                 val id: String,           // readonly property
                 // private property
                 private val message: String = "Happy Birthday")
{

    // read-only property initialised in init block
    val fullname: String
    init {
        // firstName and surname only visible in init
        fullname = "$firstName $surname"
    }

    override fun toString(): String {
        return "GamePlayer[$id, $fullname, $age]"
    }

    fun birthday() {
        val oldAge = age
        age++
        println("$message $fullname, you were $oldAge you are
now $age")
    }
}
```

In this case firstName and surname are *constructor parameters*, they are therefore only accessible within the init{} block of the class.

However age, id and message are properties accessible anywhere within the body of the class, with age and id also being publicly accessible.

In this class there is also a *member level property* filename which is initialised within the init{} block.

When an instance of the GamePlayer class is created all five parameters to the constructor must be provided. However, once the class has been instantiated only the public properties age, id and filename are externally accessible.

Within the body of the class age, id, filename and message are accessible as illustrated by the birthday() member function.

The following program illustrates how the GamePlayer class is used:

```
fun main() {
    val player = GamePlayer("John", "Hunt", 36, "123AA")
    // age is a read-write property initialised in constructor
    println(player.age)
    player.age = player.age + 1
    println(player.age)
    // id read-only property initialised in the constructor
    println(player.id)
    // fullname is a readonly property
    println(player.fullname)
    // Can invoke the birthday member function
    player.birthday()
}
```

Of course it is not possible to access firstName and surname as they are only constructor parameters and thus not accessible outside of the init{} block.

The output from this program is:

```
36
37
123AA
John Hunt
Happy Birthday John Hunt, you were 37 you are now 38
```

Member Level Properties

As mentioned in the previous section, properties can be defined as member level properties, these are properties that are defined within the body of the class (or indeed object) but that are not initialised within the constructor. These member level properties:

- may be vals or vars,
- may be public (by default) or private,
- may be initialised when they are declared or
- may be initialised within an init{} block.

The following example defines two member level properties fullname and favouriteGame both of which are initialised within the init{} block:

```kotlin
class GamePlayer(firstName: String,   // constructor param
                 surname: String,     // constructor param
                 var age: Int,        // read-write property
                 val id: String,      // readonly property
                 // private property
                 private val message: String = "Happy Birthday")
{

    val fullname: String  // read-only property
    var favouriteGame: String // read-write property

    init {
        fullname = "$firstName $surname"
        favouriteGame = ""
    }
}
```

Alternatively the member level properties could have been initialised as part of their declaration:

```kotlin
class GamePlayer(firstName: String,   // constructor param
                 surname: String,     // constructor param
                 var age: Int,        // read-write property
                 val id: String,      // readonly property
                 // private property
                 private val message: String = "Happy Birthday")
{

    val fullname: String = "$firstName $surname"
    var favouriteGame: String = ""
}
```

Note that firstName and surname are also visible when the member level properties are declared as logically their declaration and initialisation are all part of the instance initialisation process.

Property Visibility

Properties are public by default, however it is also possible to mark a property as being private; this is true for both constructor properties and for member level properties. This is illustrated below:

```kotlin
class Person(private val id: String, val name: String) {
    private var desk: String = "at home"
}
```

In this case the properties id and desk are only accessible within the body of the class Person; they are not visible externally to the class. However as id is a constructor property a value must be provided for this property when the class is instantiated.

Note that private properties may be vals or vars (that is they may be *read-only* or *read–write* properties).

Property Declaration Modifiers

There are two member property modifiers const and lateinit as well as the option to indicate that a property should be initialised *lazily* which affect the way in which a property is declared. Each of these will be discussed in this section.

Applying const to val Properties

The const property declaration modifier keyword is used to indicate to the compiler that a val property is a *compile time* constant. There are two important constraints associated with a const val, these are:

- It *can only* be used with val member level properties and
- the values used must be *derivable* at compile time (that is it must not depend on any runtime calculations or operations). It is thus limited to use with fundamental types such as Int, Short, Byte, Long, Float, Double and Boolean plus Strings.

This is illustrated in the following object where a set of val properties are marked as const:

```
object MathUtils {
    // Specifying useful compile-time
    // constant properties
    const val ZERO = 0;
    const val MIN: Int = -100
    const val MAX = 100
}
```

It is useful to do this for several reasons:

- it makes it explicit to the compiler that this is a value which is set at compile time,
- the compiler may be able to perform some optimisations such as inline the value directly within your code,
- other developers will understand the semantics of this as being a compile time constant.

Applying lateinit to var Properties

The lateinit property modifier *can only* be applied to var properties. It is used to indicate that the var property will be initialised at a *later* date; and not at the point that it is declared nor within an init{} block. Essentially the developer takes responsibility for ensuring that the var property will be initialised before it is first used. If they do not then a runtime error will be generated.

For example, the following code defines an object MyUtils that has a lateinit var title. It also defines a member function printTitle() that will access the String held in the title property and print out its length as well as the String itself.

```
object MyUtils {
    // Lateinit allows value to be provided later on
    lateinit var title: String

    fun printTitle() {
        println(title.length)
        println(title)
    }
}
```

In this case the title is a public member var property and thus code external to the MyUtils object is expected to provide a String to be used.

The following code illustrates this:

```
fun main() {
    MyUtils.title = "KVaders"
    MyUtils.printTitle()
}
```

The output from this program is:

```
7
KVaders
```

However, if the client code of the MyUtils objects does not initialise the title, for example as shown below:

```
fun main() {
    MyUtils.printTitle()
}
```

Then the printTitle() member function will try to obtain the length of the uninitialised title property and a runtime error will be shown to the user:

```
Exception in thread "main"
kotlin.UninitializedPropertyAccessException: lateinit property
title has not been initialized
   at MyUtils.printTitle(MyUtils.kt:8)
   at MyUtilsKt.main(MyUtils.kt:15)
   at MyUtilsKt.main(MyUtils.kt)
```

Using `lateinit` can therefore allow the developer a great deal of flexibility, however this flexibility must be used with care.

There are three important restrictions on the use of lateinit:

- can only be used with var (read–write properties),
- it is *not* possible to use `lateinit` with *nullable* properties,
- `lateinit` *cannot* not be used with basic or fundamental types such as Byte, Short, Int, Long, Float, Double, Boolean etc.

Applying Lazy Initialisation to val Properties

A third option is to initialise a *read-only* val property *lazily*. For example the following standard definition of a *val* is initialised immediately the first time that the object `Utils` is referenced:

```
object Utils {
    val myString: String = "Hello"
}
```

However, you can use the `by lazy` to indicate that the *val* should only be evaluated the first time it is accessed:

```
object Utils {
    val myLazyString: String by lazy { "Hello" }
}
```

This can be used to improve the performance of a system where some property is expensive to initialise (either in terms of time and/or resources) but is only infrequently required.

Once the property has been initialised then the value will be reused for any subsequent access.

Summary

As a quick reference summary note the following:

- the keyword `const` can only be used with val (real only) properties,
- a `const` property's value must be *derivable* at compile time which means that it is limited to basic type such as Int, Double, Boolean, Float, Short etc. And Strings,
- by `lazy` can only be used with vals,
- `lateinit` can only be used with vars,
- `lateinit` cannot be used for nullable properties,
- `lateinit` cannot be used for basic / primitive types e.g. Int, Float, Boolean etc.,
- by `lazy` is thread safe, `lateinit` relies on user code to handle multiple threads of execution acting the property,
- can check `lateinit` using the `isInitialized` attribute (introduced in Kotlin 1.2) for example:

```
nthis::title.isInitialized
```

Creating Custom Property Setters and Getters

Let us revisit what a property is; a property is an item of data, held within an instance of a class or within an object, that can be accessed, possibly externally to that instance or object, either as a *read-only* property or as a *read–write* property.

Behind the scenes to support his idea, Kotlin creates a *field* to store the value in and a reader (also known as a getter) member function and a writer (also known as a setter) member function associated with each property. If the property is marked as val, then it would only create the reader or getter function. Indeed if you were to look at a Kotlin class that had one or more properties from the Java would, you would find that it possessed methods of the form `get<Name of Property>()` and `set<Name of Property>()`.

Depending upon the context in which you reference the property, Kotlin knows whether to invoke the reader or writer. For example if you are attempting to access the value of the property then it knows to invoke the reader. Where as if you are attempting to set the value of the property it knows to use the writer member function.

Kotlin also allows a programmer to override the default readers and writers if required; it is just that the default behaviour provided by Kotlin generally meets the requirements of most developers.

If you wish to define your own readers and writers then you can.

For the reader element of a property you define a `get()` function and for the writer side of the property you define a `set()` function (hence the terms getters and setters).

The syntax for a val is

```
val <name-of-property>: Type get() {}
```

The syntax for a var is

```
var <name-of-property>: Type get() {} set(value) {}
```

The following partial code illustrates this idea:

```
class GameObject {

    val y: Int
        get() = // calc current y location

    val x: Int
        get() = // calc current x location
        Set(value) = // set the current x location


    var name: String
        get() = // read name from somewhere
        set(value) = // set the name somewhere
}
```

In the above outline code the val property has a get() function defined for it and the var name property has both a get() and a set(value) function defined.

Note that the return type of the get() member function is the same as the type specified for the property.

The type of the parameter passed into set() member function is also the same as the type of the property.

Using an Implicit Backing Field

The following code illustrates the implementation of the x and y *getter* and *setter* functions.

```kotlin
class GameObject {
    var x = 0
        // implicit backing 'field' generated by compiler
        get() = field
        set(value) {
            if (value >= 0) {
                field = value
            }
        }

    var y: Int = 0
        get() = field
        set(value) {
            if (value >= 0) {
                field = value
            }
        }
}
```

This example uses what is known as an *implicit* backing field. This is used to store the value for the property and is represented by the keyword `field`. The Kotlin compiler will generate a unnamed internal variable to hold the value that is hidden from the developer.

In these examples the `get()` function merely returns the `field` value and thus the shorthand member function declaration form is being used. In fact as this is all the `get()` function does it could be omitted and the Kotlin compiler will provide the implementation.

The setters both check that the value supplied is valid. If the value is valid then the backing `field` is updated with the new value. Note that the name of the parameter for the setter function can be whatever you like although it is common practice to call it value. In this case if the value presented is negative it is ignored; in practice this should be indicated back to the code calling this possible by raising an exception - this will be covered in a later chapter.

We can now use the `GameObject` class and its properties x and y as follows:

```kotlin
fun main() {
    val obj = GameObject()
    println("initial obj.x: ${obj.x}, obj.y: ${obj.y}")
    obj.x = 10
    obj.y = 10
    println("updated obj.x: ${obj.x}, obj.y: ${obj.y}")
}
```

If we run this program the output generated is:

```
initial obj.x: 0, obj.y: 0
updated obj.x: 10, obj.y: 10
```

As you can see the initial values for the properties x and y were zero. Having set the properties to 10 then the output is updated.

Using an Explicit Backing Field

If you choose you can use your own backing field to hold the value represented by the property. There are two issues to note about this:

- The first is that the only way to do this is to create a hidden property that is used by the public properties. This hidden property can be made private as this is one way to ensure that it is not publicly available. However a private property is still accessible from anywhere within the body of the class (or object). Developers must therefore be careful not to use the hidden value rather than the published property. For this reason the common convention is to prefix the hidden property name with an underbar to indicate that it should not be used.
- The second is that you must be careful not to name the internal property with the same name as the property itself, otherwise things get recursive and will generate a run time error.

As such the following illustrates the previous GameObject now using an explicit backing field for a new property background:

```kotlin
class GameObject {
    // ... Code hidden for brevity

    // Can explicitly specify own backing field
    private var _background: String? = null
    var background: String?
        get() {
            if (_background == null) {
                _background = "blue"
            }
            return _background
        }
        set(value) { _background = value }

}
```

The background var allows client code to set the colour of the property. In this case if no background colour has been set when the getter is called then the background colour is set to blue. The actual field holding the value is _background which is of course a hidden (private) property in its own right as that is the only option in Kotlin.

Properties Without a Backing Field

In some cases it may be useful to make something look like a property but in reality it is just a hard coded value. For example:

```kotlin
class GameObject {
    // .. Code removed for brevity

    // Doesn't use a backing field but looks like a property
    val isHome: Boolean
        get() {
            return false
        }
}
```

In this example, to client code it appears that the GameObject has a property isHome. However, the getter of this property merely returns the Boolean value false.

Modifying Setter Visibility

The *visibility* of the *getter* function for a property is always the same as that of the property itself. However, this does not have to be true for the *setter* function (whether it relies on the default implementation or whether a custom implementation is used). In either case the *setter* function can have a different visibility to that of the property.

This is sown below:

```kotlin
class GameObject {
    // ... Code hidden for brevity
    // Appears as a val outside the class
    // but internally can be set
    var location: Location = Location()
        private set

}
```

In this case the *setter* function has private visibility where as the property (and its getter function) are public. This means that as far as client code of the GameObject is concerned the property appears to be a *read-only* val property. However, internally to the GameObject the property appears to be a *read–write* property with both getter and setter functionality.

GameObject with Properties

For ease of reference the complete listing for the GameObject class is given below:

```
class Location

class GameObject {
    var x = 0
        get() = field // implicit backing field generated
        set(value) {
            if (value >= 0) {
                field = value
            }
        }

    var y: Int = 0
        get() = field
        set(value) {
            if (value >= 0) {
                field = value
            }
        }

    // Doesn't use a backing field but looks like a property
    val isHome: Boolean
        get() {
            return false
        }

    // Can explicitly specify own backing field
    private var _background: String? = null
    var background: String?
        get() {
            if (_background == null) {
                _background = "blue"
            }
            return _background
        }
        set(value) { _background = value }

    // Appears as a val outside the class
    // but internally can be set
    var location: Location = Location()
        private set

}
```

Online Resources

An online resource on properties is:

- https://kotlinlang.org/docs/reference/properties.html Documentation on properties and fields in Kotlin.

Exercises

In this exercise you will create a custom definition for the balance property such that
an opening balance is provided when the instance is created which is used to update
a property balance that is read-only externally but read–write internally to the class.

```kotlin
fun main() {
    val acc1 = Account("123", "John", 10.05, "current")
    val acc2 = Account("345", "Denise", 23.55, "savings")
    val acc3 = Account("567", "Phoebe", 12.45, "investment")

    println(acc1)
    println(acc2)
    println(acc3)

    acc1.deposit(23.45)
    acc1.withdraw(12.33)
    println("balance: ${acc1.balance}")

    println("balance: ${acc1.balance}")
    acc1.withdraw(300.00)
    println("balance: ${acc1.balance}")

    Account.printInstancesCreated()
}
```

The output from this might be:

```
New Account created for John of current
New Account created for Denise of savings
New Account created for Phoebe of investment
Account('123', 'John', 10.05, type='current')
Account('345', 'John', 23.55, type='savings')
Account('567', 'Phoebe', 12.45, type='investment')
balance: 21.17
balance: 21.17
balance: -278.83
3 instances of Account class created
```

Chapter 11
Scope and Conditional Functions

Introduction

Kotlin provides *five* functions whose sole purpose is to execute a block of code within the context of an instance or an object. When you call such a function on an instance with a *lambda* expression, it forms a temporary scope (hence the term *scope function*). In this scope, you can access the instance directly typically using the `this` reference or in two cases using the `it` *implicit* parameter.

There are five higher order *scope* functions:

- `apply{}`, `let{}`, `run{}`, `with{}`, and `also{}`

In addition there is the `runCartching{}` exception handling scope function which will be discussed in the chapter on Error and Exception Handling.

Each of these *scope* functions and their typical usages will be discussed in the remainder of this chapter.

The User Class

Several of the examples in the reminder of this chapter make use of the following class:

```kotlin
class User(val name: String) {
    var id: String = ""
    var game: String = ""

    override fun toString(): String {
        return "User(name='$name', id='$id', game='$game')"
    }
}
```

It is provided here for reference.

© The Author(s), under exclusive license to Springer Nature Switzerland AG 2021
J. Hunt, *Beginner's Guide to Kotlin Programming*,
https://doi.org/10.1007/978-3-030-80893-8_11

The Apply Scope Function

The `apply` scope function binds the receiving instance/object to the `this` variable within the *lambda* function provided. This allows the body of the *lambda* to reference the public interface of the instance/object directly without needing to reference it via a named parameter (or indeed explicitly using the `this` reference).

It is typically used to allow some code to run that will be used to initialise data or execute behaviour on a newly created instance *before* any other code has access to the instance.

The following illustrates a typical usage of the apply scope function:

```
val user = User("John").apply {
    this.id = "123"
    // can reference this.game implicitly
    game = "Nightfall"
}
println("user: $user")
```

In this code we create an instance of the class `User`. Then before the instance is assigned to the val `user` we run the code in the `apply` block. This code initialises the `id` and the `game` properties of the `User`. Note that within the code block we have used `this.id` to illustrate that the `this` variable is available, however it is not required as illustrated by the reference to the `game` property on the `User` instance. In this case referencing the `game` property within the apply lambda is exactly the same as writing `this.game`.

The result of running this code snippet is:

```
user: User(name='John', id='123', game='Nightfall')
```

Also note that the result returned by the `apply{}` scope function is the instance of the class `User`. That is `apply{}` returns the object it is applied/bound to.

The Also Scope Function

The `also` scope function is an alternative to the `apply` scope function. It also returns the object it is applied to, it can also be used to initialise an instance prior to the instance being accessed by other code and like `apply` it returns the receiving object/instance.

However, unlike `apply` the receiver is bound to the implicit parameter `it`. Thus it is not possible to reference the public interface of the instance or object directly, all references must be made via the `it` parameter.

For example:

```
val user2 = User("John").also {
    println(it)
    it.id = "456"
    it.game = "Monopoly"
}
println("user2: $user2")
```

The effect of running this code is:

```
user2: User(name='John', id='456', game='Monopoly')
```

If you prefer not to use the implicit it parameter you can define your own parameter, for example:

```
val user3 = User("John").also {u ->
    println(u)
    u.id = "456"
    u.game = "Monopoly"
}
println("user3: $user3")
```

In this case the receiving object/instance is bound to the parameter u.

The Run Scope Function

Th run scope function is also used to bind to an instance/object. The bound instance/object is then accessible via the this reference from within the run block. However, the result of the run scope function is the *result* returned by the *lambda* function that it executes.

```
user.run{
    print("Please input the users favourite game: ")
    val favouriteGame: String ? = readLine()
    game = favouriteGame ?: ""
}
println("user: $user")
```

The output from this code block is:

```
Please input the users favourite game: Assassins Creed
user: User(name='John', id='123', game='Assassins Creed')
```

In this example the `run` scope function has bound the `this` reference to the instance held in the val `user`. In this case we have mimicked some operation that has generated a new favourite game for the user.

Note that because the `readLine()` function returns a *nullable* String it is necessary to use a *nullable operator* to extract the value or use a default. In this case we have used the *elvis* operator to either take the value held in `favouriteGame` or, if the value is `null`, to use an empty String.

Note that the result of executing the `run` scope function is the result returned by the *lambda* function. In the above example the result returned will therefore be Unit as the last expression is an assignment and assignments always return Unit.

The Let Scope Function

The `let` scope function has the same purpose as the `run` function but slightly different semantics. The use of `let` indicates that we wish to execute some behaviour within the context of the receiving instance/object. As such the receiver is bound to the implicit parameter `it` by default (although this can be overridden).

Within the *lambda* applied to the `let` scope function it is necessary to access the bound object/instance via the `it` reference (there is no implicit `this`).

For example:

```
val s2 = user.let { it.name.toUpperCase() }
println("s2 $s2")
val s3 = user.let {
    println(it)
    println(it.name)
    it.name.toUpperCase()
}
println("s3 $s3")
```

The output generated by this code is:

```
s2 JOHN
User(name='John', id='123', game='Nightfall')
John
s3 JOHN
```

In both these examples of the `let` scope function, the instance held in `user` is bound to the `it` parameter. The `name` property is then accessed. In both cases the last thing that the *lambda* function does is to convert the name into upper case. As this is the last expression in the lambda it is returned as the result of the *lambda* and thus this is also the result of the `let` scope function.

If you do not want to use the `it` parameter you can override this to give a more semantically meaningful name to the reference inside the lambda function:

```
val r1 = user.name.let{
    name -> name.toUpperCase()
}
println("r1: $r1")
```

This example binds the String held in the `user.name` property to the parameter `name` within the *lambda* function applied to the `let` scope function. Within the body of the *lambda* we can then reference the `name` directly and invoke the `toUpperCase()` member function on it.

The with Scope Function

The `with` scope function takes a first parameter which is the object/instance to be bound and a second parameter which is the function to apply (although typically the *trailing lambda function syntax* is usually adopted).

The `with` scope function allows a sequence of operations to be written all relating to the object passed to the associated *lambda* function. Within the *lambda* function the bound instance/object is accessible via the `this` reference. Which means that the public interface of the receiver is directly accessible to the code within the lambda. This helps to avoid repeatedly referencing the instance/object.

An example of using the `with` scope function is given below.

```
val label = with(user) {
    This.id = "new${this.id}"
    game = "new$game" // implicit reference to this
    println(this)
    this.toString()
}
println("label: $label")
```

The output from this code is:

```
User(name='John', id='new123', game='newNightfall')
label: User(name='John', id='new123', game='newNightfall')
```

Scope Functions and Nullability

Scope functions are often used in combination with *nullable* types. This is because it is possible to combine the *scope* function with the use of the *safe dot* operator (? .) so that the scope function is only invoked if a value is not null.

For example:

```
val service: Service? = getService("bookService")

val result: String? = service?.run {
    port = 8080
    query("get")
}

println("result: $result")
```

In this case the run scope function lambda is only executed if the value held in service is not null.

If service is null then the run scope function is not run and the result val is set to null.

If service is *not null* then the run scope function is executed and the services' port is set to 8080 and the member function query is called on the service. The result of the run scope function is then the data returned from query("get") call.

Scope Function Categories

Scope functions can be categorised by the way they bind the object/instance they are applied to. Specifically:

- `run`, `with`, and `apply` refer to the context object/instance as *this,*
- `let` and `also` refer to the context object as *it.*

Another way to categorise the scope functions is based on what is the result returned from the scope function:

- `apply` and `also` return the bound instance/ object,
- `let`, `run` and `with` return the lambda function result.

This is illustrated in the following table:

Scope function	Receiver bound to	Returns	Typical Uses
run	this	lambda result	run behaviour on this
with	this	lambda result	execute behaviour with bound object
apply	this	this	configure 'this'
let	it	lambda result	run behaviour on this
also	it	it	configure 'it'

Conditional Functions

There are two *higher order* conditional functions provided in Kotlin. These are functions which will either return `null` or the receiver object depending upon some conditional element. The conditional element is a *lambda* function that must return a Boolean.

The first conditional function is the `takeIf` function. This takes a lambda function as an argument If the lambda function returns true then the receiving instance or object is returned, if the lambda returns false then null is returned.

The conditional functions are often combined with the scope functions to provide a functional style of programming that captures the if then style of imperative programs.

For example:

```
service.takeIf { service.port > 1024 }?.run {
     println(query("get"))
}
```

This code example says:

Take the value in service if service.port is greater than 1024 otherwise take the value null. The safe dot operator will then only execute the run lambda if the result returned from takeIf is not null.

A second conditional function is takeUnless. This is the inverse of the takeIf function. For example:

```
service.takeUnless{service.port > 1024 }?.run {
    println(query("get"))
}
```

In this example takeUnless will take the value held in service unless the port is greater than 1024. In which case the run block will only execute if the service point is less than or equal to 1024.

Exercises

In this exercise you will use both the run{} and the apply{} scope functions.

Use the run{} scope function to determine what message to present to a user. The message will differ depending on whether they are in credit or not. For example, if they are in credit then print a message "You are a good customer; you are in credit". However, if they are not in credit then they should have a message "You need an overdraft".

The second part of the exercise is to create a new instance of a current Account for Jasmine. However, Jasmine has deposited 10.55 when she opened the account. Ensure that the deposit is registered against the account (which has an opening balance of 0.0) before any client code can access the Account.

Chapter 12
Class Inheritance

Introduction

Inheritance is a core feature of Object Oriented Programming. It allows one class to *inherit* data and/or behaviour from another class and is one of the key ways in which reuse is enabled within classes.

This chapter introduces inheritance between classes in Kotlin.

What is Inheritance?

Inheritance allows features defined in one class to be *inherited* and reused in the definition of another class. For example, a `Person` class might have the properties `name` and `age`. It might also have behaviour associated with a `Person` such as `birthday()`.

We might then decide that we want to have another class `Employee` and that employees also have a `name` and an `age` and will have birthdays. However, in addition an `Employee` may have an employee `id` property and a `calculatePay()` behaviour.

At this point we could duplicate the definition of the `name` and `age` properties and the `birthday()` behaviour in the class `Employee` (for example by cutting and pasting the code between the two classes).

However, this is not only inefficient; it may also cause problems in the future. For example we may realise that there is a problem or bug in the implementation of `birthday()` and may correct it in the class `Person`; however, we may forget to apply the same fix to the class `Employee`.

In general, in software design and development it is considered best practice to define something once and to reuse that something when required.

© The Author(s), under exclusive license to Springer Nature Switzerland AG 2021
J. Hunt, *Beginner's Guide to Kotlin Programming*,
https://doi.org/10.1007/978-3-030-80893-8_12

In an object oriented system we can achieve the reuse of data and/or behaviour via inheritance. That is one class (in this case the `Employee` class) can *inherit* features from another class (in this case `Person`). This is shown pictorially below:

In this diagram the `Employee` class is shown as inheriting from the `Person` class. This means that the `Employee` class obtains all the data and behaviour of the `Person` class. It is therefore as though the `Employee` class has defined three properties `name`, `age` and `id` and two member functions `birthday()` and `calculatePay()`.

Terminology Around Inheritance

The following terminology is commonly used with inheritance in most object oriented programming languages including Kotlin:

- *Class* A class defines a combination of data and behaviour that operates on that data.
- *Subclass* A subclass is a class that inherits from another class. For example, an `Employee` might inherit from a class `Person`. Subclasses are classes in their own right. Subclasses are also referred to as child or derived classes.
- *Superclass* A superclass is the parent of a class. It is the class from which another class inherits. For example, `Person` might be the superclass of `Employee`. In Kotlin, a class can have exactly one superclass. Superclasses are also referred to as the parent or base class.
- *Single or multiple inheritance* Single and multiple inheritance refer to the number of super classes from which a class can inherit. For example, Kotlin is a single inheritance system, in which a class can only inherit from one class. Python by contrast is a multiple inheritance system in which a class can inherit from one or more classes.

The following diagram illustrates the terms superclass, class and subclass with respect to a class hierarchy based around a class Employee.

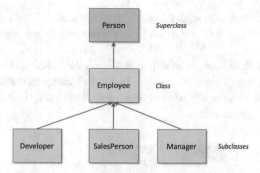

Note that a set of classes, involved in an inheritance hierarchy, such as those shown above is often named after the class at the root (top) of the hierarchy; in this case it would make these classes part of the Person class hierarchy.

Types of Hierarchy

In most object oriented systems there are two types of hierarchy; one refers to *inheritance* (whether single or multiple) and the other refers to *instantiation*. The inheritance hierarchy has already been described. It is the way in which one class inherits features from a superclass.

The instantiation hierarchy relates to instances or objects rather than classes and is important during the execution of the program.

There are two types of instance relationships: one indicates a *part-of* relationship, while the other relates to a *type of* relationship (it is referred to as an *is-a* relationship). This is illustrated below:

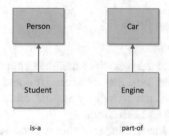

The difference between an *is-a* relationship and a *part-of* relationship is often confusing for new programmers (and sometimes for those who are experienced in non object oriented languages). The above figure illustrates that a Student *is-a* type of Person whereas an Engine is *part-of* a Car. It does not make sense to say that a student is part-of a person or that an engine is-a type of car!

In Kotlin, *inheritance* relationships are implemented by the sub-classing mechanism. In contrast, part-of relationships are implemented using properties in Kotlin.

The problem with classes, inheritance and is-a relationships is that on the surface they appear to capture a similar concept. In the following figure the hierarchies all capture some aspect of the use of the phrase *is-a*. However, they are all intended to capture a different relationship.

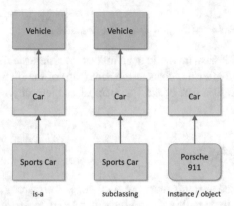

The confusion is due to the fact that in modern English we tend to overuse the term *is-a*. For example, in English we can say that an Employee is a type of Person or that Andrew is a Person; both are semantically correct. However, in Kotlin classes such as Employee and Person and an instance such as Andrew are different things. We can distinguish between the different types of relationship by being more precise about our definitions in terms of a programming language such as Kotlin.

Purpose of Subclasses

Subclasses are used to refine the behaviour and data structures of a superclass.

A parent class may define some generic/shared properties and member functions; these can then be inherited and reused by several other (sub) classes which add subclass specific properties and behaviour.

In fact, there are only a small number of things that a subclass should do relative to its parent or super class. If a proposed subclass does not do any of these then your selected parent class is not the most appropriate super class to use.

A subclass should modify the behaviour of its parent class or extend the data held by its parent class. This modification should refine the class in one or more of these ways:

- Changes to the external protocol or interface of the class, that is it should extend the set of member functions or properties provided by the class.

- Changes in the implementation of the member functions; i.e. subclasses can replace the implementation inherited form the parent class.
- Changes in the implementation of the set or get behaviour of properties.
- Additional behaviour that references inherited behaviour.

If a subclass does not provide one or more of the above, then it is incorrectly placed. For example, if a subclass implements a set of new member functions, but does not refer to the properties or member functions of the parent class, then the class is not really a subclass of the parent (it does not extend it).

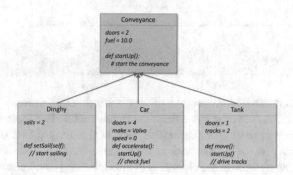

As an example, consider the class hierarchy illustrated above. A generic root class has been defined. This class defines a `Conveyance` which has doors, fuel (both with default values) and a member function, `startUp()` that starts the engine of the conveyance.

Three subclasses of `Conveyance` have also been defined: `Dinghy`, `Car` and `Tank`. Two of these subclasses are appropriate, but one should probably not inherit from `Conveyance`. We shall consider each in turn to determine their suitability.

- The class `Tank` overrides the number of doors inherited, uses the `startUp()` member function within the member function `move()`, and provides a new property. It therefore matches our criteria.
- Similarly, the class `Car` overrides the number of doors and uses the member function `startUp()`. It also uses the instance variable `fuel` within a new member function `accelerate()`. It therefore also matches our criteria.
- The class `Dinghy` defines a new property `sails` and a new member function `setSail()`. As such, it does not use any of the features inherited from `Conveyance`. However, we might say that it has extended `Conveyance` by providing this property and member function. We must then consider the features provided by `Conveyance`. We can ask ourselves whether they make sense within the context of `Dinghy`. If we assume that a dinghy is a small sail-powered boat with no cabin and no engine, then nothing inherited from `Conveyance` is useful. In this case, it is likely that `Conveyance` is misnamed, as it defines some sort of a *motorised conveyance*, and the `Dinghy` class should not have extended it.

Kotlin Class Hierarchy

Kotlin supports single inheritance between classes. This means that a class can only inherit from one single class. The root of the class hierarchy in Kotlin is the class Any. All classes in Kotlin eventually inherit from this class either directly or through intermediate classes.

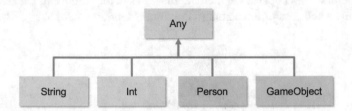

The above diagram illustrates some of the classes that inherit from (or extend) the class Any in Kotlin. As you can see there are fundamental class such as Int as well as built-in classes such as String. However it is also true of user defined classes such as Person and for objects such as GameObject.

Any behaviour defined in the class Any is thus inherited by all classes and objects in Kotlin. Any defines the following:

- A zero parameter constructor.

It also defines the following member functions:

equals(other: Any?): Boolean This member function is used to indi-cate whether some other object is "equal to" this one. Implementations must fulfil the following requirements:

- Reflexive: for any non-null value x, x.equals(x) should return true.
- Symmetric: for any non-null values x and y, x.equals(y) should return true if and only if y.equals(x) returns true.
- Transitive: for any non-null values x, y, and z, if x.equals(y) returns true and y.equals(z) returns true, then x.equals(z) should return true.
- Consistent: for any non-null values x and y, multiple invocations of x.equals(y) consistently return true or consistently return false, provided no information used in equals comparisons on the objects is modified.

hashCode(): Int Returns a hash code value for the object. The general contract of hashCode is:

- Whenever it is invoked on the same object more than once, the hashCode member function must consistently return the same integer, provided no information used in equals comparisons on the object is modified.
- If two objects are equal according to the equals() member function, then calling the hashCode member function on each of the two objects must produce the same integer result.

`toString(): String` Returns a string representation of the object.

In addition `Any` also defines the scope functions (also, apply, let, run etc.) and conditional functions (takeIf, takeUnless) and the function `to()` which creates a `Pair` from the current instance and a second instance (Pairs will discussed in the section on data containers/collections in Kotlin).

Kotlin Classes and Inheritance

A class that is defined as extending a parent class has the following syntax:

```
class SubClassName : BaseClassName(<constructor params>) {
    class-body
}
```

Note that the parent class is specified by providing the name of the that class following a colon (:) after the name of the new (child) class.

We can make the class `Person` extendable with one modification; we must mark it as `open`:

```
open class Person(val name: String ="", var age: Int = 0) {

    fun birthday() {
        println("Happy birthday you were $age")
        age++
        println("You are now $age")
    }

}
```

The keyword `open` indicates that a class can be extended.

By default in Kotlin classes are *closed* (the equivalent of final in Java). This means that unless you mark a class as `open` it cannot be extended.

We could now define the class `Employee` as being a class whose definition builds on (or inherits from) the class `Person`:

```
open class Employee(name: String,
                    age: Int,
                    val id: String): Person(name, age) {

    var rateOfPay: Double = 7.5

    fun calculatePay(hoursWorked: Int): Double {
        return hoursWorked * rateOfPay
    }

}
```

In the above example we do several things:

1. The class is called `Employee`. It extends the class `Person`. This is indicated by including the name of the class being inherited following the colon after the the Employee constructor in the class declaration.
2. Following the name of the parent class we indicate the parent class *constructor* to be invoked. In this case the constructor that takes a String and an Int (for the name and age constructor properties). This is important as the parent class's constructor is used to initialise instances of that class. This allows whatever initialisation is required for `Person` to happen.
3. All instances of the class `Person` have a name, and age and have the behaviour `birthday()`.
4. All instances of the class `Employee` have a name, and age and an id as well as a `rateOfPay` property. `Employee` instances also have the member functions `birthday()` and `calculatePay(houseWorked)`.
5. The member function `calculatePay()` defined in the `Employee` class can access the properties name and age just as it can access the property id.
6. Note that the parameters to the `Employee` constructor are made up of two constructor parameters name and age and a constructor property id. This is because the name and age parameters are used merely to pass the values supplied up to the `Person` class constructor. Where as the id will be a new property defined for instances of the class `Employee`.

As we marked the `Employee` class as open, we can go further and we can subclass `Employee`, for example with the class `SalesPerson`:

```
class SalesPerson(name: String,
                  age: Int,
                  id: String,
                  val region: String,
                  val sales: Double) : Employee(name, age, id) {
    fun bonus(): Double {
        return sales * 0.5
    }

}
```

Now we can say that the class `SalesPerson` has a name, an age and an id as well as a region and a sales total. It also has the member functions `birthday()`, `calculatePay(hourseWorked)` and `bonus()`.

In this case the `SalesPerson` declaration indicates that `Employee` class constructor, that takes three parameters for the name, age and id, is invoked. This is because it is the constructor in the next class up in the hierarchy that we need to run when a class is initialisation.

We can now write code such as:

```
fun main() {
    val p = Person("Jasmine", 21)
    println("Person - ${p.name} is ${p.age}")
    println("----------------")
    val e = Employee("Adam", 23, "ABC123")
    println("Employee(${e.id}) - ${e.name} is ${e.age}")
    println("----------------")
    val s = SalesPerson("Phoebe", 32, "XYZ987", "South West",
905.55)
    println("SalesPerson(${s.id}) - ${s.name} is ${s.age} for
region ${s.region} with ${s.sales} sales")
}
```

With the output being:

```
Person - Jasmine is 21
----------------
Employee(ABC123) - Adam is 23
----------------
SalesPerson(XYZ987) - Phoebe is 32 for region South West with
905.55 sales
```

It is important to note that we have not done anything to the class Person by defining Employee and SalesPerson; that is it is not affected by those class definitions. Thus, a Person *does not* have an employee id. Similarly, neither an Employee nor a Person have a region or a sales total.

In terms of behaviour, instances of all three classes can run the member function birthday(), but.

- only Employee and SalesPeron instances can run the member function calculcatePay() and
- only SalesPerson objects can run the member function bonus().

Objects and Inheritance

In Kotlin it is not only classes that can be involved in inheritance; objects can also extend an *open* class.

If an object extends a open class then the object is also an instance of the super-class. It will inherit all the data and behaviour from the superclass. The syntax for this is:

object <objectName> **:** superclass()

The colon after the object's name is followed by the superclass that the object inherits from.

However, you should note that it is not possible to extend an object.

The following illustrates how an object can extend an open class:

```
open class Logger {
    fun log() = println("log")
}

object HelloWorldLogger : Logger() {
    fun doSomething() = log()
}
```

In this case the `HelloWorldLogger` is an example of the type `Logger` as well as an object of type `HellWorldLogger`. It could therefore be used in any context where an implementation of the `Logger` class is required.

Note that the constructor to invoke is still required when specifying the superclass. This is because the constructor in the class will be used to initialise the state of the object just as it will be used to initialise the state of an instance. This does not break the rule that objects do not have constructors as technically speaking the object does not have a constructor here; it is merely invoking the constructor defined in the super class.

The `HelloWorldLogger` object could now be used as shown below:

```
fun main(){
    HelloWorldLogger.doSomething()
}
```

The output from this program would be:

```
log
```

Anonymous Objects and Inheritance

Anonymous objects can also extend open classes. In this case the `: < superclass>` declaration comes straight after the keyword `object`.

As with named objects it is also necessary to indicate which constructor will be invoked in the parent class.

An anonymous object inheriting from a class is illustrated below:

```
open class LogIt {
    fun log() = println("log")
}

fun main() {
    val obj = object : LogIt() {
        var x: Int = 0
        val y = 42
    }
    println("obj.x = ${obj.x}, obj.y = ${obj.y}")
    obj.log()
}
```

In this case the anonymous object extends the LogIt class and thus inherits the log() member function. The anonymous object can also define its own member functions and member properties as required. In this case it defines the properties x and y which are both of type Int.

The output from this program is presented below:

```
obj.x = 0, obj.y = 42
log
```

The Class Any and Inheritance

Every class in Kotlin extends one or more superclasses. This is true even of the class User shown below:

```
class User(val name: String, val age: Int)
```

This is because if you do not specify a superclass explicitly then the Kotlin compiler automatically adds in the class Any as a parent class. Thus the above is exactly the same as the following declaration which explicitly specifies the class Any as the superclass of Person:

```
class User(val name: String, val age: Int) : Any()
```

Both listings above define a class called User that extends the class Any.

The fact that all class eventually inherit from the class Any means that behaviour defined in Any is available for all classes everywhere in Kotlin.

Also note that if you do not specify a superclass in Kotlin, then the Kotlin compiler not only selects Any as the superclass it also calls the zero parameter constructor for you on the class Any.

Inheritance and Member Functions

Overriding Member Functions

Overriding occurs when a member function is defined in a class (for example the class Person) and also in one of its subclasses (for example Employee). It means that instances of Person and Employee both respond to requests for this member function to be run, but each has their *own* implementation of the member function.

For example, let us assume that we define the member function toString() in these classes (so that we have a string representation of their instances to use with the println() function). The *pseudo* code definition of this in Person might be:

```
function toString() {
    return result "Person(${name} is $age)")
}
```

In Employee, it might be defined as:

```
function toString() {
    return result "Employee($id)"
}
```

The member function in Employee replaces the version in Person for all instances of Employee. If we ask an instance of Employee for the result of toString(), we get the string "Employee(<some_id>)". If you are confused, think of it this way:

> If you ask an object to perform some operation, then to determine which version of the member function is run, look in the class used to create the instance. If the member function is not defined there, look in the class's parent. Keep doing this until you find a member function which implements the operation requested. This is the version which is used.

As a concrete example, see the classes Person, Employee and SalesPerson below; in which the toString() member function in Person is overridden in Employee and then again in SalesPerson. Notice that to do this we must use the keyword override before the keyword fun. If we do not do this then the compiler will generate an error. In Kotlin we need to explicitly confirm to the compiler that we know we are *overriding* (in effect hiding the definition of a member function or property defined in the superclass).

```kotlin
open class Person(val name: String = "", var age: Int = 0) {

    fun birthday() {
        println("Happy birthday you were $age")
        age++
        println("You are now $age")
    }

    override fun toString()= "Person($name, $age)"

}

open class Employee(name: String,
                    age: Int,
                    val id: String) : Person(name, age) {

    var rateOfPay: Double = 7.5

    fun calculatePay(hoursWorked: Int): Double {
        return hoursWorked * rateOfPay
    }

    override fun toString()= "Employee($name, $age, $id)"

}

class SalesPerson(name: String,
                  age: Int,
                  id: String,
                  val region: String,
                  val sales: Double) : Employee(name, age, id) {
    fun bonus(): Double {
        return sales * 0.5
    }

    override fun toString()=
            "SalesPerson($name, $age, $id, $region, $sales)"

}
```

Instances of these classes will be convertible to a string using the `toString()` member function, but the version used by instances of `Employee` will differ from that used with instances of `Person`, for example:

```kotlin
fun main() {
    val p = Person("Jasmine", 21)
    val e = Employee("Adam", 23, "ABC123")
    val s = SalesPerson("Phoebe", 32, "XYZ987", "South West",
905.55)

    println(p)
    println(e)
    println(s)
}
```

This program generates as output:

```
Person(Jasmine, 21)
Employee(Adam, 23, ABC123)
SalesPerson(Phoebe, 32, XYZ987, South West, 905.55)
```

As can be seen from this the Employee class prints the name, age and id of the employee while the Person class only prints the name and age properties. In turn the SalesPerson prints the name, age, id, region and sales total.

Also note from this example, an open class can be extended by an *open* class or a *closed* class. If the subclass is not marked with the keyword open then it defaults to *closed* and cannot be extended.

Declaring Member Functions as Open

It is also possible to override member functions in your own classes, however to override a member function that member function must be marked as open. If a member function is not marked as open it cannot be overriden as it is by default closed (and is thus the equivalent of being marked final in Java).

To mark a member function as *open* the keyword open precedes the fun keyword when the member function is being declared, for example:

```
open class Base {
    open fun print(): Unit = println("Base print")
}

class Derived: Base() {
    override fun print(): Unit = println("Derived print")
}
```

In the above classes, the class Base defines a single member function print() : Unit that is marked as open and thus can be overriden. In the subclass Derived we can therefore redefine the member function print() : Unit but we must use the keyword override to allow us to do so.

We can now use the Base and Derived classes as shown below:

```
fun main() {
    val base = Base()
    base.print()

    println("----------")

    val derived = Derived()
    derived.print()
}
```

The output from this program is:

```
                    Base print
                    ----------
                    Derived print
```

Inheritance and Properties

It is not only member functions that can be overridden; it is also possible to override properties. Both constructor properties and member properties can be overriden in a subclass.

As with member functions it is necessary to mark a property as *open* to allow it to be overridden; if you do not do this then the property will be *closed* and cannot be overriden in a subclass.

To mark a property as *open* the declaration of the property must be preceded by the keyword `open`. The overriding property (in the subclass) must be marked with the keyword `override`.

A simple example of doing this is shown below:

```
open class Base {
    open val label: String = "Base"
    open fun print(): Unit = println("Base print")
}

class Derived: Base() {
    override val label: String = "Derived"
    override fun print(): Unit = println("Derived print")
}
```

In the above classes the `Base` class declares a property and a member function as being `open` and the whole class is marked as `open`. In the subclass `Derived`, both the `label` property and the `print()` member function are overridden.

Notice that it is still necessary to use the `override` keyword when overriding a property declaration.

A simple program using these two classes is given below:

```
fun main() {
    val base = Base()
    println(base.label)
    base.print()

    println("----------")

    val derived = Derived()
    println(derived.label)
    derived.print()
}
```

The output from this program is:

```
Base
Base print
----------
Derived
Derived print
```

A further example illustrates some of the options available when defining and overriding properties:

```
open class Cat {
    open val dangerous = false
    open val name: String = "Sammy"
    override fun toString(): String = "$name is " +
                    (if (dangerous) "dangerous" else " timid")

}

class Tiger(override val name: String) : Cat() {
    override val dangerous = true
}
```

In this example, a member level property name in the class Cat is overridden by a constructor property in the class Tiger. In turn the member level property dangerous is overridden by a member level property in the class Tiger.

As a final example, the following code illustrates both that a constructor property can be overriden and that once the property is marked as open in the root class, it is open for all subclasses:

```
open class Trade(val tradeId: String,
                 open val stock: String = "IBM",
                 open var quantity: Int = 0)

open class EquityTrade(id: String,
                       override val stock: String = "MSoft",
                       qty: Int) : Trade(id, quantity = qty)

class ShortEquityTrade(id: String,
                       override val stock: String = "Short",
                       qty: Int) : EquityTrade(id, qty=qty)
```

Extending Behaviour Using Super

We have already seen that it is possible to override behaviour defined in a parent class so that the version in the current class meets that needs of that class. The member function toString() is a typical example of this. In numerous examples we have redefined toString() to create a String based on the data held by a particular instance rather than use the generic version. To do this we used the keyword override and ensured that the member function signature (its name, parameters and return) matched those defined in the parent class.

However, rather than completely override the version of the member function defined in the parent class we can chose to extend its behaviour. This is done by defining a new version of a member function in a subclass and then using the keyword *super* to invoke the version defined higher up the inheritance hierarchy.

This is illustrated below for a member function print():

```
open class Base {
    open fun print(): Unit = println("Base")
}

class Derived : Base() {
    override fun print(): Unit {
        println("Derived before")
        super.print()
        println("Derived After")
    }
}
```

In this case the Base class defines an *open* member function print(). In the Derived class the member function print() is overridden. However, the Derived class's version of print() contains the statement super.print() in it. This means that when you call print() on the Derived class it will print out the contents of the version in Derived but in the middle it will call the version defined in Base.

This is illustrated by the following program:

```
fun main() {
    val derived = Derived()
    derived.print()
}
```

The output from this program is:

```
Derived before
Base
Derived After
```

You can clearly see the printouts from both the `Derived.print()` member function and the `Base.print()` member function displayed.

The effect of the overridden `print()` member function in `Derived` is that it calls the parent class's version of `print()`. This means that in effect it *extends*, rather than *replaces*, the behaviour of the original version of `print()`.

Note that `super` tells Kotlin to start searching up the class hierarchy for a version of `print()` defined above the current class in the hierarchy. In this case it is defined in the parent class, but it could have been defined in a parent of `Base` – that is it starts searching in `Base` and will continue searching up the class hierarchy until it finds another definition of `print()` to execute.

Casting and Inheritance

Consider the following class hierarchy:

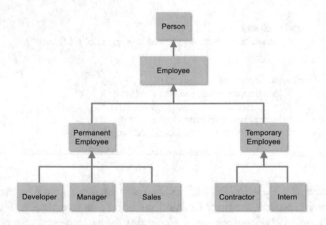

We might refer to this class hierarchy as the *Person* hierarchy as the `Person` class is the root of all the classes. Within this hierarchy instances of all the classes can also be considered to be of type `Person`. In fact on this diagram, the only direct subclass of Person is Employee. As such all the subclass of Employee are both examples of a Person and an Employee.

This means that it is possible to treat an instances of the Sales or Manager class as if they were instances of the class Employee or indeed of class Person.

This can be done by assigning an instance of the Sales or Manager class to a variable of type Employee. This is referred to as *casting* and casting back up a class hierarchy is done automatically by the Kotlin compiler as it will always be a safe cast. This is because all the features of an Employee are always available for all subclass of Employee (even if the internal implementation is different). In Kotlin this means that whatever properties and member functions have been defined in Employee will be available in all subclasses either because they were inherited or because they were overridden.

Thus it is possible to write the following:

```kotlin
fun main() {
    var e: Employee = Employee("John", 55, 1234)
    val s = Sales("Adam", 20, 3456, ''South West'', 500.0)
    e = s
    println(e)
}
```

From the point of view of the variable e what we can say is that it will hold an instance of a class that is at last an Employee but may be an instance of a subclass of Employee. However, the only behaviour that will be able from an API point of view, via the variable e, will be the behaviour (including properties) defined at the Employee level (or indeed inherited by Employee from Person etc.).

When we run this code however, it is the type of thing that is referenced by the variable e that will determine which version of the toString() member function will be executed at runtime. This is referred to as *runtime binding*. Thus the output from this program is:

```
Sales(3456, "Adam", 20, "South West", 500.0)
```

Smart Casting

Casts down the class hierarchy in Kotlin are more complicated. In some cases the Kotlin compiler can determine whether the cast will work. This is referred to as the Kotlin compiler inferring a *smart cast*. In such situations the Kotlin compiler analyses the code and calculates what type might actually be held in a variable and thus whether it is possible to perform an assignment.

For example:

```
fun main() {
    var e: Employee = Employee("John", 55, 1234)
    val s = Sales("Adam", 20, 3456)
    e = s
    val  salesPerson: Sales = e
}
```

In the above example, the val salesPerson is of type Sales. It can therefore only held references to an instance of the Sales class.

However, it is legal to for the var e to hold a reference to an instance of any of the subclasses of the class Employee. This means that the var e could hold a reference to an instance of the Sales class, but equally it could hold a reference to a Manager etc.

Therefore without analysing the code that precedes the assignment of e to salesPerson it is impossible to say whether this will cause a problem or not! Indeed in some other languages this would be illegal and cause a compile time error to be generated.

The Kotlin compiler however can infer smart casts by analysing the preceding code. In this case it will find that e holds a reference to an instances of the class Sales as it is assigned the value held in s in the preceding line. Thus the assignment will be safe. The compiler will therefore allow the assignment to the salesperson variable.

In other situations it either may not be able to determine the value held in a variable or it may determine that the variable does not hold a references to an appropriate instance of a given class; in which case a compiler error will be generated.

Checking the Type

It is possible to check the actual type being referenced by a variable using the is and the !is (is not) operators. These can be used with the name of a type to verify if a variable contains an instance of that type. This is illustrated below using the when expression:

```
fun main() {
    val any: Any = "Hello"
    when (any) {
        is String -> {
         println("any contains a String")
         println(any.length)
        }
        !is String -> {
         println("any does not contain a string")
         println(any::class.simpleName)
        }
    }
}
```

In this short program we create a variable any of type Any. This means that any can contain a reference to an instances of *any* class in Kotlin (or indeed any object).

The when expression first checks to see if any contains a String using the is operator. If any does hold a reference to a String then the code prints out a message and the length of the string.

The when expression also contains a second test that checks to see if the contents of any is not a String using the !is operator. In this case a message is printed out to indicate that it is not a string and the actual type is obtained using a member function reference ::class.simpleName.

The output from this program is:

```
any contains a String
5
```

If we now change the initialisation of any to be

```
val any: Any = 43.5
```

And now rerun the program the output is:

```
any does not contain a string
Double
```

Explicit Casts

In the previous section the Kotlin compiler could determine that the contents of any was actually a String and thus the statement any.length did not cause a compilation issue.

However, the compiler does not always succeed in doing this either because a value may be generated outside the current code analysis scope (for example in a function invoked from a third party library).

As an example, consider the function getData(): Any. It could return any type of thing in the Kotlin type system. This means that it can be very hard for the compiler to determine what the actual type returned by getData() actually is.

We can illustrate that using the following program:

```
fun main() {
    val any: Any = getData()
    println(any.length)
}
```

This program may not compile if the smart cast cannot be determined for the val any. Thus the statement `println(any.length)` may generate a compile time error specifying that the property `length` is unresolved for the type `Any`.

It is therefore necessary for the programmer to explicitly define the cast to the type String so that we can access the `length` property.

The casting operator in Kotlin is the `as` operator. It is used to cast the value in a `val` or `var` to another type, for example:

```
val message: String = any as String
```

The above would now treat the value in `any` as a String and thus the type of the variable `message` can be `String`. We can now access the `length` property via `message`. The modified program using the `as` operation is now:

```
fun main() {
    val any: Any = getData()
    val message: String = any as String
    println(message.length)
}
```

The output from this program is now:

5

Safe Casts

One issue with the `as` operator and the code illustrated in the Explicit Cast section is that from the code in the `main()` function we cannot actually say that `any` holds a String; we have merely assumed that. Without looking at the function `getData()` we can't be sure that a String is actually returned. If in fact `getData()` returns the value `42.5` then there will be a runtime error such as:

```
Exception in thread "main" java.lang.ClassCastException: class
java.lang.Double cannot be cast to class java.lang.String at
CastingExampleAppKt.main(CastingExampleApp.kt:11)
  at CastingExampleAppKt.main(CastingExampleApp.kt)
```

We could check for this of course using the `is` operator, for example:

```
if (any is String) {
    val message: String = any as String
    println(message.length)
}
```

However, this is a common enough pattern that the Kotlin language provides what is known as the *safe cast* operator **as?**. This operator either performs the cast if it is valid or returns null if it is not. For example:

```
fun main() {
    val any: Any = getSomeData()
    val message: String? = any as? String
    println(message?.length)
}
```

In this program we are now using the safe cast operation as? which requires the type of message to be *nullable*. In turn this means that we now use the *safe dot* operator to invoke the length of the message.

When we run this program if getSomeData() returns a String then the output generated is:

5

However, if the getSomeData() function returns the Double 42.5 then the value null will be output and no exception will be raised.

Closing a Member

Closing Member Functions

One issue with the ability to mark a member function as open in a root class is that it is then *open* for all subclasses of the root class. This may not be what is required; if you wish to *close* a member function in a subclass then it is necessary to mark that member function as final in the appropriate subclass.

```
open class Food {
    open fun eatMe() = println("Food - eatMe()")
}

open class Cake: Food() {
    final override fun eatMe() = println("Cake - eatMe()")
}

open class Biscuit: Food() {
    override fun eatMe() = println("Biscuit - eatMe()")
}
```

In the above example the class Food defines an open member function eatMe(). This is overridden in both the class Cake and the class Biscuit.

In the `Biscuit` class this member function is still open and can be overridden in subclasses of `Biscuit`.

However, in `Cake` class the member function is marked as both overridden and `final`. This means that subclass of `Cake` cannot override `eatMe()`.

Closing Properties

It is also possible to close a property (either a member property or a constructor property). This is also done using the `final` keyword. This is illustrated below:

```
open class Food(open val type: String = "generic")

open class Cake(
           final override val type: String = "Sponge"): Food()

open class Biscuit(override val type: String = "Sweet"): Food()

fun main() {
    val c = Cake()
    println(c.type)
}
```

In this case the property type in the base class `Food` is marked as `open` and thus can be overridden in subclasses. However the override defined in the `Cake` class is marked as `final` and thus subclasses of the `Cake` class cannot override the property `type`. In contrast in the class `Biscuit` subclasses can still override the `type` property.

Inheritance Summary

To recap on the concept of inheritance. Inheritance is supported between classes in Kotlin. For example, a class can extend (subclass) another class. A subclass inherits all the member functions and properties defined for the parent class but may override these in the subclass.

In terms of inheritance we say:

- A subclass inherits from a super class.
- A subclass obtains all code and properties from the super class.
- A subclass can add new code and properties.
- A subclass can override inherited code and properties.
- A subclass can invoke inherited behaviour or access inherited properties.

The above is also true for objects.

Online Resources

There are many resources available online relating to class inheritance including:

- https://kotlinlang.org/api/latest/jvm/stdlib/kotlin/-any/ Documentation for the Kotlin root class `Any`.
- https://kotlinlang.org/spec/inheritance.html Kotlin language specification on inheritance.
- https://en.wikipedia.org/wiki/Inheritance_(object-oriented_programming) Wikipedia page on class inheritance.

Exercises

The aim of these exercises is to extend the `Account` class you have been developing from the last two chapters by providing `DepositAccount`, `CurrentAccount` and `InvestmentAccount` subclasses.

Each of the classes should extend the `Account` class by:

1. `CurrentAccount` adding an overdraft limit as well as redefining the withdraw member function.
2. `DepositAccount` by adding an interest rate.
3. `InvestmentAccount` by adding an investment type property.

These features are discussed below:

The `CurrentAccout` class can have an `overdraftLimit` property. This can be set when an instance of a class is created and altered during the lifetime of the object. The overdraft limit should be included in the `toString()` member function used to convert the account into a String.

The `CurrentAccount withdraw()` member function should verify that the balance never goes below the overdraft limit. If it does then the `withdraw()` member function should not reduce the balance instead it should print out a warning message.

The `DepositAccount` should have an interest rate associated with it which is included when the account is converted to a string.

The `InvestmentAccount` will have a `investmentType` property which can hold a string such as 'safe' or 'high risk'.

This also means that it is no longer necessary to pass the type of account as a parameter - it is implicit in the type of class being instantiated.

For example, given this code snippet:

```
fun main() {
    val acc1 = CurrentAccount("123", "John", 10.05, -100.00)
    val acc2 = DepositAccount("345", "Denise", 23.55, 0.5)
    val acc3 = InvestmentAccount("567", "Phoebe", 12.45,
                                  "high risk")

    println(acc1)
    println(acc2)
    println(acc3)

    acc1.deposit(23.45)
    acc1.withdraw(12.33)

    println("balance: ${acc1.balance}")
    acc1.withdraw(300.00)
    println("balance: ${acc1.balance}")

    Account.printInstancesCreated()

}
```

Then the output might be:

```
New Account created for John
New Account created for Denise
New Account created for Phoebe
CurrentAccount('123', 'John', 10.05) - overdraft -100.0
DepositAccount('345', 'Denise', 23.55) - interestRate 0.5
InvestmentAccount('567', 'Phoebe', 12.45) - type high risk
balance: 21.17
Withdrawal would exceed your overdraft limit
balance: 21.17
3 instances of Account class created
```

Chapter 13
Abstract Classes

Introduction

This chapter presents *abstract classes*. An abstract class is a class that you cannot instantiate and that is expected to be extended by one or more subclasses. Typically some aspect of the abstract class needs to be implemented by its subclasses.

Abstract Classes as a Concept

An abstract class is a class from which you cannot create an instance. It is typically missing one or more elements required to create a fully functioning instance.

In contrast a non-abstract (or *concrete*) class leaves nothing undefined and can be used to create a working instance or object.

You may therefore wonder what use an *abstract* class is?

The answer is that you can group together elements which are to be shared amongst a number of subclasses, without providing a complete implementation. In addition, you can force subclasses to provide specific member functions and/or properties ensuring that implementers of a subclass at least supply appropriate data and behaviour. You should therefore use abstract classes when:

- you wish to specify data or behaviour common to a set of subclasses, but insufficient for a single instance or object,
- you wish to force subclasses or objects to provide specific behaviour or data.

In many cases, the two situations go together. Typically, the aspects of the class to be defined as abstract are specific to each class, while what has been implemented is common to all classes.

J. Hunt, *Beginner's Guide to Kotlin Programming*,
https://doi.org/10.1007/978-3-030-80893-8_13

Abstract Classes in Kotlin

Abstract classes cannot be instantiated themselves but can be extended by subclasses. These subclasses can be concrete classes or can themselves be abstract classes (that extend the concept defined in the root abstract class).

Abstract Classes can be used to define generic (potentially abstract) behaviour that can be extended by other Kotlin classes and act as an abstract root of a class hierarchy. They can also be used to provide a formal way of specifying behaviour that must be provided by a concrete class.

Abstract Classes can have:

- zero or more abstract member functions or properties,
- zero or more concrete member functions and properties.

There are many built-in abstract classes in Kotlin including (but not limited to):

- data structures such as `kotlin.collections`,
- the `Number` abstract class in package `kotlin`,
- streams/input and output packages.

In fact, abstract classes are widely used internally within Kotlin itself and many developers use abstract classes without ever knowing they exist or understanding how to define them.

To define an abstract class Kotlin uses:

- the keyword `abstract` before the keyword `class`
- Within an abstract class it is possible to define abstract member functions using:
- The `abstract` keyword before `fun` without defining the body of the member function
- It is also possible to define abstract properties using:
- the `abstract` keyword before `val` or `var`
- without a value assigned to the property
- This is true for both constructor properties and member level properties.

Defining an Abstract Class and Member Functions

An example of an abstract class is presented below:

```
abstract class Conveyance {
    protected var fuel = 5.0
    private var running = false

    fun startup() {
        running = true
        consumeFuel()
        while (fuel > 0) {
            consumeFuel()
        }
        running = false
    }

    // Abstract member function returning Unit
    abstract fun consumeFuel()
    // Abstract member function return Boolean
    abstract fun drive(distance: Int): Boolean
}
```

Within the definition of Conveyance, we can see that the startup() member function is defined, but the member function consumeFuel() is specified as *abstract* and does not have a member function body.

The conveyance class also defines a second abstract member function drive(Int): Boolean. This member function must also be defined in subclasses.

Any class which has one or more *abstract* member functions is necessarily abstract and *must* therefore be marked as abstract. However, a class can be abstract without specifying any abstract member functions.

Any subclass of Conveyance must implement the consumeFuel() and drive(Int): Boolean member functions or it must be marked as abstract. Each subclass can define how much fuel is consumed in a different manner or how a conveyance is driven etc.. The following section introduces the class Car which provides a concrete class which builds on Conveyance.

Note that an abstract class is implicitly open; that is it is expected to be extended and therefore there is no need to explicitly specify that the class is open.

If a class is marked as abstract then it is not possible to create an instance of that class.

Subclassing an Abstract Class

Given an abstract class Conveyance we can define a concrete class Car that extends it and implements the abstract functions.

To create a subclass of an abstract class we use the : symbol to represent inheritance and must indicate which constructor will be invoked for the parent class. We will then need to define the *concrete* version of any abstract member functions in the parent class. Such member functions must include the keyword override before the keyword fun in their definition. For example:

```
class Car : Conveyance() {

    override fun consumeFuel() {
        fuel -= 1.0
        println("consuming, ")
    }

    override fun drive(distance: Int): Boolean {
        println("Driven $distance")
        return true
    }
}
```

The above definition of the class `Car` defines the `consumeFuel()` and `drive(Int): Boolean` member functions. Both functions must have exactly the same signature as the versions defined within the abstract class (that is the capitalisation of names must be the same, the return types must match as must the parameter types). Both member functions must also be preceded by the keyword `override`.

We can now create instances of the class `Car` and invoke the `consumeFuel()` and `drive()` member functions.

The following program illustrates the use of the `Car` class:

```
fun main() {
    val c: Conveyance = Car()
    c.startup()
    val result = c.drive(10)
    println(result)
}
```

In this program the type of the val `c` is `Conveyance` however this is merely to show that instances of `Car` can be treated as a `Car` or a `Conveyance` (or indeed as something of type `Any`).

The output from this program is given below:

```
consuming,
consuming,
consuming,
consuming,
consuming,
Driven 10
true
```

Abstract Properties

In Kotlin, member functions are not the only things that can be declared as abstract, it is also possible to declare *properties* as abstract. An abstract class can have zero or more abstract properties, these abstract properties:

- can be constructor properties or member level properties,
- can be vals or vars,
- must be prefixed by the keyword abstract.

For example, the following CommercialVehicle abstract class defines an abstract property owner and an abstract member function load():

```
abstract class CommercialVehicle {

    // Abstract property
    abstract val owner: String

    // Abstract member function
    abstract fun load(contents: String)

}
```

Any concrete subclasses of CommercialVehicle must provide an implementation of both the member function and the abstract property. To provide a concrete implementation of the abstract property it is necessary to prefix the property declaration with the keyword override and to provide a way to initialise the property.

The following class illustrates this:

```
class Lorry(override val owner: String) : CommercialVehicle() {
    override fun load(contents: String) {
        println("loading $contents")
    }
}
```

The class provides a concrete implementation of the property owner by making this a constructor property marked with the keyword override.

Thus the value of the owner property must be supplied when the class is instantiated meeting the requirement for defining the val property. It also provides a concrete implementation of the member function load().

We can now use the class Lorry in a simple program:

```
fun main() {
    val l = Lorry("Smith and Co.")
    l.load("Hay")
}
```

The output from this is:

```
loading Hay
```

Abstract Subclasses

The subclass of an abstract class may itself be *abstract* in which case it must be marked as `abstract`.

An abstract subclass may be abstract either because it defines one or more abstract members (that is a property or a member function that is abstract) or because it does not implement one or more of the abstract members inherited from the parent class.

For example, the class `Van` is abstract as it does not implement the `owner` property nor the `load()` member function:

```
class Van(override val owner: String) : CommercialVehicle() {

}
```

However, in this example the class has not been marked as `abstract`, this will result in a compile time error being generated:

```
Class 'Van' is not abstract and does not implement abstract base
class member public abstract fun load(contents: String): Unit
defined in CommercialVehicle
```

To solve this problem we must add the keyword `abstract` before the keyword `class` in the definition of the class Van. For example:

```
abstract class Van(override val owner: String) :
CommercialVehicle() {}
```

Online Resources

Some online references for Abstract Classes include:

- https://kotlinlang.org/docs/reference/classes.html The standard Library documentation on Abstract Classes.
- http://kotlin-quick-reference.com/103-R-abstract-classes.html Quick reference on Abstract classes.
- https://en.wikipedia.org/wiki/Abstract_type Wikipedia entry on Abstract types.

Exercises

The aim of this exercise is to define an Abstract Class.

The Account class of the project you have been working on throughout the last few chapters is currently a concrete class and is indeed instantiated in earlier test applications.

Modify the Account class so that it is an Abstract Class which will force all *concrete* examples to be a subclass of Account.

Chapter 14
Interfaces, Delegation and Enumerated Types

Introduction

The Kotlin type system is comprised of more than just classes and objects; it includes interfaces and enumerated types. In this chapter we will explore the concept of an *interface* and what components can be defined within an interface. We will also consider a Kotlin language facility that allows an interface to be implemented via delegation.

The chapter concludes by looking at enumerated types. An enumerated type is a type consisting of a set of named values also called elements or members of the enumeration. These values have a specific name and an ordering.

Kotlin Interfaces

The interface construct is another element in the Kotlin type system. An interface is a specification of a set of properties or member functions that a class should implement. An interface can contain

- abstract properties,
- abstract member functions,
- concrete member functions,
- a companion object.

The syntax for an interface is:

```
access-modifier interface interface-name {
    abstract properties
    abstract member function signatures ...
    member functions
    companion object
}
```

Note that the order of these declarations is not significant.
An interface type can be used to:

- define a common protocol to be implemented by a class or object in terms of properties and member functions,
- to share behaviour across a wide range of classes and objects.

Interfaces are widely used within Kotlin for both purposes.

Defining an Interface

An interface definition can have any number or combination of concrete member functions, abstract member functions, abstract properties and a companion object.
Some points to note about interfaces:

- Interfaces *do not have* constructors (either primary or auxiliary).
- Interfaces *cannot* define concrete properties.
- An interface may or may not extend one or more other interfaces.

A simple example of an interface definition is presented below.

```
interface Organizer {
    val owner: String
    fun add(appointment: String, date: String)
    fun get(date: String): String?
    fun remove(date: String): Boolean
}
```

This represents the most basic definition of an interface and only contains abstract specifications. In this case it contains the specification for an abstract val property `owner` of type String. It also contains the signatures of three abstract member functions `add()`, `get()` and `remove()`.

This means that any class or object implementing the `Organizer` interface must provide an implementation of the `owner` property and the `add()`, `get()` and `remove()` member functions. Any class that does provide all these implementations must be marked as `abstract`.

In addition the interface also specifies the signature of the member functions, that is that the `get()` member function takes a String parameter and should return a *nullable* String and that the `remove()` member function takes a String parameter and should return a Boolean etc.

It is not necessary to define the property or the member functions as being *abstract* because they are abstract by default.

It may appear at this point that an interface is the same as an abstract class, however they differ in a number of ways:

* Any class can implement one (or more) interfaces. A class can inherit from only one parent class.
* Interfaces can inherit from zero or more interfaces.
* A class cannot extend an interface (it can only implement it or "fill it out").
* Interfaces are a compile time feature; they influence the static analysis of the program being compiled. Abstract classes involve run time issues associated with member function selection, execution, etc.
* Interfaces can be implemented by any class from anywhere in the class hierarchy whether that class explicitly specifies a super class or not. Thus, you can define an interface which is implemented by classes in completely different hierarchies.

Implementing an Interface

Classes and objects can *implement* one or more interfaces. This is done by listing the interface (or interfaces) to be implemented following the colon (:) after the class name and any constructor present. Thus the syntax is

```
class <className>(<primary-constrcutor>) : <interface> {}
```

Or for an object

```
object <object-name> : <interface>
```

Whether the implementing type is a concrete class or an object it must *implement* all the abstract elements defined in the interface.

An example of a class implementing the `Organiser` interface is given below:

```
class Calendar(override val owner: String) : Organizer {
    override fun add(appointment: String, date: String) {
        println("$appointment - $date")
    }
    override fun get(date: String): String? {
        return null
    }
    override fun remove(date: String): Boolean {
        return false
    }
}
```

This class meets the contract defined in the Organise interface as it provides an implementation of all the element in the Organiser. That is it has a concrete val property `owner` that is defined as part of the constructor. It also has concrete implementations of the three member functions.

Note however that is has been necessary to use the `override` keyword with the property `owner` and the three member functions. This is required by Kotlin and indicates, in this case, that it is implementing a member defined in the interface. If you omit the `override` keyword then a compiler error will be generated.

If a class does not implement all the abstract elements of the interface (such as an abstract member function or an abstract property) then the class must be marked as being abstract, otherwise you will generate a compile time error. In this way you are guaranteed that if an instance is created form a class that implements an interface, then that instance will have an implementation for all the abstract elements in the interface.

Objects Can Implement Interfaces

An object can also *implement* an interface, however in this case it *must always* implement all the abstract members of the interface as it is not possible to mark an object as abstract (as it is not possible to extend an object). An example of an object implementing the Organiser interface is given below:

```kotlin
object Diary : Organizer {
    override val owner: String = "John"

    override fun add(appointment: String, date: String) {
        println("add $appointment - $date")
    }



        override fun get(date: String): String? {
            return null
        }

        override fun remove(date: String): Boolean {
            return false
        }
    }
```

As with the class, the object implements the three member functions and defines a member level property val `owner`.

1. Interfaces and Types.
2. In addition to acting as a contract with a class or an object that specifies what that class (or object) must provide, an interface can also be used as a type specifier. This means that you can define an interface and then use it to specify the type a var or val can hold.

In Kotlin, the `Organiser` is a type as are its sub types `Calendar` and `Diary`. This means that an instance of the `Calendar` class is:

- of type `Calendar`,
- of type `Any` (via inheritance) and
- of type `Organiser` by virtue of the class implementing the interface.

3. In turn the object `Diary` is also of type `Organiser` as it implements the interface.
4. Thus either an instance of the `Calendar` class or the object `Diary` can be treated as an `Organiser`. This is illustrated below:

```
fun main() {
    val cal = Calendar("John")
    cal.add("Dentist", "Monday")
    val org: Organizer = cal
    org.add("Garage", "Tuesday")
    Diary.add("Opticians", "Wednesday")
    val diary: Organizer = Diary
    diary.add("Doctors", "Thursday")
}
```

The output from this program is:

```
Dentist - Monday
Garage - Tuesday
add Opticians - Wednesday
add Doctors - Thursday
```

5. The `Organiser` type can also be used to specify the type of a parameter to a function or a member function:

```
class Home {
    // ...
    fun add (Organizer temp) {
        // ...
    }
}
```

This means that the member function `add(Organiser)` can take an instance of any class or object that implements the `Organizer` interface.

6. Implementing Multiple Interfaces

A class or object can implement zero or more interfaces. This means that when a class or object is defined there can be a comma separated list of interfaces following the colon (:). For example:

```kotlin
interface Organizer {
    val owner: String
    fun add(appointment: String, date: String)
    fun get(date: String): String?
    fun remove(date: String): Boolean
}

interface Printer {
    fun prettyPrint()
}

interface Speaker {
    fun saySomething()
}

class Application(override val owner: String) : Organizer,
                                                Printer,
                                                Speaker {


    // Speaker member function
    override fun saySomething() {}
    // Printer member function
    override fun prettyPrint() {}
    // Organizer member functions
    override fun add(appointment: String, date: String) {}
    override fun get(date: String): String? = null
    override fun remove(date: String): Boolean = false


}
```

In this case the class `Application` implements the `Organiser`, `Printer` and `Speaker` interfaces. It therefore has to implement all the abstract members defined across all these interfaces. In this case

- the `Organiser` interface defines an abstract val property `owner`, and three abstract member functions `add()`, `get()` and `remove()`,
- the `Printer` interface specifies one abstract member function `prettyPrint()`,
- the `Speaker` interface defines an abstract member function `saySomething()`.

An `object` can also implement multiple interfaces in a similar manner, for example:

```
object MyObject: Organizer, Printer, Speaker {

    // Organizer member property
    override val owner: String = "John"

    // Speaker member function
    override fun saySomething() {}
    // Printer member function
    override fun prettyPrint() {}
    // Organizer member functions
    override fun add(appointment: String, date: String) {}
    override fun get(date: String): String? = null
    override fun remove(date: String): Boolean = false


}
```

Extending a Class and Implementing Interfaces

A class or object can extend another class and also implement one or more interfaces.
This allows a class or object to inherit behaviour from a named class as well as
implement the abstract members in multiple interfaces. The parent or super class
is specified after the colon (:) along with the interfaces. In Kotlin the order that
this is done is not significant, although it is common to place the class first in the
comma separated list. This should not be confusing as a class always indicates which
constructor should be run where as interfaces do not have a constructor.

An example of defining a class that extends an *open* class is given below. The
class TechnicalAuthor extends the Author class and implements the interfaces
Writer and Speaker:

```
interface Writer {
    fun writeSomething()
}

interface Speaker {
    fun saySomething()
}

open class Author(val name: String)
```

```
        class TechnicalAuthor(name: String) : Author(name),
                                              Writer,
                                              Speaker {
            override fun saySomething() {
                print("hello")
            }

            override fun writeSomething() {
                print("writers block")
            }
        }
```

In this example, the class TechnicalAuthor passes a constructor parameter name up to the super class Author and implements the interfaces Writer and Speaker. However the class could also have been defined using a different order for the super class and the interfaces, for example:

```
        class TechnicalAuthor(name: String) : Writer,
                                              Speaker,
                                              Author(name) {
            // ..
        }
```

Or indeed even:

```
        class TechnicalAuthor(name: String) : Writer,
                                              Author(name),
                                              Speaker {
            // ..
        }
```

All of the above are equivalent.

Inheritance by Interfaces

Interfaces can also inherit from zero or more interfaces. Thus, for example we can define a hierarchy of interfaces where a single interface can extend zero or more other interfaces.

This is illustrated below:

```
interface Workers {
    fun doWork()
}
interface Employers: Clonable {
    fun printSelf()
}
interface Records : Workers, Employers {
    fun doSomething()
}
```

In this case the interface `Employers` extends the interface `Cloneable`. In turn the interface `Records` extends the interfaces `Workers` and `Employers` (and by inheritance `Clonable`).

When an interface extends more than one interface then the result is the union of all declarations in the inherited interfaces. Thus any class or object implementing `Records` must implement the member functions:

- `doSomething()` from `Records`,
- `printSelf()` from `Employers` and
- `doWork()` from `Workers`
- plus anything defined in `Cloneable`.

Interfaces and Concrete Member Functions

As mentioned at the start of this chapter, interface definitions can have any number or combination of concrete member functions in addition to the abstract specification of properties and member functions. This is illustrated in the following interface:

```
interface Speaker {
    fun saySomething()
    fun sayHello() {
        println("Speaker - Hello World")
    }
}
```

The `Speaker` interface defines a *concrete* member function `sayHello()` and an *abstract* member function `saySomething()`.

When a class or object implements the `Speaker` interface they inherit any concrete member functions and must implement any abstract member functions or properties.

For example, the class `Person` implements the `Speaker` interface. It therefore inherits the `sayHello()` member function and must implement the `saySomething()` member function:

```
class Person : Speaker {
    override fun saySomething() {
        println("Person - Howdy")
    }
}
```

This is illustrated below where the `Person` class is instantiated and then the `sayHello()` member function is invoked on that instance:

```
fun main() {
    val p = Person()
    p.sayHello()
    p.saySomething()
}
```

The output from this program is:

```
Speaker - Hello World
Person - Howdy
```

Multiple Interfaces with the Same Concrete Member Functions

Interfaces can contain concrete member functions and classes or objects can implement multiple interfaces. This means that there is the possibility that a class or object could implement two or more interfaces that have concrete member functions with the same signature.

For example given the following two interfaces:

```
interface Speaker {
    fun saySomething()
    fun sayHello() {
        println("Speaker - Hello World")
    }
}
interface Translator {
    fun sayHello() {
        println("Translator - Bonjour")
    }
}
```

Any type implementing these two interfaces would find that the member function `sayHello()` was duplicated. This would be identified by the compiler and an error similar to the following would be generated;

```
Class 'Employee' must override public open fun sayHello(): Unit
defined in interfaces.Speaker because it inherits multiple
interface member functions of it
```

This error makes it clear that the implementing class must override the member function `sayHello()` to deal with the potential confusion between the behaviour implemented in the two interfaces.

This could be done simply by defining a local implementation in the implementing class. For example the class `Employee` does just that by providing its own definition of the sayHello() member function thus hiding both versions defined in the two interfaces:

```
class Employee : Speaker, Translator {
    override fun saySomething() {
        println("Employee- Say Something")
    }

    override fun sayHello() {
        println("Employee - sayHello()")
    }
}
```

In this case the class `Employee` overrides the definition of `sayHello()` defined in both the interfaces.

However, in some cases it may be useful to invoke the behaviour defined in one (or more) of the interfaces. This can be done from within the implementing class or object using the `super<interface—name>.<member name>`syntax.

This is illustrated below:

```
class Employee : Speaker, Translator {
    override fun saySomething() {
        println("Employee- Say Something")
    }

    override fun sayHello() {
        super<Speaker>.sayHello()
    }
}
```

In this revised version of the class Employee the `sayHello()` member function invokes the version of `sayHello()` defined in the `Speaker` interface.

This last version of the class `Employee` is used in the following short program:

```
fun main() {
    val e = Employee()
    e.sayHello()
    e.saySomething()
}
```

The output from this program is:

```
Speaker - Hello World
Employee- Say Something
```

Interface Companion Objects

Interfaces can also have companion objects. Such companion objects can provide functionality and properties that can only be accessed directly from the interface or from within concrete member functions defined within the interface.

An interface companion object is defined in exactly the same way as a class companion object using the keywords companion object.

This is illustrated in the Printer interface definition below:

```
interface Printer {
    fun prettyPrint()

    fun printLabel() {
        println(label)
        printMe()
    }

    companion object {
        private const val label = "Label"
        fun printMe() {
            println("Printer - printMe")
        }
    }
}
```

This interface defines an abstract member function prettyPrint(), a concrete member function printLabel() and a companion object containing a constant val property label and a member function printMe(). Within the concrete member function printLabel() both the private property label and the member function printMe() as accessible as they are defined in the interface's companion object.

For this example, we can implement the Printer interface in a class called ShoppingBasket:

```
class ShoppingBasket : Printer {
    override fun prettyPrint() {
        println("ShoppingBasket - prettyPrint")
    }
}
```

This means that the `ShoppingBasket` class must implement the `prettyPrint()` member function and inherits the `printLabel()` member function. However, it does not inherit the companion object nor does it have direct access to the companion objects members.

This is illustrated in the following main function:

```
fun main() {
    // Can call member function on interface
    Printer.printMe()
    // Compile error
    // ShoppingBasket.printMe()
    val basket = ShoppingBasket()
    // Compile error
    // basket.printMe()
    basket.prettyPrint()
    // Compile error
    // Printer.prettyPrint()
}
```

We have commented out all lines which would generate a compiler error. This illustrates several things:

1. It is possible to access the interface's companion object's members via the interface name, for example `Printer.printMe()`.
2. It is not possible to access the interface companion object members from the implementing class; thus you *cannot* write `ShoppingBasket.printMe()`.
3. An instance of the class implementing the interface also does not inherit and cannot directly access, the interfaces companion object and its members thus `basket.printMe()` is *invalid*.
4. It is not possible to invoke an abstract member function on an interface thus `Printer.prettyPrint()` is also *invalid*.

The output from the program is:

```
Printer - printMe
ShoppingBasket - prettyPrint
```

Marker Interfaces

A marker interface is an interface that declares no member functions, types or properties. Instead it is used to indicate additional semantics of a type (class, object or further interfaces). For example see the `Serializable` interface; this is a marker interface indicating the semantics of being able to be serialised (converted into a binary format for transmission over a network or to be saved into a file to be deserialised at a later date).

Marker interfaces can be used where:

1. it is useful to semantically indicate a role or concept that other entities may play within the application. However, these entities may be of varying types (from classes, to objects to further interfaces) and may inherit behaviour from various different places in the type hierarchy.
2. semantically there is a common concept, but there is little or no common behaviour or data representation between the concrete implementations of the generic domain concept.
3. client classes may need to know something about the type of an object without actually needing to know the specific type (at least at the interface level).

Using an interface as the basis of a marker is particularly convenient in Kotlin as a type may implement any number of interfaces. For example, the following code defines two marker traits, one called `Decorator` and one called `Service`.

```kotlin
interface Decorator
interface Service
```

Any type can implement one or more interfaces, thus any type can implement a marker interface and any other interfaces as required. For example:

```kotlin
object MyPrinter : Decorator, Service {
    fun print() {
        println("MyPrinter")
    }
}
```

Semantically this tells us that `MyPrinter` is a type of `Decorator` and that it is also a type of `Service`.

Delegation

The *delegation pattern* is an object oriented design pattern. The purpose of the delegate design pattern is to use instance composition to achieve code reuse without using inheritance.

In delegation, an instance handles a request for some behaviour (i.e. for some member function to run) by delegating to a second instance (the *delegate*). The delegate is a helper instance of a difference class to the original message receiver. In the delegate pattern, this is accomplished by holding a reference to a delegate within the original instance and mirroring the member functions in the delegate with member functions in the receiver that merely pass the request onto the delegate.

The basic idea behind the delegation pattern is shown below. There is a type (class or object0 that is the Delegator. This delegates responsibility for some behaviour to a delegate. This delegate is often defined as an interface or an abstract class. One or more concrete implementations are then provided for the Delegate that can be plugged in as required.

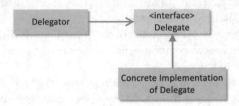

To illustrate this we will first define an interface and a class that implements that interface:

```
interface Role {
    fun printRole(): Unit
}

class TellerRole(val name: String) : Role {
    override fun printRole() = println("Role: $name")
}
```

For example, given an interface Role and a default implementation of that interface (the TellerRole) we could now create a class that implemented the interface Role by delegating (or forwarding) the result onto an instance of TellerRole:

```
class Cashier(name: String) : Role {
    private val tellerRole: TellerRole = TellerRole(name)
    override fun printRole() = tellerRole.printRole()
}
```

We could now describe the class Cashier as *delegating* the implementation of the Role interface to the TellerRole private property.

The above works, however we have had to define a private val property to hold the TellerRole instance and we have had to define a member function printRole() to handle the forwarding.

This is a very common pattern which may be repeated many times; to avoid the amount of boiler plate code required here, Kotlin provides the by operator. The by operator allows a class to explicitly specify that an interface is being implemented using the delegation pattern by another class.

The by operator follows the name of the interface with the name of the class that will be used to implement the interface. Note that the appropriate constructor must also be invoked for this delegate class. For example:

```
class User(name: String) : Role by TellerRole(name)
```

Instances of the class User still implement the Role interface via delegation to an instance of the TellerRole class however it is now explicit in the specification of the class and avoids the developer having to write a set of boiler plate member functions and properties.

An example of using the User class is given below:

```
fun main() {
    val user = User("Player1")
    user.printRole()
}
```

The output from this program is given here:

```
Role: Player1
```

Note that you can implement any number of interfaces in this way by using a series of <interface> by <class>declarations separated by a comma. For example assuming we have a set of interfaces Role, Accessor and Printable then we could delegate the responsibility for each to a separate class:

```
class User(name: String) : Role by TellerRole(name),
                           Accessor by Person(name),
                           Printable by Printer()
```

Enumerated Types

An enumerated type (also called an enum) is another part of the Kotlin type system. It consists of a set of named values called the elements or members of the enumerated type. The values are names associated with an integer index that starts from zero. The values can also posses properties that allow them to represent other values.

Kotlin Enums

In Kotlin an enumerated type is defined using the keywords enum class. This is illustrated below for a simple enumerated type representing directions:

```
enum class Direction {
    NORTH, SOUTH, EAST, WEST
}
```

Note that the values that comprise the enumerated type are defined as named constants in a comma separated list.

In this case the enumerated type Direction defines the values NORTH, SOUTH, EAST and WEST. There is also an explicit ordering defined for the values in an enumerated type. In this case NORTH comes before SOUTH and SOUTH comes after NORTH.

It is possible to define a property or a local var or val as having the type Direction. The val or var can then be assigned one of the values defined for the enumerated type Direction, for example:

```
val d: Direction = Direction.NORTH
```

Each value in the enumerated type has two principal attributes.

1. Name. The name is the same as the name of the value, thus the name of the NORTH value above is NORTH.
2. ordinal (Zero based). Thus NORTH has the ordinal value 0, SOUTH has the ordering value 1 and EAST has the ordinal value 2 etc.

These values are accessible through name() and ordinal() member functions.

Each value also has default implements of the equals(), hashcode(), toString() and compareTo() member functions defined. This means that it is possible to print out an enumerated value using the toString() member function, to compare two values using equals() and to check the ordering of values using operators such as < or > (that use compareTo() under the hood).

These ideas are illustrated in the following program:

```
fun main() {
    val d = Direction.NORTH
    println(d)
    println("d.name: ${d.name}")
    println("d.ordinal: ${d.ordinal}")

    if (d == Direction.NORTH) {
        println("We are heading North")
    }
    println(d < Direction.SOUTH)
}
```

The result of running this program is:

```
NORTH
d.name: NORTH
d.ordinal: 0
We are heading North
true
```

Ordering Enumerated Type

The typical use of enumerated types is associated with having an ordered sequence of values where the ordering is significant.

This is illustrated below for the DaysOfWeek enumerated type. There is a very definite ordering to the days of the week, with Monday coming before Tuesday and Friday coming at the end of the week. In an application it may be useful to be able to reason about this ordering explicitly.

The following code example illustrates this idea:

```kotlin
enum class DaysOfWeek {
    MONDAY, TUESDAY, WEDNESDAY, THURSDAY, FRIDAY
}

fun main() {
    val day = DaysOfWeek.WEDNESDAY
    println(day)
    println(day < DaysOfWeek.FRIDAY)
    println(day < DaysOfWeek.MONDAY)
}
```

The output from this program is:

```
WEDNESDAY
true
false
```

Providing Additional Enum Data

It is also possible to define constructor member properties for enumerated types. These can be used to initialise values represented by an enumerated value other than the default ordinal values.

For example, the following CompassDirections enumerated type has a constructor val property defined for it called bearing. This is an integer that is used to represent the number of degrees associated with a particular `CompassDirection`.

```
enum class CompassDirections(val bearing: Int) {
    NORTH(0), SOUTH(180), EAST(90), WEST(270)
}
```

Notice that when each of the enumerated values is defined it is now provided with an appropriate value for `bearing`.

We can now use the `CompassDirection` enumerated type and its set of values in a simple program to illustrate accessing the `bearing` property associated with a enumerated `CompassDirection`:

```
fun main() {
    val d = CompassDirections.WEST
    when (d) {
        CompassDirections.WEST -> println("Heading " +
d.bearing)
        else -> println("Unknown heading")
    }
}
```

The output from this is:

$$println(d < Direction.SOUTH)$$

Online Resources

The following provide further information on interfaces, the delegation pattern and enums classes:

1. https://kotlinlang.org/docs/interfaces.html Interfaces in Kotlin documentation.
2. https://en.wikipedia.org/wiki/Delegation_pattern Wikipedia delegation design pattern.
3. https://kotlinlang.org/docs/enum-classes.html Enumerated types in Kotlin.

Exercises

The aim of this exercise is to define an interface for our account types and also to create an enumerated type for the types of investment accounts.

First create rename your `Account` to `AbstractAccount`.

Next create an interface called Account. Note that this interface should have the following abstract properties:

1. A val `accountNumber: String`
2. A val `holder: String`
3. A val `balance: Double`. Note this is a val not a var in the interface. The class has a private setter and makes it a var but that is internal to the class. The public API to the class makes it look like the balance is a val property - which we need to reflect in the Kotlin interface Account.

The interface should also have two abstract member functions `deposit()` and `withdraw()`. Both these abstract member functions should take a `Double` as a parameter.

In the `AbstractAccount` class make it implement the Account interface.

Note you will need to mark the `deposit()` and `withdraw()` member functions with `override`. You will also need to mark the properties with `override`.

Next create an enum class called `InvestmentAccountTypes` which will define three classes of investment account, High, Medium and Low risk.

Now change the `InvestmentAccount` class so that the type field is an `InvestmentAccountTypes` not a string and instantiate it with an appropriate value, for example:

```
val acc3 = InvestmentAccount("567", "Phoebe", 12.45,
InvestmentAccountTypes.High)
```

Chapter 15
Packages

Introduction

Packages are a language construct used in Kotlin to organise larger programs. This chapter introduces packages as well as visibility modifiers.

Packages

You can bring a set of related functions, properties, classes and objects together in a single compilation unit by defining them all within one directory. By default, this creates an implicit (unnamed) package; classes and objects in the same directory can access properties and member functions that are only visible in the current package. However, such a group of functions, properties, classes and objects cannot be accessed by code defined in another directory with a different name. This is therefore an acceptable approach when creating *sample* code or exploring the language, however for real world applications the is *not* appropriate.

A much better approach is to group the classes together into an explicit *named* package.

Packages are encapsulated units which can possess classes, objects, interfaces, functions, properties and enumerated types. Packages are extremely useful as they:

- **Help organise your code base**. They allow you to associate related types, functions and properties.
- **Provide a namespace**. They resolve naming problems which would otherwise cause confusion.
- **Support visibility/access controls**. They allow some privacy for objects, classes, member functions, properties and functions that should not be visible outside the

© The Author(s), under exclusive license to Springer Nature Switzerland AG 2021
J. Hunt, *Beginner's Guide to Kotlin Programming*,
https://doi.org/10.1007/978-3-030-80893-8_15

package. You can provide a level of encapsulation such that only those elements which are intended to be public can be accessed from outside the package.

Indeed the Kotlin language and associated third party libraries provides a wide range of packages which, as your applications develop and particularly if you use Android, you will need to work with.

Declaring a Package

An explicit package is defined by the `package` keyword at the start of the file in which one or more functions, classes, objects, enumerated types, interfaces or properties are defined:

package benchmarks

The package statement must be the first *executable* line in a file (comments are not executable code).

Package names should be *unique* to ensure that there are no name conflicts. Kotlin adopts a naming convention by which a package name is made up of a number of components separated by a full stop/period. These components correspond to the location of the files. Thus if the files in a particular package are in a directory called benchmarks, within a directory called tests, then the package name is given as:

package tests.benchmarks

Notice that this assumes that all files associated with a single package are in the *same* directory. It also assumes that files in a separate package will be in a different directory. Any number of files can become part of a package, however any one file can only be part of/specify a single package.

A further convention that Kotlin adopts is that to ensure that your packages are unique, that you should prefix your packages with your domain name in reverse. For example, if you worked for a company called Midmarsh Technology and your web domain was www.midmarsh.com then your packages would all start `com.midmarsh`, for example:

package com.midmarsh.util

How Packages Relate to Directories

Packages relate to the directory structure in which the `.class` files generated from your source code are stored. This structure is created by the compiler and is based on the package names. Each part of the package name maps onto a directory with each full stop (`.`) acting as a separator between parts of the package name. For example, given the following code:

package com.jjh.util

When this is compiled, the compiler will generate a directory structure that match the `com.jjh.util` package name.

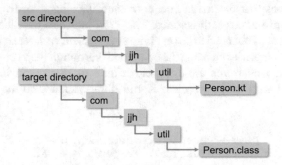

In this diagram the *source* code is stored under a directory called `src` while the `.class` files created by the compiler are stored under the *target* directory.

Note that the source code directory also follows the convention that the package name elements match onto directories, however for the source code this is just a convention; it is not enforced (although many IDEs will complain if you do not follow this convention).

However, it is enforced for the *target* directory, the class `Person` must be compiled into `Person.class` file which must be stored within a directory structure `com/jjh/util`.

Finding a Package

All components in the package are relative to the contents of the `CLASSPATH` variable. This environment variable tells the Kotlin compiler and Virtual Machine runtime where to start looking for class definitions.

Thus, if the CLASSPATH variable is set to `C:\jjh\kotlin` then the following path is searched for the elements of the package `com.midmarsh.utils`:

```
c:\jjh\kotlin\com\midmarsh\utils
```

Notice how the whole path is a combination of the value in the CLASSPATH environment variable and the directory structure indicated by the package name.

All the files associated with the com.midmarsh.util package should therefore be in this directory.

The Kotlin compiler can be told where to place the .class files using the -d compiler option (which indicates the destination directory). For example, in the previous digram the source code is under src directory but the .class files are under the target directory, thus we might compile this code using:

```
kotlinc src/*.kt -d target
```

Which assumes that the kotlinc command is being issued in the directory above both the src and target directories. The '*/kt' indicates the files to compile.

The classpath does not need to be set via an environment variable, it is also possible to set it when a program is run using the command line option -cp or -classpath. This can be done wether you are using either the kotlin command or using the java command with the appropriate Kotlin libraries added to the classpath, for example:

```
java -classpath target;… MyApp
kotlin -classpath target;… MyAppKt
```

This is often hidden from the developer as IDEs such as IntelliJ handle this for you.

It is also command to create a Jar file that wraps all the directory structure and .class files up into a single file (which makes it much easier to deploy). This can be created using the jar command for example:

```
jar -cvf target/* MyApp.jar
```

Importing a Package

It is possible to access a type, function or property from one package in another in either by using a fully qualified name or by importing the type, function or property into the current file. We will look at both approaches in this section.

Using the Fully Qualified Name

A class `Person` defined in a package `com.jjh.util` has a fully qualified name:

- `com.jjh.util.Person`

This fully qualified name can be used to reference the class directly, for example:

```
val p1 = com.jjh.util.Person("John", 55)
```

This allows code in a separate package to access the definition of the class `Person` and create a new instance of that class. The same is true for objects, functions and top level properties. For example let us assume that there is a function `printer(Person)` defined in the same `com.jjh.util` package then we could reference that via:

```
com.jjh.util.printer(p1)
```

Importing a Type, Function or Property

Always referencing elements in other packages using their fully qualified names is certainly possible but it is rather long winded and would result in quiet verbose code.

In Kotlin it is possible to import objects, classes, enumerated types, interfaces, functions and properties from one package into another packaging using the `import` statement.

The `import` statement follows any package declaration in a file and comes before any type, function or property declarations.

An example of importing the class `Person` from the package `com.jjh.util` into a package `com.jjh.payroll` is given below:

```
package com.jjh.payroll

import com.jjh.util.Person
```

This makes the class `Person` directly accessible within the current file within the package `com.jjh.payroll`. Within this file the type `com.jjh.util.Person` can be referenced just using the name `Person`.

Importing does not affect the size of the class file being created as importing is actually a visibility thing; it does not bring the definition of the class Person into the current file; it only makes it visible.

In addition importing a class, function or property into a file only makes it visible within that file; it is not made visible to the package as a whole. Any other files in the same package must import their own elements as required.

Import Options

There are in fact several ways and things that can be imported. You can import a specific type, function or property. This is the example illustrated in the previous section for the class Person, here are some other examples:

```
import com.jjh.util.Person      // import the class Person
import com.jjh.util.MyObject     // import an object

// import top level property MAX
import com.jjh.util.MAX

// import a function prettyPrint
import com.jjh.util.prettyPrint

// import public elements from the package
import com.jjh.util.*
```

As the above examples show you can import anything from a package including objects, classes, properties and functions. It is also possible to import all public elements in a package using the *asterisk* (*) wild card.

It is also possible to import member functions and properties from within an object and then reference them directly, for example given an object Course with a property present, you can write:

```
import com.jjh.util.Course.present
```

The above code *imports* the property present from the object Course in the package com.jjh.util. If this is done then within the rest of the file it is possible to merely reference the property present to get to the property; it is not necessary to prefix it with the name of the object.

It is also possible to import all elements from an object using the asterisk (*) wildcard, for example:

```
import com.jjh.util.Course.*
```

Now all public *properties* and *member functions* are accessible within the current file.

You can also import values from within an enumerated type, for example:

```
import com.jjh.util.VehicleTypes.SUV
```

It is now possible to access the enum value SUV directly in the current file.

Dealing with Name Clashes

In some cases you might find that the name of a package element (such as a class or object) clashes with the name of another element in another package. In such situations you can either resort to using fully qualified names as these ensure that even if the class Person is defined in a package com.jjh.util and a package com.staff then their fully qualified named will be different, for example:

```
val p1 = com.jjh.util.Person()
val p2 = com.staff.Person()
```

Here the use of fully qualified names completely differentiates between the two classes.

However, having to use fully qualified names is quiet long and laborious; Kotlin provides an alternative, you can use an *alias* for a class so that any potential clashes are avoided. This is done by appending an as<newName> to the end of the import statement. For example:

```
import com.jjh.util.Person as User
import com.staff.Person
```

In the above example the class com.jjh.util.Person will be know as User in the current file, while the class com.staff.Person can be referenced just using Person.

Kotlin Default Imports

Several packages are imported by default into your code by the Kotlin compiler, these are listed below:

- `java.lang` provides access to default Java types such as String and is only available when Kotlin is being executed using the JVM runtime environment.
- `kotlin.jvm` Functions and annotations specific to the Kotlin Java platform.
- `kotlin` Core functions and types.
- `kotlin.annotation` Library support for Kotlin annotations.
- `kotlin.collections` Collection types
- `kotlin.comparisons` Helper functions for creating Comparators (since 1.1)
- `kotlin.io` API for files and streams
- `kotlin.ranges` ranges and progressions library
- `kotlin.sequences` lazily evaluated collections
- `kotlin.text` functions for text and regular expressions.

Visibility Modifiers

All the components in a package are *public* by default. That is, they are visible anywhere that the package is accessible. However, this is just the default. You can change the visibility of an object, class, interface, enumerated type, constructor, member function, function, top level and member properties by using a *modifier* keyword before the declaration keyword.

There are four visibility modifiers:

- `public` This is the *default* for all package elements as well as for member functions and properties. No explicit modifier is required to declare something as public. However the keyword `public` does exist and can be applied to any element although it is redundant.
- `private` The effect of the `private` keyword depends on where it is being applied, there are two situations in which you can mark somethings private:

  - *private top level elements* such as classes, objects, interfaces, enumerated types, functions and properties are only accessible in current file,
  - *private members elements* elements (such as constructors, properties or member functions) are only accessible in same class or object.

- `protected` Member functions or properties can be marked as `protected` which indicates that they are only accessible to the *current class* and *subclasses*. They are not accessible anywhere else. Note that the subclasses can be defined anywhere in any package. Also note that it is not possible to mark top level package elements as protected; that is you cannot mark a top level class as protected.
- `internal` This indicates that the associated element is only accessible within the same *module*. Modules are used by developers within the IntelliJ IDE to help them organise larger, more complex systems. They are frequently used within Android applications to help organise the code base.

It should also be noted that although a property can have one visibility, its *setter* function can have a different visibility. The *getter* functions alway have the same visibility as the property. However, the *setter* functions can have a different visibility; a common idiom is to define a property that is a `var` with the *getter* being public but the *setter* being private to a particular scope (such as a class, object or package). For example:

```
var name: String
    private set(value) = field = value
```

The above declares a public property `name`. However although it is a `var` the setter is marked as private. Thus the property is *read-only* externally to wherever it is defined but *read-write* internally. Note that we did not have to explicitly specify the `get()` function as that is implied by the definition of the property.

Visibility Modifiers and Constructors

It is possible to apply a visibility modifier to a constructor. However you must use the long hand form of declaring a constructor. That is you must explicitly use the keyword `constructor` when defining the constructor. If you do that you can *prefix* the `constructor` keyword with a visibility modifier, for example:

```
package com.jjh.util

class Session private constructor(val id: String)
```

This indicates that the class `Person` can only be instantiated from within the class.

This may at first seem nonsensical; however it is usual that such a class would have an associated *companion object* with a factory member function on it that is used to create instances of the class. This is illustrated below.

```
class Session private constructor(val id: Int) {

    // Companion (singleton) object
    companion object {
        private var count = 0
        fun create(): Session {
            count++
            return Session(count)
        }
    }

    override fun toString(): String {
        return "UserSession($id)"
    }

}

fun main() {
    val session1 = Session.create()
    println(session1)
    val session2 = Session.create()
    println(session2)
}
```

In this example, the Session class has a companion object that defines a create() member function. This member function can create instances of the class Session as it is defined within the class Session and thus has access to the private constructor.

However, no code outside of the class can access the constructor. In this case it is done to ensure that each Session created has a unique id.

Online Resources

See the Kotlin reference documentation for:

- https://kotlinlang.org/docs/reference/packages.html Kotlin packages.
- https://kotlinlang.org/spec/packages-and-imports.html Kotlin specification packages and imports.
- http://kotlin-quick-reference.com/95-R-imports-packages.html Kotlin imports and packages quick reference.

Exercise

The aim of this exercise is to create a package for the classes you have been developing.

You should move your `Account`, `CurrentAccount`, `DepositAccount` and `BalanceError` classes into a separate package called `fintech.accounts`. This means that you will need to create the appropriate directory structure/package structure in your IDE. You will also need to add the package declaration to the start of each file within the package.

Save the `main()` function into a separate package, for example called `fintech.main`. In this package store your `main()` function in a file called `Main.kt`. You will now need to import the account classes from the `fintech.accounts` package into `Main.kt`.

Your test application will now look like:

```kotlin
package fintech.main

import fintech.accounts.*

fun main() {
    val acc1 = CurrentAccount("123", "John",
                                        10.05, -100.00)
    val acc2 = DepositAccount("345", "Denise",
                                        23.55, 0.5)
    val acc3 =
        InvestmentAccount("567",
                                        "Phoebe",
                                        12.45,

InvestmentAccountTypes.HighRisk)

    println(acc1)
    println(acc2)
    println(acc3)

    acc1.deposit(23.45)
    acc1.withdraw(12.33)

    println("balance: ${acc1.balance}")
    acc1.withdraw(300.00)
    println("balance: ${acc1.balance}")

    AbstractAccount.printInstancesCreated()
}
```

Chapter 16
Nested/Inner Types

Introduction

Nested and inner types are types that are defined with the scope of an outer (or top-level) type. This chapter introduces nested as well as inner types and considers where and when they can be defined.

What are Nested/Inner Types

Nested types can be defined within:

- Classes, objects, enumerated types and interfaces.

The nested types defined within another type can be:

- Classes, objects, interfaces and enumerated types.

All of these types can be defined inside another, top level type. They are not part of the outer type per say but are part of the namespace created by the outer type.

Inner types are different to nested types. An Inner type is a type defined within the scope of another type and is part of that type. You can define an inner classes and anonymous objects within a class, object, enumerated type or interface.

Additionally, you can define function and member function level inner classes and anonymous objects. These are classes and anonymous objects that are defined within a function or member function.

The attributes that a nested/inner type possess will depend on whether they are *nested* types or *member inner* types or function/*member function inner* types.

© The Author(s), under exclusive license to Springer Nature Switzerland AG 2021
J. Hunt, *Beginner's Guide to Kotlin Programming*,
https://doi.org/10.1007/978-3-030-80893-8_16

Nested Types

A *nested* top level type (class, object, enum or interface) is exactly like a normal top level type, except that it has been placed within an existing type. Such types can be used in the same way as any other top level type.

Thus defining nested types within an existing type is really a *namespace* thing. That is nested types are grouped together within an outer type for convenience and may be treated like any normal type. Although, they must be referenced either via their outer type or imported directly using the import statement, for example import `outerClassName.innerClass-Name`.

Thus such types may be referenced by program elements outside of the top level type. This means that:

- instances can be created from nested classes,
- nested interfaces can be used with objects and classes,
- nested objects can be referenced,
- nested enumerated types can be accessed,
- nested abstract classes can be extended.

Nested classes and objects can implement any interfaces and extend any required class.

Some examples of top level nested types are given below:

```
package com.midmarsh.inner

class Util {

    // Top level nested class defined within
    // the scope of Util namespace
    class Printer {
        fun print(msg: String) {
            println(this.javaClass.name + " - " + msg)
        }
    }


    // Top level interface defined within the scope
    // of the Util namespace
    interface Printable {
        fun convert(): String?
    }
```

```
    // Top level object defined within the scope
    // of the Util namespace
    object Session {
        val id = 2
        fun doSomething() {
            println("Do Something")
        }
    }

    // Abstract top level class defined within the scope
    // of the Util namespace
    abstract class DefaultPrintable : Printable {
        abstract val name: String?
    }
}
```

The class Util acts as the top level class that contains *four* nested types. In this case there is a:

- nested class Printer,
- nested interface Printable,
- nested object Session and
- nested abstract class DefaultPrintable.

To reference any of the nested types they must either be referenced using their fully qualified name, for example:

```
val printer = com.midmarsh.inner.Util.Printer()
```

Or if the com.midmarsh.inner package has been imported, then the nested types can be referenced via the name of the outer class:

```
import com.midmarsh.inner.*
val printer = Util.Printer()
```

Alternatively the members of the Util class can be imported directly either using the wildcard asterisk format:

```
import com.midmarsh.inner.Util.*

fun main() {
    Session.doSomething()
}
```

A final option is to specifying the elements from the `Util` class that should be imported:

```
import com.midmarsh.inner.Util.Session

fun main() {
    Session.doSomething()
}
```

As previously mentioned, it is not only classes that can have nested types; enumerated types, objects and interfaces can have them as well. The following illustrates an object that contains a set of nested types:

```
object MyObject {
    class Author(val name: String)
    interface Reviewable {
        fun review(): BooleanArray
    }
    object InnerObject {
        fun prettyPrint() {
            println("prettyPrint")
        }
    }
    enum class DaysOfWeek {
        MONDAY, TUESDAY, WEDNESDAY, THURSDAY
    }
}
```

In this case the object `MyObject` contains a nested class, interface, object and an enum class (enumerated type).

To complete the set here is an example of an interface containing a set of nested types:

```
interface Processable {
    class InnerClass(val id: String)
    object InnerObject{
        val name: String = "Title"
    }
    fun doSomething(): Boolean
}
```

This interface definition contains a nested class, a nested object and a member function signature that will need to be provided by any class implementing this interface. This is illustrated below:

```
class Processor: Processable {
    override fun doSomething(): Boolean {
        println("DoSomething")
        return true
    }
}
```

Note that the class `Processor` does not have access to the `InnerClass` nor the `InnerObject` directly. To access them it must user the `Processable` namespace, for example `Processable.InnerObject`.

Finally, the following code illustrates the same use of nested types within an enumerated type:

```
enum class DaysOfWeek {
    MONDAY, TUESDAY, WEDNESDAY, THURSDAY, FRIDAY;
    object Util {
        const val DAY_TOTAL = 5
    }
    class Printer {
        override fun toString() = "Printer()"
    }
    interface Printable {
        fun convert(): String?
    }
}
```

Member Inner Classes/Anonymous Objects

Inner member classes and anonymous objects are defined within the scope of an existing type but outside of any member function or `init{}` block.

The keyword `inner` is used to indicate that an *inner* class (rather than a nested class) is being defined. This is important as missing out the keyword `inner` changes the type being defined significantly.

An inner class or anonymous object is defined at the *member level* of an existing type. They possess very specific attributes which include being:

- defined within the scope of an existing type including classes, objects, enumerated types and interfaces,
- able to access the outer class/object properties and member functions. This is also true of an member inner type within an interfaces where the inner type can access the concrete member functions of the interface,

- able to access outer class "this" variable. This can be done using `this@<outerclassname>` syntax,
- able to be an interface specification,
- able to have default (public), private, protected or internal visibility,
- able to be an abstract class,
- able to be an anonymous object.

For example, in the following class Calculator, an inner member class is defined that is used to perform a calculation as a separate `Worker` instance.

```
class Calculator(private val value: Int) {
    private var count = 0
    var result = 0
        private set

    // Inner class defined within the scope of Calculator
    inner class Worker(val id: Int) {
        fun performCalculation() {
            for (i in 0 until value) {
                result += i
            }
        }
    }

    val worker: Worker
        get() = Worker(count++)

}
```

The class `Calculator` has a private constructor property val `value`. It also has a var `result` that has a private `set()` function. Note that this means that the `result` property is a *read-only* property to anything defined outside of the `Calculator` class but is a *read–write* property internally to the class.

The `Calculator` class also has a `count` private var property that is used when creating `Worker` instances in the `get()` function of the `worker` property. Notice that this means that from outside of this class worker, it appears to be a *read-only* property, however internally to the class the *getter* function generates a new `Worker` each time the client code calls `get()`.

The `Worker` class is an *inner* class that has its own `id` val property and a member function `performCalculation()`.

The `performCalculation()` member function accesses the outer class's `value` property and updates the `result` property of the outer class. The inner class can do this because, although the `value` property is a private property and the `result` *setter* function is marked as `private`, the *inner* class is defined within the scope of the outer class and thus has direct access to all the private elements of the class.

The following program uses the `Calculator` class and illustrates how the `Worker` can be accessed:

```kotlin
fun main() {
    val calc = Calculator(5)
    val worker = calc.worker
    worker.performCalculation()
    println("calc.result: " + calc.result)
}
```

When this program is run the output is:

```
calc.result: 10
```

As a further example, the following code illustrates defining an inner anonymous object within a class. This is also able to access the outer class properties and member functions:

```kotlin
class Calculator(private val value: Int) {
    val p = object {
        val x = 10
        val y = value
    }
}
```

Member Function Inner Classes/Objects

These are classes or anonymous objects that are defined within a member function.

They have the scope of the enclosing block, thus they may only be visible for part of a member function's execution. They can access the enclosing types properties and member functions and any local vals, vars or parameters.

An example of a member function inner class is given below:

```kotlin
object CalculateFib {
    fun printFibSequence(number: Int) {
        val separator = ","

        // Class defined within the scope of a member function
        class Fib {
            fun printFib(n: Int) {
                var n1 = 0
                var n2 = 1
                var n3 = 0
                for (i in 2 until n) {
                    n3 = n1 + n2
                    print("$separator $n3")
                    n1 = n2
                    n2 = n3
                }
            }
        }
        print("0 $separator 1") // printing 0 and 1

        val fib = Fib()
        fib.printFib(number)
    }
}
```

In this example, the member function `printFibSequence()` is given a number to generate the fibonacci sequence for. In mathematics the Fibonacci numbers form a sequence called the *Fibonacci sequence*. Within the fibonacci sequence each number is the sum of the two preceding ones, starting from 0 and 1. The beginning of the sequence is thus: 0, 1, 1, 2, 3, 5, 8, 13, 21, 34 etc.

To calculate the fibonacci sequence the `printFibSequence()` member function defines a member function inner class called `Fib`. This member function inner class has a single member function `printFib(Int)` this member function calculates the fibonacci sequence and prints out each number generated. To do this it references the separate local val defined within the `printFibSequence()` outer member function.

A simple example using the CalculatorFib object is given

```kotlin
fun main(args: Array<String>) {
    CalculateFib.printFibSequence(10)
}
```

The output from this program is:

```
0, 1, 1, 2, 3, 5, 8, 13, 21, 34
```

Function Inner Classes/Objects

It is also possible to define function inner classes and anonymous objects. These are classes and anonymous objects defined within the scope of a function. As such they can access any local vals or vars and parameters available within the function.

A simple example of a function level inner class is given below using the `main()` function:

```kotlin
fun main() {
    class Person(val name: String) {
        override fun toString() = "Person($name)"
    }
    val p = Person("John")
    println(p)
}
```

In this case the class `Person` is only accessible from within the function `main()`.

Online Resources

See the Kotlin reference documentation for:

- https://kotlinlang.org/docs/reference/nested-classes.html. Nested and Inner classes.

Exercise

- The aim of this exercise is to create an inner class `DefaultTransaction` to represent a financial transaction. A `DefaultTransaction` instance will be returned by the `deposit()` and `withdraw()` member functions to represent the financial transaction that has taken place.
- A `DefaultTransaction` should possess:
- the amount to be deposited or withdrawn,
- whether it was a deposit or withdrawal,
- the local date and time at which the depositor or withdrawal took place (you can use `java.time.LocalDateTime`) for this,
- the resulting balance at the point that the depositor or withdrawal occurred.
- a `toString()` member function should be defined as appropriate.

This should be defined as an inner class within the `Account` class that implements the `Transaction` interface.

The transaction interface is given below.

```
interface Transaction {
    val amount: Double
    val type: String
    val datetime: LocalDateTime
    val transactionBalance: Double
}
```

Note that the member functions in the `Account` interface will need to be updated to return a Transaction.

Note in the `CurrentAccount` you will need to decide what to return if the withdrawal will take the customer over the over draft limit. For now you can set the amount for the transaction to 0.0 and the type to "failed–exceeded overdraft".

Finally you should now be able to print the result of calling deposit or withdraw on any account:

```
println(acc1.deposit(23.45))
println(acc1.withdraw(12.33))

println("balance: ${acc1.balance}")
println(acc1.withdraw(300.00))
println("balance: ${acc1.balance}")
```

The output from this code is:

```
Transaction(23.45, deposit, 2021-04-26T16:11:48.975260,
transactionBalance=56.95)
Transaction(12.33, withdrawal, 2021-04-26T16:11:48.977125,
transactionBalance=8.840000000000002)
balance: 21.17
Withdrawal would exceed your overdraft limit
Transaction(0.0, failed - exceeded overdraft,
2021-04-26T16:11:48.977300, transactionBalance=21.17)
balance: 21.17
```

Chapter 17
Data Classes

Introduction

We have now explored Kotlin classes, nested classes and inner classes, however there is another type of class in Kotlin called a Data Class.

Data classes can be used to represent data-oriented concepts. That is concept that represent data but tend not to have much related functionality. Such a class might contain several properties but other than member functions for equality or string conversions they do not contain any behaviour. This chapter presents Data Classes.

Defining Data Classes

A data class is defined in the same way as a normal class, with the addition of the keyword data placed in front of the class keyword. For example:

```
data class Person(val name: String = "Denise",
                  var age: Int = 0)
```

The above definition creates a new *data* class called Person that has two constructor properties name and age. This illustrates that the constructor properties can be vals or vars, although it is far more common for all the constructor properties in a data class to be vals.

It is not possible to define plain constructor parameters in data class.

In fact there are several effects of marking the class as a *data* class as well as restricting the constructor parameter types, these are:

- The class definition must start with the keyword data.
- It must have at least one constructor property.
- All constructor parameters must be vals or vars.

© The Author(s), under exclusive license to Springer Nature Switzerland AG 2021
J. Hunt, *Beginner's Guide to Kotlin Programming*,
https://doi.org/10.1007/978-3-030-80893-8_17

- A default implementation of `toString()` member function will be provided any the compiler. This default `toString()` provides the name of the data class and the constructor properties.
- A default value based implementation of the `equals()` member function (used by `==` and `!=` operators). In this compiler provided implementation equality is based on the primary constructor properties and their values. It thus provides a form of structural equality based purely on the constructor properties.
- A default `copy()` member function to create a copy of an object. This is used to create a copy of the data class based on the constructor properties. The `copy()` function allows one or more of the constructor property values to be overridden for the new instance.
- A default implementation of the `hashcode()` member function. This is a unique code used to represent a unique instance in memory and which is suitable for use in a hash map data structure (which relies on a key to value mapping).
- Data classes cannot be abstract, open, sealed or inner classes.
- Data classes can extend any appropriate superclass.
- Data classes are implicitly closed/final and cannot be extended.
- The super class of a data class *cannot* define a member function `copy()`.
- Data classes can implement any number of interfaces.

Another example of a data class is given below, this is an immutable class (that is once created the values held cannot be changed). It is immutable because all the properties defined for the data class are vals and thus are read-only properties. This is a very common pattern for data classes:

```
data class GameContent(val x: Double, val y: Double)
```

The `GameContent` data class can be used within a program in exactly the same way as any other class, for example:

```
fun main() {
    val inst1 = GameContent(10.0, 10.0)
    println(inst1)
    val inst2 = GameContent(10.0, 10.0)
    // uses default implementation of toString()
    println(inst2)
    println("x: ${inst2.x}, obj2.y: ${inst2.y}")
    // uses default implementation of equals()
    println(inst1 == inst2)
    // Uses default implementation of hashCode()
    println(inst1.hashCode())
}
```

In this program two instances of the data class `GameContent` are created. Both are initialised with the values 10.0 for their x and y coordinates. The program then illustrates some of the features listed above.

- When a data class instance is printed the default `toString()` generated for the data class will print out the name of the data class and the values of x and y.
- The equality operator (==) will use the `equals()` member function which was generated by the compiler for the data class.
- The `hashCode()` member function was also generated for the data class.

The output from this program is:

```
GameContent(x=10.0, y=10.0)
GameContent(x=10.0, y=10.0)
x: 10.0, obj2.y: 10.0
true
75497472
```

Data Classes with Non Constructor Properties

Data classes can be defined with any number of member level properties such as that defined in the data class `Ship` below:

```
data class Ship(val x: Double,
                val y: Double) {
    // following property is not used by
    // toString, equals, hashcode etc.
    var image: String = "ship.png"
}
```

However, it is only the constructor properties that are used in the `toString()`, `copy()`, `equals()` and `hashCode()` member functions. Thus in this case the value of the `image` property will be ignored by all of these member functions.

This is illustrated below where two instances of the data class `Ship` are created. Their constructor parameters are equal, however the `image` property of the first ship has been changed.

```
fun main() {
    val ship1 = Ship(10.0, 10.0)
    println(ship1)
    println(ship1.image)
    ship1.image = "default.png"
    println(ship1)
    val ship2 = Ship(10.0, 10.0)
    println(ship1 == ship2)
}
```

The output from this program is:

```
Ship(x=10.0, y=10.0)
ship.png
Ship(x=10.0, y=10.0)
true
```

This output illustrates that:

1. The `image` property is not included in the `toString()` implementation
2. Even though the `image` property is different for `ship1` and `ship2`, the `equals()` member function still thinks they have structural equality.

Data Classes and Inheritance

Data classes can extend any *open* class. As usual this means that they will inherit all the properties and member functions defined in the parent class. They can also override any open properties or member functions etc. A simple example is given below:

```
open class GameEntity

data class GamePiece(val x: Double,
                     val y: Double): GameEntity()
```

However, a data class is implicitly *closed*/final and therefore cannot itself be extended.

Data Classes and Interfaces

Data classes can implement any number of interfaces. As usual this means that the data class must implement any abstract members defined in the interface and will inherit any concrete member functions defined in the interface. For example:

```
data class GamePiece(val x: Double,
                     val y: Double): Cloneable
```

Or an example with multiple interfaces:

```
data class GamePiece(val x: Double,
                     val y: Double): Cloneable, Serializable
```

Copying Data Classes

It is useful to be able to make copies of data classes, particularly as the default pattern is to define immutable data classes.

The Kotlin compiler provides a default implementation of the `copy()` member function that allows you to create a copy of a data class instance while overriding one or more property values (even if they are vals).

This is illustrated below for the data class `Ship` we presented earlier:

```kotlin
fun main() {
    ship1.image = "default.png"
    println("ship1: $ship1")
    println("ship1.image: ${ship1.image}")
    val otherShip = ship1.copy(x = 20.0)
    println("othership: $otherShip")
    println("otherShip.image: ${otherShip.image}")
}
```

In this program we make a copy of the original `ship1` using the `copy()` member function and overriding the value held in the property x. The means that we end up with two instances of the data class ship; `ship1` and `otherShip`.

The `otherShip` has the value `20.0` for the property x which was supplied when the copy was made. The value for the property y however was copied from the original `ship1` and is thus `10.0`.

However, the property `image` was not involved in the `copy()` operation and thus the "default.png" String was not copied over. This means that the `otherShip` still has the default value provided when the data class was instantiated.

The output is shown below:

```
ship1: Ship(x=10.0, y=10.0)
ship1.image: default.png
othership: Ship(x=20.0, y=10.0)
otherShip.image: ship.png
```

Data Classes and De-structuring

It is possible to unpack values from data classes into distinct variables. This can be done at the point that the receiving variables are defined using the syntax:

```
val/var (<variable-list>) = data-class-instance
```

However, this only works for constructor properties (any member level properties are not included).

An example of doing this for the Ship data class is given below:

```
fun main() {
    val ship = Ship(10.0, 10.0)
    val (x, y) = ship
    println("x $x, y $y")
}
```

In this case two vals are being created called x and y; they will be populated with the constructor property values held in ship. Note that the names of the vals are not significant as the values are extracted/restructured based on their positions in the constructor rather than on the property names.

The output generated from this code is:

```
x 10.0, y 10.0
```

The variables used to hold the extracted values must be declared at the point that the destructing happens but can be a val or a var, for example:

```
fun main() {
    val ship = Ship(10.0, 10.0)
    val otherShip = ship.copy(x = 20.0)
    var (a, b) = otherShip
    println("a $a, b $b")
}
```

The output from this program is:

```
a 20.0, b 10.0
```

It is also possible to indicate that you are not interested in certain values using the underbar syntax (_). This is necessary as the values are extracted based on their position, thus if we are only interested in the y value for the ship we still need to indicate that it is the second property defined within the data class constructor. However using the underbar (_) we can indicate this and ignore the value in x, for example:

```
val (_, y1) = ship
println("y1: $y1")
```

The output from this code snippet is:

```
y1: 10.0
```

Exercise

The aim of this exercise is to create a data class to represent a Customer for our *fintech* system.

In this simple example, the Customer data class will have a name, an address and an email. All three of these properties will be vals and will hold Strings.

You should be able to create a Customer using:

```
val customer1 = Customer("John",
                         "10 High Street",
                         "john@gmail.com")
```

Next change the type of the account holder property to Customer.

You will now need to create a customer for each account instance, for example:

```
val customer1 = Customer("John",
                         "10 High Street",
                         "john@gmail.com")
val acc1 = CurrentAccount("123", customer1, 10.05, -100.00)

val customer2 = Customer("Denise",
                         "11 Main Street",
                         "denise@gmail.com")
val acc2 = DepositAccount("345", customer2, 23.55, 0.5)

val customer3 = Customer("Phoebe",
                         "12 Market Square",
                         "phoebe@gmail.com")
val acc3 =
    InvestmentAccount("567",
                      customer3,
                      12.45,
                      InvestmentAccountTypes.HighRisk)
```

Chapter 18
Sealed and Inline Classes and Typealias

Introduction

There are two further types of classes in Kotlin specifically Sealed Classes and inline Classes. This chapter will explore each of these. The chapter will conclude by introducing type aliases.

Sealed Classes

Sealed classes are useful for managing closely related hierarchies.

Sealed Classes in Kotlin 1.4

For Kotlin 1.4 and earlier versions of the language, a sealed class is a special type of class with the following properties:

- A sealed class is a class that can only be extended within the *same file* that it is defined in. That is only the classes and objects within the *same file* as the sealed class can extend it. Note that sub-sub classes can be defined anywhere as they only indirectly inherit from the sealed class.
- Sealed classes are implicitly *abstract* and therefore it is not possible to instantiate a sealed class directly.
- A sealed class is implicitly *open* and as such it is possible to extend a sealed class using a class or object.
- The sealed class can be referenced anywhere that it is visible so that it can be used as the type for parameters, vals, vars or the return type for functions/member functions.
- A sealed class is indicated using the keyword sealed before the keyword class.

© The Author(s), under exclusive license to Springer Nature Switzerland AG 2021   279
J. Hunt, *Beginner's Guide to Kotlin Programming*,
https://doi.org/10.1007/978-3-030-80893-8_18

An example of a very simple sealed class is given below along with the subclasses that extend it within the *same file*:

```
sealed class Trade

class EquityTrade(val name: String) : Trade()
class FxTrade(val currency1: String,
              val currency2: String) : Trade()
class InterestRateSwap(val fixedRate: Double,
                       val floatingRate: Double) : Trade()
class Swaption(val data: String) : Trade()
```

In this case a simple sealed class called Trade has been defined. In practice this class acts as a *marker class* as it provides no properties nor does it define any member functions.

The sealed class Trade is then extended by the classes EquityTrade, FxTrade, InterestRateSwap and Swaption. Assuming that this is the entire contents of the file then we know that there are no other direct subclasses of the sealed class Trade within the code base.

Sealed classes can have a public primary and any number of auxiliary constructors, they can have constructor and member level properties and member functions.

The following code extends the definition of the Trade sealed class with a constructor property id, a counterParty var member level property and a member function printId():

```
sealed class Trade(protected val id: Int=0) {
    var counterParty: String = ""
    fun printId() {
        println(id)
    }
}

class EquityTrade(val name: String) : Trade()
class FxTrade(val currency1: String,
              val currency2: String) : Trade()
class InterestRateSwap(val fixedRate: Double,
                       val floatingRate: Double) : Trade()
class Swaption(val data: String) : Trade()
```

Although the Trade sealed type can only be extended in the *current file*, it can be used as a type in other files. The following code resides in a separate file but is able to reference the Trade type as a parameter type for the function describe(Trade):

```
    fun describe(x: Trade): String {
        return when (x) {
            is EquityTrade -> "EquityTrade"
            is FxTrade -> "FxTrade"
            is InterestRateSwap -> "An InterestRateSwap"
            is Swaption -> "A Swaption"
            else -> "Unknown"
        }
    }

    fun main() {
        println(describe(EquityTrade("IBM")))
        println(describe(FxTrade("GBP", "USD")))
        println(describe(InterestRateSwap(5.0, 3.4)))
        println(describe(Swaption("Bermudan")))
    }
```

The output from this program is:

```
            EquityTrade
            FxTrade
            An InterestRateSwap
            A Swaption
```

It is not only classes that can extend a sealed class. The following example illustrates how a set of objects can be used to create singleton instances of a sealed class Genre:

```
        sealed class Genre

        object Fiction : Genre() {
            override fun toString() = "Fiction"
        }

        object Technical : Genre() {
            override fun toString() = "Technical"
        }

        object History : Genre() {
            override fun toString() = "History"
        }
```

Sealed Classes and Interfaces in Kotlin 1.5

Kotlin 1.5 also introduces the concept of a sealed interface and relaxes the restrictions on sealed classes. From Kotlin 1.5 onwards a sealed class can be implemented within the same module rather than just within the same file. This means that if your application is defined completely within a single module (the default) then a sealed class is just like any other class. However, if your application is comprised of multiple modules (as may be the case with an Android application) then a sealed class is only accessible within the current module.

As from Kotlin 1.5 it is also possible to define a sealed interface. The sealed interface can be implemented by any class, data class or object defined in the same module. A sealed interface is implemented using the keyword sealed before the keyword interface, for example:

```
sealed interface Vehicle

object PetrolCar : Vehicle
class DieselCar: Vehicle
interface ElectricCar : Vehicle
```

Note that in Kotlin 1.5 sealed interfaces are considered experimental so may change in later versions of the language.

Inline Classes

Kotlin 1.3 introduced a new type of class called the inline class. This type of class was experimental in Kotlin 1.3, was in beta in Kotlin 1.4 and was stable (fully released) in Kotlin 1.5.

An inline class can be used to represent *value* style classes. A value class is a type where the actual value being represented by the class is held directly by a variable, at runtime (within the JVM) rather than needing to access that value via a reference (an address in memory). This can be more efficient for simple types like Int.

Examples of value types include Booelan, Int and Double which can have the values true, false, 32, 45.7 etc. Inline classes effectively allow developers to create user defined value types that will be as efficient as native Kotlin value types at runtime, but allow more semantic meaning to be defined for developers, for their code and for those maintaining the code base.

To define an inline class in Kotlin it is necessary prefix the keyword class by the keyword inline.

Inline Class Constraints

Inline (value) classes are treated as special by the Kotlin compiler. That is, the compiler will determine if it can inline the value held by the class directly. This avoids the need to allocate runtime instances and is thus more efficient and faster (as no allocation must be made and no reference must be followed).

To ensure that the compiler can treat an instance of the class in this way it is necessary for the programmer to ensure that no instance allocation is performed within the type. Thus an inline class cannot hold within itself a reference to a non-Value type (that is it cannot hold a reference to an instance of the class Person).

To be an inline class the compiler must also ensure that the class being defined:

- has a single public val parameter for the underlying type (that is the fundamental or basic type being wrapped),
- has an underlying type that must be one of Byte, Short, Int, Long, Float, Double, String or Boolean,
- is immutable by nature (that is it should not change itself but return a new instance whenever a change in value is required),
- *cannot* have any auxiliary constructors,
- *cannot* define any nested types such as classes, objects or interfaces,
- is not used in tests used to determine their type,
- must not override the equals() or hashcode() member functions,
- cannot have any initialisation blocks (i.e. no init{ } blocks).

However, they can have

- any member functions as required,
- properties that do not use a backing field.

Simple Inline Class Example

The following inline class meets the criteria defined in the last section. That is, the inline class Name has a single *val* property value of type String, it is marked with the keyword inline, it has one property length which is defined relative to the value property (and thus does not use a backing field) and has a simple member function greet().

```
inline class Name(val value: String) {
    val length: Int
        get() = value.length

    fun greet() {
        println("Hello, $value")
    }
}
```

The following simple application illustrates how this class may be used:

```
fun main() {
    val name = Name("Kotlin")
    name.greet()
    println(name.length)
}
```

In this example, we create a new instances of the Name class and store it in a local val name. We then invoke the member function greet() and access the property length. Note that this looks very much as it would if name held *a normal class*. The result is then printed out. The effect of running this application is shown below:

```
Hello, Kotlin
6
```

Interestingly the compiler actually replaces the references to Name with the primitive held within the instance at compile time. The method greet() will be replaced with the String "Hello, Kotlin" and name.length will be repeated with "Kotlin".length. Thus there is virtually no overhead in using the inline Name class compared with using the String class directly.

This raises the question "Why bother?". The answer is two fold:

- Name is more semantically meaningful than *String*. That is *String* is a generic way of representing a set of characters. The inline class Name represents the concept of the name of something.
- Name also allows member functions to be defined that allow semantically meaningful operations to be provided that can also indicate what is being done at a higher level of abstraction than the basic type String would allow.

Additional Inline Class Concepts

Inline classes are implicitly treated as *closed*/final classes, thus ensuring that they cannot be extended by other classes. That is, it is not possible to combine the keywords inline and open together.

This is important as it restricts the need for polymorphism and thus allows the compiler to inline the values being represented.

Inline *classes* are implicitly assumed to have structural *equality* and *hashcodes*. That is, their equals() and hashcode() member functions are treated as being defined as:

```
    override fun equals(other: Any?): Boolean {
            return when (other) {
                null -> false
                is <sameType> -> (other.value == value)
                else -> false
            }
        }
    }
    fun hashCode() = value.hashCode
```

Where value equates to the underlying property (such as String, Double, or Int). In other words if the underliers have the same value then the value types are equal otherwise they are not equal. In addition the *hashcode* of a value type of the *hashcode* of its underlier.

Typealias

A type alias allows you to provide an alternative name for an existing type. It is used extensively to provide Kotlin like names for Java types. Within your own programs it can be used:

- to create domain specific names for existing types,
- to provide more meaningful name for generic types,
- or semantic names for function types.

To do this use the typealias keyword followed by the new name you want to give to a type. The syntax is:

```
    typealias <new-name> = <existing-name>
```

For example, the following code creates three type aliases:

```
    class Person(val name: String, val age: Int)
    data class Node(val value: Any)

    typealias Player = Person
    typealias NodeSet = Set<Node>
    typealias Test<T> = (T) -> Boolean
```

Within the code the developer can now refer to the class Player or to the collection NodeSet or the function type Test <T>.

However, this is just a programmer convenience, as it is an *alias* that only has meaning at compile time.

The compiler does not introduce a new type, instead it will replace the typealias with the actual name so that at runtime the code will use the class Person, the collection Set <Node> (which indicates this is a set of Nodes) and the function type (T) -> Boolean.

Chapter 19
Operator Overloading

Introduction

We will explore Operator Overloading in this chapter; what it is, how it works and why we want it.

Why Have Operator Overloading?

Operator overloading allows user defined *classes* to appear to have a natural way of using operators such as +, -, , > or == as well as logical operators such as & (and) and | (or).

This leads to more succinct and readable code as it is possible to write code such as:

```
val q1 = Quantity(5)
val q2 = Quantity(10)
val q3 = q1 + q2
```

It feels more natural for both developers and those reading the code. The alternative would be to create member functions such as add() and write code such as

```
val q1 = Quantity(5)
val q2 = Quantity(10)
val q3 = q1.add(q2)
```

Which semantically might mean the same thing but feel less *natural* to most developers.

© The Author(s), under exclusive license to Springer Nature Switzerland AG 2021
J. Hunt, *Beginner's Guide to Kotlin Programming*,
https://doi.org/10.1007/978-3-030-80893-8_19

Why Not Have Operator Overloading?

If operator overloading is such a good idea, why don't all programming languages support it? Interestingly Java does not support operator overloading!

One answer is because it can be abused! For example, what is the meaning of the following code:

```
val p1 = Person("John")
val p2 = Person("Denise")
val p3 = p1 + p2
```

It is not clear what '+' means in this context; in what way is Denise being added to John; does it imply they are getting married? If so, what is the result that is held in p3?

The problem here is that from a design perspective (which in this case may be purely intuitive but in other cases may relate to the intention of an application) the plus operator does not make sense for the type Person. However, there is nothing in the Kotlin language to indicate this and thus anyone can code any operator into any class!

As a general design principle; developers should follow the semantics of built-in types and thus should only implement those operators which are appropriate for the type being developed. For example, for arithmetic value types such as Quantity it makes perfect sense to provide a plus operator but for domain specific data-oriented types such as Person it does not.

Implementing Operator Overloading

To implement operators such as '+' in a custom or user defined class it is necessary to implement specific member functions that are then *mapped* to the arithmetic or logical operators used by users of the class.

These member functions are considered *special* in that they are pre-mapped by Kotlin and the Kotlin compiler will understand how to convert the + operator into the appropriate member function.

As an example, let us assume that we want to implement the '+' and '−' operators for our Quantity type. We also want our Quantity type to hold an actual value and be able to be converted into a string for printing purposes.

We can make the Quantity type a class or a data class. Although operators can be applied to either type of class we will make our Quantity type a *data* class as it will then automatically obtain member functions such as toString(), equals() and hashCode(). We will also make our Quantity data class *immutable* and thus it will use only vals to define its constructor properties. Both the use of a *data*

Introduction   289

class and the decision to make it *immutable* are common approaches when working
with classes such as `Quantity`.

To implement the '+' and '−' operators we need to provide two special member
functions one will provide the implementation of the '+' operator and one will provide
the implementation of the '−' operator. Such member functions will be prefixed with
the keyword `operator`:

- '+' operator is implemented by a member function with the signature
- **operator fun**plus(other: Quantity): Quantity
- '−' operator is implemented by a member function with the signature
- **operator fun**plus(other: Quantity): Quantity.

Where other represents another Quantity which will be either added to, or
subtracted from, the current Quantity instance.

The member functions will be mapped by the Kotlin compiler to the operators
'+' and '−'; such that if someone attempts to add two quantities together then the
plus(Quantity) member function will be called etc.

The definition of the class Quantity is given below:

```
data class Quantity(val value: Int) {
    operator fun plus(other: Quantity): Quantity =
                            Quantity(value + other.value)
    operator fun minus(other: Quantity): Quantity =
                            Quantity(value - other.value)
}
```

Using this class definition, we can create two instances of the type `Quantity`
and add them together:

```
fun main() {
    val q1 = Quantity(5)
    val q2 = Quantity(10)
    println("q1 = $q1, q2 = $q2")

    val q3 = q1 + q2
    println("q3 = $q3")
}
```

If we run this program we get:

```
q1 = Quantity(value=5), q2 = Quantity(value=10)
q3 = Quantity(value=15)
```

As the `Quantity` class is immutable, when two quantities are added tougher a
new instance of the class `Quantity` is created. This is analogous to how integers
work, if you add together $2+3$ then you get 5; neither 2 or 3 are modified however;

instead a new integer 5 is generated—this is an example of the general design principle; developers should follow the semantics of built-in types; `Quantity` instances act like numbers.

Overloading the Operator Member Functions

One issue with the current implementation of `Quantity` is that it is only possible to add two quantities together, what about if we want to add an Int to a `Quantity`?

To do this we will need to overload the `plus()` and `minus()` member functions. That is we will need to define additional versions of the `plus()` and `minus()` member functions that take different types of parameters such as `Int`, for example:

```
data class Quantity(val value: Int) {
    operator fun plus(other: Quantity): Quantity =
                        Quantity(value + other.value)
    operator fun minus(other: Quantity): Quantity =
                        Quantity(value - other.value)

    operator fun plus(increment: Int): Quantity =
                        Quantity(value + increment)
    operator fun minus(decrement: Int): Quantity =
                        Quantity(value - decrement)
}
```

In this second version of the `Quantity` class we have two versions of the `plus` member function and two version of `minus` member function. Each version takes a different type of parameter, one takes a `Quantity` the other takes an `Int`. This is a common thing to do to allow different types to be used with operators as required by your application.

This means we can now modify our application such that we can add an integer to a Quantity:

```
fun main() {
    val q1 = Quantity(5)
    val q2 = Quantity(10)
    println("q1 = $q1, q2 = $q2")

    val q3 = q1 + q2
    println("q3 = $q3")

    val q4 = q3 + 7
    println("q4 = $q4")
}
```

This program now generates the following output:

```
q1 = Quantity(value=5), q2 = Quantity(value=10)
q3 = Quantity(value=15)
q4 = Quantity(value=22)
```

Mutable Data Types

Not all types are naturally immutable and not all operators can be used with immutable types. For example, *increment* and *decrement* operators cannot be used with immutable types as they operate on the instance itself. That is the increment operator, when used with a var a, such as a++, is equivalent to writing a= a+ 1 which might be most naturally implemented as modifying the *current* value.

The data class Counter is defined to be mutable, that is its value can be changed directly.

```
data class Counter(var value: Int) {

    operator fun plusAssign(c: Counter) {
        value += c.value
    }

    operator fun minusAssign(c: Counter) {
        value += c.value
    }

    operator fun plus(other: Counter) {
        value = value + other.value
    }
    operator fun minus(other: Counter) {
        value = value - other.value
    }
    operator fun plus(other: Int) { value = value + other }
    operator fun minus(other: Int) { value = value - other }
}
```

This means that the operator member functions plus and minus are changed so that they do not return a value, instead they affect the current instance directly. It also means that we can now implement += and −+ related operator member functions. These are the plusAssign() and minusAssign() member functions.

We can now use these operators in a program with the Counter data class, for example:

```
fun main() {
    val c1 = Counter(1)
    val c2 = Counter(5)

    c2 += c1
    println("c2 += c1: $c2")
}
```

Here we are using the += operator which will call the plusAssign() operator member function and modify the value of the Counter referenced by c1.

The output from this program is:

```
c2 += c1: Counter(value=6)
```

Numerical Operators

There are five different numerical operators plus the rangeTo operator (represented by ..) that can be implemented by special member functions; these operators are listed in the following table.

Operator	Expression	Member function
Addition	q1+ q2	q1.plus(q2)
Subtraction	q1- q2	q1.minus(q2)
Multiplication	q1 * q2	q1.times(q2)
Division	q1 / q2	q1.div(q2)
Modulo (Remainder)	q1%q2	q1.rem(q2)
Range operator	q1..q2	q1.rangeTo(q2)

We have already seen examples of add and subtract; this table indicates how we can also provide operators for multiplication and division etc.

The updated Quantity class is given below for the five numerical operators (excluding the range operator):

```
data class Quantity(val value: Int) {
    operator fun plus(other: Quantity): Quantity =
                    Quantity(value + other.value)
    operator fun minus(other: Quantity): Quantity =
                    Quantity(value - other.value)

    operator fun times(i: Int): Quantity = Quantity(value * i)
    operator fun div(i: Int): Quantity = Quantity(value / i)
    operator fun rem(i: Int): Quantity = Quantity(value % i)
}
```

This means that we can now extend our simple application that uses the
`Quantity` class to include some of these additional numerical operators:

```kotlin
fun main() {
    val q1 = Quantity(5)
    val q2 = Quantity(10)
    println("q1 = $q1, q2 = $q2")

    println("q1 + q2 = ${q1 + q2}")
    println("q2 - q1 = ${q2 - q1}")
    println("q2 * 3 = ${q2 * 3}")
    println("q2 / 2 = ${q2 / 2}")
    println("q2 % 3 = ${q2 % 3}")
}
```

The output from this is now:

```
q1 = Quantity(value=5), q2 = Quantity(value=10)
q1 + q2 = Quantity(value=15)
q2 - q1 = Quantity(value=5)
q2 * 3 = Quantity(value=30)
q2 / 2 = Quantity(value=5)
q2 % 3 = Quantity(value=1)
```

Unary Prefix Operators

A **unary operator** is an operator that only has *one* operand. That is it is only applied
to a single value. This is in contrast to binary operators such as multiple or divide
which have two operands (i.e. two values to which they are applied).

There are three unary prefix operators available in Kotlin:

- Unary positive (+) The result of the unary positive operator is the value of its
  operand.
- Unary negative (−) this operator produces the negative of the operand value, this
  -x will produce the negative of the value held in x, if x has the value 2 then -x will
  produce −2. However, if x has the value −2 then -x will produce the value 2.
- Not operator (!) This operator logically inverse the value of its operand. For
  example !flag will logically invert the value of flag, if flag has the value true then
  !flag return false, in turn if the value of flag is false then !flag returns the value
  true.

The operators and their member functions are listed in the following table.

Operator	Expression	Member Function
Unary positive	+ a	a.unaryPlus()
Unary negative	−a	a.unaryMinus()
Not	!a	a.not()

Postfix Increment and Decrement Operators

Another style of unary operator are the *increment* or *decrement* operator.

These are operators that apply to the operand they are used with. The increment operator will increment the value by 1 while the decrement operator will decrement the value by 1. For example given a value x with the value 1 then x++ will increment x to 2. In turn x−− will reduce the value of x by one.

One confusing aspect of these operators is that they shouldn't mutate the object on which the increment or decrement operation was invoked. Instead they should return a new value which will be stored into the variable to which they were applied.

There are two increment and decrement operators as shown below:

Operator	Expression	Member Function
Increment	a++	a.inc()
Decrement	a−−	a.dec()

An example of defining the dec() and inc() operator member functions for the Counter class is given below:

```
data class Counter(var value: Int) {
    // ... Additional operator omitted for clarity

    operator fun inc():Counter = Counter(value + 1)
    operator fun dec():Counter = Counter(value - 1)
}
```

This means that we can now apply the increment and decrement operators to a *var* of type Counter (note this must be a *var* as we are changing the value of the var):

```
fun main() {
    var c = Counter(1)
    c++
    println(c)
}
```

The output from this is:

```
Counter(value=2)
```

Comparison Operators

Numerical types (such as integers and real numbers) also support comparison operators such as equals, not equals, greater than, less than as well as greater than or equal to and less than or equal to.

Kotlin allows these comparison operators to be defined for user defined types/classes as well.

Just as numerical operators such as '+' and '−' are implemented by special member functions so are comparison operators. For example the '<' operator is implemented by a member function called `compareTo()` and a logical test of its result.

The complete list of comparison operators and the associated special member functions is given in the following table.

Operator	Expression	Member function
Less than	q1 < q2	q1.compareTo(q2) < 0
Less than or equal to	q1 <= q2	q1.compareTo(q2) <= 0
Equal to	q1== q2	q1.equals(q2)
Not equal to	q1 != q2	!q1.equals(q2)
Greater than	q1 > q2	q1.compareTo(q2) > 0
Greater than or equal to	q1 >= q2	q1.compareTo(q2) >= 0

We can add these definitions to our `Quantity` class to provide a more complete type that can be used in comparison style tests (such as `if` statements). However, the `equals()` functionality is already provided as we marked the class as a `data` class. We therefore only need to implement the `compareTo()` member function to provide a complete set of logical operators.

The updated `Quantity` class is given below (with some of the numerical operators omitted for brevity):

```kotlin
data class Quantity(val value: Int) {
    operator fun plus(other: Quantity): Quantity =
                        Quantity(value + other.value)
    operator fun minus(other: Quantity): Quantity =
                        Quantity(value - other.value)

    // Additional numerical operators omitted for brevity

    operator fun compareTo(other: Quantity): Int =
                    value.compareTo(other.value)
}
```

This now means that we can update our sample application to take advantage of these comparison operators:

```kotlin
fun main() {
    val q1 = Quantity(5)
    val q2 = Quantity(10)
    println("q1 = $q1, q2 = $q2")

    println("q1 < q2: ${q1 < q2}")
    println("q1 < q2: ${q1 <= q2}")
    println("q1 < q2: ${q1 == q2}")
    println("q1 < q2: ${q1 != q2}")
    println("q1 < q2: ${q1 > q2}")
    println("q1 < q2: ${q1 >= q2}")
}
```

The output from this is now:

```
q1 = Quantity(value=5), q2 = Quantity(value=10)
q1 < q2: true
q1 < q2: true
q1 < q2: false
q1 < q2: true
q1 < q2: false
q1 < q2: falsee
```

Augmented Assignment Operators

This category of operators provide a set of shorthand operators that can be used to apply a numerical operator and an assignment in one go. For example a+ = b is a shorthand form for a = a + b. These operators are presented in the following table:

Operator	Expression	Member function
Plus assignment	q1 + = q2	q1.plusAssign(q2)
Minus assignment	q1 − = q2	q1.minusAssign(q2)
Times assignment	q1 * = 2	q1.timesAssign(2)
Divide assignment	q1 / = 2	q1.divAssign(2)
Modules assignment	q1 % = 2	q1.remAssign(2)

We can now modify the class Counter to define these augmented assignment operators:

```
data class Counter(var value: Int) {

    // Additional numerical operators omitted for brevity

    operator fun plusAssign(c: Counter) {
        value = value + c.value
    }
    operator fun minusAssign(c: Counter) {
        value = value - c.value
    }
    operator fun timesAssign(i: Int) { value = value * i}
    operator fun divAssign(i: Int) { value = value / i}
    operator fun remAssign(i: Int) { value = value % i}
}
```

Note that we have chosen the parameter types used with the operators based on what makes sense for the Counter type. Thus we have decided that you cannot multiple a Counter by a Counter but you can multiple a Counter by an integer.

We can now uses these operators with an instance of the class Counter:

```
fun main() {
    var count = Counter(10)
    count /= 2
    println(count)
    count *= 3
    println(count)
}
```

The output from this program is:

```
Counter(value=5)
Counter(value=15)
```

One point to note about the numerical operators and the augment assignment operators is that there can be ambiguity in which operator to apply. For example, if we define both the *plus* operator member function and the *plusAssign* operator member function then when we write `count+  = Counter(1)` the compiler will not know which operator member function to use and will generate a compiler time error as shown below:

```
Assignment operators ambiguity. All these functions match.
public final operator fun plus(other: Counter): Unit defined in
com.jjh.ops.Counter
public final operator fun plusAssign(c: Counter): Unit defined
in com.jjh.ops.Counter
```

At which point you can decide how to handle this by either only defining one of the operators or by changing the parameter types of one or more of the member functions.

Containment (in) Operators

These operators are used with types that contain values such as collections. They can be used to check that a value is held within the type being tested. There are two operators `in` and `!in` but it is only necessary to implement a single operator member function called `contains()`:

Operator	Expression	Member function
Contained in	`a in b`	b.contains(b)
Not contained in	`a !in b`	!b.contains(a)

As these operators do not really make sense for the `Quantity` type, we will not define them. For example, what would it mean to say:

$$q1 \text{ } \textbf{in} \text{ } q2$$

In what way is q2 *in* q2?

Infix Named Operators

It is also possible to define what are known as *infix named* operators.

These are operators that are similar to those described above but use a *name* rather than a symbol (such as + or −). These are often just referred to as *named* operators.

Infix named operators have the following characteristics:

- named operators are binary operators that are applied to two operands (values),

- they are defined using the keyword `infix` before the member function definition.

Once defined they can be used without resorting to the *dot* notation to invoke the associated behaviour.

The following revised `Quantity` class definition defines two *infix named* operators `add` and `sub`.

```
data class Quantity(val value: Int) {
    infix fun add(i: Int): Quantity = Quantity(value + i)
    infix fun sub(i: Int): Quantity = Quantity(value - +i)
}
```

This class can now be used as shown below:

```
fun main() {
    val q1 = Quantity(5)
    println("q1 add 5: ${q1 add 5}")
    println("q1 sub 5: ${q1 sub 5}")
}
```

The output from this program is:

```
q1 add 5: Quantity(value=10)
q1 sub 5: Quantity(value=0)
```

Summary

Only use operators when they make sense and only implement those operators that work/make semantic sense for the type you are defining. In general, this means

- Arithmetic operators should only be used for values types with a numeric property.
- Comparison operators typically only make sense for classes that can be ordered.
- Containment (In) operators typically work for types that in some way contain other a collection of data items.

Online Resources

Some online resources on operator overloading include:

- https://kotlinlang.org/docs/reference/operator-overloading.html for information on operator overloading in Kotlin.
- https://www.programiz.com/kotlin-programming/operator-overloading Tutorial on operator overloading.

Exercises

The aim of this exercise is to define some operators for the Account classes to make it more natural to work with them. For example, it should be possible to *add* an amount to an account and *subtract* an amount from an account.

Exactly how you implement this is up to you. One approach is to merely wrap the add and sub member functions around the deposit and withdraw member functions. To obtain a suitable return type you can then merely retrieve the transactionBalance from the tractions instance.

You should be able to run the following code:

```
println(acc1 + 10.55)
println(acc1 - 5.0)
```

Chapter 20
Error and Exception Handling

Introduction

This chapter considers exception and error handling and how it is implemented in Kotlin. The chapter first introduces the object oriented model of exception handling as well as how to define custom exceptions and exception chaining. The chapter then explores the functional approach to exception handling in Kotlin.

Errors and Exceptions

When something goes wrong in a computer program someone needs to know about it. One way of informing other parts of a program (and potentially those running a program) is by generating an error object and propagating that through the code until either something *handles* the error and sorts thing out or the point at which the program is entered is found.

If the error propagates out of the program, then the user who ran the program needs to know that something has gone wrong. Typically they are notified of a problem via a short report on the error that occurred and a stack trace of where that error can be found. The stack trace shows the sequence of calls (both functions and member functions) that were invoked up until the point at which the error occurred.

You may have seen these yourself when writing your own programs. For example, the following program will cause an exception to be generated as it is not possible to convert the string "42a" into an integer:

```
package com.jjh.exp.basic

fun main() {
    val numberString = "42a"
    println(numberString.toInt())
}
```

© The Author(s), under exclusive license to Springer Nature Switzerland AG 2021
J. Hunt, *Beginner's Guide to Kotlin Programming*,
https://doi.org/10.1007/978-3-030-80893-8_20

When we run this program we obtain a stack trace in the output console of your program, such as that displayed within the IntelliJ IDE. This is because the exception is not handled by the program and instead it has propagated out of the program and a stack trace of the code that was called is presented. Note the line numbers are included which helps with *debugging* the problem.

```
Run:     ThrowingAnExceptionKt
  ▶  ↑    Exception in thread "main" java.lang.NumberFormatException Create breakpoint : For input string: "42a"
  🔧  ↓        at java.base/java.lang.NumberFormatException.forInputString(NumberFormatException.java:68)
     ⇉        at java.base/java.lang.Integer.parseInt(Integer.java:652)
  📷  ⇉        at java.base/java.lang.Integer.parseInt(Integer.java:770)
  🔖  🖨        at com.jjh.exp.basic.ThrowingAnExceptionKt.main(ThrowingAnException.kt:5)
     🗑        at com.jjh.exp.basic.ThrowingAnExceptionKt.main(ThrowingAnException.kt)
```

What is an Exception?

In Kotlin, almost everything is an instance of some type including integers, strings, booleans and indeed Exceptions and Errors. In Kotlin the Exception/Error types are defined in a class hierarchy with the root of this hierarchy being the `kotlin.Throwable` type.

All built-in errors and exceptions eventually extend from the `kotlin.Throwable` type.

The `Throwable` class has two subclasses: `Error` and `Exception`.

- Errors are exceptions generated at runtime from which it is unlikely that a program can recover (such as out of memory errors).
- Where as Exceptions are issues that your program should be able to deal with (such as attempting to read from the wrong file).
- A third type of exception is a RuntimeException. RuntimeExceptions represents bugs in your code and should not occur.

Part of the class hierarchy is shown below:

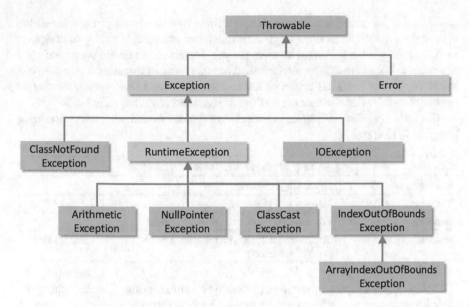

The above diagram illustrates the class hierarchy for some of the common types of errors and exceptions in Kotlin.

When an exception occurs, this is known as *raising* an exception and when it is passed to other code to handle the error or exception this is known as *throwing* an exception. The code which receives and handles the error exception is described as having *caught* the exception. These are terms that will hopefully become more obvious as this chapter progresses.

As stated above all exceptions inherit from `kotlin.Throwable`.

On the JVM runtime these are actually a set of *typealiases* that map the Kotlin types to the underlying Java (JVM) runtime exceptions, for example:

- `kotlin.Throwable` maps to java.lang.Throwable
- `kotlin.Exception` maps to java.lang.Exception
- `kotlin.NullPointerException` maps to java.lang.NullPointerException.

What Is Exception Handling?

An exception moves the flow of control from one place to another. In most situations, this is because a problem occurs which cannot be handled locally but that can be handled in another part of the system.

The problem is usually some sort of error (such as dividing by zero), although it can be any problem (for example, identifying that the postcode specified with an address does not match). The purpose of an exception, therefore, is to handle an error condition when it happens at runtime.

It is worth considering why you should wish to handle an exception; after all the system does not allow an error to go unnoticed. For example, if we try to divide by zero, then the system generates an error for you. However, in general we do not want programs to fail or crash in an uncontrolled manner. We can therefore use exceptions to identify that an issue has occurred and to determine how to correct it, for example we might request that the user correct the mistake and rerun the calculation.

The following table illustrates terminology typically used with exception/error handling in Kotlin.

Exception	An error which is generated at runtime
Raising an exception	Generating a new exception
Throwing an exception	Triggering a generated exception
Handling an exception	Processing code that deals with the error
Handler	The code that deals with the error (referred to as the catch block or exception handler)

Different types of error produce different types of exception. For example, if the error is caused by trying to divide an integer by zero then the exception generated might be an `ArithmeticException`.

The actual type of exception is represented by exception instances and can be caught and processed by exception handlers. Each handler can deal with exceptions associated with its class of error or exception (and its subclasses).

An exception is instantiated when it is thrown. The system searches back up the execution stack (the set of functions or member functions that have been invoked in reverse order) until it finds a handler which can deal with the exception. The associated handler then processes the exception. This may involve performing some remedial action or terminating the current execution in a controlled manner. In some cases, it may be possible to restart executing the code.

As a handler can only deal with an exception of a specified class (or subclass), an exception may pass through a number of handler blocks before it finds one that can process it.

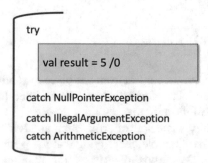

The above figure illustrates a situation in which an exception is generated due to a divide by zero issue. This exception is called an `ArithemticException`.

This exception is thrown when the integer 5 is divided by 0 and is passed up the execution stack where it encounters a catch exception handler defined for an `NullPointerException`. This handler cannot handle the `ArithmeticException` as it is a different type and so it is passed to the next catch block. It then encounters a catch exception handler for an `IllegalArgumentException`. Again, it cannot deal with a `ArithmeticException` and the exception is passed to the final catch exception handler which can handle the `ArithmeticException`. This handler then processes the exception.

Handling an Exception

You can catch an exception by implementing the `try catch` construct. This construct is broken into three parts:

- `try` block. The `try` block indicates the code which is to be monitored for the exceptions listed in the catch expressions.
- `catch` clauses. You can use one or more optional `catch` clause to indicate what to do when certain classes of exception/error occur (e.g. resolve the problem or generate a warning message). There can be any number of `catch` clauses in sequence checking for different types of error/exceptions.
- `finally` clause. The optional finally clause runs after the try block exits (whether or not this is due to an exception being thrown). You can use it to clean up any resources, close files, etc.

This language construct may at first seem confusing, however once you have worked with it for a while you will find it less daunting.

As an example, consider the following function which divides a number by zero; this will throw the `ZeroDivisionError` when it is run for any number:

```
fun runcalc(x: Int){
    x / 0
}
```

If we now call this function, we will get the exception stack trace in the standard output:

```
fun main() {
    runcalc(5)
}
```

This is shown below:

```
/Library/Java/JavaVirtualMachines/jdk-14.0.1.jdk/Contents/Home/bin/java ...
Exception in thread "main" java.lang.ArithmeticException Create breakpoint : / by zero
    at com.jjh.exp.basic.BasicExceptionHandlingKt.runcalc(BasicExceptionHandling.kt:4)
    at com.jjh.exp.basic.BasicExceptionHandlingKt.main(BasicExceptionHandling.kt:8)
    at com.jjh.exp.basic.BasicExceptionHandlingKt.main(BasicExceptionHandling.kt)
```

However, we can handle this by wrapping the call to `runcalc` within a `try` block and providing a `catch` clause. The syntax for the `try-catch` construct is:

```
try {
    <code to monitor>
} catch (<variabe-name>: <type of exception to monitor for>) {
    <code to call if exception is found>
}
```

A concrete example of this is given below for a `try` block that will be used to monitor a call to `runcalc`:

```
fun main() {
    try {
        runcalc(5)
    } catch (exp: ArithmeticException) {
        println("Opps")
    }
}
```

which now results in the string 'Oops' being printed out instead of the exception stack trace:

```
/Library/Java/JavaVirtualMachines/jdk-14.0.1.jdk/Contents/Home/bin/java ...
Opps
```

This is because when `runcalc` is called the '/' operator throws a the `ArithmeticException` which is passed back to the calling code which has an `catch` clause specifying this type of exception. This *catches* the exception and runs the associated code block which in this case prints out the string 'Oops'.

If we want to log the error and allow the program to proceed we can use the `printStackTrace()` member function, for example:

```
fun main() {
    try {
        runcalc(5)
    } catch (exp: ArithmeticException) {
        println("Opps")
        exp.printStackTrace()
    }
}
```

In fact, we don't have to be as precise as this; the catch clause can be given the class of exception to look for and it will match any exception that is of that exception type or is an instance of a subclass of the exception. We therefore can also write:

```
fun main() {
    try {
        runcalc(5)
    } catch (exp: Exception) {
        println("Opps")
        exp.printStackTrace()
    }
}
```

The Exception class is a grandparent of the ArithmeticException thus any ArithmeticException instance is also a type of Exception and thus the catch block matches the exception passed to it. This means that you can write one catch clause and that clause can handle a whole range of exceptions.

Multiple Catch Blocks

If you don't want to have a common block of code handling your exceptions, you can define different behaviours for different types of exception. This is done by having a series of catch clauses; each monitoring a different type of exception:

```
fun main() {
    try {
        runcalc(5)
    } catch (exp: NullPointerException) {
        println("NullPointerException")
    } catch (exp: IllegalArgumentException) {
        println("IllegalArgumentException")
    } catch (exp: ArithmeticException) {
        println("ArithmeticException")
    } catch (e: Exception) {
        println("Duh!")
    }
}
```

In this case the first catch monitors for a NullPointerException but the other catches monitor for other types of exception. Thus the second catch monitors for IllegalArgumentException, the third for the ArithmeticException etc.

Note that the catch (e: Exception) is the last catch clause in the list. This is because NullPointerException, IllegalArgumentException and ArithmeticException are all eventual subclasses of Exception and thus this clause would catch any of these types of exception. As only one catch block is allowed to run; if this catch handler came fist the other catch handers would never ever be run.

Accessing the Exception Object

It is possible to gain access to the exception instance being caught by the *catch clause* as it is available within the catch handler code block. You can name this parameter whatever you like, however names such as e, exp, ex are commonly used. For example:

```
fun main() {
    try {
        runcalc(5)
    } catch(exp: Exception) {
        println("Opps")
        println(exp)
        println(exp.message)
        exp.printStackTrace()
    }
}
```

Which produces:

```
/Library/Java/JavaVirtualMachines/jdk-14.0.1.jdk/Contents/Home/bin/java ...
Opps
java.lang.ArithmeticException: / by zero
/ by zero
java.lang.ArithmeticException Create breakpoint : / by zero
    at com.jjh.exp.basic.BasicExceptionHandlingKt.runcalc(BasicExceptionHandling.kt:6)
    at com.jjh.exp.basic.BasicExceptionHandling3Kt.main(BasicExceptionHandling3.kt:5)
    at com.jjh.exp.basic.BasicExceptionHandling3Kt.main(BasicExceptionHandling3.kt)
```

Jumping to Exception Handlers

One of the interesting features of exception handling in Kotlin is that when an Error or an Exception is raised it is immediately *thrown* to the exception handlers (the catch blocks). Any statements that follow the point at which the exception is raised are not run. This means that a function or member function may be terminated early and further statements in the calling code will not be run.

As an example, consider the following code. This code defines a function divide(Int, Int) that divides two integers returning the result. Note that function logs *entry* and *exit* from the function.

The divide() function is called from within a try statement of the main() function. Notice that there is a println() statement each side of the call to divide(Int, Int). There is also a handler for the ArithmeticException.

```
fun divide(x: Int, y: Int): Int {
    println("entering divide($x, $y)")
    val result = x / y
    println("exiting divide $result")
    return result
}

fun main() {
    println("Starting")
    try {
        println("Before the call to divide")
        val result = divide(6,2)
        println("After the call to divide: $result")
    } catch (exp: ArithmeticException) {
        println("Opps")
    }
    println("Done")
}
```

When we run this program the output is

```
Starting
Before the call to divide
entering divide(6, 2)
exiting divide 3
After the call to divide: 3
Done
```

In this example we have run every statement with the exception of the catch clause as the ArithmeticException was not thrown.

If we now change the call to divide(Int, Int) such that we pass in 6 and 0 we will throw the ArithmeticException.

```kotlin
fun main() {
    println("Starting")
    try {
        println("Before the call to divide")
        val result = divide(6,0)
        println("After the call to divide: $result")
    } catch (exp: ArithmeticException) {
        println("Opps")
    }
    println("Done")
}
```

Now the output is:

```
Starting
Before the call to divide
entering divide(6, 0)
Opps
Done
```

The difference is that the second println statement in divide(Int, Int) has not been run; instead after printing 'entering divide(6, 0)' and then raising the error we have jumped strait to the catch clause and run the println statement in the associated exception handling block of code.

This is partly why the term *throwing* is used with respect to error and exception handling; because the error or exception is raised in one place and thrown to the point where it is handled, or it is thrown out of the application if no catch clause is found to handle the error/exception.

The Finally Clause

An optional finally clause can also be provided with the try statement. This clause is the last clause in the construct and must come after any catch classes.

It is used for code that you want to run whether an exception occurred or not. For example, see the following program:

```kotlin
fun main() {
    println("Starting")
    try {
        println("Before the call to divide")
        val result = divide(6,2)
        println("After the call to divide: $result")
    } catch (exp: ArithmeticException) {
        println("Opps")
    } finally {
        println("Always runs")
    }
    println("Done")
}
```

The `try` block will run, if no error is thrown then the `finally` code will run, we will therefore have as output:

```
Starting
Before the call to divide
entering divide(6, 2)
exiting divide 3
After the call to divide: 3
Always runs
Done
```

If however we pass in 6 and 0 to `divide(Int, Int)`:

```kotlin
fun main() {
    println("Starting")
    try {
        println("Before the call to divide")
        val result = divide(6,0)
        println("After the call to divide: $result")
    } catch (exp: ArithmeticException) {
        println("Opps")
    } finally {
        println("Always runs")
    }
    println("Done")
}
```

We will now cause an exception to be thrown in the `divide(Int, Int)` function which means that the `try` block will execute, then the `ArithmeticException` wil be thrown, it will be handled by the `catch` clause and then the `finally` clause will run. The output is now:

```
Starting
Before the call to divide
entering divide(6, 0)
Opps
Always runs
Done
```

As you can see in both cases the finally clause is executed.

The `finally` clause can be very useful for general housekeeping type activities such as shutting down or closing any resources that your code might be using, even if an error has occurred.

Throwing an Exception

An error or exception is thrown using the keyword `throw`. The syntax of this is

```
throw <Exception/Error type to throw>()
```

For example:

```
fun functionBang() {
    println("entering functionBang")
    throw RuntimeException("Bang!")
    println("exiting functionBang")
}
```

In the above function the second statement in the function body will create a new instance of the `RuntimeException` class and then `throw` it allowing it to be caught by any exception handlers that have been defined.

We can handle this exception by writing a `try` block with an `catch` clause for the `RuntimeException` class. For example:

```
fun main() {
    try {
        functionBang()
    } catch (exp: RuntimeException) {
        println(exp.message)
    }
}
```

This generates the output:

```
entering functionBang
Bang!
```

You can also *re-throw* an error or an exception; this can be useful if you merely want to note that an error has occurred and then re-throw it so that it can be handled further up in your application. To do this you use the `throw` keyword and the parameter used to hold the exception for the `catch` block. For example:

```kotlin
fun main() {
    try {
        functionBang()
    } catch (exp: RuntimeException) {
        println(exp.message)
        throw exp
    }
}
```

This will re throw the `RuntimeException` caught by the `catch` clause. However, in this case there is nothing to handle the exception and therefore it propagates out of the program causing the program to terminate and generate a exception stack trace:

```
entering functionBang
Bang!
Exception in thread "main" java.lang.RuntimeException: Bang!
    at
com.jjh.exp.raise.RaisingAnExceptionKt.functionBang(RaisingAnExc
eption.kt:5)
    at
com.jjh.exp.raise.RaisingAnExceptionKt.main(RaisingAnException.k
t:11)
    at
com.jjh.exp.raise.RaisingAnExceptionKt.main(RaisingAnException.k
t)
```

Try Catch as an Expression

In Kotlin most statements are actually expressions that return a value. The try-catch-finally expression is no different. You can assign the value returned by the `try{}` block (or the `catch{}` block if an error occurs) to a value.

For example, the following listing instantiates the class `Rational` and stores that instance into the *val* `result` unless an exception is thrown.

If an exception is thrown then if the exception is of type `RuntimeException` then a default `Rational` instance is returned by the `catch` block.

Thus the val `result` with either have an instance created from with in the `try` block or an instance created within the `catch` block:

```
class Rational(val numerator: Int, d: Int) {
    val denominator: Int

    init {
        if (d == 0)
            throw RuntimeException(
                     "Denominator cannot be Zero")
        denominator = d
    }

    override fun toString()=
        "Rational($numerator, $denominator)"

}

fun main() {
    val result = try {
        Rational(5, 0)
    } catch (exp: RuntimeException) {
        Rational(5, 1)
    }
    println(result)
}
```

The output from this is:

```
Rational(numerator=5, denominator=1)
```

However, care should be taken when using the `try-catch` expression with a `finally` block. The `finally` block is *optional* but when present runs after the `try` block and if an exception occurs it also runs after any `catch` block has run. For example:

```
val result = try {
    throw RuntimeException("oops")
} catch (e: RuntimeException) {
    3
} catch (e: Throwable) {
    0
} finally {
    2
}
println("result1: $result1")
```

The question here is what is the value of `result`? It will either be the value returned from the `try` block if there is no exception or it will be the value returned from the `catch` block.

Notice that although the `finally` block is executed any value returned from that block will be ignored. Thus the output generated for the above code is:

```
result1: 3
```

One common idiom or pattern used with `try-catch` expressions is that they can represent the whole body of a function or member function. This ensures that the `try` expression encapsulates all the functionality in the function block. For example:

```
fun func() = try {
        Rational(5, 0)
    } catch (exp: RuntimeException) {
        Rational(5, 1)
    }
```

Defining an Custom Exception

You can define your own exception types, which can give you more control over what happens in particular circumstances. To define an exception, you create a subclass of the `Exception` class or one of its subclasses.

For example, to define a `InvalidAgeException`, we can extend the `Exception` class and generate an appropriate message:

```
class InvalidAgeException(val invalidAge: Int,
                          message: String): Exception(message)
```

This class can be used to explicitly represent an issue when an age is set on a `Person` which is not within the acceptable age range.

We can use this with the class `Person` that we defined earlier in the book; this version of the `Person` class defined `age` as a property and attempted to validate that an appropriate age was being set. We can modify this class so that if the value being used for `age` is less than zero or greater than 120 then we will throw an `InvalidAgeException`. For example:

```kotlin
class Person(val name: String, _age: Int) {

    var age: Int = 0
        private set(value) {
            if (value < 0 || value > 120) {
                throw InvalidAgeException(value,
                    "Age must be between 0 and 120")
            } else {
                field = value
            }
        }

    init {
        age = _age
    }

}
```

Note that the age set() function now throws an InvalidAgeException,
so if we write:

```kotlin
fun main() {
    try {
        val p1 = Person("Adam", -1)
        println(p1)
    } catch (exp: InvalidAgeException) {
        println(exp.invalidAge)
        println(exp.message)
        println(exp)
    }
}
```

When this code runs and we try and create an instance of the Person class
with an age of -1 the set() function for the age property will throw the
InvalidAgeException passing in information to help any exception handler
determine the issue with the data and what that data was.

When the above code runs we will see:

```
-1
Age must be between 0 and 120
com.jjh.exp.people.InvalidAgeException: Age must be between 0
and 120
```

Chaining Exceptions

A feature that can be useful when creating your own exceptions is to chain them to a generic underlying exception. This can be useful when a generic exception is thrown, for example, by some library or by the Kotlin system itself, and you want to convert it into a more meaningful application exception.

For example, let us say that we want to create an exception to represent a specific issue with the parameters passed to a function `divide()`, but we don't want to use the generic `ArithmeticException`, instead we want to use our own `DivideByYWhenZeroException`. This new exception could be defined as:

```
class DivideByYWhenZeroException(
            message: String = "",
            cause: Throwable? = null): Exception(message, cause)
```

This exception is defined to handle an underlying cause. The `cause` is defined as a *nullable* Throwable type (which means that it can be used with any type of Exception or Error). It is then passed up to the parent class exception along with the `message`. Notice that the cause is optional as we have provided a default value `null`.

And we can use it in a function `divide()`:

```
fun divide(x: Int, y: Int): Int {
    try {
        return x / y
    } catch (exp: ArithmeticException) {
        throw DivideByYWhenZeroException("Divide by Zero", exp)
    }
}
```

We have used the throws keyword when we are instantiating the `DivideByYWhenZeroException` and passed in the original exception in to the constructor as a argument. This chains our exception to the original exception that indicates the underling problem.

We can now call the `divide()` function as shown below:

```
fun main() {
    divide(6, 0)
}
```

This produces a stack trace as given below:

```
Exception in thread "main"
chained.DivideByYWhenZeroException: Divide by Zero
    at
chained.ChainedExceptionExampleKt.divide(ChainedExceptionExam
ple.kt:12)
    at
chained.ChainedExceptionExampleKt.main(ChainedExceptionExampl
e.kt:17)
    at
chained.ChainedExceptionExampleKt.main(ChainedExceptionExampl
e.kt)
Caused by: java.lang.ArithmeticException: / by zero
    at
chained.ChainedExceptionExampleKt.divide(ChainedExceptionExam
ple.kt:10)
    ... 2 more
```

As can be seen you get information about both the (application specific) `DivideByYWhenZeroException` and the original
`ArithmeticException`—the two are linked together.

Nesting Exception Handlers

It is also possible to nest one `try catch` expression or statement inside another.

As a handler can only deal with an exception of a specified class (or subclass), an
exception may pass through a number of handler blocks before it finds one that can
process it.

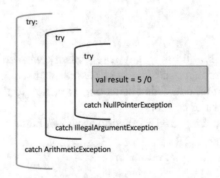

The above figure illustrates a situation in which an `ArithemticException`
is generated due to a divide by zero issue. The exception is thrown when
the integer 5 is divided by 0 and is passed up the execution stack where it
encounters an exception handler defined for an `NullPointerException`.
This handler cannot handle the `ArithmeticException` as it is a different
type and so it is passed further up the execution stack. It then encounters a

handler for an `IllegalArgumentException`. Again, it cannot deal with a `ArithmeticException` and the exception is passed further up the execution stack until it finds a handler defined for the `ArithmeticException`. This handler then processes the exception.

This example is illustrated in code below:

```kotlin
fun main() {
    try {
        try {
            try {
                println("In here")
                val result = 5 / 0
            } catch (exp: NullPointerException) {
                println("Its an NullPointerException")
            }
        } catch (ire: IllegalArgumentException) {
            println("Its an IllegalArgumentException")
        }
    } catch (ae: ArithmeticException) {
        println("Its an ArithmeticException")
        ae.printStackTrace()
    }
}
```

Limitations of Try-Catch

For those of you who are familiar with exception handling in other languages such as Java, C# etc. you will see that Kotlin's try-catch-finally construct is very similar. However, it is not without its drawbacks. The need to work with some resources (such as database connections or connections to a file) in multiple places can result in some awkward programming solutions. In general there are three key problems with this approach:

- The syntax results in scoping issues leading to unnecessarily complicated constructs as well as the need to nest `try-catch` block within either the try, catch or finally part of the top level construct! For example, to open a network connection you might write something like:

```
var connection: Connection? = null
try {
    connection =
    // … Use the connection
} catch (exp: ConnectionException) {
    // … Log the error occurred when opening the connection
} finally {
    try {
        connection.?close()
    } catch (expo: Exception) {
        // … Log the exception caused when closing the
connection
    }
}
```

- It forces developers to use vars for local variables as in the above code connection must be accessible in at least two different code blocks. This goes against the general approach of using vals in Kotlin programs.
- Multi-threaded code can be difficult to deal with using the try-catch-finally construct. For example, how should you react to an exception which occurs in a separate thread but which impacts the data being accessed? In fact the try-catch-finally construct primarily assumes that the exception is handled in the current execution thread (that is the exception is completely handled within the thread in which it occurred). This is not ideal for a concurrent program and seems at odds with the coroutine model implemented by Kotlin (see later in this book for chapters on Kotlin coroutines).

It can also be argued that the try-catch-finally approach is not particularly functional and is more procedural in nature. As Kotlin is a hybrid language this is not necessarily an issue in its own right, but it does highlight that alternative approaches can be developed based on the functional programming model.

Functional Exception Handling

Kotlin 1.3 added a new type of run scope function called runCatching{}. This scope function supports functional style exception handling.

It also introduce the kotlin.Result type which encapsulates whether the runCatching{} block was successful or not.

Using runCatching{}

To use the runCatching{} scope function all you have to do is embed the code to be monitored within the body of the runCatching block, for example:

```
runCatching {
    "32".toInt()
}
```

This scope function will attempt to convert the String "32" to an Integer. The scope function `runCatcing{}` will return a result representing success or failure of the block of code.

Thta is, `runCatching{}` allows the behaviour defined within the scope block to execute. It then generates a *result* which is a discriminated union that encapsulates:

- a *successful* outcome representing a value generated by the `runCatching{}` block or
- a *failure* which holds a reference to the `Throwable` instance (the exception) that caused the code to fail.

It is possible to check the *result* instance to identify whether it represents a *success* or *failure* using the `isSuccess` and `isFailure` properties.

For example:

```
fun main() {

    val result1 = runCatching {
        "32".toInt()
    }
    println(result1)
    println(rresult11.isSuccess)

    val result2 = runCatching {
        "32a".toInt()
    }
    println(result2)
    println(result2.isFailure)
}
```

This example attempts to convert a String to an integer for the val `result1` and the val `result2`. The String used for `result1` can be converted to an `Int` (the integer 32) but the String used for `result2` cannot be converted into an integer (as it contains the character 'a'). Thus the first expression should succeed, but the second should fail. The output of this program is:

```
Success(32)
true
Failure(java.lang.NumberFormatException: For input string:
"32a")
true
```

As you can see from this the value held in r1 is a Success type but the value held in r2 is a Failure type. The Failure also contains information about the problem that occurred and the value associated with it.

Accessing the Failure Exception

To access the exception associated with the Failure you can use the exceptionOrNull() member function, for example:

```
val result2 = runCatching {
    "32a".toInt()
}
println(r2)
println(r2.isFailure)
println(r2.exceptionOrNull())
```

The output from this block of code is:

```
Failure(java.lang.NumberFormatException: For input string:
"32a")
true
java.lang.NumberFormatException: For input string: "32a"
```

Accessing the Successful Value

To obtain the value held in the Result if it is successful there are a set of getter style member functions available:

- getOrDefault(<defaultValue>) Returns the encapsulated value if this instance represents success or the defaultValue if it is failure.
- GetOrElse{<onFailure function>} Returns the encapsulated value if this instance represents success or the result of the onFailure function for the encapsulated Throwable exception if it is failure.
- getOrNull() Returns the value generated or null.
- getOrThrow() Returns the encapsulated value if this instance represents success or re-throws the encapsulated Throwable exception if it is failure.

Examples of each of these getter member functions are given below:

```
val result0 = runCatching {
    "32".toInt()
}.getOrDefault(-1)
println("result0 $result0")

val result1 = runCatching {
    "32a".toInt()
}.getOrElse {
    println(it)
    0
}
println("result1 $result1")

val result2 = runCatching {
    "32a".toInt()
}.getOrNull()
println("result2 $result2")

val result3 = runCatching {
    "32a".toInt()
}.getOrThrow()
println("result3: $result3")
```

The output from this code block is:

```
result0 32
java.lang.NumberFormatException: For input string: "32a"
result1 0
result2 null
Exception in thread "main" java.lang.NumberFormatException: For
input string: "32a"
    at
java.base/java.lang.NumberFormatException.forInputString(NumberF
ormatException.java:68)
    at java.base/java.lang.Integer.parseInt(Integer.java:652)
    at java.base/java.lang.Integer.parseInt(Integer.java:770)
    at exp.func.FunctionalStyleExceptionHandlingAppKt.main
```

Treating Result as a Container

Result is actually a type of container and therefore it is also possible to apply *higher order functions* such as map and filter to the result generated by runCatching{}, for example:

```
runCatching { "32".toInt() }
    .map { println(it) }

runCatching { "32a".toInt() }
    .map { println(it) }
```

In this case the map function is being applied to the result instance. The result either *contains* a value if it is a success or it contains a Throwable (which is *not* considered to be a value returned by the block). As such map will be applied to a successful result but will have no effect of there if an exception thrown. The result generated by this code snippet is thus just:

32

This comes for the first runCatching{} block. The second runCatching{} block generates an exception and there is therefore no successful result to apply map to. This approach is fine if you are not interested in the exception and just want to do something if everything goes ok. However in many situation s you want to at least log the fact that an exception happened and may want to take some remedial action.

Recovery Operations

The recover{} operation can be used to handle an exception situation and *recover* from it. It can therefore be combined with map to provide some exception handling behaviour followed by the map operation. This is an approach favoured by many in the functional programming community.

For example:

```
runCatching { "32a".toInt() }
    .recover {
        it.printStackTrace()
        -1
    }
    .map { println(it) }
```

In this case we are mimicking the *try-catch* behaviour where the catch behaviour provides an alternative value to use. Thus in this case, if the String to be converted to an Int cannot be represented as an Int we will default to the value -1 however we are also logging the exception so that it does not fail silently.

The output from this code is therefore:

```
java.lang.NumberFormatException: For input string: "32a"
   at
java.base/java.lang.NumberFormatException.forInputString(NumberF
ormatException.java:68)
   at java.base/java.lang.Integer.parseInt(Integer.java:652)
   at java.base/java.lang.Integer.parseInt(Integer.java:770)
   at
.exp.func.FunctionalStyleExceptionHandlingAppKt.main(FunctionalS
tyleExceptionHandlingApp.kt:47)
   at
exp.func.FunctionalStyleExceptionHandlingAppKt.main(FunctionalSt
yleExceptionHandlingApp.kt)
-1
```

Providing Explicit OnFailure and OnSuccess Behaviour

In many situations developers want to one thing if the code works successful but do a different thing if it fails. This may be because there is no obvious recovery step. For example, if an error occurs while trying to connect to a server then there may not be a way to recover from that if the server is unavailable.

To support this scenario kotlin.Result provide the onFailure{} and onSuccess{} functions. These *higher order functions* take a function that is run depending on whether the kotlin.Result represents a success or failure scenario. These functions can be chained together for the result instance.

The order in which the functions are chained together is not significant and as such they can be chained to getter using result.onSuccess{}.onFailure{} or result.OnFailure{}.onSuccess{}.

Within both function blocks the variable it is used to represent the information supplied. For the onFailure{} block it represents the exception that was thrown. In the onSuccess{} block it represents the result generated by the runCatching{} block.

An example of using onSuccess and onFailure is given below:

```kotlin
runCatching {
    "32a".toInt()
}.onFailure {
    when (it) {
        is NumberFormatException -> {
            print("Oops - number wasn't formatted correctly: ")
            println(it.message)
        }
        is Exception -> {
            println("some other exception")
            it.printStackTrace()
        }
        else -> throw it
    }
}.onSuccess {
    println("All went well")
    println(it)
}
```

The onSuccess block will print out a message and the value generated.

The onFailure block will use a when expression to check the type of the exception. Depending upon the exception type, different message are printed out. If the issue is not a NumberFormatException or any type of Exception (it must then be an Error) it is thrown out of the runCatching{}.onFailure{].onSuccess{} chain.

The output from this code is:

```
Oops - number wasn't formatted correctly: For input string:
"32a"
```

This is quiet a common functional style of exception handling.

Online Resources

For more information on Kotlin errors and exceptions see:

1. https://kotlinlang.org/docs/reference/exceptions.html. The reference library documentation for built-in exceptions.
2. https://kotlinlang.org/api/latest/jvm/stdlib/kotlin/run-catching.html. runCatching function.

Exercises

This exercise involves adding error handling support to the CurrentAccount class.

In the CurrentAccount class it should not be possible to withdraw or deposit a negative amount.

Define an exception/error class called AmountException. The AmountException should take the account involved and an error message as parameters.

Next update the deposit() and withdraw() member functions on the Account and CurrentAccount classes to throw an AmountException if the amount supplied is negative.

You should be able to test this using:

```
try {
    acc1.deposit(-1.0)
} catch (exp: AmountException) {
    exp.printStackTrace()
}
```

This should result in the exception stack trace being printed out, for example:

```
fintech.accounts.AmountException: Cannot deposit negative
amounts
   at
fintech.accounts.AbstractAccount.deposit(AbstractAccount.kt:71)
   at fintech.main.MainKt.main(Main.kt:23)
   at fintech.main.MainKt.main(Main.kt)
```

Next modify the class such that if an attempt is made to withdraw money which will take the balance below the over draft limit threshold a BalanceException is thrown. This is again an application specific or custom exception that you can define.

The BalanceException exception should hold information on the account that generated the error.

This means that you can refactor the withdraw() member function in the CurrentAccount so that it does not print a message out to the user and it does not return a default zero transaction. Instead it throws the BalanceException which is a more explicit representation of the situation. The BalanceException can take the same message string as was previously printed out, for example:

```
if (amount < 0) {
    throw AmountException("Cannot deposit negative amounts")
}
```

Test your code by creating instances of `CurrentAccount` and taking the balance below the overdraft limit.

You should see something similar to:

```
Exception in thread "main" fintech.accounts.BalanceException:
Withdrawal would exceed your overdraft limit
  at
fintech.accounts.CurrentAccount.withdraw(AbstractAccount.kt:101)
  at fintech.main.MainKt.main(Main.kt:23)
  at fintech.main.MainKt.main(Main.kt)
```

Write code that will use `try` and `catch` blocks to catch the exception you have defined.

You should be able to add the following to your test application:

```
try {
    println("balance: ${acc1.balance}")
    acc1.withdraw(300.00)
    print("balance: ${acc1.balance}")
} catch (exp: BalanceException) {
    println("Handling Exception")
    println("Problem occurred on account: ${exp.acc}")
}
```

The output from this is:

```
Handling Exception
Problem occurred on account: CurrentAccount('123',
'Customer(name=John, address=10 High Street,
email=john@gmail.com)', 21.17) - overdraft -100.0
```

Chapter 21
Extension Functions and Properties

Introduction

In this chapter we will look at both Extension Functions and Extension Properties as well as Infix Extension Operators.

Such extensions are extensions to existing types either to provide additional functionality, to meet some library or framework requirements or just to make the type they are applied to easy to use in Kotlin.

Extensions

Kotlin provides the ability to extend a type with new behaviour without having to modify that type or inherit from the type or to wrap that type etc. This is done via special declarations called *extensions*.

This means that in Kotlin a type such as a class can have its behaviour and data extended even when:

- The type is closed or final and thus cannot normally be extended.
- When you do not have access to the source code and thus cannot change the type.
- The additional functionality or data is only required in one or a small number of situations and you do not wish to pollute the interface for the type in the general case.
- You want to extend the behaviour or data of a built-in type without modifying that type.

Extensions can provide these additional features (sometimes also known as the pimp my type design pattern).

There are three types of extension:

- *extension functions* that add functionality,
- *extension properties* that add data,

- *infix extension operators* that add additional named operators.

Each of these will be discussed in the remainder of this chapter.

Extension Functions

An extension function is a member function defined outside the scope of a type. It is defined using the syntax:

```
fun <Type>.<Extension Function Name>() { … function body … }
```

Or using the shorthand form:

```
fun <Type>.<Extension Function Name>() = expression
```

For example, to add additional behaviour to the built-in *closed/final* class String we can write:

```
fun String.hasLength(len: Int) = this.length == len

fun String.mult(len: Int): String {
    var result: String = ""
    for (i in 0..len) {
        result += this
    }
    return result
}
```

This add the member functions hasLength(Int) and mult(Int) to the class String.

We can now use this new functionality in our own programs:

```
fun main() {
    val s = "John"
    println("s.hasLength(4): ${s.hasLength(4)}")

    println("-".mult(25))
}
```

The output from this is:

```
s.hasLength(4): true
-------------------------
```

It therefore appears that the `String` class supports this behaviour. Of course if you look at the documentation for the class `String` you will not find these member functions listed. Indeed if you do not define these extension functions in your own code you will find that the above `main()` function will not even compile.

This illustrates the way in which extension functions add behaviour to an existing type.

Extension Properties

An extension property is a property defined outside the scope of a type. An extension property is defined using the syntax:

```
val <Type>.<Extension Property Name>
    get() { … function body … }
```

And for a var it can be defined as:

```
var <Type>.<Extension Property Name>
    get() { … function body … }
    set(value) { … function body … }
```

For example, to add additional properties to the built in *closed*/final class `String` we can write:

```
val String.size get() = this.length
```

This will define a new property `size` on the class `String`. The *read-only* (val) property `size` has a `get()` function that uses the `length` property already defined on the class `String` to generate the size of the String.

We can therefore now write:

```
fun main() {
    val s = "John"
    println("s.size: ${s.size}")
}
```

This generates the output:

```
s.size: 4
```

It is also possible to define a *read–write* property, however the `set()` function *cannot* introduce a backing field for the property; it is therefore necessary to access existing properties or handle the state in some other way.

For example given the class Person:

```
class Person(var name: String = "",
             val age: Int = 0) {
    override fun toString() = "Person($name, $age)"
}
```

We can define a *read–write* extension property that uses the existing var name property to get and set the property tag:

```
var Person.tag
    get() = name
    set(value) { name = value }
```

We can now use this new *read–write* tag property in our applications as an *alias* for the name property:

```
fun main() {

    val p = Person("John", 21)
    println(p.tag)

    p.tag = "Bob"
    println("p: $p")

}
```

The output generated by this program is:

```
John
p: Person(Bob, 21)
```

Infix Extension Operators

It is also possible to add named infix extension operators. These are infix operators that are defined outside the scope of a given type using the syntax:

```
infix fun <Type>.<operator name>() {
    ... operator function body ...
}
```

For example, to add a new named infix operator to the *closed* class `String` we could write:

```
infix fun String.m(len: Int): String {
    var result: String = ""
    for (i in 0..len) {
        result += this
    }
    return result
}
```

This adds a new operator 'm' to the class `String` (which represents the ability to multiple the string a specific number of times).

We can now use this in our own applications as shown below:

```
fun main() {

    // Infix operator example
    println("-" m 25)
    // same as
    println("-".m(25))

}
```

Not that this illustrates that the infix operator extension function can be called using traditional member function syntax or using operator syntax.

The output from the above program is:

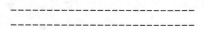

Extensions Scope

It is possible to encapsulate extensions within a class or an object. In this case the extension is only available within the scope of the class or the object. This limits the availability of the extension but also limits the extent to which the interface to the type is polluted by the extensions within the code.

To define an extension function for the class String which is limited to the class MyClass you can define new member level functions that follow the synt:ax.

```
class <classname> {
   fun <TypeToExtend>.<function-name>() { … function body … }
}
```

For example:

```
class MyClass {
      // Extension function for a String
      // But only accessible from within class
      fun String.rev(): String {
          return this.reversed()
      }
      fun printMe(s: String) {
          println(s.rev())
      }
}
```

The extension function rev for the class String is only accessible from within the class MyClass. Thus the member function printMe() can access rev() on a String but code outside of the class cannot.

We can do a similar thing with objects, for example:

```
object MyObject {
      fun String.rev(): String {
          return this.reversed()
      }
      fun printMe(s: String) {
          println(s.rev())
      }
}
```

Online Resources

More information on Kotlin extensions and the *pimp my type* design pattern see:

- https://kotlinlang.org/docs/reference/extensions.html Introduces Kotlin Extensions.
- http://blog.rcard.in/jvm/programming/design-pattern/2019/12/15/pimp-my-library-pattern.html Pimp My Type Design Pattern.

Exercises

This exercise involves defining an extension function for the `AbstractAccount` class. This extension function should be defined in a separate file to the `AbstractAccount` class. It should be called `prettyPrint`. It should pretty print information about the account.

Note to obtain the actual class of the instance running a member function or extension function you can use `this::class`—this is referred to as the class reference syntax.

You should now be able to run:

```
acc1.prettyPrint()
```

An example of the sort of output from this is:

```
class fintech.accounts.CurrentAccount
   Customer(name=John, address=10 High Street,
email=john@gmail.com)
   123
   26.720000000000002
```

Part III
Data Containers

Chapter 22
Arrays

Introduction

Earlier in this book we looked at some Kotlin built-in types such as String, Int and Double as well as Boolean. These are not the only built-in types in Kotlin; another group of built-in types are collectively known as container types. This is because they contain other types (such as a collection of Strings or Ints).

There are in effect two categories of container types Arrays and Collections. Arrays are always mutable but of fixed size where as collections may be mutable or immutable, that may grow in size (and may have different characteristics depending upon the type of collection being used). This chapter introduces Arrays and the next chapter introduces Collections.

Kotlin Arrays

Arrays are a common way in which multiple values can be held together in one place. Arrays in Kotlin have several features:

- Arrays are another part of the type system in Kotlin. Thus `Array <String>` specifies something of type String array, that is an array that can hold Strings.
- Arrays in Kotlin are instance of the class Array.
- Arrays are mutable that is the values they hold can be changed.
- Once created the size of an Array is fixed, it cannot grow.
- Arrays know their size.
- Arrays have a range of common behaviours defined for them that allow developers to obtain elements at the start or end of an array, a subset of an array known as a slice etc.

© The Author(s), under exclusive license to Springer Nature Switzerland AG 2021
J. Hunt, *Beginner's Guide to Kotlin Programming*,
https://doi.org/10.1007/978-3-030-80893-8_22

- Arrays hold elements of data in an order specified by an index. Like many other languages the elements of an array are indexed from zero, which means that an array with 10 elements is indexed from 0 to 9.
- Index access is supported using the [index] notation.

Creating Arrays

There are several ways in which a new array can be created. Each of these are discussed din this section.

Using Class Array

Arrays can be created via the class Array using an initial size and a function that will be used to initialise the values held by the array.

This is the long hand form which is very flexible but not commonly used for basic arrays:

```
val asc = Array(5) { i -> (i * i).toString() }
```

Using Specialised Array Classes

Arrays can be created using a specialised version of the array type.

This is more common, for example to create an array of size 5 that can hold Int values you can use IntArray:

```
val intArray1 = IntArray(5)
```

In fact there are specialised array classes for all of the primitive types in Kotlin.

The specialised array types should be used in preference to the generic Array class as they are more efficient as they avoid a JVM concept known as boxing (which has overheads in terms of memory and performance).

The available specialised array types are ByteArray, ShortArray, IntArray, LongArray, DoubleArray, FloatArray and BooleanArray.

Using Factory Function arrayOf

Arrays can be created using the library factory function `arrayOf()`.

The `arrayOf()` function is a generic function that can create an array of a given size for a specified type. The following illustrate several examples of using this function:

```
val data = arrayOf<Int>(5) // Array of Int
val data2 = arrayOf<String>("John", "Denise") // Array of
Strings
val data3 = arrayOf("John", "Denise") // String can be inferred
val personArray = arrayOf(Person("John"),
                          Person("Denise"),
                          Person("Adam"),
                          Person("Phoebe"))
```

Alternatively, the `arrayOfNulls()` library function can be used to create an array of a given size filled with null values:

```
val strings = arrayOfNulls<String>(5)
```

Note that as this is an array of null values, it is necessary to indicate the *type* of the array created. In the above example an array of Strings is created.

Specialised arrayOf Functions

For the primitive type arrays there are specialised version of the `arrayOf()` factory function. These specialised functions are used to create arrays of the specified primitive type. The functions are `intArrayOf()`, `byteArrayOf()`, `shortArrayOf()`, `longArrayof()`, `floatArrayOf()`, `doubleArrayOf()` and `booleanArrayOf()`.

As an example here is the `intArrayOf()` factory function being used to create an array of 4 elements with the initial values 2, 4, 6 and 8:

```
val intArray2 = intArrayOf(2, 4, 6, 8)
```

Create Empty Arrays

An empty array can be created using emptyArray() or via the factory function arrayOf(). Here are some examples of using the emptyArray() factory function to create a set of empty arrays:

```
val someStrings = emptyArray<String>()
val friends = emptyArray<Person>()
val anything: Array<Any> = emptyArray()
val names: Array<String> = emptyArray()
val data = arrayOf<String>()
```

An empty array is an instance of the class Array which has a length zero. This can be useful for testing purposes but also in situations where it is necessary to provide an array instance but there is no data to populate that array.

Note that in the above example the type of the emptyArray() is indicated by the type of the vals for anything, names and data. Thus Kotlin is inferring the appropriate type of empty array to create. However, for someStrings and friends the type of the empty array to create is specified when invoking the emptyArray function. This is referred to as a *generic* function where the specific type to be used is included between angle brackets following the function name but before the parentheses.

Create an Array of Different Types

It is also possible to create an array that can hold different types of things, for example:

```
val things = arrayOf("John", 2, true)
```

In this case things will hold an array of any Comparable type of thing (i.e. Array <Comparable>) this is because Comparable is the lowest common denominator between the String "John", the Int 2 and the Boolean true.

A Comparable is something that can be *compared*. Comparable is an interface which is implemented by a wide range of types in Kotlin including Strings, Ints and Booleans.

Working with Arrays

Arrays of Reference Types

We can create an array of Strings either by using the `Array` class directly and providing a function to initialise the values of the array or using the `arrayOfNulls` factory function, for example:

```
// Array of 4 elements initialised to null
val names = arrayOfNulls<String>(4)
// Array of 4 elements initialised to the empty string
val alternativeNames = Array<String>(4){ "" }
```

Both of these create an array capable of holding 4 string instances.

Of course if you know the default values that you want to use with the String array you can provide them via the `arrayOf()` function and a comma separated list of values:

```
val names2 = arrayOf("John", "Denise", "Phoebe", "Adam")
```

This creates an array of four elements containing the strings "John", "Denise", "Phoebe" and "Adam". We can change any of these fields by specifying the appropriate index and replacing the existing value with a new string:

```
names2[2] = "Jasmine"
```

The above statement replaces the string "Phoebe" with the string "Jasmine". Remember arrays are indexed from Zero thus the first position has index 0, the second has index 1 and so on.

Merely being able to put values into an array would be of little use; we can also access the array locations in a similar manner:

```
println("The name in index 2 is ${names2[2]}")
```

The above statement results in the following string being printed:

```
The name in index 2 is Jasmine
```

As arrays are instances we can also obtain information from them. For example, to find out how many elements are in the array we can use the property size:

```
println("anything.size: ${anything.size}")
```

Working with Primitive Type Arrays

We can also work with primitive type arrays in a similar manner to the String array example in the previous section. However, we now use the appropriate specialised array class such as `IntArray` or `DoubleArray`. Such an array also has a property size and values can be set using index access and accessed in the same8 way. For example:

```
val moduleMarks = IntArray(5)
println("moduleMarks: $moduleMarks")
println("moduleMarks.size: ${moduleMarks.size}")

moduleMarks[0] = 26
moduleMarks[1] = 15
moduleMarks[2] = 56
moduleMarks[3] = 72
moduleMarks[4] = 34

println("moduleMarks[0]: ${moduleMarks[0]}")
```

The output from this block of code is:

```
moduleMarks: [I@1218025c
moduleMarks.size: 5
moduleMarks[0]: 26
```

Note the slightly strange way in which an array is printed (the '[' indicates that it is an array and the following I indicates that it is an *Int array*.

Working with User Defined Types

It is also possible to create arrays of user defined types such as the class `Person`. This is done in exactly the same way as creating an array of Strings, for example:

```
data class Person(val name: String)
val personArray = arrayOf(Person("John"),
                          Person("Denise"),
                          Person("Adam"),
                          Person("Phoebe"))
```

This will create an `Array <Person>` instance that is stored in the `personArray` val. The personArray will have a size of 4 indexed 0 to 3.

Iteration and Arrays

Iterating Over an Array

The `for` statement can be used with any iterable type of thing. Earlier in this book we iterated over a range of values for example from `0until 10` etc. In Kotlin arrays are *iterable* so we can iterate over all the values in an array, using the `in` operator for example:

```
val moduleMarks = intArrayOf(26, 15, 56, 72, 34)

// Iterate over values in Int Array
for (item in moduleMarks) {
    println("item: $item")
}
```

The output from this code block is:

```
item: 26
item: 15
item: 56
item: 72
item: 34
```

Iterating Over the Indices for an Array

It is also possible to use the *indices* for each element in the array. This is done using the `indices` property of an array and the `in` operator. The `indices` property returns a range which is from 0 to the last index in the array. Thus if you have an array of 10 elements then the indices will return a range from 0 to 9. This is illustrated below:

```kotlin
val moduleMarks = intArrayOf(26, 15, 56, 72, 34)
for (index in moduleMarks.indices) {
    println("index: $index - value ${moduleMarks[index]}")
}
```

The output from this code block is given below:

```
index: 0 - value 26
index: 1 - value 15
index: 2 - value 56
index: 3 - value 72
index: 4 - value 34
```

Multi-Dimensional Arrays

As in most high level languages multi dimensional arrays can be defined in Kotlin. This can be done in several ways, but the following illustrates the simplest approach for an array of Int:

```kotlin
// Create a 2D array of Ints
val seats = arrayOf(
        arrayOf(0, 0, 0, 0, 1),
        arrayOf(0, 0, 0, 1, 1),
        arrayOf(0, 0, 1, 1, 1),
        arrayOf(0, 0, 0, 1, 1),
        arrayOf(0, 0, 0, 0, 1))
```

Note that the type of the val seats is actually Array <Array<Int>>. It is therefore useful to consider what this actually means. It states that the val seats can hold references to an Array of Arrays of Ints.

Thus if you did this long hand for a val and explicitly defined the type for the val, you would:

1.   Define the variable family as hold a reference to an array of arrays

```kotlin
var family: Array<Array<String>>
```

2.   Create the multi-dimensional array

```
family = arrayOf (
        arrayOf("John", "Denise", "Phoebe", "Adam"),
        arrayOf("Paul", "Fi", "Andrew", "James")
)
```

Note that we have explicitly here created an array of arrays of Strings.

3.   Access the sub arrays:

```
val family0 = family[0]
for (name in family0) {
    println(name)
}
```

This code block accesses the first element of the family Array of Arrays which returns the first Array of Strings. We can then iterate over these values in turn. The output of this code is thus:

```
John
Denise
Phoebe
Adam
```

We can also change an individual element of the sub array using the double index operations [ ] [ ], for example:

```
family[0][2] = "Jasmine"
for (name in family[0]) {
    println(name)
}
```

This code block accesses the first array element (index 0) and then in that array accesses the third element (index 2) and updates it. The cod then loops through the first array element and prints out each value, the result is:

```
John
Denise
Jasmine
Adam
```

As you can see from this last example, multi-dimensional arrays are accessed in exactly the same way as single dimensional arrays with one indices following another (note each is within its own set of square brackets—[ ]).

Ragged Arrays

It is also possible to have *ragged arrays* as the second dimension is made up of separate array instances. For example, the following code defines a two dimensional array in which the first row has *four* elements and the second has *five* elements.

```kotlin
val family = arrayOf (
        arrayOf("John", "Denise", "Phoebe", "Adam"),
        arrayOf("Paul", "Fi", "Andrew", "James", "Joselyn")
)
```

You can always find out the size of an array (or an array of arrays) using the size property, thus you can find out that the outer array has 2 elements, the first inner array has 4 elements and the second inner array has 5 elements, for example:

```kotlin
println("family.length: ${family.size}")
println("family(0).length: ${family[0].size}")
println("family(1).length: ${family[1].size}")
```

Of course the way that multi-dimensional arrays are implemented in Kotlin means that you can easily implement any number of dimensions as required.

Array Operations/Functions

In addition to the size property there are a whole range of member functions defined for Arrays that can be used to find the first element in an array or the last, make a copy of an array, obtain a slice (sub section) of an array or convert an array into a list. None of these member functions modify the original array. However you can also *reverse* the array which changes the underlying array itself.

These features are illustrated below:

```kotlin
fun main() {
    val names = arrayOf("John", "Denise", "Adam", "Phoebe")
    println(names)
    println("size(): ${names.size}")
    println("first(): ${names.first()}")
    println("last(): ${names.last()}")
    println("copyOf(): ${names.copyOf()}")
    println("sliceArray(2..3): ${names.sliceArray(2..3)}")
    names.reverse()
    println("reversed array: $names")
    for (name in names) { print("$name, ") }
    println("\nasList(): ${names.asList()}")
}
```

The output from this program is:

```
[Ljava.lang.String;@1c20c684
size(): 4
first(): John
last(): Phoebe
copyOf(): [Ljava.lang.String;@448139f0
sliceArray(2..3): [Ljava.lang.String;@6f496d9f
reversed array: [Ljava.lang.String;@1c20c684
Phoebe, Adam, Denise, John,
asList(): [Phoebe, Adam, Denise, John]
```

Chapter 23
Collections

Introduction

Collection classes are often used as the basis for more complex or application specific data structures and data types.

The collection types support various types of data structures (such as lists and maps) and ways to process elements within those structures. This chapter introduces the collection types in Kotlin.

Collections Library

The Collections library is one of the main categories within the set of Kotlin libraries that you will work with. It provides types (Interfaces, Objects and Classes) that support various data structures (such as Lists, Sets and Maps) and ways to process elements within those structures. A *collection* is a single instance representing a group of instances (or objects). That is they are a *collection* of other things.

The Kotlin collections framework is defined within the `kotlin.collection` package. This package provides a collections framework for holding references to objects, instances and values. The Collection types also define a group of higher order functions, such as the foreach function that can be used to apply an operation to each of the elements held in a collection (this is discussed in the next chapter).

The Kotlin collection library is split into *Mutable* and *Immutable* concepts. The result is that Lists, Sets, Maps etc. can be mutable or immutable. Thus all the mutable collections can be updated, added to, removed from etc. In practice this means that you can change the contents of the mutable collection after it has been created. All immutable collections however, once created cannot change their content. Thus when you create an immutable list then the elements that comprised that list cannot be removed, added to etc.

© The Author(s), under exclusive license to Springer Nature Switzerland AG 2021   351
J. Hunt, *Beginner's Guide to Kotlin Programming*,
https://doi.org/10.1007/978-3-030-80893-8_23

The concepts of mutability and immutability (and their meaning for different collection types) are represented via a hierarchy of interfaces. The core elements of this hierarchy are presented below:

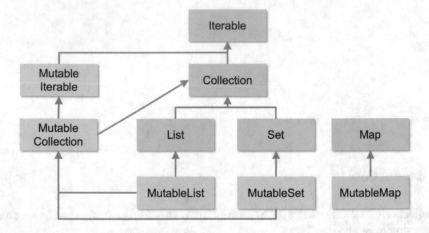

In this diagram all the *immutable* interfaces capture the core essence of that type of Collection. These are represented in blue in the diagram. Thus all collections are `Iterable` as represented by the Iterable interface. This concept is extended by the concept of being a Collection as represented by the interface `Collection` extending the interface `Iterable`. Within this Lists are immutable types of collections that are indexed and have an order. In contrast Sets are immutable collections that are not indexed, do not have an order and do not allow duplicates. Maps are separate as they represent an associated between a set of Key to Value pairs.

Additionally, the diagram illustrates that each of the core interface concepts has an associated *mutable* version. Thus the `List` interface is extended by the `MutableList` interface, in turn the `Set` interface is extended by the `MutableSet` and the `Map` interface is extend day the `MutableMap` interface. In addition there are also `MutableIterable` and `MutableCollection` interfaces.

Various implementations of each interface are provided that capture what interface is implanted and in what way for example the `ArrayList` class implements the List concept using a backing array where as the `HashSet` class implements the Set interface using a hashing member function.

Kotlin Collection Types

In this chapter and the next few chapters we will look at the following core collection clas

- **Lists** Lists hold a collection of objects that are ordered and mutable (changeable), they are indexed and allow duplicate members.

- **Sets** Sets are a collection that is unordered and unindexed. They are mutable (changeable) but do not allow duplicate values to be held.
- **Map** A Map is an unordered collection that is indexed by a key which references a value. The value is returned when the key is provided. No duplicate keys are allowed. Duplicate values are allowed. Dictionaries are mutable containers.
- **Pairs** Pairs represent a collection of exactly two values. They are ordered and immutable (cannot be modified), allow duplicate members and are indexed.
- **Triples** Triples represent a collection of exactly three values. They are ordered and immutable (cannot be modified), allow duplicate members and are indexed.

Like arrays collections are *generic* containers and thus can hold any type of instance of object within your Kotlin runtime environment. This includes system provided and user defined types.

Chapter 24
Lists

Introduction

This chapter presents the Kotlin List collection.

Lists

Lists have the following characteristics:

- Lists are ordered.
- Lists are indexed.
- By default lists are immutable.
- Lists allow duplicates.
- Lists maintain the order in which items are added or inserted.
- Lists are iterable.
- MutableLists are growable, that is as you add elements to a list it can grow.

Immutable Lists can be created using the `listOf()` factory function which can take a comma separated lists of the value to be used to initialise the list. For example:

```
val list1 = listOf("John", "Paul", "George", "Ringo'')
```

In this case we have created a list of four elements with the first element being indexed from zero, we thus have:

J. Hunt, *Beginner's Guide to Kotlin Programming*,
https://doi.org/10.1007/978-3-030-80893-8_24

List Creation

Using Classes Directly

Lists can be created by instantiating the appropriate class such as `ArrayList`. For example:

```
val list0: List<String> = ArrayList()
val list1: MutableList<String> = ArrayList()
println("myList0: $list0")
println("myList1: $list1")
```

Note that the `ArrayList` class implements both the `List` and the `MutableList` interface. It is therefore your choice whether you view the `ArrayList` as being *mutable* or not. If it is referenced through the variable `list0` then it will appear *immutable*, however it is accessed via the val `list1` it will reaper *mutable*.

Using Factory Functions

The example illustrated in the previous sub section is *not* idiomatic Kotlin, that is it is not the recommended way of creating lists in Kotlin. Instead you should use either the `listOf()` or `mutableListOf()` factory functions. These are the `List` equivalent of the `arrayOf()` factory function.

Using these factory functions you choose whether you want to create a *mutable* or *immutable* list, although note the default is an *immutable* list and you must explicitly choose the `mutableListOf()` function to create a mutable version:

```
val myList1 = listOf<String>("One", "Two", "Three")
val myList2 = listOf("One", "Two", "Three")
val myList3 = mutableListOf("Denise", "Adam", "Phoebe")
val myList4 = listOf<String>()   // Create an empty list
```

The type can be inferred for all lists that provide a default set of values. However an empty list has no values and thus Kotlin cannot infer the appropriate type to use in which case you must specify the type using the generic `<type>` syntax.

Unlike Arrays the default `toString()` member function provided for a list will print the contents of the list, for example:

```
println("myList1: $myList1")
println("myList2: $myList2")
println("myList3: $myList2")
println("myList4: $myList4")
```

Will generate the following output:

```
myList1: [One, Two, Three]
myList2: [One, Two, Three]
myList3: [One, Two, Three]
myList4: []
```

Nested Lists

Lists can be nested within Lists; that is a List can contain, as one of its elements, another List. For example, the following diagram illustrates the nesting of a tree of Lists:

We can thus create the following structure of nested Lists:

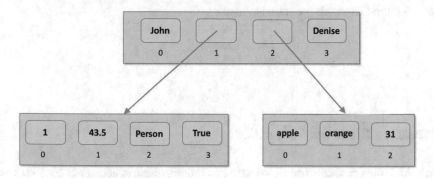

In code this can be defined as:

```
data class Person(val name: String)
```

```
fun main() {
    val list1 = listOf(1, 43.5, Person("Phoebe"), true)
    val list2 = listOf("apple", "orange", 31)
    val rootList = listOf("John", list1, list2, "Denise")
    println(rootList)
}
```

When the rootList is printed we get:

```
[John, [1, 43.5, Person(name=Phoebe), true], [apple, orange,
31], Denise]
```

Note the square brackets inside the outer square brackets indicating nested lists.

Accessing List Data

Obtaining the Size of a List

Like Arrays lists have a property size that will tell you how many elements they contain. In addition they have a property lastIndex which tells you the index of the last element in the list. As lists are indexed from zero (just as Arrays are) then the size of a list might be 3 but the last index would be 2. For example:

```
fun main() {
    val list = listOf("John", "Paul", "Bill")
    println("list.size: ${list.size}")
    println("list.lastIndex: ${list.lastIndex}")
}
```

The output from this program is thus:

```
list.size: 3
list.lastIndex: 2
```

Accessing Elements from a List

You can access elements from a list using an index (within square brackets [ ]). The index returns the element at that position, for example:

```
fun main() {
    val list = listOf("John", "Paul", "George", "Ringo")
    println(list[1])
}
```

This will print out the element at index 1 which is Paul (lists are indexed from Zero so the first element is the zeroth element).

Note that the index access operation [ ] is actually implemented by the underlying operation member function get() on the List interface. You could therefore write:

```
println(list.get(1)) // more common to use index access
```

However, the use of the get() member function is not considered idiomatic Kotlin and so should not generally be used.

Updating Elements Using an Index

Indexed access can also be used to update the value at an index within a mutable list. However such a list must be a *mutable* list. It is therefore necessary to create it using the `mutableListOf()` factory function. For example:

```
val mutableList = mutableListOf("John", "Paul", "George",
"Pete")
mutableList[3] = "Ringo"
println(mutableList)
```

The output from this is:

```
[John, Paul, George, Ringo]
```

In actual fact the index update operator maps to the `set()` member function on the List interface, you could therefore also write:

```
mutableList.set(3, "Ringo") // more common to use index access
```

Rather than use an index update. However, this is not considered idiomatic Kotlin and so should not generally be used.

Obtaining a Slice or Sub List

It is also possible to extract a slice (or *sublist*) from a list.

This is done using the `slice()` member function which takes a *range* indicating the start and end index to use for the slice (note this is the index not the position). For example `slice(1.0.3)` indicates a slice starting at the *oneth* element and extending up to the *third* element. The following illustrates this:

```
println("Take a slice of a list")
val group = listOf("John", "Paul", "George", "Ringo")
println(group)
println(group.slice((1..3)))
```

Which produces:

```
Take a slice of a list
[John, Paul, George, Ringo]
[Paul, George, Ringo]
```

Adding to a List

You can add an item to a list using the add() member function of the
MutableList interface. This changes the actual list; it does not create a copy
of the list and thus the list must be mutable. The syntax of this member function is:

<list>.add(<value>)

As an example, consider the following list of strings, to which we append a fifth
string:

```
fun main() {
    val list1= mutableListOf("John", "Paul", "George", "Ringo")
    list1.add("Pete")
    println(list1)
}
```

This will generate the output:

[John, Paul, George, Ringo, Pete]

You can also add all the items in a list to another list using the addAll() member
function:

```
fun main() {
    val list1= mutableListOf("John", "Paul", "George", "Ringo")
    list1.add("Pete")
    println(list1)
    list1.addAll(listOf("Albert", "Bob"))
    println(list1)
}
```

The output from this code snippet is:

[John, Paul, George, Ringo, Pete]
[John, Paul, George, Ringo, Pete, Albert, Bob]

Note that strictly speaking addAll() takes a collection and thus a set or a list
could be added to a list.

Inserting Into a List

You can also insert elements into an existing mutable list. This is done using the add() member function of the List interface. The syntax of this member function is:

```
<list>.add(<index>, <value>)
```

This version of the add() member function takes an index indicating where to insert the value and the value to be inserted.

For example, we can insert the string "Paloma" in between the *Zeroth* and *oneth* item in the following list of names:

```
println("Inserting an element")
val aList = mutableListOf("Adele", "Madonna", "Cher")
println(aList)
aList.add(1, "Paloma")
println(aList)
```

The result is:

```
Inserting an element
[Adele, Madonna, Cher]
[Adele, Paloma, Madonna, Cher]
```

In other words, we have inserted the string "Paloma" into the index position 1 pushing "Madonna" and "Cher" up one within the List.

List Concatenation

It is possible to concatenate two lists together using the concatenation operator '+':

```
val l1 = mutableListOf("Apple", "Orange")
val l2 = listOf("Banana", "Pear")
val l3 = l1 + l2
println(l3)
```

This code snippet generates:

```
[Apple, Orange, Banana, Pear]
```

Removing from a List

We can remove an element from a mutable list using the `remove()` and `removeAt(Int)` member functions. The syntax for these member function is:

`<list>.remove(<object>)`

`<List>.removeAt(index)`

This will remove the element from the list; if the element is not in the list then an error will be generated by Kotlin.

```
println("Removing from a list")
val anotherList = mutableListOf("Gary", "Mark", "Robbie",
"Jason", "Howard")
println(anotherList)
anotherList.remove("Robbie")
println(anotherList)
anotherList.removeAt(2)
println(anotherList)
```

The output from this is:

```
Removing from a list
[Gary, Mark, Robbie, Jason, Howard]
[Gary, Mark, Jason, Howard]
[Gary, Mark, Howard]
```

Checking for List Membership

It is possible to check whether a value is *contained* within a list using the `contains()` member function. If you are interested in a values position within a list you can use the `indexOf()` member function. This returns either the index position of a value or -1 if the value is not in the receiving list. For example:

```
println("Checking an element is in a list")
val names = listOf("Adam", "Jasmine", "Phoebe", "Gryff")
println("names.contains(\"Adam\"): ${names.contains("Adam")}")
println("names.contains(\"Bob\"): ${names.contains("Bob")}")
println("names.indexOf(\"Adam\"): ${names.indexOf("Adam")}")
println("names.indexOf(\"Bob\"): ${names.indexOf("Bob")}")
```

The output generated is:

```
Checking an element is in a list
names.contains("Adam"): true
names.contains("Bob"): false
names.indexOf("Adam"): 0
names.indexOf("Bob"): -1
```

Iterating Over Lists

You can iterate over the contents of a List (that is process each element in the list in turn). This is done using the for loop in which the iteration is performed over the List:

```
fun main() {
    val myList1 = listOf<String>("One", "Two", "Three")
    println("Iterating over a list")
    for (item in myList1) {
        println(item)
    }
}
```

This prints out each of the elements in the the list in turn:

```
Iterating over a list
One
Two
Three
```

Note that the order of the elements in the list is preserved.

It is also possible to iterate over the indices for the values in the list. This is done using the indices property of the list:

```
fun main() {
    println("Accessing index and value in a list")
    for (index in myList1.indices) {
        println("index: $index - value ${myList1[index]}")
    }
}
```

This program generates the output:

```
Accessing index and value in a list
index: 0 - value One
index: 1 - value Two
index: 2 - value Three
```

List Member Functions

Kotlin has a set of built-in member functions that you can use on lists.

Member Function	Description
`first()`	Returns the first element in the list
`last()`	Returns the last element in the list
`takeLast(Int)`	Takes the last *n* elements in the list
`isEmpty()`	Returns true if the list contains no elements otherwise false
`isNotEmpty()`	Returns true fi the list contains elements otherwise false
`asReversed()`	Returns the values in the receiving list in their reverse order

Some of these are illustrated in the following program:

```kotlin
fun main() {
    val list = listOf("One", "Two", "Three")
    println("list.first(): ${list.first()}")
    println("list.last(): ${list.last()}")
    println("list.takeLast(2): ${list.takeLast(2)}")
    println("list.isEmpty(): ${list.isEmpty()}")
    println("list.isNotEmpty(): ${list.isNotEmpty()}")
    println("list.asReversed(): ${list.asReversed()}")
}
```

The output from this is:

```
list.first(): One
list.last(): Three
list.takeLast(2): [Two, Three]
list.isEmpty(): false
list.isNotEmpty(): true
list.asReversed(): [Three, Two, One]
```

Online Resources

See the Kotlin reference documentation for:

- https://kotlinlang.org/docs/reference/collections-overview.html Kotlin Collections Overview.
- https://kotlinlang.org/api/latest/jvm/stdlib/kotlin.collections/   Kotlin `kotlin.collections` package.

- https://kotlinlang.org/docs/reference/constructing-collections.html constructing collections.
- https://kotlinlang.org/docs/reference/list-operations.html List specific operations.

Exercises

The aim of this exercise is to work with a collection/container such as a list.

To do this we will return to your `Account` related classes.

You should modify your `Account` class such that it is able to keep a history of transactions.

We already created a `DefaultTransaction` inner class in an earlier exercise.

Note that the initial amount in an account can be treated as an initial deposit.

The history could be implemented as a *mutable list* containing an ordered sequence to transactions.

Each time a withdrawal or a deposit is made a new transaction record should be added to a transaction history list.

The history could be a read-only property.

You should be able to run the following code at the end of your Accounts application:

```
for (transaction in acc1.history) {
    println(transaction)
}
```

Depending upon the exact set of transactions you have performed (deposits and withdrawals) you should get a list of those transactions being printed out

```
Transaction(10.05, deposit, 2021-04-26T16:56:09.839615,
transactionBalance=20.1)
Transaction(23.45, deposit, 2021-04-26T16:56:09.843016,
transactionBalance=56.95)
Transaction(12.33, withdrawal, 2021-04-26T16:56:09.843162,
transactionBalance=8.840000000000002)
Transaction(10.55, deposit, 2021-04-26T16:56:09.843928,
transactionBalance=42.27)
Transaction(5.0, withdrawal, 2021-04-26T16:56:09.844017,
transactionBalance=21.720000000000002)
```

Chapter 25
Sets

Introduction

This chapter presents the Kotlin Set collection.

Sets

A Set is an unordered (un indexed) collection of *immutable* objects that does not allow duplicates. Sets have the following characteristics:

- Sets are unordered.
- Sets are not indexed.
- By default sets are immutable.
- Sets do not allow duplicates.
- Sets do not maintain the order in which items are added or inserted.
- Sets are iterable.
- MutableSets are growable, that is as you add elements to a set it can grow.

Creating Sets

An immutable set can be created using a named class such as HashSet or by using a factory function such as the setOf() and mutableSetOf() factory functions. Some examples are given below:

© The Author(s), under exclusive license to Springer Nature Switzerland AG 2021
J. Hunt, *Beginner's Guide to Kotlin Programming*,
https://doi.org/10.1007/978-3-030-80893-8_25

```kotlin
fun main() {
    val set1: Set<String> = HashSet()
    val set2: MutableSet<String> = HashSet()
    // More idiomatic Kotlin
    val set3 = setOf<String>("One", "Two", "Three")
    val set4 = setOf("A", "B", "C")
    val set5 = mutableSetOf("Chasing Pavements",
                            "Rumour Has it",
                            "Turning Tables")

    println(set1)
    println(set2)
    println(set3)
    println(set4)
    println(set5)
}
```

The first two statements create new sets using the HashSet class directly. The HashSet class implements both the Set and the MutableSet interfaces and thus can be used as either type of set.

In this example, set1 is declared to hold reference to an immutable Set and thus set1 cannot be modified. In turn set2 holds a reference to a MutableSet and thus this set can be modified. In both sets the values can be Strings.

Both set3 and set4 hold references to *immutable* sets of Strings and use the more idiomatic Kotlin style of creating a set.

Finally set5 holds a reference to a mutable set of Strings. When this program runs the output generated is:

```
[]
[]
[One, Two, Three]
[A, B, C]
[Chasing Pavements, Rumour Has it, Turning Tables]
```

Set Properties and Member Functions

Like both Arrays and Lists, a Set knows its own size and can indicate whether it is empty or not:

```kotlin
fun main() {
    val set5 = mutableSetOf("Chasing Pavements",
        "Rumour Has it",
        "Turning Tables")
    println(set5.size)
    println(set5.isEmpty())
    println(set5.isNotEmpty())
}
```

This produces:

```
3
false
true
```

Accessing Elements in a Set

Unlike Lists it is not possible to access elements from a Set via an index; this is because they are *unordered* containers and thus there are no stable indexes available. However, they are *iterable* containers.

Elements of a Set can be iterated over using the for statement:

```
for (item in set) {
    println(item)
}
```

This applies the println() function to each item in the set in turn.

Working with Sets

Checking for Presence of an Element

You can check for the presence of an element in a set using the contains() member function. This returns true or false depending on whether the value is contained in the set:

```
// Checking that an element is in a list
println(set.contains("Rumour Has it"))
```

This will print true if "Rumour Has it" is a member of the set.

Adding Items to a Set

It is possible to add items to a MutableSet using the add() member function:

```
fun main() {
    val set5 = mutableSetOf("Chasing Pavements",
        "Rumour Has it",
        "Turning Tables")
    // Can only add a value once
    println(set5)
    set5.add("Skyfall")
    println(set5)
    set5.add("Skyfall")
    println(set5)
}
```

This generates:

```
[Chasing Pavements, Rumour Has it, Turning Tables]
[Chasing Pavements, Rumour Has it, Turning Tables, Skyfall]
[Chasing Pavements, Rumour Has it, Turning Tables, Skyfall]
```

As you can see from this "Skyfall" has only been added once.

If you want to add more than one item to a Set you can use the addAll()
member function:

```
set5.addAll(listOf("Hello", "Rolling In the Deep", "Hello"))
println(set5)
```

Generating:

```
[Chasing Pavements, Rumour Has it, Turning Tables, Skyfall,
Hello, Rolling In the Deep]
```

The argument to addAll() can be any type of Collection including a set or a
list. The addAll() member function however will still only add a value once, this
is illustrated above as "Hello" is only added once.

Removing an Item

To remove an item from a mutable set, use the remove() member function. The
remove() function removes a single item from a Set.

```
fun main() {
    val set5 = mutableSetOf("Chasing Pavements",
        "Rumour Has it",
        "Turning Tables")
    set5.remove("Rumour Has it")
    println(set5)
}
```

This generates:

```
[Chasing Pavements, Turning Tables]
```

Nesting Sets

We can of course also nest Lists in Sets and Sets in List. For example, the following structure shows Sets (the ovals) hold references to Lists (the rectangles) and vice versa:

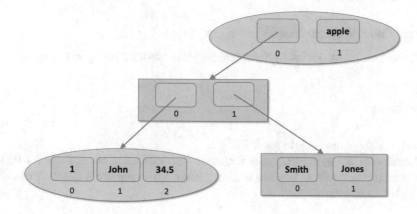

In code this would look like:

```
fun main() {
    val set1 = setOf(1, "John", 34.5)
    val list1 = listOf("Smith", "Jones")
    val list2 = listOf(set1, list1)
    val set2 = setOf(list2, "apple")
    println(set2)
}
```

which produces:

```
[[[1, John, 34.5], [Smith, Jones]], apple]
```

Set like Operations

You can also perform mathematical set like operations with Sets in Kotlin.

To merge two collections into one, use the `union()` function. It can also be used in the infix form, for example `a union b`.

To find an intersection between two collections (elements present in both sets), use the `intersect()` function.

To find collection elements not present in another collection, use the `subtract()` function.

Both the `intersect()` and `subtract()` functions can be called in the infix form as well, for example, `a intersect b`.

Online Resources

See the Kotlin reference documentation for:

- https://kotlinlang.org/docs/reference/set-operations.html Set specific operations.

Exercises

The aim of this exercise is to use a Set.

Create two sets of students, one for those who took an exam and one for those that submitted a project. You can use simple strings to represent the students, for example:

```
// Set up sets
val exam = setOf("Andrew", "Kirsty", "Beth", "Emily", "Sue")
val project = setOf("Kirsty", "Emily", "Ian", "Stuart")

// Output the basic sets
println("exam: $exam")
println("project: $project")
```

Using these sets answer the following questions:

- Which students took both the exam and submitted a project?
- Which students only took the exam?
- Which students only submitted the project?

- List all students who took either (or both) of the exam and the project.

  The output from the associated project might look like:

  ```
  exam: [Andrew, Kirsty, Beth, Emily, Sue]
  project: [Kirsty, Emily, Ian, Stuart]
  Students who took both the exam and the project [Kirsty, Emily]
  Students only took the exam [Andrew, Beth, Sue]
  Students only took the project [Ian, Stuart]
  Students who took either (or both) of the exam and the project
  [Andrew, Kirsty, Beth, Emily, Sue, Ian, Stuart]
  ```

Chapter 26
Maps

Introduction

This chapter considers the Map collection type in Kotlin.

Maps

A Map is a set of *associations* between a key and a value that is unordered, changeable (mutable) and indexed. Pictorially we might view a Map as shown below for a set of countries and their capital cities. Note that in a May the keys must be unique but the values do not need to be unique.

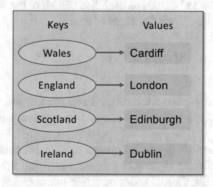

J. Hunt, *Beginner's Guide to Kotlin Programming*,
https://doi.org/10.1007/978-3-030-80893-8_26

Creating a Map

Maps can be created using the mapOf() and mutableMapOf() factory functions. Each Map has the type used to represent the key and the type used to represent the value in the Map.

These Map factory function are illustrated below:

```
fun main() {
    val map1: Map<Int, String> = mapOf(
            1 to "John",
            2 to "Denise")

    val map2 = mapOf(
            1 to "John",
            2 to "Denise")

    val map = mutableMapOf(
            "Ireland" to "Dublin",
            "UK" to "London",
            "France" to "Paris",
            "Spain" to "Madrid")

    println(map1)
    println(map2)
    println(map)

}
```

When defining values to be used to initialise the Map, the to operator is used to associate keys with values. Thus the expression:

```
"Ireland" to "Dublin"
```

is used to create an *association* for the key Ireland to the value Dublin. Note that values can be any type within Kotlin and thus a value could be a List, a Set or indeed another Map.

The first two statements in the above program create immutable Maps which map an Int to a String. The third statement creates a mutable map that holds a set of key:value pairs for the Capital cities of different countries.

When this code is run we see:

```
{1=John, 2=Denise}
{1=John, 2=Denise}
{Ireland=Dublin, UK=London, France=Paris, Spain=Madrid}
```

Map Properties

Maps have a set of characteristics such as their size, whether they are empty, their keys and the values they hold. These can be accessed using three properties (size, keys and values) and a member function isEmpty():

```
fun main() {
    val map = mapOf(
            "Ireland" to "Dublin",
            "UK" to "London",
            "France" to "Paris",
            "Spain" to "Madrid")
    println(map.size)  // return the sie off the map
    println(map.keys) // return a set of the keys
    println(map.values) // returns a collection of vales
    println(map.isEmpty()) // returns true or false
}
```

Th output from this is:

```
4
[Ireland, UK, France, Spain]
[Dublin, London, Paris, Madrid]
false
```

Working with Maps

Accessing Items via Keys

You can access the values held in a Map using their associated key. This is specified using either the square bracket ('[ ]') notation (where the key is within the brackets) or the get() member function. The get() is an *operator* member function that is invoked when you use the more idiomatic Kotlin index [ ] operator. Both approaches either return the value associated with the key or null:

```
fun main() {
    val map = mapOf(
            "Ireland" to "Dublin",
            "UK" to "London",
            "France" to "Paris",
            "Spain" to "Madrid")
```

```
// Returns value for key or Null
println(map.get("UK"))
// Returns value for key or null (more common style)
println(map["UK"])

println(map.get("USA"))
println(map["USA"])
}
```

The output of this is:

```
London
London
null
null
```

If you do not want the value null to be returned if the key is not present then you can use the getOrDefault() member function instead, for example:

```
println(map.getOrDefault("Germany", "Not known"))
```

Which will generate:

```
Not known
```

Adding a New Entry

A new entry can be added to a MutableMap using the idiomatic Kotlin approach via the index accessor and the new value to be assigned to that key. Alternatively you can use the operator member function put (kay, value) which is indirectly invoked when you use the index approach. For example:

```
fun main() {
    val map = mutableMapOf(
        "Ireland" to "Dublin",
        "UK" to "London",
        "France" to "Paris",
        "Spain" to "Madrid")
    // Mutable map operations
    map.put("Italy", "Rome")
    // more common format
    map["Germany"] = "Berlin"
    println(map)
}
```

Which produces:

```
{Ireland=Dublin, UK=London, France=Paris, Spain=Madrid,
Italy=Rome, Germany=Berlin}
```

Changing a Keys Value

The value associated with a key can be changed in a mutable map by reassigning a
new value using the square bracket notation, for example:

```
cities["UK"] = "Swansea"
print(cities)
```

which would now show 'Swansea' as the capital of the UK:

```
{Ireland=Dublin, UK=Swansea, France=Paris, Spain=Madrid,
Italy=Rome, Germany=Berlin}
```

Removing an Entry

An entry into the `MutableMap` can be removed using the `remove()` member
function. This function removes the entry with the specified *key* from the map.
    The following example removes the value for the key "Germany":

```
fun main() {
    val cities = mutableMapOf(
        "Ireland" to "Dublin",
        "UK" to "London",
        "Germany" to "Berlin",
        "France" to "Paris",
        "Spain" to "Madrid")
    // Mutable map operations
    println("cities: $cities")
    cities.remove("Germany")
    println("cities: $cities")
}
```

The output from this code snippet is thus:

```
cities: {Ireland=Dublin, UK=London, Germany=Berlin,
France=Paris, Spain=Madrid}
cities: {Ireland=Dublin, UK=London, France=Paris, Spain=Madrid}
```

Values, Keys and Items

There are two properties that allow you to obtain a view onto the contents of a Map, these are `values` and `keys` properties.

- The `values` property returns a mutable collection of the map's values.
- The `keys` property returns a mutable set of the onto a map's keys.

The following code uses the `cities` dictionaries with these two member functions:

```
println(cities.values)
println(cities.keys)
```

The output from the is:

```
[Dublin, London, Paris, Madrid]
[Ireland, UK, France, Spain]
```

Iterating Over Keys

You can loop through a Map using the `for` loop statement and the Maps `keys` property. The `for` loop processes each of the *keys* in the Map in turn. This can be used to access each of the values associated with the keys, for example:

```
for (key in map.keys) {
    print("$key -> ${map.get(key)}, ")
    print("$key -> ${map.get(key)}, ")
}
println()
```

Which generates the output:

```
Ireland -> Dublin, UK -> London, France -> Paris, Spain ->
Madrid, Italy -> Rome, Germany -> Berlin,
```

Iterating Over Values

If you want to iterate over all the values directly, you can do so using the Maps' `values` property. This returns a collection of all the values, which of course you can then iterate over:

```
            for (value in map.values) {
                print("$value, ")
            }
            println()
```

This generates:

```
    Dublin, London, Paris, Madrid, Rome, Berlin,
```

Iterating Over Map Entries

A final option is to iterate over the *key-value* entires in the Map directly. This can be done by applying the `for` loop to directly to the Map rather than to either the `keys` or the `values`:

```
            for (mapEntry in map) {
                println (mapEntry)
            }
```

This produces:

```
            Ireland=Dublin
            UK=London
            France=Paris
            Spain=Madrid
            Italy=Rome
            Germany=Berlin
```

Checking Key Membership

You can check to see if a key is a member of a map using the `contains()` member function:

```
            println(map.contains("UK"))
```

Nesting Dictionaries

The *key* and *value* in a map must be an valid Kotlin type; thus anything can be used as a key or a value.

One common pattern is where the *value* in a Map is itself a container such as a List, Pair, Set or even another Map.

The following example uses Lists to represent the months that make up the seasons:

```kotlin
fun main() {
    val seasons = mapOf(
        "Spring" to listOf("Mar", "Apr", "May"),
        "Summer" to listOf("June", "July", "August"),
        "Autumn" to listOf("Sept", "Oct", "Nov"),
        "Winter" to listOf("Dec", "Jan", "Feb")
    )
    println(seasons["Spring"])
    println(seasons["Spring"]?.get(1))
}
```

The output is:

```
[Mar, Apr, May]
Apr
```

Each season has a `List` for the value element of the entry. When this `List` is returned using the `key` it can be treated just like any other `List`.

Note that it was necessary to use the *safe dot* operator as the index access to a map key can return `null`.

Online Resources

See the Kotlin reference documentation for:

* https://kotlinlang.org/docs/reference/map-operations.html Map specific operations.

Exercises

The aim of this exercise is to use a Map as a simple form of data cache.

Calculating the factorial for a very large number can take some time. For example calculating the factorial of 150,000 can take several seconds. We can verify this using a `timer()` function that records the start and end time of a calculation and runs a function between the two time stamps.

Note that the range of values supported by the types such as Int and Long are limited and are not sufficient to represents the results of calculating the factorial of a number such as 30 or above. To allow larger numbers to be represented the following program uses the `java.math.BigInteger` type. This type is used to represent immutable arbitrary-precision integers. To convert any integer into a Biginteger use `toBigInteger()`, for example `0.toBigInteger()`.

To time how long a function (or indeed member function) takes to run you can use `kotlin.system.measureTimeMillis{}`. This takes a lambda function that is executed and timed. For example:

```
val timeInMillis = measureTimeMillis {
    func(parameter)
}
```

The following program runs several factorial calculations on large numbers and prints out the time taken for each:

```
package timers

import java.math.BigInteger
import kotlin.system.measureTimeMillis

val cache = mutableMapOf<BigInteger, BigInteger>()
val BigIntegerZero = 0.toBigInteger()
val OneBigInteger = 1.toBigInteger()

fun timer(func: (BigInteger) -> BigInteger?,
          parameter: BigInteger) {
    println("Starting to execute function for $parameter")
    val timeInMillis = measureTimeMillis {
        func(parameter)
    }
    println("The function took $timeInMillis ms")
}

fun factorial(number: BigInteger): BigInteger? {
    return if (number < BigIntegerZero) {
        null
    } else if (number == BigIntegerZero) {
        cache[number] = OneBigInteger
        OneBigInteger
```

```
        } else {
            var factorial = OneBigInteger
            var i = OneBigInteger
            while (i.compareTo(number) == -1) {
                factorial *= i
                i = i.inc()
            }
            cache[number] = factorial
            factorial
        }
    }

fun main() {

    println("Starting timer test")
    timer(::factorial, 25000.toBigInteger())
    timer(::factorial, 25000.toBigInteger())
    timer(::factorial, 50000.toBigInteger())
    timer(::factorial, 50000.toBigInteger())
    timer(::factorial, 150000.toBigInteger())
    timer(::factorial, 150000.toBigInteger())
    println("Done")

}
```

An example of the output generated by this program is given below:

```
Starting timer test
Starting to execute function for 25000
The function took 224 ms
Starting to execute function for 25000
The function took 145 ms
Starting to execute function for 50000
The function took 834 ms
Starting to execute function for 50000
The function took 491 ms
Starting to execute function for 150000
The function took 4568 ms
Starting to execute function for 150000
The function took 4658 ms
Done
```

As can be seen from this, in this particular run, calculating the factorial of 25,000 took 224 ms, while the factorial of 150,000 took 4658 ms etc.

In this particular case we have decided to re run these calculations so that we have actually calculated the factorial of 25,000, 50,000 and 150,000 twice.

The idea of a *cache* is that it can be used to save previous calculations and reuse those if appropriate rather than have to perform the same calculation multiple times. The use of a cache can greatly improve the performance of systems in which these repeat calculations occur.

There are many commercial caching libraries available for a wide variety of languages including Kotlin. However, at their core they are all somewhat Map like; that is there is a *key* which is usually some combination of the operation invoked and the parameter values used. In turn the *value* element is the *result* of the calculation.

These caches usually also have eviction policies so that they do not become overly large; these eviction policies can usually be specified so that they match the way in which the cache is used. One common eviction policy is the *Least Recently Used* (or LRU) policy. When using this policy once the size of the cache reaches a predetermined limit the Least Recently Used value is evicted etc.

For this exercise you should implement a *simple* caching mechanism using a Map (but *without* an eviction policy).

The cache should use the parameter passed into the `cachedFactorial()` function as the key and return the stored value if one is present.

The logic for this is usually:

1. Look in the cache to see if the key is present.
2. If it is return the value.
3. If not perform the calculation.
4. Store the calculated result for future use.
5. Return the value.

Note as the `cachedFactorial()` function is exactly that a function; you will need to think about using a global *read-only* property to hold the cache.

Once the cache is used with the `cachedFactorial()` function, then each subsequent invocation of the function using a previous value should return almost immediately. This is shown in the sample output below. In this output you can see that subsequent method calls, with the same parameter values, return in less than a millisecond.

```
Starting cached timer test
Starting to execute function for 25000
The function took 223 ms
Starting to execute function for 25000
The function took 0 ms
Starting to execute function for 50000
```

```
The function took 771 ms
Starting to execute function for 50000
The function took 0 ms
Starting to execute function for 150000
The function took 4729 ms
Starting to execute function for 150000
The function took 0 ms
Done
```

Chapter 27
Pairs and Triples

Introduction

In this chapter Pairs and Triples are presented.

Pairs and Triples are an *immutable* ordered collections of objects; that is each element in a `Pair` or `Triple` has a specific position (its index) and that position does not change over time. Indeed, it is not possible to add or remove elements from the Pair or Triple once it has been created.

A Pair is comprised of exactly two elements and a Triple is comprised of exactly three elements.

Creating Pairs and Triples

Creating Pairs

Pairs are defined using either the `Pair` class and its constructor or the `to` operator. For example:

```kotlin
fun main() {
    val pair1 = Pair<Int, String>(1, "John")
    val pair2 = Pair(2, "Denise")
    val pair3 = Pair("Adam", "Jasmine")
    val pair4 = "Phoebe" to "Gryff" // shorthand form

    println(pair1)
    println(pair2)
    println(pair3)
    println(pair4)
}
```

Each of the pairs in the above code contain exactly two elements.

© The Author(s), under exclusive license to Springer Nature Switzerland AG 2021
J. Hunt, *Beginner's Guide to Kotlin Programming*,
https://doi.org/10.1007/978-3-030-80893-8_27

The first two pairs contain an `Int` and a `String` while the third and fourth pairs contain two Strings.

The first definition of a pair for `pair1` explicitly specifies the types used for the first and second elements in the pair. The remaining definitions rely on Kotlin to infer the types of the two elements of the Pair.

Pairs 1, 2 and 3 use the long hand form where by a pair is created using the class name `Pair` and the constructor which takes two parameters.

Pair 4 is created using the shorthand form via the `to` operator.

The output from this program is:

```
(1, John)
(2, Denise)
(Adam, Jasmine)
(Phoebe, Gryff)
```

Creating Triples

Triples are created using the `Triple` class and its constructor that takes exactly three parameters. For example:

```kotlin
fun main() {
    val triple1 = Triple<Int, String, String>(1, "John",
"Denise")
    println(triple1)

    val triple2 = Triple(1, "John", "Denise")
    println(triple2)
}
```

Each Triple in the above code contain exactly three elements.

Both Triples contain an `Int` and two Strings. The first Triple also explicitly specifies the types for the three elements held in the Triple. The second decollation relies on Kotlin to infer the types of the three elements.

The output from the above code is:

```
(1, John, Denise)
(1, John, Denise)
```

Working with Pairs and Triples

Accessing Elements of a Pair or Triple

The elements of a `Pair` can be accessed using the named properties `first` and `second`. The elements of a `Triple` can be accessed using the named properties `first`, `second` and `third`.
   For example:

```kotlin
fun main() {
    val pair = Pair(1, "John")
    println(pair)
    println(pair.first)
    println(pair.second)

    val triple = Triple(1, "John", "Denise")
    println(triple)
    println(triple.first)
    println(triple.second)
    println(triple.third)
}
```

which generates the output:

```
(1, John)
1
John
(1, John, Denise)
1
John
Denise
```

Copying Pairs and Triples

Although both Pairs and Triples are *immutable*, a `copy()` member function is provided that allows a copy of a Pair or Triple to be made with one or more of the values held in the Pair or Triple overwritten.
   The `copy()` member function has two named parameters `first` and `second` for a Pair and three named parameters `first`, `second` and `third` for a Triple.
   Examples of using `copy()` with both a Pair and a Triple are given below:

```
val pair = Pair(1, "John")
println(pair.copy(first = 3))
val triple = Triple(1, "John", "Denise")
println(triple.copy(first=3))
```

The output from this is:

```
(3, John)
(3, John, Denise)
```

Converting Pairs and Tiples to Lists

A Pair or Triple can be converted into a list using the toList() member function, for example:

```
val pair = Pair(1, "John")
println("pair1.toList(): ${pair1.toList()}")
val triple = Triple(1, "John", "Denise")
println("triple2.toList(): ${triple2.toList()}")
```

This generates the following output:

```
pair1.toList(): [1, John]
triple2.toList(): [1, John, Denise]
```

Destructuring Pairs and Triples

The elements held in a Pair or Triple can be *destructured* in a similar way to data held in data classes. That is, it is possible to *unpack* values from Pairs and Triples into distinct variables. This can be done at the point that the receiving vals or vars are defined using the syntax:

val/var (<variable-list>) = pair or triple

An example of doing this for a Pair and a Triple is given below:

```kotlin
fun main() {
    val pair = Pair(1, "John")
    val (x, y) = pair
    println("x: $x, y: $y")
    val triple = Triple(1, "John", "Denise")
    val (a, b, c) = triple
    println("a: $a, b: $b, c: $c")
}
```

The output generated from this code is:

```
x: 1, y: John
a: 1, b: John, c: Denise
```

Nested Pairs and Triples

Pairs and Triples can be nested within Pairs and triples; that is a `Pair` can contain, as one of its elements, another `Pair` or indeed a `Triple` (and vice versa).

For example, the following diagram illustrates the nesting of a group of Pairs within a Triple:

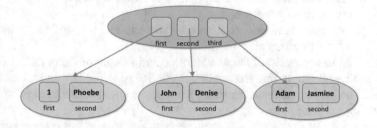

In code we could define this structure as:

```kotlin
fun main() {
    val pair1 = Pair(1, "Phoebe")
    val pair2 = Pair("John", "Denise")
    val pair3 = Pair("Adam", "Jasmine")
    val triple1 = Triple(pair1, pair2, pair3)
    println(triple1)
}
```

The output from this is:

```
((1, Phoebe), (John, Denise), (Adam, Jasmine))
```

Note the *nesting* of round brackets in the printout illustrating where one Pair or Triple is contained within another.

In fact, a `Pair` or `Triple` can have nested within it not just other Pairs and Triples but any type of container, and thus it can contain Lists, Sets, Maps etc. This provides for a huge level of flexibility when constructing data structures for use in Kotlin programs.

Things You Can't Do with Pairs and Triples

It is not possible to add or remove elements from a `Pair` or `Triple`; they are *immutable*. It should be particularly noted that none of the functions or member functions presented above actually change the original pair or triple they are applied to.

Exercises

- The aim of this exercise is to create a concordance program in Kotlin using the Pair and Map collection classes.
- For the purposes of this exercise a concordance is an alphabetical list of the words present in a text or texts with a count of the number of times that the word occurs.
- Your concordance program should include the following steps:
- Ask the user to input a sentence.
- Split the sentence into individual words (you can use the `split()` member function of the `String` class for this).
- Use a Map to keep a list of the words found and a count of the number of times they are found. To do this you could use the String as the key and a Pair as the value. The pair can contain the string itself and a count of the number of times the string has been found.
- Produce a list of the words with their counts. You can do this by accessing the `values` property of the map—which will return a sequence of Pairs (where each pair is the string of interest and the count of the number of times it appears).

An example of how the program might operate is given below:

```
Please enter text to be analysed: cat sat mat hat cat hat cat
(cat, 3)
(sat, 1)
(mat, 1)
(hat, 2)
```

Chapter 28
Generic Types

Introduction

This chapter introduces *Type Parameterisation* aka Generic Types. We have already seen examples of type parameterisation in the collection types where a List can be parameterised to hold only Strings, Person instances or integers etc. In this chapter, we will look at how you can create your own parameterised types and the options available for controlling the types that can be used with those parameterisations.

The Generic Set Class

As a concrete example of type parameterisation, we can refer back to the Set class from a few chapters ago. The Set class allows the type of element that it will hold to be specified between angle brackets '<..>' after the name of the class when declaring a val or var. It can also be used with the factory function setOf() to indicate the type of Set being created.

Of course, this being Kotlin it is also possible to allow the compiler to infer the type to use with the Set based on the contents of the collection. For example, sets 1 to 4 defined below are all sets that will contain only Strings, while set5 is a MutableSet that can only contain Strings:

```kotlin
fun main() {
    val set1: Set<String> = HashSet()
    val set2: MutableSet<String> = HashSet()
    // More idiomatic Kotlin
```

© The Author(s), under exclusive license to Springer Nature Switzerland AG 2021
J. Hunt, *Beginner's Guide to Kotlin Programming*,
https://doi.org/10.1007/978-3-030-80893-8_28

```
val set3 = setOf<String>("One", "Two", "Three")
val set4 = setOf("A", "B", "C")
val set5 = mutableSetOf("Chasing Pavements",
                        "Rumour Has it",
                        "Turning Tables")

println(set1)
println(set2)
println(set3)
println(set4)
println(set5)
}
```

Thus all of the above vals reference sets that can only contain Strings. It is therefore not possible to add a `Person` instance or an `Int` to such a set.

Equally, if we wanted a set to be limited to only holding integers then we could use `Set <Int>` and to only hold `Person` types then we would use `Set <Person>` (or the equivalent factory function such as `setOf <Int> (1, 2, 3)` or `setOf <Person> (Person("Phoebe"), Person("Gryff")))`.

In all of the above examples the class Set is referred to as a *generic* class. If you look at the definition of Set in the Kotlin documentation then you will see that it is defined as being something like:

```
Set<E>
```

Which indicates that Sets can hold elements of a type E where E is a placeholder for the type to be defined. Thus in `Set <String>` and `Set <Int>` the placeholder E has been replaced by `String` and `Int` respectively. The result of applying a type to a Set is a *parameterised* Set.

Writing a Generic Type

It is possible to create user defined or custom generic types. To do this the generic type is specified after the name of the class or interface being defined. This is done using angle brackets followed by one or more labels to use for the generic type. If more than one generic type is being defined then a comma separated list of labels is used. The labels can be anything you want but it is common to use single letters and for these letters to be related to the class or interface being created. For example, T is often used to represent a type, although E might be used for a container of elements or K and V for something that rates keys to values.

The following class defines a generic type `Bag` that can hold a single data item of type T:

```
class Bag<T>(private var data: T) {

    fun get(): T {
        return data
    }

    fun set(value: T) {
        data = value
    }
}
```

The class Bag is defined using the generic type syntax as Bag<T>. This means that within the body of the class we can refer to T as if it was a concrete type. In this case it means that the private val data is marked as being of type T. In turn the member function get() returns a value of type T and the set() member function takes a value of type T.

To use the class Bag either the programmer must specify the type to use with the Bag (such as String or Int) or the Kotlin compiler must be able to infer the type.

In the following program we create two bags, one that can only hold Strings and one that can only hold Ints.

```
fun main() {
    val bag1 = Bag<String>("Phoebe")
    println(bag1.get())
    bag1.set("Gryff")
    println(bag1.get())

    val bag2 = Bag(42)
    println(bag2.get())
    val temp: Int = bag2.get()
    println(temp)
    bag2.set(35)
    println(bag2.get())
}
```

The first Bag can hold a String and this is explicitly indicated when we create the Bag. Thus the string "Phoebe" and the String "Gryff" can be stored in the Bag. The get() member function will return a String and the set() member function will receive a String.

In turn the second Bag is inferred to hold an Int. Thus the result returned by the get() member function will now be a value of type Int. In turn the value passed into the set() member function must be an Int.

The output generated by the above program is:

```
Phoebe
Gryff
42
42
35
```

Declaration-Site Variance

Kotlin allows the programming to indicate that a generic type is only used to produce data. This is done by using the keyword out before the type in the Type Parameter (i.e. within the angle brackets). For example given some DataSource class, we can write:

```
class DataSource<out T>(val data: T) {
    fun next(): T {
        return data
    }
}
```

In this case Kotlin makes it explicit that the type T is expected to be used when data is generated, there are no member functions that consume data of type T defined. If we now write:

```
fun main() {
    val source = DataSource<Any>("Phoebe")
    println(source.next())
}
```

Then the source can produce any thing that is of type Any or a subclass of Any. Since Any is the root of the Kotlin class hierarchy this means that the data source can be a producer of instances of any type in Kotlin including Strings, Ints, Persons, any object etc.

Where as if we now write:

```
val source = DataSource<Person>()
```

This limits the DataSource to producing instances of the class Person or any subtype of the class Person.

In fact Kotlin goes further than this by checking that if you have marked a type as being out then it will only be used in *out-positions* or *producer* locations within the class. For example, as return types for member functions rather than as parameters to a member function.

Interestingly if you now look at the definition of the Set interface in Kotlin you will find that it is defined as:

```
interface Set<out E>
```

Which indicates that the type E will only be used by member functions that supply data from a Set (remember that Sets are by default immutable).

In addition to the out keyword, Kotlin as provides the complimentary version, the in keyword. It is also used with Type Parameterisation, but this time it is used to indicate that a generic type can only be *consumed* that is it can only be used in *in-positions* that is as parameters to member function and not as the return type of a member function. This is known as making a type parameter contra variant.

For example, if we define:

```
class DataConsumer<in T> {
    fun consume(data: T): Boolean {
        return true
    }
}
```

Now we can use the DataConsumer class by specifying a concrete type to use. However, it will only be able to consume (or receive) data of that type, no member functions can be defined that return data of type T.

We can thus use the DataConsumer as shown below:

```
fun main() {
    val consumer = DataConsumer<String>()
    val success = consumer.consume("Theeban")
    println(success)
}
```

Generic Functions

It is not only classes that can have type parameters; it is also possible to have generic functions.

When a generic function is being defined, the type parameter information is placed before the name of the function, for example:

```
fun <T> printer(item: T) {
    print(item)
}
```

398   28   Generic Types

To call a generic function, the type of the argument can be specified at the call site *after* the name of the function, for example:

```
printer<String>("Jasmine")
```

Or

```
printer<Int>(42)
```

However, in many cases the type can be inferred from the context/values being passed in. As such it is more common to write:

```
printer("Jasmine")
printer(42)
```

In both of these cases the type of T is being inferred, first the type is inferred to be a String and in the second it is inferred to be an Int.

Generic Constraints

If you want to limit the type used for the Type Parameterisation you can specify an *upper bound*. This indicates that the type used must be a subtype of that specified in the type constraint. The constraint is indicated using a colon (:) followed by the upper bound type. For example, if we wish to indicate the type specified to be one that implements the Comparable interface we can write:

```
fun <T : Comparable<T>> sort(list: List<T>): List<T> {
    return list.sorted()
}
```

This indicates that the type T used with the sort function must be a subtype of the Comparable interface.

Integers and Strings are sub type of Comparable and so we are able to write:

```
println(sort<String>(listOf("Jasmine", "Adam", "John")))
println(sort(listOf(1, 5, 4, 2)))
```

However, the data class Person given below does not implement the Comparable interface and therefore is not compatible with the constraint defined for T. Thus the following code does not compile:

```
data class Person(val name: String, val age: Int)
println(sort(listOf(Person("Phoebe", 23),
                    Person("Gryff, 21"))))
```

Creating a Parameterised Type

1.   Queue collections

Queues are very widely used within Computer Science and in Software Engineering. They allow data to be held for processing purposes where the guarantee is that the earlier elements added will be processed before later ones.

There are numerous variations on the basic queue operations but in essence all queues provide:

* Queue creation.
* Add an element to the back of the queue (known as enqueuing).
* Remove an element from the front of the queue (known as dequeuing).
* Find out the length of the queue.
* Check to see if the queue is empty.
* Queues can be of fixed size or variable (growable) in size.

The basic behaviour of a queue is illustrated by:

Here there are five elements in the queue, one element has already been removed from the front and another is being added at the back. Note that when one element is removed from the front of the queue all other element moved forward one position. Thus, the element that was the second to the front of the queue becomes the front of the queue when the first element is dequeued.

Many queues also allow features such as:

* *Peek* at the element at the front of the queue (that is see what the first element is but do not remove it from the queue).

- Provide *priorities* so that elements with a higher priority are not added to the back of the queue but to a point in the middle of the queue related to their priority.

In the remainder of this section we will create a parametrised Queue type.

2.   The MyQueue Mutable class

You can create your own types that are parameterised types. For example, the mutable collection class MyQueue, presented in the following listing, is a programmer defined parameterised type. It defines a placeholder T that will be used to represent various concrete types. Note by convention the letter T is used to indicate a type to specify (but we could use any letter or sequence of letters thus if the types for a key and a value were being specified we might use K and V).

```
package com.jjh.collections

class MyQueue<T> {

    private val content = mutableListOf<T>()

    val head: T
        get() = content.first()

    val size: Int
        get() = content.size

    fun enqueue(item: T) = content.add(item)

    fun dequeue(): T = content.removeFirst()

    override fun toString(): String {
        return "MyQueue(content=$content)"
    }

}
```

The class MyQueue uses T as if it were an actual type in the body of the class. Thus the type of element held by the MutableList is T, the type of element that can be enqueued using the enqueue() member function is T and the result returned by the dequeue() member function is T. The type of the head property is also T.

This class is used in exactly the same way as one of the built-in collection classes as shown below:

```
fun main() {
    val q = MyQueue<String>()
    q.enqueue("John")
    q.enqueue("Denise")
    q.enqueue("Gryff")
    q.enqueue("Jasmine")
    println(q)
    println("q.head: " + q.head)
    val name = q.dequeue()
    println(name)
    println("q.head: " + q.head)
    q.enqueue("Phoebe")
    println("q.head: " + q.head)
    println(q)
}
```

The output from this is:

```
MyQueue(content=[John, Denise, Gryff, Jasmine])
q.head: John
John
Denise
Denise
MyQueue(content=[Denise, Gryff, Jasmine, Phoebe])
```

In the above example, the type String is used to parameterise MyQueue such that it now holds Strings. The effect is that the letter T is replaced by the type String throughout the instance of the MyQueue class referenced by the variable q. Thus the type of the head property is String, the type used as a parameter to enqueue() is String and the type returned by dequeue() is String. Thus it is the same as writing:

```
val head: String
    get() = content.first()
...
fun enqueue(item: String) = content.add(item)

fun dequeue(): String = content.removeFirst()
```

However, we can also create a MyQueue of Ints, for example:

```
val q2 = MyQueue<Int>()
q2.enqueue(12)
q2.enqueue(42)
println(q2)
println(q2.head)
```

This is now the equivalent of writing:

```
val head: Int
    get() = content.first()
...
fun enqueue(item: Int) = content.add(item)

fun dequeue(): Int = content.removeFirst()
```

As well as `String` and `Int` any type can be used as the concrete type including `Double`, `Boolean` as well as user defined types such as the class `Person` or the interface `Model`.

Thus a parameterised class and type parameterisation provide a powerful construct for creating type safe, reusable code.

Note that you can create generic type parameterised Classes and Interfaces as both can be instantiated with a concrete type. You cannot create generic Objects as you do not instantiate an Object (this is handled for you by the Kotlin runtime).

Exercises

The aim of this exercise is to create your own generic `Stack` class in Kotlin. You should be able to create your `Stack` class as shown below:

```
class Stack<T>(val contents: MutableList<T> =
mutableListOf<T>()) {
    // ...
}
```

Stacks are a very widely used data type within computer science and in software applications. They are often used for evaluating mathematical expressions, parsing syntax, for managing intermediate results etc.

The basic facilities provided by a `Stack` include:

1. Stack creation.
2. Add an element to the top of the stack (known as pushing onto the stack).
3. Remove an element from the top of the stack (known as popping from the stack).
4. Find out the length of the stack.
5. Check to see if the stack is empty.
6. Stacks can be of fixed size or a variable (growable) stack.

The basic behaviour of a stack is illustrated by:

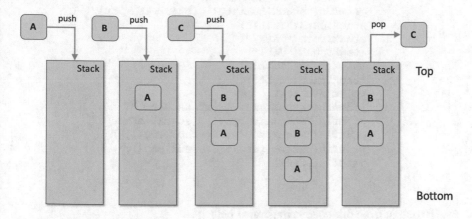

This diagram illustrates the behaviour of a Stack. Each time a new element is pushed onto the Stack, it forces any existing elements further down the stack. Thus the most recent element is at the *top* of the stack and the oldest element is at the *bottom* of the stack. To get to older elements you must first pop newer elements off the top etc.

Many stacks also allow features such as:

1. *Top* which is often an operation that allows you to peek at the element at the top of the stack (that is see what the element is but do not remove it from the stack).

The Stack class should provide:

1. A push (element) member function used to add an element to the Stack.
2. A pop () member function to retrieve the top element of the Stack (this member function removes that element from the stack).
3. A top () member function that allows you to peek at the top element on the stack (it does not remove the element from the stack).
4. A size property which will indicate the number of elements in the stack.
5. An isEmpty property to indicate whether the stack contains any elements.
6. A toString () member function so that the stack can be printed appropriately.
7. A data property which returns the underlying data structure you are using to hold the data, for example a MutableList etc.

One you have created your Stack class you should be able to run the following code:

```
fun main() {
    val stack = Stack<String>()
    println("stack.isEmpty: ${stack.isEmpty}")
    stack.push("Task1")
    stack.push("Task2")
    stack.push("Job1")
    stack.push("Task3")
    stack.push("Job2")
    println(stack)
    println("stack.size: ${stack.size}")
    println("stack.isEmpty: ${stack.isEmpty}")
    println("Stack.top(): ${stack.top()}")
    println("Stack.top(): ${stack.pop()}")
    println(stack)
}
```

The output from this code is illustrated below:

```
stack.isEmpty: true
Stack([Task1, Task2, Job1, Task3, Job2])
stack.size: 5
stack.isEmpty: false
Stack.top(): Job2
Stack.top(): Job2
Stack([Task1, Task2, Job1, Task3])
```

Chapter 29
Functional Programming and Containers

Introduction

Kotlin provides several functions that are widely used to implement functional programming style solutions in combination with collection container types.

These functions are *higher-order functions* that are applied to a collection and are given a function that will be used in various ways with the data in the receiving collection.

This chapter introduces several functions forEach(), filter(), map(), flatMap(), sortedBy(), fold(), foldRight() and reduce().

ForEach

The forEach() function is a higher order function that can be used to apply a function (which can be a callable reference to a named function, an anonymous function or most commonly a *lambda* function) to each item of data in an iterable. It is thus the functional programming equivalent of a for loop.

The result of forEach is Unit and thus it is used where no return values are expected.

An iterable is any type of container that supports the ability to iterate over its contents. Many types are iterable including arrays, sets, lists, maps, pairs and triples.

The format of foreach is:

```
iterable.forEach(function)
```

This can of course be used with the *trailing lambda syntax* used with lambda functions and higher order functions in Kotlin.

The following code creates a list of Strings and applies the forEach() higher order function to this list. Three styles are illustrated:

© The Author(s), under exclusive license to Springer Nature Switzerland AG 2021
J. Hunt, *Beginner's Guide to Kotlin Programming*,
https://doi.org/10.1007/978-3-030-80893-8_29

- The first uses a *named* function (in this case the built-in function `println()` with a callable reference (created using the box operator).
- The second uses an *anonymous* function.
- The third approach uses a *lambda* function and the *trailing lambda syntax* format. Two examples are given one where an explicitly named parameter is used and one where the implicit parameter `it` is used.

The listing is given below:

```kotlin
val myList = listOf("Zero", "One", "Two")

// Using a named function via a callable reference
myList.forEach(::println)

// Using an anonymous function
myList.forEach(fun(s: String) = println(s))

// Lambda function applied to each element in the list
myList.forEach { s -> println(s) }
myList.forEach { println(it) }
```

The output from each of the `forEach` examples above is the same as each generates:

```
Zero
One
Two
```

Note that for the *lambda* functions we have allowed the Kotlin compiler to infer the type of the variable s (and indeed the implicit parameter `it`). However, the type is determined by the type of elements held in the collection that `forEach` is applied to. Thus the type of s is `String` and we could have written this long hand if we had so desired:

```kotlin
myList.forEach { s: String -> println(s) }
```

We can apply `forEach` to any type of iterable container including Sets, Lists, Maps, Pairs and Triples as well as Arrays.

The following examples applies the `forEach` function to an array:

```kotlin
val myArray = arrayOf("Adam", "Jasmine", "Phoebe", "Gryff")
myArray.forEach { println(it) }
```

This generates:

```
Adam
Jasmine
Phoebe
Gryff
```

It is also possible to apply forEach to a Map. In the case of a Map there are three options; apply forEach to all the keys, all the values or to all the key-value pairs:

```
print("Keys: ")
map.keys.forEach { print("$it, ") }
print("\nValues: ")
map.values.forEach { print("$it, ") }
print("\nKey-Value pairs: ")
map.forEach{ (k, v) -> print("$k -> $v, ") }
println()
```

This code generates:

```
Keys: Ireland, UK, Spain,
Values: Dublin, London, Madrid,
Key-Value pairs: Ireland -> Dublin, UK -> London, Spain ->
Madrid,
```

Note that when forEach is applied to the whole Map then two parameters are supplied to the *lambda* function representing the key and the value.

Finally, there is a variation on the basic forEach function that allows you to obtain the *index* for a value in a collection as well as that value. This is the forEachIndexed() function. The function passed to forEachIndexed() must take *two* parameters, the index of the value and the value itself. This is illustrated below:

```
val myList = listOf("Zero", "One", "Two")
myList.forEachIndexed { i, s -> println("index: $i value: $s") }
```

The output from this is:

```
index: 0 value: Zero
index: 1 value: One
index: 2 value: Two
```

Filter

The filter() function is a higher order function that takes a *predicate* function (i.e. a function that returns true or false) to be used to filter out elements from a collection. The result of the filter() function is a new iterable containing only those elements selected by the predicate function.

That is, the function passed into filter() is used to test all the elements in the collection that filter is applied to. Those where the test filter returns true are included in the list of values returned. Note that the order of the elements is preserved.

The syntax of the filter() function is:

```
iterable.filter(function)
```

Note that the receiver of the filter() function is anything that is iterable which includes all Lists, Pairs, Triples, Sets and Maps, Arrays and many other types etc.

The predicate function passed in to filter() can be an *anonymous* function, a *lambda* function or a *named* function (via a callable reference).

The result returned will be an *iterable* containing all those elements that passed the test function.

Here are some examples of using filter() with a simple list of integers:

```kotlin
fun main() {
    fun isEven(i :Int) = i % 2 == 0

    val data = listOf(1, 3, 5, 2, 7, 4, 10)
    println("data; $data")

    // Filter using a named function
    val d1 = data.filter(::isEven)
    println("d1: $d1")

    // Filter using an anonymous function
    val d2 = data.filter(fun(i: Int) = i % 2 == 0)
    println("d2: $d2")

    // Filter for even numbers using a lambda function
    val d3 = data.filter{it % 2 == 0}
    println("d3: $d3")
}
```

The output from this is:

```
data; [1, 3, 5, 2, 7, 4, 10]
d1: [2, 4, 10]
```

```
d2: [2, 4, 10]
d3: [2, 4, 10]
```

Note that the type of d1, d2 and d3 is inferred by Kotlin and is List <Int>.

One difference between the *named* function example and the *anonymous* and *lambda* function examples is that with a *named* isEven() function it is more obvious what the role is of the test function. The *anonymous* function and the *lambda* function do exactly the same, but it is necessary to understand the test function itself to work out what they are doing.

It is also worth pointing out that defining a named function such as isEven() may actually pollute the namespace of the package if it is defined at the top level as there would then be a function that others might decide to use even though the original designer of this code never expected anyone else to use the isEven() function. This is why *lambda* functions are often used with filter(). However in the above code we have defined isEven() within the scope of the main() function, it is therefore not available anywhere outside of this function.

Of course, you are not just limited to applying filter() to an iterable containing fundamental built-in types such as Ints, Floats, Booleans or indeed Strings; any type can be used. For example, if we have a class Person such as:

```kotlin
class Person(val name: String, val age: Int) {
    override fun toString()= "Person($name', $age)"
}
```

Then we can create a list of instances of the class Person and then filter() out all those over 21:

```kotlin
fun main() {
    val data = listOf(
        Person("Alun", 56),
        Person("Nikki", 51),
        Person("Megan", 21))

    println("data: $data")

    // Use a lambda to filter out People over 21
    val d1 = data.filter{it.age <= 21}
    println("d1: $d1")
}
```

The output from this is:

```
data: [Person(Alun', 56), Person(Nikki', 51), Person(Megan',
21)]
d1: [Person(Megan', 21)]
```

Map

The map () function is another higher order function available in Kotlin. The map () function applies the supplied function to all items in the receiver *iterable*. It returns a new *List* of the results generated by the applied function.

It is the functional equivalent of a for loop applied to an iterable where the results of each iteration round the for loop are gathered up into a new List collection.

The map () function is very widely used within the functional programming world and it is certainly worth becoming familiar with it.

The function signature of map is:

```
iterable.map(function)
```

The function passed into the map () function is applied to each item in the *iterable*. The result returned from the function is then gathered up into a new List.

The following example applies map () to a list of integers. Each version of the function passed to map increments the value passed to it by 1:

```
fun main() {

    fun increment(i: Int) = i + 1

    val data = listOf(1, 3, 5, 2, 7, 4, 10)
    println("data: $data")

    // Apply a named function via map
    val d1 = data.map(::increment)
    println("d1: $d1")

    // Apply an anonymous function via map
    val d2 = data.map(fun(i: Int) = i + 1)
    println("d2: $d2")

    // Apply a lambda function via map
    val d3 = data.map { it + 1 }
    println("d3: $d3")
}
```

The output of the above example is:

```
data: [1, 3, 5, 2, 7, 4, 10]
d1: [2, 4, 6, 3, 8, 5, 11]
d2: [2, 4, 6, 3, 8, 5, 11]
d3: [2, 4, 6, 3, 8, 5, 11]
```

Map   411

As with the `filter()` function, the function to be applied can either be defined inline as an *anonymous* function or a *lambda* function or it can be *named* function as illustrated by `increment()`. Either can be used, the advantage of the `increment()` named function is that it makes the intent of the function explicit; however, it can pollute the namespace of the package. Which is why we have defined it within the scope of the `main()` function; thus it cannot be used outside of the scope of `main()`.

As with the `filter()` function, it is not only built-in types such as Ints that can be processed by the function supplied to map; we can also use user defined types such as the class Person. For example, if we wanted to collect all the ages for a list of Person we could write:

```kotlin
fun main() {
    val data = listOf(
        Person("Alun", 56),
        Person("Nikki", 51),
        Person("Megan", 21)
    )
    println("data: $data")

    val ages = data.map { it.age }
    println("ages: $ages")
}
```

Which creates a list of the ages of the three people:

```
data: [Person(Alun', 56), Person(Nikki', 51), Person(Megan',
21)]
ages: [56, 51, 21]
```

Flatten

The `flatten()` function is *not* a higher order function instead it is a function that can flatten a list of containers of containers down into a single level of container. It is thus often used with the higher order container functions described in this chapter.

For example, given a list of lists such as the `data` list below, we can use `flatten()` to remove one level of nesting:

```
fun main() {
    val data = listOf(
        listOf("John", "Paul", "George", "Ringo"),
        listOf("Freddie", "Brian", "Roger", "John")
    )
    println("data: $data")

    val flattenedData = data.flatten()
    println("flattenedData: $flattenedData")
}
```

In the above program the val data holds a list containing references to two sub-lists. One contains the Strings, "John", "Paul", "George" and "Ringo" while the second list contains the strings "Freddie", "Brian", "Roger" and "John". When we apply the flatten() function to this list a new list is generated which directly contains the all the strings.

This output from the above program is:

```
data: [[John, Paul, George, Ringo], [Freddie, Brian, Roger,
John]]
flattenedData: [John, Paul, George, Ringo, Freddie, Brian,
Roger, John]
```

Notice that one level of square brackets (used to indicate a list) have been removed in the flattenedData.

FlatMap

The flatMap() higher order function essentially combines the map() function with a call to flatten().

That is the function passed to flatMap() is mapped to the receiver. The result of the map() part of the operation is a List. The function flatten() is then applied to this results list. The overall result of flatMap() is then returned.

As a simple example, consider the following program:

```
fun main() {
    val listOfLists = listOf(listOf(1, 2), listOf(4, 5))
    println("listOfLists: $listOfLists")
    println("---------------")
```

```
    val data1 = listOfLists.map { it.filter { i -> i > 1 } }
    println("data1: $data1")
    val data2 = data1.flatten()
    println("data2: $data2")

    println("---------------")

    val result = listOfLists.flatMap { it.filter { i -> i > 1 }
}
    println("Result: $result")
}
```

This program creates a list of lists. The inner most lists contain integers (that is a list of 1, 2 and a list of 4, 5). The code first applies the map() function and then the flatten() function to illustrate their combined behaviour. The flatMap() function is then applied to this list of lists. The *lambda* applied to the inner lists itself applies a filter to each list which will filter out any inner list values less then 2. However, this results in the generation of two lists that are then flattened automatically.

The output from this program is:

```
listOfLists: [[1, 2], [4, 5]]
---------------
data1: [[2], [4, 5]]
data2: [2, 4, 5]
---------------
Result: [2, 4, 5]
```

Sorting Iterables

Kotlin provides two functions that can be used to *sort* the contents of an iterable, sorted() and sortedBy{}.

The sorted() function sorts the contents of an iterable using the natural ordering of a type.

The sortedBy{} function is a higher order function that uses a supplied function to generate how a type should be ordered.

An example of using both sorted() and sortedBy{} are given below:

```
fun main() {
    val myList = listOf("Zero", "Fifteen", "One", "Two")
    println(myList)

    println(myList.sorted())

    println(myList.sortedBy { s -> s.length })
}
```

The sorted() function will sort the list of strings using their natural ordering, where as the sortedBy{} function uses the *lambda* passed to it. In this case the lambda returns the length of each string and thus the list will be sorted based not he strings lengths.

Note that a *named* function or an *anonymous* function could have been used as well as a *lambda*.

The output generated by this program is:

```
[Zero, Fifteen, One, Two]
[Fifteen, One, Two, Zero]
[One, Two, Zero, Fifteen]
```

Fold

The fold() function applies a function to an iterable and combines the result returned for each element together into a single result. It thus *reduces* or *folds* the iterable down to a single value.

The fold() function takes two parameters, the value to be used to initialise the accumulated value and the function to apply to each element in the iterable.

One point that is sometimes misunderstood with fold() is that the function passed into it takes two parameters, which are the previous result and the next value in the sequence; it then returns the result of applying some operation to these parameters.

The fold() function applies the function passed to it to the elements in the iterable from left to right, that is the element with index zero is precessed first etc.

The signature of the fold() function is:

```
iterables.fold(initialValue, function)
```

Of course the trailing lambda syntax can be used with fold so that it is often written as:

```
iterables.fold(initialValue){ function }
```

One obvious use of `fold` is to sum all the values in a list:

```kotlin
fun main() {
    val data = listOf(1, 3, 5, 2, 7, 4, 10)
    println("data; $data")

    val result = data.fold(0){total, element -> total + element}
    println("result: $result")
}
```

The output generated for this code is:

```
data; [1, 3, 5, 2, 7, 4, 10]
result: 32
```

Of course we could use a *named* function or an *anonymous* function as well as a *lambda* function. For example:

```kotlin
fun adder(total: Int, value: Int) = total + value
val result2 = data.fold(0, ::adder)
println("result2: $result2")
```

This also generates the output:

```
result2: 32
```

Although it might appear that `fold` is only useful for numbers such as integers; it can be used with other types as well. For example, let us assume that we want to calculate the average age for a list of people, we could use `fold` to add together all the ages and then divide by the length of the data list we are processing:

```kotlin
fun main() {
    val data = listOf(
        Person("Alun", 56),
        Person("Nikki", 51),
        Person("Megan", 21)
    )

    println("data: $data")

    val totalAge = data.fold(0)
                        {total, element -> total + element.age}

    val averageAge = totalAge / data.size
    println("Average Age: $averageAge")
}
```

In this code example, we have a data list of three People. We then use the fold function to apply a *lambda* to the data list. The lambda takes a total and adds a person's age to that total. The value zero is used to *initialise* this running total. When the lambda is applied to the data list, we will add 56, 51 and 21 together. We then divide the final result returned by the size of the data list (3) using the / (division) operator. Finally, we print out the average age:

```
data: [Person(Alun', 56), Person(Nikki', 51), Person(Megan',
21)]
Average Age: 42
```

FoldRight

The foldRight() function performs exactly the same operation as fold() exception that it starts from the *right* hand end of the iterable rather then the left hand end. That is given the list:

$$\textbf{val } data = listOf(1, 3, 5, 2, 7, 4, 10)$$

It will start by applying the supplied function to the value 10, then 4, then 7 etc. until it reaches the value 1. It is thus the equivalent of reversing a list and then applying fold to the reversed list.

An example of using foldRight is given below:

```
fun main() {
    val data = listOf(1, 3, 5, 2, 7, 4, 10)
    println("data; $data")

    val result = data.foldRight(0) { total, element -> total +
element }
    println("result: $result")
}
```

The output from this program is:

```
                data; [1, 3, 5, 2, 7, 4, 10]
                result: 32
```

Reduce

The `reduce()` function is a higher order function that acts as a shorthand form for the most common usage of the `fold` function. That is it is used to *reduce* all the values in an iterable down to a single value. However, unlike `fold` it is not possible to define your own *initial* value for the running total as it is always initialised to zero.

An example of using `reduce()` is given below:

```
fun main() {
    val data = listOf(1, 3, 5, 2, 7, 4, 10)
    println("data; $data")

    val result = data.reduce{ total, element -> total + element
}
    println("result: $result")
}
```

This program produces the following output:

```
                    data; [1, 3, 5, 2, 7, 4, 10]
                    result: 32
```

Labelled Return from Lambdas

This section describes one of the difference between *anonymous* functions and *lambdas* and considers examples of labelled returns from *lambdas* used with container higher order functions.

We will start this section by looking at how the `return` statement works when used within an anonymous function. When `return` is used with *anonymous* function it returns from that anonymous function. For example, in the following function `processList0()` the anonymous function used with the `forEach()` higher order container function includes a `return` statement when the value passed to it is 3. This means that when the anonymous function is applied to each of the values in the list (1, 2, 3, 4, 5) then when it reaches the number 3 the *anonymous* function will immediately return and will not print the value out. However, it only returns from the anonymous function and thus the `forEach()` function will continue to apply the higher order function to the remainder of the values in the list. Once this has completed the function will then print out the message "Done".

```
fun processList0() {
    println("Starting processList0")
    listOf(1, 2, 3, 4, 5).forEach(
        fun (i: Int) {
            if (i == 3) return // Return from anonymous function
            print("$i, ")
        }
    )
    println("\nDone")
}


fun main () {
    processList0()
}
```

When this program is run the output is:

```
Starting processList0
1, 2, 4, 5,
Done
```

Which is much as you might expect.

However, now let us re-write this function using a *lambda* function:

```
fun processList1() {
    println("Starting processList1")
    listOf(1, 2, 3, 4, 5).forEach {
        if (it == 3) return // global return for the function
        print("$it, ")
    }
    println("\nDone")
}

fun main () {
    processList1()
}
```

Now when we run this program the output generated is:

```
Starting processList1
1, 2,
```

Notice that the numbers 3 and 4 nor the String "Done" are printed out.

This is because the return inside the *lambda* does not return from the *lambda* it instead returns from the *enclosing context*, which in this case is the function processList1. It thus returns from the *outer function* instead of the lambda.

This is because *lambdas* are treated by default as being *inlineable* and thus the return relates to the *contained function*. This is why in general we do not use returns from within lambdas and rely instead on the implicit return of the last expression to execute within the lambda (and in fact why Kotlin restricts the use of return within lambdas in most cases).

However, in some cases such as that presented in processList1(), there may be a reason why we want to return from the inner lambda rather than the outer function.

To do this we can *label* the higher order container function and indicate that the return is scoped within the labelled container operation. This is done using the label syntax used with break and continue. For example the forEach function can be labelled with <label>@ and when the return statement is invoked it can indicate the label to return to via return @<label>.

This is illustrated below:

```
fun processList2() {
    println("Starting processList2")
    listOf(1, 2, 3, 4, 5).forEach lit@{
        // local return to the caller of the lambda,
        // i.e. the forEach loop
        if (it == 3) return@lit
        print("$it, ")
    }
    println("\nDone with explicit label")
}

fun main () {
    processList2()
}
```

The output from this program is now:

```
Starting processList2
1, 2, 4, 5,
Done with explicit label
```

As you can see we now have the equivalent behaviour to that exhibited by the *anonymous* function.

In fact this is such a common pattern that Kotlin gives us a shorthand form that avoids the need to label container higher order functions such as forEach.

In the shorthand form it is only necessary to *label* the return using the notation return @<contianer-function> such as return@forEach (where the lambda is defined within a forEach function).

For example:

```
fun processList3() {
    println("Starting processList3")
    listOf(1, 2, 3, 4, 5).forEach {
        // local return forEach loop - shorthand form
        if (it == 3) return@forEach
        print("$it, ")
    }
    println("\nDone with implicit label")
}

fun main () {
    processList3()
}
```

The output from this program is now:

```
Starting processList3
1, 2, 4, 5,
Done with implicit label
```

Online Resources

More information on map, filter, flatMap and reduce can be found using the following online resources:

• https://kotlinlang.org/docs/reference/collection-operations.html Summary of container related operations.

Exercises

Using the Stack class you created in the last chapter, explore the use of forEach, map and filter.

You should now be able to use the forEach, filter and map functions with the Stack class as shown below:

```kotlin
fun prettyPrintItem(element: String) {
    println("\telement: '$element'")
}

fun main() {
    val stack = Stack<String>()
    stack.push("Task1")
    stack.push("Task2")
    stack.push("Job1")
    stack.push("Task3")
    stack.push("Job2")
    println(stack)

    // Apply functions to stack contents using
    // forEach, map and filter
    println("Printing the stack contents using forEach")
    stack.contents.forEach(::prettyPrintItem)

    println("Stack contents as uppercase strings")
    val capsList = stack.contents.map{ it.toUpperCase() }
    println(capsList)

    println("Found all elements representing Jobs")
    val filteredList =
        stack.contents.filter{ it.startsWith("Job") }
    println(filteredList)

}
```

The output from the above sample `main()` function might look like:

```
Stack([Task1, Task2, Job1, Task3, Job2])
Printing the stack contents using forEach
  element: 'Task1'
  element: 'Task2'
  element: 'Job1'
  element: 'Task3'
  element: 'Job2'
Stack contents as uppercase strings
[TASK1, TASK2, JOB1, TASK3, JOB2]
Found all elements representing Jobs
[Job1, Job2]
```

Part IV
Concurrent Kotlin

Chapter 30
Coroutines

Introduction

In this chapter we will introduce Kotlin *coroutines*. We will first discuss asynchronous programming/concurrency in computer programs. We will then consider *threading* which is the underlying mechanism used to support concurrency in programs running on the JVM including Kotlin. We will then discuss why *threading* is too low a level for many applications and introduce Coroutines as the Kotlin higher level solution to concurrency.

Concurrency

Concurrency is defined by the dictionary as.

two or more events or circumstances happening or existing at the same time.

In Computer Science concurrency refers to the ability of different parts or units of a program, algorithm or problem to be *executed at the same time*, potentially on multiple processors or multiple cores.

Here a processor refers to the central processing unit (or CPU) of a computer while core refers to the idea that a CPU chip can have multiple cores or processors on it.

Originally a CPU chip had a single core. That is the CPU chip had a single processing unit on it. However, over time, to increase computer performance hardware manufacturers added additional *cores* or processing units to chips. Thus a dual-core CPU chip has two processing units while a quad-core CPU chip has four processing units. This means that as far as the operating system of the computer is concerned, it has multiple CPUs on which it can run programs.

Running processing at the same time, on multiple CPUs, can substantially improve the overall performance of an application.

© The Author(s), under exclusive license to Springer Nature Switzerland AG 2021
J. Hunt, *Beginner's Guide to Kotlin Programming*,
https://doi.org/10.1007/978-3-030-80893-8_30

For example, let us assume that we have a program that will call three independent functions, these functions are:

- make a backup of the current data held by the program,
- print the data currently held by the program,
- run an animation using the current data.

Let us assume that these functions run sequentially, with the following timings:

- the *backup* function takes 13 s,
- the *print* function takes 15 s,
- the *animation* function takes 10 s.

This would result in a total of *38* s to perform all three operations. This is illustrated graphically below:

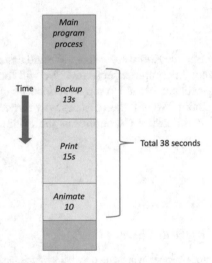

However, the three functions are all completely *independent* of each other. That is they do not rely on each other for any results or behaviour; they do not need one of the other functions to complete before they can complete etc. Thus we can run each function *concurrently*.

If the underlying operating system and program language being used support multiple processes, then we can potentially run each function in a separate process at the same time and obtain a significant speed up in overall execution time.

If the application starts all three functions at the same time, then the *maximum* time before the main process can continue will be 15 s, as that is the time taken by the *longest* function to execute. However, the main program may be able to continue as soon as all three functions are started as it also does not depend on the results from any of the functions; thus the delay may be negligible (although there will typically be some small delay as each process is set up). This is shown graphically below:

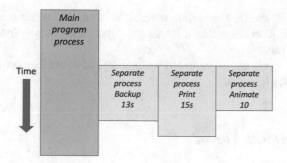

Parallelism

A distinction its often made in Computer Science between *concurrency* and *parallelism*.

In *concurrency*, separate independent tasks are performed potentially at the same time.

In *parallelism*, a large complex task is broken down into a set of *subtasks*. The subtasks represent part of the overall problem. Each subtask can be executed at the same time. Typically it is necessary to combine the results of the subtasks together to generate an overall result. These subtasks are also very similar if not functionally exactly the same (although in general each subtask invocation will have been supplied with different data/parameters).

Thus parallelism is when *multiple copies* of the same functionality are run at the same time, but on different data.

Some examples of where parallelism can be applied include:

- *A web search engine.* Such a system may look at many, many web pages. Each time it does so it must send a request to the appropriate web site, receive the result and process the data obtained. These steps are the same whether it is the BBC web site, Microsoft's web site or the web site of Cambridge University. Thus the requests can be run sequentially or in parallel.
- *Image Processing.* A large image may be broken down into slices so that each slice can be analysed in parallel.

Threads

For any JVM language, including Kotlin, the `Thread` class represents an activity that is run in a separate thread of execution within a single process. These threads of execution are lightweight, pre-emptive execution threads. A thread is a *lightweight* process because it does not possess its own address space and it is not treated as a separate entity by the host operating system; it is not a separate operating system process. Instead, it exists within a single machine process using the same address space as other threads.

Threads are a very well established technology, however they provide fairly low level concurrency features.

The Problems with Threads

There are several issues associated with the direct use of Threads to implement concurrency, including:

- Threads represent a low level API for concurrency.
- Threads are expensive in terms of CPU and System overheads.
- Threads are expensive to create, schedule and destroy.
- A thread may spend a lot of time waiting for Input/Output actions.
- A thread may spend a lot of time waiting for results produced by other treads.
- Even when threads are run natively by the operating system, there are issues such as:
- in practice the number of threads that can run at the same time (concurrently) is limited by the number of CPUs/cores available,
- if your program requires more threads than there are cores then some form of scheduler is required to coordinate the execution of the threads on the cores.

Coroutines Introduction

Coroutines are a Kotlin specific, lighter weight alternative to the JVM based Threading model. They are an abstraction layer on top of threads and thus at runtime it is still threads that execute the coroutine code for you. However, this is now done in an efficient manner, with the reuse of threads via a pool of reusable threads (referred to as a Thread Pool) and by sharing threads between coroutines.

A Thread can be shared between coroutines whenever a coroutine needs to wait for some reason (for example for some input/output operations need to be performed). This means that rather than blocking a Thread during such waits, other coroutines can make used of the Thread instead. This means coroutines use Threads in a much more efficient manner than would be the case just from directly executing behaviour within an individual Thread.

To summarise the Coroutine to Thread relationship we can say:

- coroutines are assigned to threads. The thread will then execute the coroutine for you.
- When an active coroutine is suspended, for example when waiting for input/output operations such as waiting for a database system to respond, then:

- The state of the coroutine is saved by the Kotlin runtime.
- The coroutine is removed from the Thread that is executing it.
- Another coroutine can the be assigned to the Thread.
- When the original coroutine is resumed it is assigned to the next free thread which may be a different Thread from that previously executing it.

In this way a limited number of threads can support a larger number of coroutines.

If you are confused by all this think of coroutines as a task that can be performed by a thread, however a thread can switch between tasks if the task is waiting for something to happen.

Working with Coroutines

Adding Coroutine Library Dependencies

Coroutines are not by default apart of the Kotlin environment, as such it is necessary to add the Kotlin Coroutine library to your project. In IntelliJ IDE you can do this by adding the coroutines library directly to your project (see the IntelliJ documentation for more details as this may change between versions—https://www.jetbrains.com/help/idea/library.html).

Once you have done this you can start to use the Coroutine library in your code.

Implementing a Coroutine

Coroutines can be defined using a *implicit* lambda function or as a *named* function that is marked with the keyword `suspend`.

A *suspend(ing)* function is one that can be run by the Kotlin coroutine execution/runtime but that can be suspended (without suspending the underlying thread) and can be resumed at a later point in time when the reason for its suspension has been met (for example if the coroutine is waiting for some response from a RESTful service or a database management system etc.).

This means that when we run a coroutine we need to launch that coroutine via the coroutine runtime and provide either a *lambda* or a *suspending* function.

Launching Coroutines

To use the coroutines library in Kotlin you will need to import seam or all of the contents of the `kotlin.coroutines` package. In the following program we import three elements from this package, the GlobalScope, the delay function and the launch function, for example:

```
import kotlinx.coroutines.GlobalScope
import kotlinx.coroutines.delay
import kotlinx.coroutines.launch
```

To start a coroutine we need to launch it, this can be done using the coroutine builder GlobalScope.launch{}. This allows a coroutine to be started on a separate thread (to the main application). We will return to the term *scope* with respect to coroutines below.

The GlobalScope.launch{} launcher implements a *fire and forget* policy that will start an *asynchronous* task/coroutine which will run to completion. That is there is no result returned to the main thread in which the application runs nor is there any interaction between the task and the main application - hence the term *fire* (off the task) and *forget* (about it in the main program).

The following program launches a simple coroutine using a *lambda* function passed to the launch member function (using the trailing lambda syntax). The coroutine prints out a message and then sleeps for 5,000 ms using the delay() function. This function delays/sleeps a coroutine for a given amount of time without blocking the underlying thread and resumes the coroutine after a specified time (potentially in another thread):

```kotlin
import kotlinx.coroutines.GlobalScope
import kotlinx.coroutines.delay
import kotlinx.coroutines.launch

fun main() {

    println("Main -> Launching fire-and-forget task")

    GlobalScope.launch {
        println("coroutine ---> Starting Task")
        delay(5000)
        println("coroutine ---> Done Task")
    }
    println("--------------------------------")
    println("Main -> After launching coroutine")
    println("Main -> Waiting for task - press enter to
continue:")
    readLine()
    println("--------------------------------")
    println("Main -> Done")
}
```

The main() function prints out a message after the coroutine is launched and then asks the user for input so that the main program does not terminate. This is necessary as the launcher runs the coroutine in a *background* thread. On the JVM, programs automatically terminate when there are no more *foreground* threads to execute, as this coroutine runs in the background this is not sufficient to stop the program terminating, thus we cause the *main* application thread (which is a foreground thread) to wait for user input.

The output from this coroutine program is:

```
Main -> Launching fire-and-forget task
---------------------------------
Main -> After launching coroutine
Main -> Waiting for task - press enter to continue:
coroutine ---> Starting Task
coroutine ---> Done Task


---------------------------------
Main -> Done
```

Note that the output from the main application thread (the lines prefixed with 'Main -> ' are intertwined with the output from the coroutine running in the background thread.

Suspending Functions

We can define a *named* function to run as the coroutine task by prefixing the function definition with the keyword suspend. For example:

```
import kotlinx.coroutines.delay

suspend fun executeSlowTask() {
        println("Starting Task")
        delay(5000)
        println("Done Task")
}
```

Such a function is known as a *suspending* function. A *suspending* function may suspend the execution of the current coroutine without blocking the underlying thread.

This means that the executeSlowTask() function can cause a coroutine to be suspended when it reaches the delay() function. The function can then cause the coroutine to resume when the *delay* is completed. Of course the thread that is initially executing the coroutine may or may not be the same thread as is used to resume the coroutine.

The following code illustrates how the executeSlowTask() suspending function can be run within a coroutine using the GlobalScope.launch{} launcher.

```kotlin
import kotlinx.coroutines.GlobalScope
import kotlinx.coroutines.launch

fun main() {

    println("Main -> Launching fire-and-forget task")

    GlobalScope.launch {
        executeSlowTask()
    }
    println("--------------------------------")
    println("Main -> After launching coroutine")
    println("Main -> Waiting for task - press enter to


continue:")
    readLine()
    println("---------------------------------")
    println("Main -> Done")
}
```

The output from this second version of the program is given below:

```
Main -> Launching fire-and-forget task
-----------------------------------
Main -> After launching coroutine
Main -> Waiting for task - press enter to continue:
executeSlowTask -> Starting Task
executeSlowTask ->Done Task


-----------------------------------
Main -> Done
```

As before you can see that the output from the main application (running in the *main* Thread) is interspersed with the output from the suspending function executeSlowTask() running in a background thread.

Running Multiple Concurrent Coroutines

It is possible to run multiple coroutines concurrently. This can be done by launching each coroutine independently, for example:

```
GlobalScope.launch { executeSlowTask1() }
GlobalScope.launch { executeSlowTask2() }
GlobalScope.launch { executeSlowTask3() }
```

This would cause the three slow tasks to run concurrently.

Coroutine Scope

When a coroutine is launched, it is actually launched within the context of a coroutine *scope*.

In the examples presented in the previous sections we have been using the GlobalScope. This means that the lifetime of the coroutine being launched is limited only by the lifetime of the whole application. That is the *scope* of the coroutine, in terms of where and how long it can execute, is the same as the top level (or *global*) application.

Custom Coroutine Scope

There are other alternatives to the *global* scope for coroutines. One option is to create a *custom scope*. This allows an application to manage a group of coroutines together. For example the application can then cancel all coroutines with the same scope in one go if required.

Custom scopes are built on top of a *Coroutine Dispatcher*. A Coroutine Dispatcher is the part of the coroutine *runtime* that handles how coroutines are executed and is discussed in the next section.

A new custom scope can be created by instantiating a CoroutineScope instance and passing in a suitable dispatcher, for example:

```
val customScope = CoroutineScope(Dispatchers.Main)
```

This can then be used with the launch() function, to launch a coroutine within a specific scope, for example:

```
val customScope = CoroutineScope(Dispatchers.Main)
customScope.launch {
    executeSlowTask()
}
```

Coroutine Dispatchers

Coroutine Dispatches handle how coroutines are run (dispatched). That is they handle how coroutines are assigned to JVM Threads. They also handle how coroutines are suspended (which stops them running and unloads them from a particular thread) and how they are resumed (how they are reassigned to an available thread).

There are three built-in dispatchers:

- `Dispatchers.Default` This is the default dispatcher and is intended primarily for CPU intensive tasks.
- `Dispatchers.IO` This is the dispatcher that is recommended for network, disk, database or other IO operations.
- `Dispatchers.Main` (Android specific) This is the dispatcher used to run coroutines on the main Android thread. This is significant as it allows a coroutine to make changes to UI components within an Android application.

Coroutine Builders/Launchers

Coroutine Builders/Launchers are used to dispatch (start) a coroutine within a particular scope.

There are several built-in coroutine builders/launchers including:

- `launch{}` starts a coroutine that does not return a result. It is sometimes referred to as a fire and forget coroutine. It can be used to launch a *lambda* or *suspending* function from within a normal function.
- `async{}` allows the caller thread to wait for a result generated by another coroutine using `await()` function. It can only be called from within another *suspending* function. It returns a `Deferred < T >` instance – which promises to return a result. The result must be returned from the invoked coroutine using `return@async`.
- `withContext{}` allows a coroutine to be launched with a different dispatcher context from that used by the parent coroutine. For example to switch from the Default Dispatcher to the IO dispatcher.
- `coroutineScope{}` used to allow multiple coroutines to be launched in parallel and for some behaviour to execute once all coroutines complete. It can only be launched from within a suspend function. If one (child) coroutine fails then all the coroutines fail.
- `supervisorScope{}` this is similar to `coroutineScope{}`, but failure of a child coroutine does not cause all child coroutines to fail.
- `runBlocking{}` starts a coroutine and blocks the current thread. This is usually only used for testing.
- `withTimeout(millseconds){}` runs the associated coroutine. However the launched coroutine must complete within the specified time.

An example of a coroutine that returns a result using the `async{}` launcher and the `GloabalScope` is given below:

```
suspend fun executeSlowTaskWithResultAsync(): Deferred<Int> =
    GlobalScope.async {
        println("executeSlowTaskWithResultAsync --> Starting
Task")
        delay(5000)
        println("executeSlowTaskWithResultAsync --> Done Task")
        return@async 42
    }
```

Note that the return type of the `GlobalScope.async{}` is `Deferred < Int >` in the above suspending function. This is used as the return result for the whole function and indicates that this function will return a result asynchronously. It also indicates that the deferred result will be an `Int`. It then uses `return@async` to return the integer 42.

This *suspending* function can be invoked from the main application as shown below:

```
fun main() {
    println("Main -> Launching deferred result task")
    GlobalScope.launch {
        val result = executeSlowTaskWithResultAsync().await()
        println("coroutine --> result: $result")
    }
    println("Main -> After launching coroutine")
    println("Main -> Waiting for task - press enter to
continue:")
    readLine()
    println("Main -> Done")
}
```

The output from this program is:

```
Main -> Launching deferred result task
Main -> After launching coroutine
Main -> Waiting for task - press enter to continue:
executeSlowTaskWithResultAsync --> Starting Task
executeSlowTaskWithResultAsync --> Done Task
coroutine --> result: 42

Main -> Done
```

As you can see from this the result is returned from the `executeSlowTaskWithResult()` suspending function. The main launcher waits for this result using the `await()` member function of a suspending function.

As an example of the `withContext{}` launcher the following code illustrates running a coroutine using a different dispatcher:

```
suspend fun performTask() {
    println("Task 1: ${Thread.currentThread().name}")
}
```

```
suspend fun startWork() {
    println("startWork")
    withContext(Dispatchers.IO){performTask2()}
    println("end startWork")

}
```

Coroutine Jobs

Each call to a launcher such as `launch{}`, `async{}` etc. returns a *Job* instance. These jobs are instances of the `kotlinx.coroutines.Job` class. Jobs can be used to track and manage the lifecycle of coroutines. In turn calls to coroutines within a coroutine result in child jobs.

Once you have a reference to a coroutine job you can cancel a job. If the associated coroutine has children then you can also cancel child jobs.

The status of the associated coroutine can also be obtained from a job using Boolean properties such as `isActive`, `isCompleted` and `isCancelled`.

There are also a range of member functions defined for jobs including:

- `invokeOnCompletion{}` this is used to provide behaviour to run when job completed,
- `join()` which suspends the current coroutine until the receiver coroutine completes,
- `cancel(CalcellationException?)` which cancels a job,
- `cancelChildren()` which cancels child jobs of a receiver job,
- `cancelAndJoin()` cancel the receiving coroutine and wait for it to complete before continuing.

The following program illustrate some of these ideas. It creates a new coroutine using the `GlobalScope.launch{}` launcher and stores the resulting job reference in the val `job`. It then uses this job to check to see if it is still active, whether it has completed, has it been cancelled and whether it has any child jobs or not. It also registers a callback lambda to be invoked when the job completes:

```kotlin
import kotlinx.coroutines.GlobalScope
import kotlinx.coroutines.launch

fun main() {
    println("Launching fire-and-forget task")
    val job = GlobalScope.launch {
        executeSlowTask()
    }
    println("After launching coroutine")
    println("job.isActive: ${job.isActive}")
    println("job.isCompleted: ${job.isCompleted}")
    println("job.isCancelled: ${job.isCancelled}")
    println("job.children.count(): ${job.children.count()}")
    job.invokeOnCompletion { println("I am Completed") }


    println("Waiting for task - press enter to continue:")
    readLine()
    println("Done")
}
```

The output from this program is:

```
Launching fire-and-forget task
After launching coroutine
job.isActive: true
job.isCompleted: false
job.isCancelled: false
executeSlowTask -> Starting Task
job.children.count(): 0
Waiting for task - press enter to continue:
executeSlowTask ->Done Task
I am Completed

Done
```

As can be seen from this output the job is still active, has not been completed or cancelled, has zero child jobs etc. It also calls the on completion callback after the task completes.

Online Resources

See the following online resources for information on coroutines:

- https://kotlinlang.org/docs/reference/coroutines-overview.html Coroutines for asynchronous programming.

Exercise

In this exercise you will create a suspending function and run several coroutines concurrently.

Create a suspending function called printer() that takes three parameters:

- a message to be printed out,
- a maximum value to use for a period to sleep,
- the number of times that the message should be printed.

Within the function create a loop that iterates the number of times indicated by the third parameter. Within the loop.

- generate a random number from 0 to the max period specified and then sleep for that period of time. You can use the Random.nextLong(0, sleep) function for this,
- once the *sleep* period has finished print out the message passed into the function,
- then loop again until this has been repeated the number of times specified by the final parameter.

Next run the printer() function with various different parameters. Each execution of the suspending function printer() should be launched independently using the GlobalScope.

An example program to concurrently run the printer() function five times is given below:

```kotlin
import kotlin.random.Random
import kotlinx.coroutines.delay
import kotlinx.coroutines.GlobalScope
import kotlinx.coroutines.launch

fun main() {
    println("Main -> Launching fire-and-forget tasks")
    GlobalScope.launch { printer("A", 100, 10) }
    GlobalScope.launch { printer("B", 200, 5) }
    GlobalScope.launch { printer("C", 50, 15) }
    GlobalScope.launch { printer("D", 30, 7) }
    GlobalScope.launch { printer("E", 75, 12) }
    println("--------------------------------")
    println("Main -> After launching coroutine")
    println("Main -> Waiting for task - press enter to
continue:")
    readLine()
    println("--------------------------------")
    println("Main -> Done")
}
```

An example of the sort of output this could generate is given below:

1. Main -> Launching fire-and-forget tasks
2. ----------------------------------
3. Main -> After launching coroutine
4. Main -> Waiting for task - press enter to continue:
5. C, B, E, D, A, D, A, C, A, D, C, D, C, D, C, E, C, D, A, D,
   E, C, E, C, A, C, B, A, E, E, E, C, C, A, E, E, A, C, B, E,
   C, A, E, C, E, A, C, B, B,
6. ----------------------------------
7. Main -> Done

Chapter 31
Coroutine Channel Communications

Introduction

In this chapter we will discuss communications between separate coroutines. This is not an uncommon requirement within asynchronous programs.

In the last chapter we treated our coroutines as being of the so called *fire and forget* category. That is once a coroutine was launched it could run to completion and had no interaction with any other coroutines etc.

However, in many situations one coroutine needs to communication with one or more other coroutines. For example, one coroutine may be a producer of data and another coroutine (or coroutines) may be a consumer of that data.

In this chapter we will consider how channels provide for communications between coroutines, look at how multiple coroutines can send data to a channel and how multiple coroutines can receive data from channels. We will conclude by looking at buffered channels.

Coroutine Channels

Coroutine Channels provide for communications between coroutines. This differs from the use of deferred values between coroutines. A deferred value is a promise from one coroutine to another to supply a value at some point in the future. A channel allows for the transfer of a stream of data between two or more cooperating coroutines.

© The Author(s), under exclusive license to Springer Nature Switzerland AG 2021
J. Hunt, *Beginner's Guide to Kotlin Programming*,
https://doi.org/10.1007/978-3-030-80893-8_31

The idea behind channels is illustrated below:

To enable two coroutines to communicate you need to

- create a shared channel,
- have at least one coroutine that must *send* some data to the channel,
- have at least one other coroutine that must *receive* that data.

The terms *send* and *receive* above relate to the functions defined on a `Channel`. That is Channels have a suspending *send* function and a suspending *receive* function. This means that several coroutines can use channels to pass data to each other in a non-blocking fashion. Thus you can have multiple senders and multiple receivers.

For example, to send data to a channel:

```
channel.send(data)
```

And to receive data from a channel:

```
val data = channel.receive()
```

It is also possible to *close* a channel to indicate that there will be no more data sent. A channel can be closed using the `close()` member function:

```
channel.close()
```

There are four types of channels, and they differ in the number of values they can hold at a time. These four are:

- **Rendezvous Channel** used to coordinate the *send* and *receive* of messages.
- **Buffered Channel** provides a predefined buffer that allows several messages to be sent before the channel blocks while waiting for receives to handle those messages.
- **Unlimited Buffered Channel** provides for an unlimited size buffer so any number of messages can be sent without blocking the sending coroutine.
- **Conflated Channel** When using this channel type, the most recent value overwrites any previous values sent but not yet received.

Examples of each of these types of channel will be given in the remainder of this section.

Note to use challenge we need to import the appropriate type form the `kotlinx.coroutines.channels` package.

Rendezvous Channel

A rendezvous channel is used to allow two or more coroutines to coordinate the sending and receiving of data. With a rendezvous channel the:

- sending coroutine suspends until a receiver coroutine invokes *receiv* on the channel,
- consuming coroutine suspends until a producer coroutine invokes *send* on the channel.

A rendezvous channel does not have a buffer so only one value can be sent at a time.

A rendezvous channel is created using the default *Channel* constructor with no arguments, for example:

```
val channel = Channel<Int>()
```

Note that the Channel is a generic type and thus the type of data handled by the channel is specified when it is created. In the above example we are creating a channel that can handle integers, if we wanted to create a channel that could handle Strings then we would write:

```
val channel = Channel<String>()
```

An example of a program that creates a shared *rendezvous* channel used by two coroutines is given below.

```
import kotlinx.coroutines.GlobalScope
import kotlinx.coroutines.channels.Channel
import kotlinx.coroutines.delay
import kotlinx.coroutines.launch

fun main() {
    val channel = Channel<Int>() // Shared rendezvous Channel

    suspend fun sendDataToChannelTask() {
        repeat(3) {
            delay(100)
            println("Sending ---> $it")
            channel.send(it)
        }
    }

    suspend fun receiveDataFromChannelTask() {
        repeat(3) {
            println("Receiving ---> ${channel.receive()}")
        }
    }
```

```
println("Main -> Launching rendezvous channel task")
GlobalScope.launch { sendDataToChannelTask() }
GlobalScope.launch { receiveDataFromChannelTask() }
println("Main -> After launching coroutines")
println("Main -> Waiting for tasks - press Enter to
Terminate:")
    readLine()
    channel.close()
    println("Main -> Done")
}
```

In the above program you can see the two functions:

- `sendDataToChannelTask()` which is a suspending function that publishes three values with a 100 ms delay between each.
- `receiveDataFromChannelTask()` which is a suspending function that receives each value but is blocked until a value is available.

The `main()` function launches both functions as coroutines and then waits for user input before terminating.

The output generated by this program is:

```
Main -> Launching rendezvous channel task
Main -> After launching coroutines
Main -> Waiting for tasks - press Enter to Terminate:
Sending ---> 0
Receiving ---> 0
Sending ---> 1
Receiving ---> 1
Sending ---> 2
Receiving ---> 2

Main -> Done
```

As can be seen from the output the sending and receiving coroutines coordinate their sending and receiving actions. That is, the receiving coroutine blocks until the sending coroutine publishes some data.

Buffered Channel

The Buffered Channel is a channel type that has a predefined buffer. The buffer size is specified when the Channel is created. For example to create a Channel that can handle Ints and has a buffer of 10 integers you can write:

```
val channel = Channel<Int>(10)
```

This means that the publishing coroutine can send 10 integers to the channel before the send operation will block that coroutine.

A modified version of the program shown in the previous section is given below. It differs in three ways:

- The channel created is now a shared *buffered* channel with a buffer of size 2.
- The receiveDataFromChannelTask() suspending function has an initial delay of 50 ms before it enters a while loop that will allow it to continue processing data while there is data available.
- Inside the wile loop of the receiveDataFromChannelTask() suspending function a further delay of 100 ms has been used to ensure that the receiver has to wait between reads. This means that the sending coroutine will always run ahead of the receiving coroutine and thus the sender will be able to send up to 2 values into the buffered channel before it is blocked.

```kotlin
import kotlinx.coroutines.GlobalScope
import kotlinx.coroutines.channels.Channel
import kotlinx.coroutines.delay
import kotlinx.coroutines.launch

fun main() {
    val channel = Channel<Int>(2) // Shared Buffered Channel

    suspend fun sendDataToChannelTask() {
        repeat(5) {
            delay(50)
            println("Sending ---> $it")
            channel.send(it)
        }
    }

    suspend fun receiveDataFromChannelTask() {
        delay(500)
        while (true) {
            delay(100)
            println("Receiving ---> ${channel.receive()}")
        }
    }

    println("Main -> Launching Buffered channel task")
    GlobalScope.launch { sendDataToChannelTask() }
    GlobalScope.launch { receiveDataFromChannelTask() }
    println("Main -> After launching coroutines")
    println("Main -> Waiting for tasks - press Enter to
Terminate:")
    readLine()
    channel.close()
    println("Main -> Done")
}
```

The output from this program is:

```
Main -> Launching Buffered channel task
Main -> After launching coroutines
Main -> Waiting for tasks - press Enter to Terminate:
Sending ---> 0
Sending ---> 1
Sending ---> 2
Receiving ---> 0
Sending ---> 3
Receiving ---> 1
Sending ---> 4
Receiving ---> 2
Receiving ---> 3
Receiving ---> 4

Main -> Done
```

Looking at the output it is possible to see that when the sending coroutinesend the 3rd value into the channel that it is blocked. It must then wait for the receiving coroutine to receive a value before it can send another value. This behaviour is repeated until the sending coroutine has sent all its values. The receiver can then read the remaining values held in the buffer.

Unlimited Buffered Channel

An unlimited buffered channel has an unlimited buffer size. Therefore any number of messages can be sent without blocking the sending coroutine. The receiving coroutine will receive buffered data when it is ready to process that data.

The unlimited buffered channel may generate an OutOfMemoryError as the unlimited size of the buffer will allow it to fill up all available memory within the application runtime.

An Unlimited Buffered Channel is created by providing UNLIMITED as the constructor parameter when instantiating a Channel. For example:

```
import kotlinx.coroutines.channels.Channel.Factory.UNLIMITED

val channel = Channel<Int>(UNLIMITED)
```

If the previous program is modified merely by changing the channel to be the above and the program is rerun then the output generated is now:

```
Main -> Launching Unlimited channel task
Main -> After launching coroutines
Main -> Waiting for tasks - press Enter to Terminate:
Sending ---> 0
Sending ---> 1
Sending ---> 2
Sending ---> 3
Sending ---> 4
Receiving ---> 0
Receiving ---> 1
Receiving ---> 2
Receiving ---> 3
Receiving ---> 4

Main -> Done
```

As you an see from this the sending coroutine publishes all its data to the unlimited buffered channel before the receiver even starts processing that data.

Conflated Channel

A Conflated Channel will conflate published but as yet un read values. That is, the most recently written value overrides the previously written values that have not yet been received (read) by any coroutines. Thus:

- the *send* member function of the channel never suspends,
- the *receive* member function receives only the latest value.

To create a Conflated Channel you create a Channel and pass in the CONFLATED value to the constructor:

```
import kotlinx.coroutines.channels.Channel.Factory.CONFLATED

val channel = Channel<Int>(CONFLATED)
```

If we now modify the preceding program by changing the channel declaration to that used above and rerun it, then the output generated is:

```
Main -> Launching rendezvous channel task
Main -> After launching coroutines
Main -> Waiting for tasks - press Enter to Terminate:
Sending ---> 0
Sending ---> 1
Sending ---> 2
Sending ---> 3
Sending ---> 4
Receiving ---> 4
```

Notice how the only value received by the consuming coroutine is the value 4. This is the last value published before the producer coroutine finishes.

Multiple Senders and Receivers

The examples presented so far all show a single sending coroutine and a single receiver coroutine; however it is possible to have multiple senders and multiple receivers.

Multiple Coroutine Channel Senders

There can be multiple senders to a channel. The values sent are processed in the order they are sent from the various different coroutines using that channel. The values will be received by the receiver in the time order that they were sent (no matter which sending coroutine published that data).

A simple program illustrating the use of two coroutines that publish data to a common rendezvous channel with one receiver is given below:

```kotlin
import kotlinx.coroutines.GlobalScope
import kotlinx.coroutines.channels.Channel
import kotlinx.coroutines.delay
import kotlinx.coroutines.launch

fun main() {

    suspend fun sendMessage(tag: String,
                            channel: Channel<String>,
                            message: String,
                            time: Long) {
        repeat (5) {
            delay(time)
            println("$tag sending --> $message")
            channel.send(message)
        }
    }

    suspend fun receiveMessage(channel: Channel<String>) {
        while (true) {
            println("Receiver --> ${channel.receive()}")
        }
    }
```

```
        println("Main -> Multiple senders and one receiver")
        val msgChannel = Channel<String>()
        GlobalScope.launch { sendMessage("Sender1",
                                         msgChannel,
                                         "Welcome",
                                         300L) }
        GlobalScope.launch { sendMessage("Sender2",
                                         msgChannel,
                                         "Hello",
                                         150L) }
        GlobalScope.launch { receiveMessage(msgChannel) }

        println("Main -> After launching coroutines")
        println("Main -> Waiting for task - press enter to
continue:")
        readLine()
        msgChannel.close()
        println("Main -> Done")
}
```

This program generates the output:

```
    Main -> Multiple senders and one receiver
    Main -> After launching coroutines
    Main -> Waiting for task - press enter to continue:
    Sender2 sending --> Hello
    Receiver --> Hello
    Sender1 sending --> Welcome
    Receiver --> Welcome
    Sender2 sending --> Hello
    Receiver --> Hello
    Sender2 sending --> Hello
    Receiver --> Hello
    Sender1 sending --> Welcome
    Receiver --> Welcome
    Sender2 sending --> Hello
    Receiver --> Hello
    Sender2 sending --> Hello
    Receiver --> Hello
    Sender1 sending --> Welcome
    Receiver --> Welcome
    Sender1 sending --> Welcome
    Receiver --> Welcome
    Sender1 sending --> Welcome
    Receiver --> Welcome

    Main -> Done
```

As you can see the output intermixes `Sender1` and `Sender2` with the *delay* used for `Sender1` *double* that used for Sender2.

Multiple Coroutine Channel Receivers

Just as there can be multiple sending coroutines there can be multiple receiving coroutines. In this scenario when the single sending coroutine publishes data to the channel, if there is an available receiving coroutine then that coroutine receives the data. Once the data has been consumed it is removed from the data stream. Thus only one receiving coroutine will receive each data item.

A simple program using multiple receiver coroutines is presented below:

```kotlin
import kotlinx.coroutines.GlobalScope
import kotlinx.coroutines.channels.Channel
import kotlinx.coroutines.delay
import kotlinx.coroutines.launch
import java.util.*

fun main() {

    suspend fun sendMessage(channel: Channel<String>,
                            message: String,
                            time: Long) {
        repeat(5) {
            delay(time)
            val messageToSend = "$message + ${Date()}"
            println("Sender sending --> $messageToSend")
            channel.send(messageToSend)
        }
    }

    suspend fun receiveMessage(tag: String,
                               channel: Channel<String>,
                               time: Long) {
        while (true) {
            delay(time)
            println("$tag --> ${channel.receive()}")
        }
    }
    println("Main -> Single sender and multiple receivers")
    val msgChannel = Channel<String>()

    // Launch Single sending coroutine
    GlobalScope.launch {
        sendMessage(msgChannel, "Welcome", 1000L)
    }
```

```
        // Launch multiple receiver coroutines
    GlobalScope.launch { receiveMessage("Receiver1",
                                         msgChannel,
                                         1000L) }
    GlobalScope.launch { receiveMessage("Receiver2",
                                         msgChannel,
                                         1500L) }


    println("Main -> After launching coroutines")
    println("Main -> Waiting for tasks - press enter to
continue:")
    readLine()
    msgChannel.close()
    println("Main -> Done")


}
```

The output from this program is:

```
Main -> Single sender and multiple receivers
Main -> After launching coroutines
Main -> Waiting for tasks - press enter to continue:
Sender sending --> Welcome + Wed Feb 03 15:01:57 GMT 2021
Receiver1 --> Welcome + Wed Feb 03 15:01:57 GMT 2021
Sender sending --> Welcome + Wed Feb 03 15:01:58 GMT 2021
Receiver2 --> Welcome + Wed Feb 03 15:01:58 GMT 2021
Sender sending --> Welcome + Wed Feb 03 15:01:59 GMT 2021
Receiver1 --> Welcome + Wed Feb 03 15:01:59 GMT 2021
Sender sending --> Welcome + Wed Feb 03 15:02:00 GMT 2021
Receiver2 --> Welcome + Wed Feb 03 15:02:00 GMT 2021
Sender sending --> Welcome + Wed Feb 03 15:02:01 GMT 2021
Receiver1 --> Welcome + Wed Feb 03 15:02:01 GMT 2021

Main -> Done
```

As you can see the data sent by the Sender coroutine is received in turn by either Receiver1 or Receiver2.

Pipelines

Pipelines are a design pattern where one coroutine produces a set of values and another coroutines consume those values, does some processing on the values, and then sends the modified values onto another channel.

The idea behind a pipeline is illustrated by the following diagram:

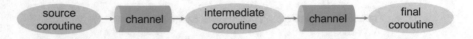

In this diagram an initial source coroutine sends data to a first channel. Another coroutine then receives that data, processes it in some way and then sends the results onto a new channel. The second channel then passes the data onto the final coroutine that consumes the results.

Depending upon the type of channels used, the final coroutine can be the controlling coroutine that determines how data is sent through the pipeline. For example, if both intermediate channels are rendezvous channels then it is only when the final coroutine consumes the data that the next data item can be sent through the whole pipeline.

A simple example application that implements the two channel pipeline illustrated above is given below.

In this pipeline an initial source numberGenerator() coroutine generates a series of integer numbers. These numbers are sent to channel1. Another coroutine running the doubler() suspending function receives data from channel1, doubles the number and sends it onto channel2. Finally a third coroutine running the printer() suspending function receives the number from channel2 and prints it out.

```kotlin
import kotlinx.coroutines.GlobalScope
import kotlinx.coroutines.channels.Channel
import kotlinx.coroutines.delay
import kotlinx.coroutines.launch

fun main() {

    suspend fun numberGenerator(channel: Channel<Int>,
                                time: Long) {
        repeat (5) {
            delay(time)
            println("numberGenerator sending --> $it")
            channel.send(it)
        }
    }


    suspend fun doubler(inputChannel: Channel<Int>,
                        outputChannel: Channel<Int>) {
```

```
            while (true) {
                val num = inputChannel.receive()
                println("doubler received --> $num")
                val newNum = num * 2
                println("doubler sending --> $newNum")
                outputChannel.send(newNum)
            }
        }

    suspend fun printer(channel: Channel<Int>) {
        while (true) {
            println("printer received --> ${channel.receive()}")
        }
    }

    // Set up channels
    val channel1 = Channel<Int>()
    val channel2 = Channel<Int>()

    // Launch the coroutines
    GlobalScope.launch {numberGenerator(channel1, 150L) }
    GlobalScope.launch { doubler(channel1, channel2) }
    GlobalScope.launch { printer(channel2) }

    // Wait for coroutines to complete
    println("Main -> After launching coroutines")
    println(
        "Main -> Waiting for task - press enter to continue:")
    readLine()
    channel1.close()
    channel2.close()
    println("Main -> Done")

}
```

The output from this is:

```
    Main -> After launching coroutines
    Main -> Waiting for task - press enter to continue:
    numberGenerator sending --> 0
    doubler received --> 0
    doubler sending --> 0
    printer received --> 0
    numberGenerator sending --> 1
    doubler received --> 1
```

```
doubler sending --> 2
printer received --> 2
numberGenerator sending --> 2
doubler received --> 2
doubler sending --> 4
printer received --> 4
numberGenerator sending --> 3
doubler received --> 3
doubler sending --> 6
printer received --> 6
numberGenerator sending --> 4
doubler received --> 4
doubler sending --> 8
printer received --> 8

Main -> Done
```

From this output you can see that

- the numbers are initially published by the `numberGenerator()` suspending function,
- they are received and processed by the `doubler()` suspending function and
- finally received (and printed) by the `printer()` suspending function.
- This is a common enough pattern that there is a simpler way to set up the different channels. This can be done by defining the suspending functions as extensions of the `CoroutineScope` object. Thus functions are defined using the syntax:
- `fun CoroutineScope.<nameOfFunction>(.. Parameters ..):`
- `ReceiveChannel<T> =`
- `produce { .. body of function...}`
- Such a function is not marked as being suspending but will be expected to return a `ReceiveChannel`. This is handled via the `produce{}` function which is used to wrap up the behaviour of the function. The `produce{}` function launches a new coroutine to produce a stream of values by sending them to a channel and returns a reference to the coroutine as a `ReceiveChannel`. Within the *lambda* passed to the `produce{}` function calls to send will automatically send the data items to the `ReceiverChannel` return from produce.
- An example of using this style of pipelining is given below:

```
import kotlinx.coroutines.CoroutineScope
import kotlinx.coroutines.GlobalScope
import kotlinx.coroutines.channels.ReceiveChannel
import kotlinx.coroutines.channels.produce
import kotlinx.coroutines.delay
import kotlinx.coroutines.launch
```

```kotlin
fun main() {

    fun CoroutineScope.numberGenerator(): ReceiveChannel<Int> =
        produce<Int> {
            var i = 0
            while (true) {
                delay(150L)
                println("numberGenerator sending --> $i")
                send(i)
                i++
            }
        }

    fun CoroutineScope.doubler(channel: ReceiveChannel<Int>):
    ReceiveChannel<Int> =
        produce {
            while (true) {
                val num = channel.receive()
                println("doubler received --> $num")
                val newNum = num * 2
                println("doubler sending --> $newNum")
                send(newNum)
            }
        }

    GlobalScope.launch {
        // produces integers from 1 and on
        val numberChannel = numberGenerator()
        // doubles integers received from number channel
        // and resends
        val doublerChannel = doubler(numberChannel)

        // Receiver used to print final results
        repeat (4) {
            println("receiving --> ${doublerChannel.receive()}")
        }
    }

    println("Main -> After launching coroutines")
    println("Main -> Waiting for task - press enter to
continue:")
    readLine()
    println("Main -> Done")

}
```

The output from this is:

```
Main -> After launching coroutines
Main -> Waiting for task - press enter to continue:
numberGenerator sending --> 0
doubler received --> 0
doubler sending --> 0
receiving --> 0
numberGenerator sending --> 1
doubler received --> 1
doubler sending --> 2
receiving --> 2
numberGenerator sending --> 2
doubler received --> 2
doubler sending --> 4
receiving --> 4
numberGenerator sending --> 3
doubler received --> 3
doubler sending --> 6
receiving --> 6
numberGenerator sending --> 4
doubler received --> 4
doubler sending --> 8
receiving --> 8
numberGenerator sending --> 5

Main -> Done
```

Exercise

In this exercise you will create three suspending functions; one suspending function
will publish data to a channel and two other receivers will handle that data when
emitted by the channel.

The channel (called msgChannel) will handle strings, it can therefore be defined
as:

```
val msgChannel = Channel<String>()
```

Each publishing suspending function and the two receivers will all be launched
independently.

The publishing suspending function should take the channel to use, and a timeout
to be used between each value being published. The strings to be published should
be held in an array of Strings such as:

```
val messages = arrayOf("Hello", "Welcome", "G'day", "Bonjour",
"Ola")
```

The suspending function should randomly select a message to be published from
the above array.

Two types of receiver should be implemented. One should be a suspending function that will receive a published message and print it. Between each receive it should sleep (delay) for a given amount of time. The parameters to this function shod be the channel to be used for communications and the delay to use as a Long.

The other receiver should be a lambda function that is defined within the launcher itself.

A sample of what the main() function might look like for this exercise is given below:

```kotlin
fun main() {

    println("Main -> Single sender and multiple receivers")
    val msgChannel = Channel<String>()

    // Launch Single sending coroutine
    GlobalScope.launch {
        sendMessageOfTheDay(msgChannel, 1000L)
    }

    GlobalScope.launch { receiveMessage(msgChannel, 1000L) }
    GlobalScope.launch {
        while (true) {
            println("\t\treceiving --> ${msgChannel.receive()}")
        }
    }

    println("--------------------------------")
    println("Main -> After launching coroutines")
    println("Main -> Waiting for tasks - press enter to
continue:")
    readLine()
    msgChannel.close()
    println("--------------------------------")
    println("Main -> Done")

}
```

The output from this sample program might look like:

```
Main -> Single sender and multiple receivers
--------------------------------
Main -> After launching coroutines
Main -> Waiting for tasks - press enter to continue:
   Sender sending --> Bonjour + Tue Apr 27 14:45:09 BST 2021
         receiving --> Bonjour + Tue Apr 27 14:45:09 BST 2021
   Sender sending --> Hello + Tue Apr 27 14:45:10 BST 2021
```

```
        receiveMessage --> Hello + Tue Apr 27 14:45:10 BST 2021
Sender sending --> Bonjour + Tue Apr 27 14:45:11 BST 2021
        receiving --> Bonjour + Tue Apr 27 14:45:11 BST 2021
Sender sending --> Ola + Tue Apr 27 14:45:12 BST 2021
        receiving --> Ola + Tue Apr 27 14:45:12 BST 2021
Sender sending --> G'day + Tue Apr 27 14:45:13 BST 2021
        receiveMessage --> G'day + Tue Apr 27 14:45:13 BST 2021


----------------------------------

Main -> Done
```

Part V
Android Development

Chapter 32
Android Overview

Introduction

In 2019 Google declared that Kotlin was its preferred development language for Android development. This chapter will therefore introduce Android Mobile device application development.

What is Android?

Android is an open software platform for mobile development. It is very widely used from smart phones, to tablets and from smart TVs to in car systems. It provides a complete system stack, from the low level operating system kernel, through the runtime environment and system provided services and libraries to application execution.

This is illustrated in the following diagram:

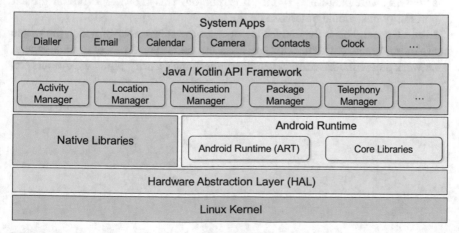

There are several different levels in this diagram represented by each of the boxes, a short summary of each of these is given below:

- **System Applications**. Android provides a set of core applications such as an email client, a calendar, a camera or a telephone dialer etc. The exact applications depends on the actual environment on which Android is running (for example the dialer may not be appropriate for Android TV and the Camera may not be appropriate for Android Auto). Custom applications can interact with these system provided applications using the Android infrastructure.

- **API Framework**. Developers have access to framework APIs that allow custom applications to either be notified of events occurring within the device (such as the device being tilted) or to interact with facilities provided by the Android platform such as the Location Manager or the Telephony Manager.

- **Native Libraries**. These are a set of libraries provided by Android that are implemented natively, that is they run directly on the underling operating system. These libraries include secure socket communications, OpenGL graphics libraries and WebKit for HTML rendering. They are exposed to Kotlin developers through the Android application framework.

- **Android Runtime**. This is divided into two parts, the Android Runtime (aka ART) itself and the set of core Android runtime libraries. The ART runs each application in its own process with its own instances of the ART. It converts byte codes into native instructions in a similar manner to the plain old JVM in a desktop application. However, it is optimised for the Android platform. The core libraries provide most of the functionality available to a Kotlin developer; they include data structures, utilities, file and network access, application infrastructure classes etc.

- **Hardware Abstraction Layer (HAL)**. This layer provides a set of standard interfaces that expose device hardware capabilities to the higher level Kotlin API Framework. It consists of multiple library modules each of which implements an interface for a specific type of hardware component, such as the camera or bluetooth modules. These Library modules are loaded on demand when they are required. They provide a level of abstraction between the software system and the actual hardware platform on which it is running. This allows Android far greater portability than would otherwise be the case.

- **Linux Kernel**. This is the underlying operating system on top of which the whole of Android runs. It provides the facilities for memory and process management, network protocols, driver management, underlying security, input and outputs etc.

From this we can see that Android is an environment for running applications written in Kotlin (or Java) on physical devices. Although the most popular devices are smart phones such as Android phones including those from Samsung and Google itself, it is also used on Android Tablets, Android Televisions and Android Auto for motor vehicles.

Android Versions

There have been numerous versions of Android released over the years. Each of these versions provides a particular range of facilities and certain versions have represented a step change in the way in which Android applications are built. For many versions there is both a code name such as *Jelly Bean* and an API level number such as 16. To add to the confusion for some codenames there are several API versions, for example *Oreo* is associated with both API level 26 and 27. Finally, each version has a release number associated with it. Thus the two releases with the codename *Oreo* are version 8.0 and 8.1 (which are at API level 26 and 27). This is illustrated below, along with when the version was released, for some key versions:

Code name	Version	Initial release	API level
No code name	1.0	23/09/08	1
No code name	1.1	09/02/09	2
Lollipop	5.0–5.1.1	12/11/14	21–22
Oreo	8.0–8.1	21/09/17	26–27
Pie	9.0	06/08/18	28
Q	10.0	03/09/19	29
R	11.0	08/09/20	30
S	12.0	September 2021	31

You will find that applications, libraries and developers will talk about things at both the code name and the API level. You may therefore find that a library specifies that it requires API Level 30 to run or that another application says that it requires Lollipop to be installed. In some cases you might find that a framework specifies the version number it requires such as version 8.0 onwards. It is therefore useful to be familiar with all of these terms.

It is worth noting that Google does not provide security updates for all versions, at the time of writing it only provided security updates for version 8.0 onwards (aka Oreo or API 26 onwards).

Another point worth noting is that there was a change in the way Android applications were run with the Lollipop/version 5.0 operating system. From this point onwards Android applications always run in their own process with their own instance of the ART (Android Runtime). Because of this you often find that discussion relating to Android consider pre Lollipop/Version 5.0 systems and post Lollipop/Version 5.0 systems.

Android Programming Languages

Both Java and Kotlin are widely used programming languages on the Android platform. Java was the original language that was used to implement Android applications and it is still very widely used.

However, on the 7th of May 2019 Google announced that Kotlin was now the *preferred* development language to be used with Android. Although it may have taken a while for development organisations and developers to switch over, by 2021 this process was accelerating and more and more applications were being developed or enhanced using Kotlin.

Another alternative is to use C++. This approach is known as native coding and is supported by the Android Native Development Kit. It represents application coding at a lower level than Kotlin. By this we mean that the code that is written does not use an intermediate runtime (such as the ART) and instead is executed directly by the underling operating system. This can have significant performance benefits but can be more complex to implement.

Android Runtime

Deploying to Android

The following diagram illustrates how a source code file written in Kotlin is converted into a form that can be deployed onto a device and executed by the Android Runtime (ART) environment:

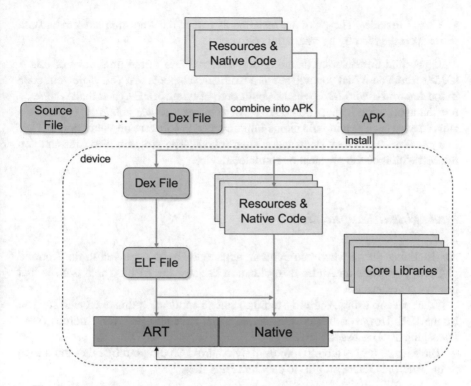

There are several points to note about this diagram:

- **Source File to Dex File**. This process has changed over the years. The actual steps performed have varied with pre Android 6.0 versions compiling Java code into byte codes and then wrapping them up as Dex files. This changed between Android 6.0 and Android 8.0 when a compiler known as *jack* (Java Android Compiler Kit) was used. Currently both Java and Kotlin files are compiled into *class* files which are then wrapped up as Dex files. Dex stands for *Dalvik Executable Format* files. Dalvik was an older version of the Android Runtime which is no longer used, however the name has been retained for Dex files. Compared to a plain *class* file, a Dex file is an executable file that can be run directly by the ART.
- **APKs**. An APK (or Android Application Package) file contains one or more Dex files plus any additional resources such as security certificates or images and any native code used by an application. Once an APK is created it can be installed onto an Android device.
- **Installing an APK**. When an APK is installed onto an Android device, the contents of the API is unpacked and made available to the ART. This involves extraction of the Dex files and converting them into ELF files. ELF stands for *Executable and Linkable Format* file. An ELF file is an executable file that can be run by the Linux operating system. Native code and other resources such as security certificates are also extracted.

- **Core Libraries**. These are pre installed as part of the Android platform and can be accessed directly by your application code.

If you find this diagram daunting don't worry, 99% of the time most of this is hidden from you. What you will see as a Kotlin developer is that you write your code in the Android Studio IDE (which is built onto of IntelliJ IDEA) and then when you run the application it must be deployed onto either a *device emulator* (which is a smart device such as a mobile phone implemented in software on your computer) or to a *physical device* such as an actual smart phone. The program then runs and you interact with it on the physical or emulated device.

Packaging an Application

As mentioned above when you build an application to be deployed to the Android platform you create an Android Application Package (an APK) which is a file that has a `.apk` extension.

When we are using Android Studio to run an application this is created for you by the IDE. However, behind the scenes a tool called `aapt2` (or Android Asset Packaging Tool) is used.

The `aapt2` tool is a build tool used by Android Studio (and by other tools such as the Android Gradle plugin) to generate APK files.

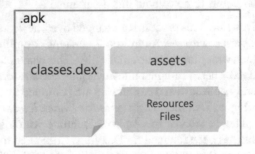

The end result is that a file is created with an `.apk` extension that contains one or more Dex files and all required supporting files and assets including any application security certificates, the `AndroidManifest.xml` file, images, sound files etc.

You may have more than one Dex files as the size of a Dex file is optimised such that if it gets too big a second Dex file will be created to ensure speed of access to the contents of the file.

Application Core Building Blocks

Core Element Types

The following diagram illustrates the core elements used to create an Android application in Kotlin. Each of these elements has a specific structure and a defined life cycle and method of operation. That is they are more than conceptual elements in an application. For example, Android understands the role of an *Activity*, it understands what a *Content Provider* is etc. And has a specific lifecycle of actions associated with these elements.

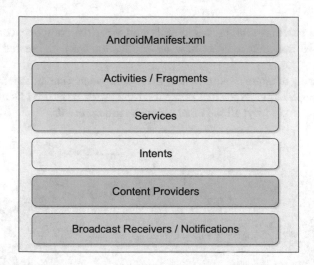

The elements presented in the above diagram are:

- **AndroidManifest.xml file**. This is an XML (eXtensible Markup Language) file that defines the application to the Android Runtime (ART) system. It tells the ART what the entry point to the application is, what security permissions are used, what services are implemented etc.
- **Activities and Fragments**. These elements represent the *User Interfaces* elements of an application. Typically an *Activity* or *Fragment* will represent all or part of a screen presented to the user. Every application is made up of at least one *Activity* and may or may not have multiple Activities or multiple Fragments used to represent additional screens.
- **Services**. Services implement one or more *non visual* behavioural aspects of an application. They typically represent the business logic of an application.
- **Intents**. Intents can be used to pass information between different applications/activities. They are mainly used to invoke other components such as when starting up a service, displaying a web page, displaying a list of contacts, dialling a phone number etc.

- **Content Providers**. Content Providers are components that can be used to share information between applications.
- **Broadcast Receivers**. Applications can *send* and *receive* broadcast messages. These messages can be sent from within the same application or from external applications.
- **Notifications**. Notifications provide a way for an application to present information to the user even when they are in the background via the Notifications Drawer.

How Core Elements Fit Together

However, the previous section merely tells you what the components available in Android are, it does not indicate how an application may be created from these components.

The following diagram illustrates how these components can fit together to create an Android application. Note that other than the AndroidManifest.xml file and the main Activity; all the other elements are *optional*.

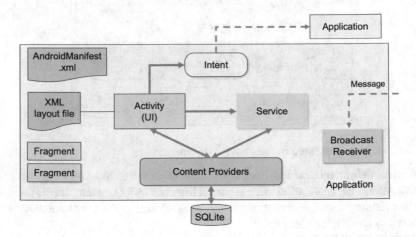

Within this diagram we can see that the green boxes relate to user interface elements. In this case there is a single main *activity* and two *fragments* which may be displayed within this activity. The actual structure of the Activities user interface is defined within an xml layout file.

The activity uses a *Service* that implements its business logic.

Both the Activity and the Service interact with a *Content Provider* that reads and writes data to an SQLite database (which is provided as part of the Android runtime).

At some point in the applications lifetime it uses an *Intent* to initiate another application (such as the Dialer application). It can also receive broadcast messages using its *Broadcast Receiver*.

Android JetPack

Android JetPack was introduced back in 2018. It is a suite of libraries designed to help developers create Android applications that following best practices, with reduced boiler plate code, and that are easier to port from one Android version to another and from one Android device to another.

The key elements provided by JetPack include:

- *Android Architecture Components* to support best practices in structuring applications.
- *Android Support Library* to make it easier to access common facilities such as when building mobile camera applications.
- *Android Studio* which is part of the JetPack world and makes it easier to create, test and run Android applications.
- Set of *guidelines* on how to build Android applications.

However, it is important to understand the basics before getting to into using Android JetPack as some of the libraries assume you understand the underpinnings of the environment.

Online Resources

See the following online resources for information on Android:

- https://developer.android.com/ Android Home Page.
- https://developer.android.com/reference Android API Reference.
- https://developer.android.com/guide Developer Guides.
- https://www.tutorialspoint.com/android/index.htm Quick set of tutorials.

Chapter 33
Applications and Activities

Introduction

In this chapter we will look at the Android Studio and a simple *Hello World* style Android application.

Android Studio

Android Studio is the development IDE for Android applications. It is built on top of the IntelliJ IDEA IDE. It extends this IDE with specific Android development tools such as the AVD Manager (which helps managed Android Virtual Devices which are emulators for things such as Smart phones or Smart TVs) and the Android SDK manager.

Android Studio is available for a wide range of platforms including Microsoft Windows 64-bit version (the 32-bit version deprecated as of December 2019), macOS X 10.10 or later and Linux 64-bit distribution capable of running 32-bit apps.

Android Studio is quiet memory hungry and the recommendation is that the host computer should have at least 8 GB of memory (although in practice more is better).

To download your own copy of Android Studio go to the URL https://developer.android.com/studio. Follow the instructions provided.

© The Author(s), under exclusive license to Springer Nature Switzerland AG 2021
J. Hunt, *Beginner's Guide to Kotlin Programming*,
https://doi.org/10.1007/978-3-030-80893-8_33

Setting Up a Project

Once you have installed the Android Studio IDE. You can create a new project and install specific versions of the Android SDK and create Android Virtual Devices (AVD) to emulate running Android applications on a Smart Phone.

Android SDKs

The Android Software Development Kit or Android SDK provides a suite of tools and a specific version of the android operating system that can be deployed to a AVD to test out applications. You will need to to install each version of the Android SDK that you want to use.

The Android SDK includes the following:

- Required libraries.
- Debugger.
- An emulator.
- API Documentation.
- Sample source code.
- Tutorials for the Android OS.

Android Studio provides the SDK Manager which is used to install and manage the versions of the Android SDK that you want to work with. For example, depending upon the version of Android Studio you are using, you should be able to find it under Tools>SDK Manager menu option.

Android Studio AVD

An Android Studio AVD (Android Virtual Device) is an emulator that will run a particular Android device with a particular Android SDK version so that you can test your Android applications without resorting to using a physical device.

The Android AVD Manager is a tool used to configure these emulators and well as to manage what is installed on them, when they should be restarted etc.

When you first run Android Studio you will typically find that there is only one AVD installed, however you can configure additional devices as required. This is done using the Tools>AVD Manager menu option. This will display the 'Select Hardware' dialog:

For example:

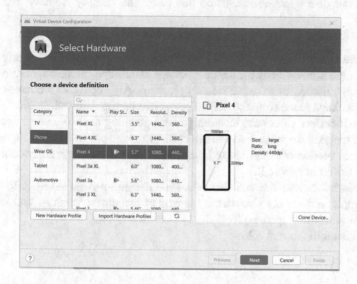

Select the device you want to install and follow through the Next button option and the screen presented to you. As part of the device set up you can specify the version of Android SDK that you want to install on that device. If the selected Android SDK is not currently installed on your local machine, then it will need to be downloaded first and Android Studio will do that for you.

Creating an Android Application

In this section we will look at how to create a new Android Application and what its constituent parts are.

Creating a New Project

You can either create a new Android development project from File>New>New project… or via the Android Studio start up screen where you can select the 'Create New Project' option.

On the dialog presented to you can select what type of *Project Template* you want to use. These templates are used to provide a skeleton of the type of project selected with the core elements in place.

We will use the 'Empty Activity' Project Template as that will give us the flexibility to create our own applications. To do this select the 'Empty Activity' then select 'Next'.

On the Configure Your Project dialog you will see the following fields:

1.   **Name**. Enter a suitable name for your project, for example HelloWorld.
2.   **Package name**. Check the default package name. You can also specify a default package name, for example `com.jjh.app`. Also note that we have changed the package name from the default generated by the Android Studio.
3.   **Save location**. Check the location you are planning to save your project in.
4.   **Language**. Also make sure you select Kotlin as the programming language (the current version of Android Studio now defaults to Kotlin but still double check that Kotlin is selected).
5.   **Minimum SDK**. You can also select the minimum Android SDK to use (for example version 8.1 Oreo which is one of the oldest versions that currently obtains security updates).
6.   This is all illustrated below:

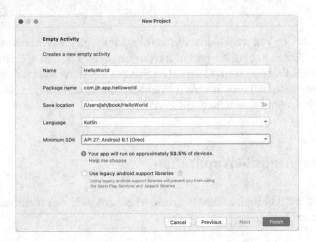

Now click Finish.

Android Studio will now create a new project for you and display this project using the Android view (note it may initially display this using the standard Kotlin view and may then update after a few moments/minutes).

Once Android Studio has completed indexing and refreshed the screen you should see something similar to:

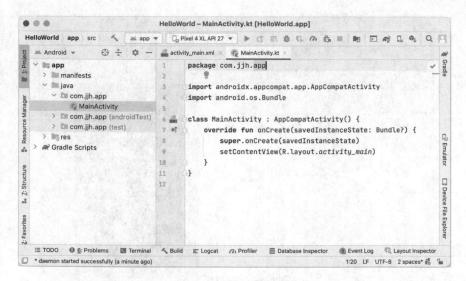

We will now open the layout editor to modify the display a bit. To do this select the res (resources) node in the Android View tree on the left hand side of the IDE. Next expand the layout node and double click on the activity_main.xml file. This is shown below:

You should now see the default display in the layout editor with both the *Design* view and the *Blueprint* view showing.

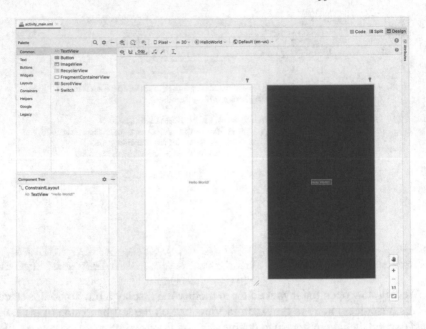

Select the Text View in the centre of the display (the element currently displaying "Hello World!"). We will now change this slightly so that your application has been configured to some extent. To do this follow these steps:

1. Change the text to say "Hello Mobile World!" You can do this by selecting the text view and then changing the text to be displayed—this is in the *properties* box on the right handside of the editor. It is under *Declared Attributes*.
2. Change the font colour to Red—to do this look at *All Attributes* and scroll down until you find `textColor` (note the spelling). Change this to the colour red—you can do this interactively from the colour dialog.
3. Change the font size to be 34sp—this is done via the `textSize` attribute under *All Attributes*.
4. Change the style of the text to be bold. This is done via the `textStyle` attribute under *All Attributes*.

Notice two things.

1. That the display updates immediately for you so that you can see what you will get.
2. That the attributes you have explicitly specified are now added to the *Declared Attributes* list.

The display should now resemble:

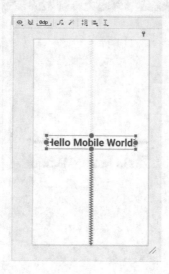

Run the Application

You can then run the application on that emulated device. Do this by ensuring that the device is selected in the run tools next to the green run button:

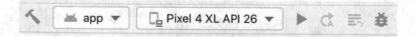

Now run the application by clicking in the green arrow button to the right of the device on which to run the app.

In your device emulator you should see the application output, it should look similar to that shown below:

Android Application

We will now examine the Android application that you have just created.

Basic Application Structure

The basic structure of the simple hello world application that we created using the Empty Activity template is given below.

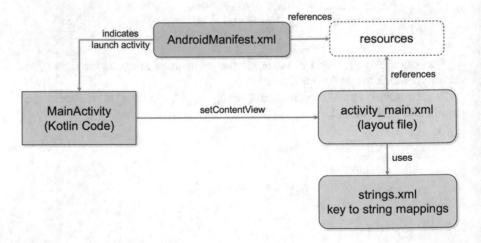

The Empty Activity template creates the core skeleton of an Android application. This skeleton is comprised of several key elements these are:

AndroidManifest.xml. This is the XML file that defines the application to the Android runtime. It notifies ART of the entry point to the application and can contain information such as the services, intents and security permissions related to the application. The `AndroidManifest.xml` file generated by the template is given below:

```xml
<?xml version="1.0" encoding="utf-8"?>
<manifest
xmlns:android="http://schemas.android.com/apk/res/android"
    package="com.jjh.app.helloworld">

    <application
        android:allowBackup="true"
        android:icon="@mipmap/ic_launcher"
        android:label="@string/app_name"
        android:roundIcon="@mipmap/ic_launcher_round"
        android:supportsRtl="true"
        android:theme="@style/Theme.HelloWorld">
        <activity android:name=".MainActivity">
            <intent-filter>
                <action
android:name="android.intent.action.MAIN" />
                <category
android:name="android.intent.category.LAUNCHER" />
            </intent-filter>
        </activity>
    </application>

</manifest>
```

Notice that the single *activity* defined within this XML file has the name `.MainActivity`. This is because the name of the activity is added to the package declaration at the top of the XML file. This declaration indicates the default package that is used with activities within the file. Also note that the activity element contains an action and a category element. The *action* element indicates that this a ativity is the entry point to the application; it is the equivalent of the `main()` function in a standalone Kotlin application. The *category* element indicates that this application should appear in the launcher window of the Android device on which the application is deployed.

MainActivity. This is the entry point for the application. ART loads this activity to run the application. That is ART instantiates the `MainActivity` class and then calls several member functions on the instance to initiate the running Android application.

activity_main.xml. This is an XML file that defines the layout of the User Interface presented by the `MainActivity`. For example, the layout file can indicate how buttons, fields, and labels are laid out across or down the screen. The layout generated by the template included a single `TextView` contained within a constraint layout. The layout file, modified as described earlier in this chapter, is given below:

```xml
<?xml version="1.0" encoding="utf-8"?>
<androidx.constraintlayout.widget.ConstraintLayout
xmlns:android="http://schemas.android.com/apk/res/android"
    xmlns:app="http://schemas.android.com/apk/res-auto"
    xmlns:tools="http://schemas.android.com/tools"
    android:layout_width="match_parent"
    android:layout_height="match_parent"
    tools:context=".MainActivity">

    <TextView
    android:layout_width="wrap_content"
    android:layout_height="wrap_content"
    android:text="Hello Mobile World!"
    android:textColor="#F40202"
    android:textSize="34sp"
    android:textStyle="bold"
    app:layout_constraintBottom_toBottomOf="parent"
    app:layout_constraintLeft_toLeftOf="parent"
    app:layout_constraintRight_toRightOf="parent"
    app:layout_constraintTop_toTopOf="parent" />

</androidx.constraintlayout.widget.ConstraintLayout>
```

strings.xml. The strings.xml file defines a set of key to string mappings that allow textual content within the User Interface to be localised. The `strings.xml` file generated by the template contains a single string entry which is the name of the application. For example:

```xml
<resources>
    <string name="app_name">HelloWorld</string>
</resources>
```

Resources. These represent other resources included in the application. The Empty Activity Template generates a set of default icons, colours, User Interface themes etc. Strictly speaking the `strings.xml` file is part of the *resources* but as it is something you are likely to need to change as development progresses we have listed it separately.

Gradle Build Files

In addition to the application code file the template also generated several *Gradle* build files. Gradle is a library dependency management and build system for JVM languages such as Java and Kotlin. It is not the only option available as *Maven* performs a similar function. However, *Gradle* is the default build system used by Android developers. Indeed Android Studio itself uses the *Gradle* build system to manage the libraries that your application uses, to build the APK files to deploy and to deploy your application to the emulator etc.

Android Application   481

The *Gradle* files are listed together under the *Gradle Scripts* node in the Android view.

```
▼   Gradle Scripts
    build.gradle (Project: HelloWorld)
    build.gradle (Module: HelloWorld.app)
```

Note that there are two *Gradle* files, one is at the *Project* level and one is at the *Module* level.

When working with Android Studio a project is made up of one or more modules. Each module can have its own *Gradle* file that is used to define the dependencies for that module as well as information such as the version of the module, how tests will be run etc. The top level *Gradle* file indicates which version of Kotlin is being used, which central library repositories to use (such as the mavenCentral and google repositories).

Actual Directory Structure

Another point to note is that the underlying directory structure differs from the way in which the Android view in the Android Studio presents the files. The underlying directory structure is in many ways more like a traditional Kotlin project than suggested by the Android view.

The reason that this layout is hidden to some extent by the Android view in Android Studio is that it aims to make it simpler to work with the code you are developing.

HelloWorld Application

The entry point for the application is the MainActivity class. This class is listed below in its entirety:

```kotlin
package com.jjh.app.helloworld

import androidx.appcompat.app.AppCompatActivity
import android.os.Bundle

class MainActivity : AppCompatActivity() {
    override fun onCreate(savedInstanceState: Bundle?) {
        super.onCreate(savedInstanceState)
        setContentView(R.layout.activity_main)
    }
}
```

This class represent the first activity run by the application. In this case the whole application is defined by a single Activity which is common practice and is considered the best development style to use.

The `MainActivity` class itself extends the `AppCompatActivity` class. This class provides backward compatibility with older versions of the Android SDK. It thus allows code to be written for later versions of the SDK using features not available on older version, but to allow that code to work on older versions as well (by emulating the newer features).

The `AppCompatActivity` class eventually extends the `Activity` class which supports the core concepts of being an *Activity* within an Android application.

The actual class hierarchy is given below. This indicates that Activities are also a type of `Context` which is a concept that reoccurs numerous times within the Android libraries. Both *Services* and *Activities* are types of *Context* and certain things require a context to be used. Note that the `Context` is an *abstract* class and normally developers will work at the `Activity` level or the `AppCompatActivity` level.

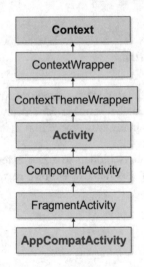

The only behaviour defined for our `MainActivity` class is in the `onCreate()` member function. This member function overrides the default behaviour that is inherited from the parent class. This function takes a *nullable* `Bundle` that represents any saved state that the Activity should restore on being started or restarted. This instance is passed up to the inherited version of `onCreate()`. It then sets the user interface up using the inherited `setContentView()` member function. It passes to this member function the parameter `R.layout.activity_main`.

The `R` class is an *autogenerated* class that provides direct access to resources and information about resources (`R` here stands for Resources). By autogenerated we mean that the class is created by the Android Studio tooling for you based on information in the current environment. In this case it refers to the contents of the `layout` directory under the `res` directory, for example:

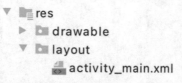

```
▼  res
   ▶   drawable
   ▼   layout
          activity_main.xml
```

The res/layout directory contains the layout XML file activity_main.xml. This appears within our code as R.layout.activity_main. If there were other layout files in the layout directory, then they could also be referenced in the same way.

Thus the Kotlin statement:

```
setContentView(R.layout.activity_main)
```

Means load the contents of the activity_main.xml file in the layout directory under res as the definition for the user interface of this activity.

The onCreate() member function is therefore used to initialise or set up the activity and its user interface.

At this point you might reasonably ask why didn't we use an init{} block. After all this block is intended for initialisation purposes. The answer is that the init{} block runs just after the instance is created but before anything outside the instance can access it. This means that it runs before the ART has an opportunity to configure the activity instance as required by the Android environment. Therefore any initialisation behaviour that refers to the Android environment (including the UI) should be placed within the onCreate() member function.

Online Resources

See the following online resources for information on Android Studio:

1. https://developer.android.com/studio Download site for Android Studio.
2. https://developer.android.com/studio/intro Android Studio User Guide.
3. https://developer.android.com/reference/kotlin/packages Android Package reference.

Chapter 34
Android Layouts and Events

Introduction

In this chapter we will look at views and layouts within an Android application.

Activity Uses Layouts

As described in the previous chapter an Activity can use an XML layout file to define the contents of its user interface. When using the Empty Activity Template to create a new project the layout file is called `activity_main.xml` and is defined within the `layout` directory of the `res` (resources) directory. For example the relationship between the layout file and the *Activity* is shown below along with the location of the files:

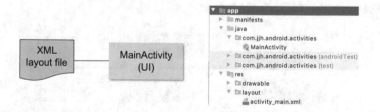

The layout file can hold any view elements. The term *view* is Androids' terminology for a graphical UI component such as a button, a label or a checkbox etc. In Android terminology the act of using an XML file to create a User Interface is known as inflating the view.

© The Author(s), under exclusive license to Springer Nature Switzerland AG 2021
J. Hunt, *Beginner's Guide to Kotlin Programming*,
https://doi.org/10.1007/978-3-030-80893-8_34

Views

Views are all instances of a *view class* of some type typically defined within the `android.widgets` package. Some of the view classes available include:

- **TextView** A user interface element that displays text to the user.
- **EditText** A user interface element for entering and modifying text.
- **Button** A user interface element the user can tap or click on to perform an action.
- **Checkbox** A checkbox is a specific type of two-state button that can be either checked or unchecked.
- **RadioButton** A radio button is a two-state button that can be either checked or unchecked. When the radio button is unchecked, the user can press or click it to check it.

Android also provides more complex views such as the Table View which can be used to create displays made up of rows and columns.

View Layouts

In this section we will look at how views are organised, defined and managed.

View Hierarchy

Strictly speaking the display used to generate the UI for an activity contains a single top level view, however this top level view can be a container that can hold sub views. These sub views can themselves be views and this results in a hierarchy of view elements. This is illustrated below:

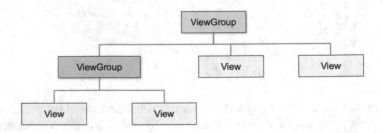

In terms of terminology all elements in a UI are views, but some views can hold other views and are known as view groups. In the above diagram the top level view is a View Group. It contains three sub views. One of these sub views is itself a view group and holds two further views.

A View Group can be a layout or a container. A Layout is a view group that has no visual representation of its own where as a container is a view group that typically has some visual aspect to it such as a tabbed display or a navigation display.

In the above diagram we might have chosen to use a simple Linear Layout for the top level view group. A `LinearLayout` is a layout that can organise its contents vertically or horizontally. Typically it does not have any visual presence itself, instead it organises the views it contains. Within this layout the sub views can indicate how they are laid out with respect to the `LinearLayout` (such as whether they match the height of the parent layout or not). This is illustrated below:

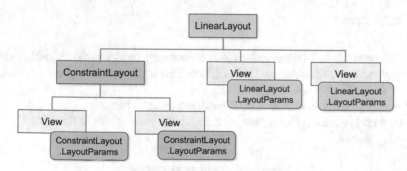

The `ConstraintLayout` is another commonly used layout and in the above diagram it is a sub layout to the top level LinearLayout. This approach of nesting one layout inside another is not uncommon.

The `ConstraintLayout` is more complex than a simple `LinearLayout` but can be used to create sophisticated user interfaces that can easily adjust to different size devices. As with the `LinearLayout` the views held within the `ConstraintLayout` specify how they are displayed with reference to the *constraints* associated with the ConstraintLayout.

View Layout Options

There are in fact several different layouts available with Android Studio. Each type of layout provides a different way of organising and managing the views it contains. Some of these are described below:

- **LinearLayout**. Organises views across or down the screen (in horizontal or vertical orientation). When the edge of the screen is reached then the layout automatically moves to the next line or row across the screen depending on the orientation.

- **FrameLayout**. A FrameLayout is used to hold a single child view, which will fill up the available space.
- **RelativeLayout**. Positions elements relative to each other within the containing layout.
- **TableLayout**. Layouts out child views based on rows and columns within the display.
- **AbsoluteLayout**. This is used to position views at specific X and Y coordinates on the screen. The use of this view is generally discouraged as different devices may have different size displays which may result in unusable UIs being created.
- **ConstraintLayout**. This is a very flexible layout which essentially replaces the RelativeLayout as it is more flexible and easier to use with the Android Studio Layout Editor. It is part of the android extensions to the core Android classes.

Linear Layout

The LinearLayout organises elements horizontally (which is the default) or vertically depending upon the orientation specified. This is very useful if you want to align a set of views in a particular orientation.

For example, if you want to have a TextView and two buttons displayed down the screen, then is easily achieved using a LinearLayout. This is illustrated by the following screen:

In this case there is a LinearLayout which does not have a visual presence itself. The LinearLayout contains a TextView with the string "Hello Mobile World!" in it. The TextView is the first element in the LinearLayout. In this case the LinearLayout has a vertical orientation thus when the second view is added it is placed below the first view. The second view is a Button and it is displayed below the text view. The second button is then placed below the first button.

The XML layout file used for this layout is given below:

```xml
<?xml version="1.0" encoding="utf-8"?>
<LinearLayout
xmlns:android="http://schemas.android.com/apk/res/android"
    xmlns:app="http://schemas.android.com/apk/res-auto"
    xmlns:tools="http://schemas.android.com/tools"
    android:layout_width="match_parent"
    android:layout_height="match_parent"
    android:orientation="vertical"
    tools:context=".MainActivity">

    <TextView
        android:layout_width="match_parent"
        android:layout_height="wrap_content"
        android:text="Hello Mobile World!"
        android:textColor="#F44336"
        android:textSize="36sp"
        android:textStyle="bold" />

    <Button
        android:id="@+id/button"
        android:layout_width="match_parent"
        android:layout_height="wrap_content"
        android:text="Button" />

    <Button
        android:id="@+id/button2"
        android:layout_width="match_parent"
        android:layout_height="wrap_content"
        android:text="Button" />
</LinearLayout>
```

Note that the TextView and the two Button definitions contain references to the layout_width and layout_height. The layout_width is set to be the same as the parents width. In this case their parent is the LinearLayout which itself has a layout_width of match_parent. Thus the TextView and the two Buttons will have the same width as the screen.

The layout_height of both the TextView and the two Buttons is set to wrap_content. This means that they will be only as high as they need to be to incorporate the visual elements displayed within them (in this case the strings being displayed).

Constraint Layout

The ConstraintLayout is a very flexible layout that uses constraints between views to organise the user interface. As such it is a very useful layout to be used when different size displays need to be supported by your application. It was added as part of AndroidX libraries, this means that to use it you must add a dependency to your grade project dependencies to include the constraint layout library:

```
implementation
'androidx.constraintlayout:constraintlayout:2.0.4'
```

The above adds the `android.constraintlayout` library version `2.0.4` to the current project.

Within the `ConstraintLayout` views are laid out according to relationships between sibling views and the parent layout. For example, in the following diagram there is a constraint between View A and View B as well as a constraint between View A and View C. The effects of these constraints is that View B must be to the right of View A and View C must be below View A. This is referred to as an order constraint.

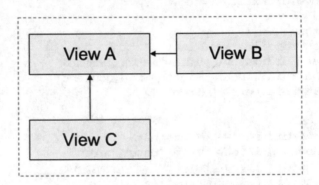

**B constrained to be right of A,
C constrained to be below A**

There are several different types of constraint:

Order Constraint This type of constraint is illustrated above.

Parent position Constraint This is used to constrain the side of a view to the corresponding edge of the layout. For example:

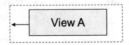

In the above diagram, the left side of the view is connected to the left edge of the parent layout.

Alignment Constraint. Using an alignment constraint you can align the edge of a view to the same edge of another view. For example:

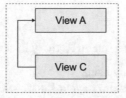

In the above diagram, the left side of View C is aligned to the left side of View A.

Baseline alignment. A baseline alignment, aligns the text baseline of a view to the text baseline of another view.

Constrain to a guideline It is also possible to add a vertical or horizontal guideline to which you can constrain views, and the guideline will be invisible to app users.

Constrain to a barrier This constraint is similar to a guideline, a barrier is an invisible line that you can constrain views to. The difference is that a barrier does not define its own position; instead, the barrier position moves based on the position of views contained within it.

Containers

A layout is a general purpose View Group, although different layouts may organise the views they hold in different ways, the layout itself is not expected to have any visual presence. Layouts also deal directly with the views that they hold.

Containers are different to plain layouts, they meet more specific requirements which usually involves some aspect of a visual presence on the screen. They also typically have additional requirements on how many and what kind of child views they can accept. In many cases a container requires an Adapter class to support their own requirements.

Examples of Containers include the ScrollView and HorizontalScrollView, the CardView, the NavigationView and the TabLayout.

- **ScrollView** and **HorizontalScrollView**. A ScrollView is a container that is used to make vertically scrollable views. A scroll view contains a single direct child. A ScrollView supports Vertical scrolling only, in order to create a horizontally scrollable view, a HorizontalScrollView is used.
- **CardView**. This is a container with rounded corners and a shadow based on its elevation with one child view.
- **NavigationView**. This is a type of view with a standard navigation menu that is used for an application. It can be displayed from the navigation drop down button.
- **TabLayout**. This layout provides a horizontal layout to display tabs. Population of the tabs to display is done through TabLayout.Tab instances.

Creating Displays

You can create the user interface for an Activity in several ways, you can:

- Write the XML layout file by hand.
- You can use the Android Studio Layout Editor which is an interactive UI design editor.
- You can create the user interface programmatically.

In this section we will look at how to use the Android Studio Layout Editor and how to create the user interface programmatically.

Working with the Layout Editor

Although it is certainly possible to write the layout XML file by hand, it is much easier to use the Android Studio Layout Editor to interactively create the layout file.

If you double click on the `activity_main.xml` file in Android Studio then the Layout Editor will automatically be opened for you. In fact we used this in the last chapter to help us change the text displayed in the application created by the Empty Activity Template. We will now return to that application.

The Layout Editor is displayed below for the application we created in the last chapter:

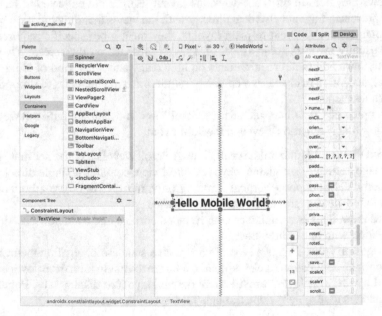

Note that by default the layout editor is organised into three areas, the *Palette* and *Component Tree* to the left, the *Attributes* pane to the right and the *layout drawing* area in the middle.

Also note that in the top right hand corner of the display are three icons labelled 'Code', 'Split' and 'Design'. These control what the Layout Editor displays; in 'Code' is shows you the XML file, in 'Split' it shows you both the XML view and the design view and in 'Design' it shows you the interactive layout design view (as shown above). If we switch to 'Split' then we can see both the XML file and the design view.

The template created a layout which had a top level ConstraintLayout, however we now want to use a LinearLayout as the top level view group. We can change thus using the Component Tree panel. In this panel select the top most node labelled ConstraintLayout. From the right mouse menu select 'Convert view …' as shown below:

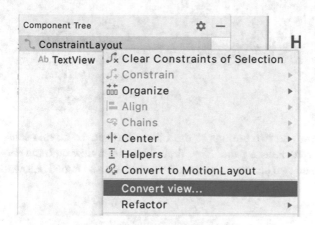

This will cause a new dialog to be displayed that will allow you to select a new layout to use, select the LinearLayout option.

The Component tree panel will now change to show that the top level ViewGroup is now a LinearLayout and the display in the design view will change to show the TextView displayed at the top of the screen.

Currently the LinearLayout has defaulted to the *Horizontal* orientation, however we want to use the *Vertical* orientation, we thus need to change the orientation. To do this right click on the LinearLayout node in the Component Tree panel and select the 'LinearLayout>Convert orientation to vertical' menu option.

Next we will select the TextView displayed in the design view and look at the *Declared Attributes* panel. It now shows that the layout_width and the layout_height are set to wrap_content:

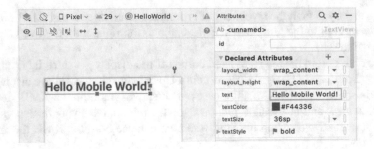

We will change the `layout_width` to match the parent width, using `match_parent`:

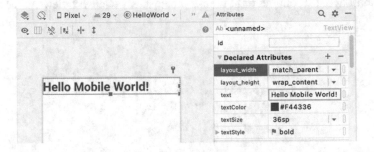

We can now add two buttons to the Linear Layout. To do this select the Button component in the Palette pane. Now drag the Button view onto the design view, do this twice to add two buttons. The buttons should each be added below the TextView, for example:

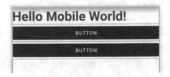

The *Component Tree* pane also reflects this hierarchy.

We can also switch to the Code view and see the resulting XML.

We have now interactively created the display described in the previous section. We can now run this version of the HelloWorld application. The display generated is:

You could now change the labels not he two buttons such that the first button has the label add and the second has the label subtract.

Each button also has an id, to make it easier to work with these buttons their ids could also be changed to be add and sub. All of this can be done via the Declared Attributes on the right and side of the layout editor.

Programmatically Creating Layout

The user interface for an Android application can be created programmatically by instantiating the appropriate views and adding them to the application using addView(). Each view added must be added with appropriate layout parameters set for the layout within which it is contained. For example, the following code snippet a Button is instantiated and the layout parameters are set for the LinearLayout. It is then added to the default linear layout (referenced via layout) using addView().

```kotlin
override fun onCreate(savedInstanceState: Bundle?) {
        super.onCreate(savedInstanceState)
        setContentView(R.layout.activity_main)

        // Set up buttons with handlers
        val addButton =  Button(this)

        button.setLayoutParams(LinearLayout.LayoutParams(
                LinearLayout.LayoutParams.MATCH_PARENT,
                LinearLayout.LayoutParams.MATCH_PARENT)

        addButton.text = "Add"
        addButton.setOnClickListener(addButtonHandler())

        layout.addView(button)
    }
```

Interacting with the Application

The previous sections have added buttons to our Android application. However, these buttons currently do not do anything when they are clicked. That is they do not trigger any behaviour when the user clicks on a button. This is because we are yet to set up any behaviour to run when a button is clicked. In this section we will look at adding such behaviour.

Event Generation

When a user interacts with an Android application, behind the scenes the ART translates key presses, taps etc. into *events*. An Event represents an action happening with respect to a view such as a button or a menu item. This event is then used to trigger appropriate behaviour registered with the view.

The operations that handle these events are known as Event Handlers and implement Event Listener interfaces. These event handlers can be registered on any type of view, including buttons, menus, lists or even the whole UI itself.

View Handler Architecture

Within the View Handler architecture, the view is the presentation aspect of an application such as a button or a menu. The Handler defines the behaviour to invoke when the user interacts with the view. Between these two elements is the Event which indicates the type of interaction performed such as a click on a button or a menu selection etc.

This is illustrated in the following diagram:

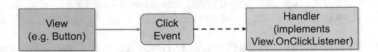

The Handler is defined by a Listener interface that indicates the type of event that can be handled. In the above example, there is a View (such as a Button) which can generate a Click event which will trigger a Handler instance that implements the `View.OnClickListener` interface.

This is actually indicative of the style of the interfaces to be implemented, that is they are all of the form `View.On<Event>Listener`. Some examples include:

- `View.OnClickListener` invoked when a view is clicked.
- `View.OnDragListener` invoked when a drag event is being dispatched to the view.
- `View.OnFocusChangeListener` invoked when the focus state of a view changes.
- `View.OnKeyListener` invoked when a key event is dispatched to this view.
- `View.OnTouchListener` invoked when a touch event is dispatched to this view.

We can now implement a class that will handle a specific event based on the interface implemented. For example to implement an event handler for the Add button created in the previous section we can write:

```
inner class AddButtonHandler : View.OnClickListener {
    override fun onClick(view: View) {
        count++
        val text = findViewById<TextView>(R.id.textView)
        text.text = "Total: ${count.toString()}"
    }
}
```

This is an inner class of our `Activity` and so can access the `findViewById()` member function available to all Activities. It implements the `View.OnClickListener` interface (which is a nested interface defined within the `View` class). The `onClick()` member function increments a count property and then updates the display with the new value of `count`.

An instance of the handler class can then be registered with a view using a setter style member function. These member functions have the form `setOn<Event>Listener(handler)`, for example:

- `fun setOnClickListener(l: View.OnClickListener?): Unit` Register a handler to be invoked when the view is clicked.
- `fun setOnFocusChangeListener(l: View.OnFocusChange Listener!): Unit` Register a handler to be invoked when focus of the view changed.
- `fun setOnDragListener(l: View.OnDragListener!): Unit` Register a drag event handler callback instance for the View.
- `fun setOnKeyListener(l: View.OnKeyListener!): Unit` Register a handler to be invoked when a key is pressed in the view.
- `fun setOnTouchListener(l: View.OnTouchListener!): Unit` Register a callback handler to be invoked when a touch event is sent to the view.

For example, to register an instance of the `AddButtonHandler` with the `addButton` in the main activities layout we can write:

```
val addButton = findViewById<Button>(R.id.add)
addButton.setOnClickListener(AddButtonHandler())
```

We can now bring this all together and update the `MainActivity` class with two OnCLickListeners, one for the *add* button and one for the *subtract* button. We can then register these handlers with the appropriate button in the `onCreate()` MainActivity member function.

The updated class is:

```kotlin
package com.jjh.android.helloworld

import androidx.appcompat.app.AppCompatActivity
import android.os.Bundle
import android.view.View
import android.widget.Button
import android.widget.TextView

class MainActivity : AppCompatActivity() {
  private var count = 0

  // Inner classes to handle user button clicks
  inner class AddButtonHandler : View.OnClickListener {
    override fun onClick(view: View) {
      count++
      val text = findViewById<TextView>(R.id.textView)
      text.text = "Total: ${count.toString()}"
    }
  }

  inner class SubtractButtonHandler : View.OnClickListener {
    override fun onClick(view: View) {
      count--
      val text = findViewById<TextView>(R.id.textView)
      text.text = "Total: ${count.toString()}"
    }
  }

  override fun onCreate(savedInstanceState: Bundle?) {
    super.onCreate(savedInstanceState)
    setContentView(R.layout.activity_main)

    // Set up buttons with handlers
    val addButton = findViewById<Button>(R.id.add)
    addButton.setOnClickListener(AddButtonHandler())
    val subButton = findViewById<Button>(R.id.sub)
    subButton.setOnClickListener(SubtractButtonHandler())
  }
}
```

Now when we run the application in our emulator we can click on the Add and Subtract buttons and the result is that the total displayed in the textView will be updated using the value held in the count property. For example:

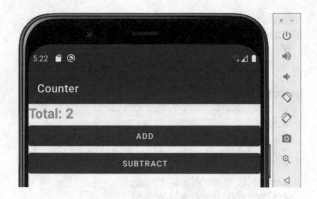

Shortcut OnClick Resource

The previous section has introduced the View Handler architecture to allow us to implement how we want to handle user interactions. However, this seems a bit long winded as we had to create a couple of inner classes and implement a specific interface.

As being able to handle a user clicking on a button is such a common event, there is actually a short cut available when working with Activities. This is the *onClick Resource*. This is a resource that can be set within the XML layout file that indicates a member function, defined within the associated Activity, that can be directly invoked when a Click event occurs.

The *android:onClick* attribute takes the name of the member function in the views context (defined within the Activity) to invoke when the view is clicked. This name must correspond to a public member function that takes exactly one parameter of type View. Thus if you specify `android:onClick="sayHello"`, you must declare a `fun sayHello(v: View): Unit` member function in your `Activity` class.

For the simple counter application we are creating, this means that we can add a member function called something like `onAddButtonClick(View)` to the `MainActivity` and add the `android:OnClick` resource to the *Add* button XML configuration information. We can do the same for the *Subtract* button using a member function called `onSubButtonCLick(View)`.

For example

```xml
<?xml version="1.0" encoding="utf-8"?>
<LinearLayout
  //...
     tools:context=".MainActivity">

 <TextView
   android:id="@+id/textView"
   android:layout_width="match_parent"
   android:layout_height="wrap_content"
   android:text="@string/total"
   android:textColor="#4CAF50"
   android:textSize="24sp"
   android:textStyle="bold" />

 <Button
   android:id="@+id/add"
   android:layout_width="match_parent"
   android:layout_height="wrap_content"
   android:onClick="onAddButtonClick"
   android:text="@string/add" />

 <Button
   android:id="@+id/sub"
   android:layout_width="match_parent"
   android:layout_height="wrap_content"
   android:onClick="onSubButtonClick"
   android:text="@string/subtract" />

</LinearLayout>
```

We must of course update the `MainActivity` class with these new member functions. Note that in doing so can remove the inner classes we previous had to define and delete the lines registering the handlers with the buttons in the onCreate() member function.

For example, the definition of the MainActivity class now looks like:

```
package com.jjh.android.helloworld

import androidx.appcompat.app.AppCompatActivity
import android.os.Bundle
import android.view.View
import android.widget.TextView

class MainActivity : AppCompatActivity() {
  private var count = 0

    // functions to handle user button clicks
    fun onAddButtonClick(view: View) {
        count++
        val text = findViewById<TextView>(R.id.textView)
        text.text = "Total: ${count.toString()}"
    }

    fun onSubButtonClick(view: View) {
        count--
        val text = findViewById<TextView>(R.id.textView)
        text.text = "Total: ${count.toString()}"
    }

    override fun onCreate(savedInstanceState: Bundle?) {
        super.onCreate(savedInstanceState)
        setContentView(R.layout.activity_main)
    }
}
```

This has significantly simplified the definition of the `MainActivity` class.

Online Resources

See the following online resources for information on Android Studio:

- https://developer.android.com/training/constraint-layout   Documentation   on working with the ConstraintLayout.
- https://developer.android.com/reference/android/view/View Documentation for views in general.

Chapter 35
Android Tic Tac Toe

Introduction

In this chapter we will explore the creation of a simple TicTacToe (or Noughts and Crosses) Android game. This sample Kotlin Android application utilises:

- Kotlin classes, member functions and properties.
- Kotlin Arrays.
- A simple piece of game playing logic.
- While loops, for loops and if statements for flow of control behaviour.
- An Android Activity and associated layout XML file.
- Event handling behaviour shared across all the buttons used for the locations in the TicTacToe grid.

The aim of the game is to make a line of 3 counters (either X or O) across a 3 by 3 grid. Each player takes a turn to place a counter. The first player to achieve a line of three (horizontal, vertically or diagonally) wins.

Classes in the Game

We will begin by identifying the key classes in the game. Note that there is not necessarily a right or wrong answer here; although one set of classes may be more obvious or easier to understand than another.

In our case we will start with what data we will need to represent our TicTacToe game.

Our key data elements include:

- the tic-tac-toe board itself,
- the players involved in the game (both computer and human),

J. Hunt, *Beginner's Guide to Kotlin Programming*,
https://doi.org/10.1007/978-3-030-80893-8_35

- the state of the game, i.e. whose go it is and whether someone has won,
- the moves being made by the players etc.,
- the counters used which are traditionally O and X (hence the alternative name 'Noughts and Crosses').
- the Android `MainActivity` used to run the application.

Based on an analysis of the data one possible set of classes is shown below:

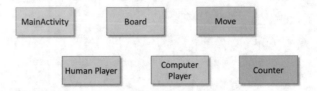

In this diagram we have

- `MainActivity` the class that act as the entry point for the Android application, will hold the board and run the application, handle user input, etc.,
- `Board` this is a class that represents the current state of the TicTacToe board or grid within the game,
- `Human Player` this class represents the human player involved in the game,
- `Computer Player` this class represents the computer playing the game,
- `Move` this class represents a particular move made by a player,
- `Counter` which can be used to represent the counters to play with; this will be either X or Y.

We can refine this a little further. For example, much of what constituents a player will be common for both the *human* and the *computer* player. We can therefore introduce a new class `Player`. This class can capture all aspects of being a player (which covers all the human players features) and then extend this class with the `ComputerPlayer` class. The `ComputerPlayer` class will then add in the features needed to provide an automated opponent.

This is illustrated below:

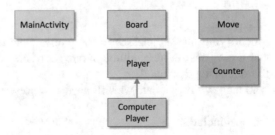

In terms of the data held by the classes we can say:

- `MainActivity` has a board.
- `Board` holds a 3 by 3 grid of cells. Each cell can be empty or contains a counter.
- `Player` Each player has a current counter which will be X or O.
- `Move` represent a players selected move; it therefore holds the counter being played and the location to put the counter in.
- `Counter` holds a label indicating either X or O.

We can now update the class diagram with data and links between the classes:

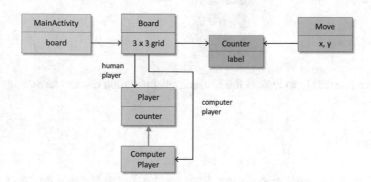

At this point it looks as though the `ComputerPlayer` class is unnecessary as it does not hold any data of its own. However, in this case the *behaviour* for the ComputerPlayer is quite different to the human player and thus it must define its own behaviour or overwrite that defined in the parent class.

The `Player` class will rely on the human user interacting with the Android application to make a move. In contrast the `ComputerPlayer` class must implement an algorithm which will allow the next move to be generated within the program.

Other behavioural aspects of the classes are:

- `MainActivity` this must handle all user interaction, create and set up the board for the game to be played, notify the user if a player has won the game or if there is a tie, trigger the computer player to make a move when the user has max their move etc.
- `Board` The Board class must allow a move to be made but it must also be able to verify that a move is legal (as cell is empty) and whether a game has been won or whether there is a draw. This latter logic could be located within the game instead; however the `Board` holds the data necessary to determine a win or a draw and thus we are locating the logic with the data.

We can now add the behavioural aspects of the classes to the diagram. Note we have followed the convention here for separating the data and behaviour into different areas within a class box:

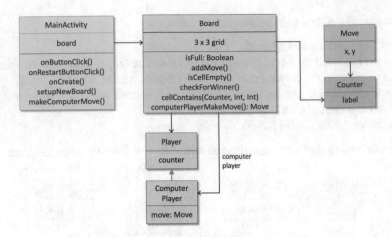

We are now ready to look at the Kotlin implementation of our class design.

Counter Class

The Counter class is given below. There will only ever be two instances of the Counter class created, one to represent X counters and one to represent O counters. These two instances are defined as val properties on the Counters' companion object.

```
package com.jjh.android.tictactoe

/**
 * Represents a Counter used on the board
 */
class Counter private constructor(private val label: String) {

    companion object {
        // Set up X and O Counter
        val X = Counter("X")
        val O = Counter("O")
    }

    override fun toString() = label

}
```

Note that the constructor is marked as private, this ensures that only code defined within the scope of the class Counter can be used to create an instance of a Counter. Thus it is only the *companion object* that will create these two instances of the Counter anywhere in this program.

Move Class

The Move class is given below; it is a data-oriented class.

```
package com.jjh.android.tictactoe
data class Move(val x: Int,
                val y: Int,
                val counter: Counter)
```

It holds the X and Y coordinates within the three by three grid for a given counter.

The Player Class

The root of the Player class hierarchy is presented below. The class maintains a reference to the counter used by the player. It also has a property isAutomatedPlayer to indicate whether it is a human or computer player. This is set to false by default but can be overriden by subclasses.

```
package com.jjh.android.tictactoe

open class Player(val counter: Counter) {

    override fun toString()= "Player($counter)"

    open val isAutomatedPlayer = false

}
```

Note that counter is defined as a Kotlin property. The class Player is extended by the classes ComputerPlayer.

The ComputerPlayer Class

This class provides an algorithmic implementation of the move property get() function.

This algorithm tries to find the best *free* cell, if this is not possible then a randomly selected empty cell location is used. If this fails it searches for the next empty grid location. The move property get function could be replaced with whatever game playing logic you want.

```kotlin
package com.jjh.android.tictactoe

import android.util.Log
import java.util.Random

class ComputerPlayer(counter: Counter,
                        private val board: Board) :
Player(counter){

    // Set up random number generator
    private val random = Random()

    // automated player property
    override val isAutomatedPlayer = true

    private fun randomlySelectMove(): Move {
        // Try to use a simplistic random selection approach
        // to find a cell to fill; if don't find a cell in 6
goes
        // then just find next free cell
        var attemptCount = 0
        var move: Move? = null
        while (move == null && attemptCount < 6) {
            // Randomly select the cell
            val row = random.nextInt(2)
            val column = random.nextInt(2)
            Log.d(TAG,
                "randomlySelectMove() - $row, $column"
            )
            // Check to see if the cell is empty
            if (board.isCellEmpty(row, column)) {
                move = Move(row, column, counter)
            }
            attemptCount++
        }
        // Random selection did not work-just find empty cell
        if (move == null) {
            for (x in 0..2) {
                for (y in 0..2) {
                    if (board.isCellEmpty(x, y)) {
                        move = Move(x, y, counter)
```

```
                                }
                            }
                        }
                    }
                return move!!
            }


    // Provide a very simple algorithm for selecting a move
    val move: Move
        get() {
            // Provide a simple algorithm for selecting a move
            return when {
                board.isCellEmpty(1, 1) -> {
                    // Choose the center
                    Move(1, 1, counter)
                }
                board.isCellEmpty(0, 0) -> {
                    // Choose the top left
                    Move(0, 0, counter)
                }
                    // Choose the bottom right
                    Move(2, 2, counter)
                }
                board.isCellEmpty(0, 2) -> {
                    // Choose the top right
                    Move(0, 2, counter)
                }
                board.isCellEmpty(0, 2) -> {
                    // Choose the top right
                    Move(2, 0, counter)
                }
                else -> {
                    randomlySelectMove()
                }
            }
        }
}
```

The Board Class

The Board class holds a 3 by 3 grid of cells in the form of a array or arrays. It also defines the member functions used to verify or make a move on the board. The checkForWinner() member function determines if there is a winner given the current board positions.

```kotlin
package com.jjh.android.tictactoe

import android.util.Log
import kotlin.random.Random

class Board {

    private val cells =
        Array(3) { arrayOfNulls<Counter>(3) }

    val firstPlayer: Player
    val humanPlayer: Player
    val computerPlayer: ComputerPlayer

    init {
        // Randomly allocate user to X or O
        if (Random.nextInt(100) > 49) {
            humanPlayer = Player(Counter.X)
            computerPlayer = ComputerPlayer(Counter.O, this)
            firstPlayer = humanPlayer
        } else {
            computerPlayer = ComputerPlayer(Counter.O, this)
            humanPlayer = Player(Counter.X)
            firstPlayer = computerPlayer
        }
    }

    val isFull: Boolean
        get() {
            for (row in cells) {
                for (c in row) {
                    if (isCellEmpty(c)) {
                        return false
                    }
                }
            }
            return true
        }

    fun computerPlayerMakeMove(): Move {
        val move = computerPlayer.move
        addMove(move)
        return move
    }
```

```kotlin
    fun addMove(move: Move) {
        val row = cells[move.x]
        row[move.y] = move.counter
    }

    private fun isCellEmpty(counter: Counter?) = counter ==
null

    fun isCellEmpty(row: Int, col: Int) = cells[row][col] ==
null

    private fun cellContains(
        counter: Counter,
        row: Int,
        column: Int) = cells[row][column] == counter

    fun checkForWinner(player: Player): Boolean {
        val c = player.counter
        // Across the top
        return cellContains(c, 0, 0) && cellContains(c, 0, 1)
&& cellContains(c, 0, 2) ||
                // Across the middle
                cellContains(c, 1, 0) && cellContains(c, 1, 1)
&& cellContains(c, 1, 2) ||
                // Across the bottom
                cellContains(c, 2, 0) && cellContains(c, 2, 1)
  && cellContains(c, 2, 2) ||
                // down the left side
                cellContains(c, 0, 0) && cellContains(c, 1, 0)
&& cellContains(c, 2, 0) ||
                // down the middle
                cellContains(c, 0, 1) && cellContains(c, 1, 1)
&& cellContains(c, 2, 1) ||
                // down the right side
                cellContains(c, 0, 2) && cellContains(c, 1, 2)
&& cellContains(c, 2, 2) ||
                // diagonal
                cellContains(c, 0, 0) && cellContains(c, 1, 1)
&& cellContains(c, 2, 2) ||
                // other diagonal
                cellContains(c, 0, 2) && cellContains(c, 1, 1)
  && cellContains(c, 2, 0)
    }

}
```

The MainActivity Class

The `MainActivity` class implements the game as an Android application. It configures the User Interface using the layout file. The `onButtonClick()` handler is shared across all the buttons in the grid and is used to either set the button to the appropriate counter or to inform the user that the button is already in use. When the human user makes a move the `onButtonClick()` handler also checks to see if the game has finished (i.e. It looks to see if one player has won or not) or if the game is a tie. If it is it notifies the user as appropriate. If not then it causes the `ComputerPlayer` to make a move.

```
package com.jjh.android.tictactoe

import android.os.Bundle
import android.util.Log
import android.view.View
import android.widget.Button
import android.widget.Toast
import androidx.appcompat.app.AppCompatActivity

import kotlinx.android.synthetic.main.activity_main.*

class MainActivity : AppCompatActivity() {

    private var board = Board()

    fun onButtonClick(view: View) {
        val buttonClicked = view as Button
        val buttonText = buttonClicked.text.toString()
        if (buttonText != " ") {
            showMessage("Cell is already in use!")
        } else {
            val player = board.humanPlayer
            var finished = checkGameStatus(player,
buttonClicked)
            if (finished) {
                restartButton.isEnabled = true
            } else {
                val buttonSelected = makeComputerMove()
                finished =
checkGameStatus(board.computerPlayer,
                                         buttonSelected)
```

```
                            if (finished) {
                                restartButton.isEnabled = true
                            }
                    }
            }
    }

    // Resets the board and the UI
    fun onRestartButtonClick(v: View) {
        setupNewBoard()
        button0.text = " "
        button1.text = " "
        button2.text = " "
        button3.text = " "
        button4.text = " "
        button5.text = " "
        button6.text = " "
        button7.text = " "
        button8.text = " "
        restartButton.isEnabled = false
    }

    override fun onCreate(savedInstanceState: Bundle?) {
        super.onCreate(savedInstanceState)
        setContentView(R.layout.activity_main)
        // Disable restart
        restartButton.isEnabled = false
    }

    private fun setupNewBoard() {
        board = Board()
        if (board.firstPlayer.isAutomatedPlayer) {
            makeComputerMove()
        }
    }

    private fun makeComputerMove(): Button {
        val move = board.computerPlayerMakeMove()
        val tag = move.x.toString() + "," + move.y
```

```kotlin
        val buttonSelected =
                mainLayout.findViewWithTag<Button>(tag)
        buttonSelected.text = move.counter.toString()
        return buttonSelected
    }

    private fun checkGameStatus(player: Player,
                                buttonClicked: Button): Boolean
{

        val counter = player.counter
        val move = Move(getButtonRow(buttonClicked),
                        getButtonCol(buttonClicked),
                        counter)
        board.addMove(move)
        buttonClicked.text = counter.toString()
        return if (board.checkForWinner(player)) {
            showMessage("Well Done $player WON!!")
            true
        } else if (board.isFull) {
            showMessage("Well Done $player WON!!")
            true
        } else {
            false
        }
    }

    private fun showMessage(message: String) {
        Toast.makeText(this,
            message,
            Toast.LENGTH_SHORT).show()
    }

    private fun getButtonRow(button: Button): Int {
        val tagString = button.tag as String
        val rowString = tagString.substring(0, 1)
        return rowString.toInt()
    }

        private fun getButtonCol(button: Button): Int {
            val tagString = button.tag as String
            val colString = tagString.substring(2, 3)
            return colString.toInt()
        }


    }
```

The Screen Layout

The User Interface of the application is defined within the `activity_main.xml` file. It was created using the Android Studio Layout Editor as shown below:

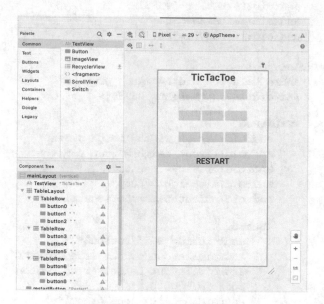

   The main part of the display is a `TableLayout` with multiple Table Rows. Each table row has three cells, in which each cell contains a button and each button has a tag associated with it. The tags represent the position of the button within the table. This information is used within the application to determine which button has been pressed by the user so that the backing model of the Board can be updated appropriately.

   The `activity_main.xml` file is given below:

```xml
<?xml version="1.0" encoding="utf-8"?>
<LinearLayout xmlns:android="http://schemas.android.com/apk/
res/android"
    xmlns:app="http://schemas.android.com/apk/res-auto"
    xmlns:tools="http://schemas.android.com/tools"
    android:id="@+id/mainLayout"
    android:layout_width="match_parent"
    android:layout_height="match_parent"
    android:orientation="vertical"
    tools:context=".MainActivity">
```

```
<TextView
    android:layout_width="match_parent"
    android:layout_height="wrap_content"
    android:gravity="center"
    android:text="TicTacToe"
    android:textColor="#3F51B5"
    android:textSize="36sp"
    android:textStyle="bold" />

<TableLayout
    android:layout_width="match_parent"
    android:layout_height="259dp">

    <TableRow
        android:layout_width="match_parent"
        android:layout_height="wrap_content"
        android:gravity="center"
        android:minHeight="80dp"
        android:orientation="horizontal">

        <Button
            android:id="@+id/button0"
            android:layout_width="wrap_content"
            android:layout_height="wrap_content"
            android:tag="0,0"
            android:onClick="onButtonClick"
            android:text=" " />

    <Button
        android:id="@+id/button1"
        android:layout_width="wrap_content"
        android:layout_height="wrap_content"
        android:tag="0,1"
        android:onClick="onButtonClick"
        android:text=" " />

        <Button
            android:id="@+id/button2"
            android:layout_width="wrap_content"
            android:layout_height="wrap_content"
            android:tag="0,2"
            android:onClick="onButtonClick"
            android:text=" " />
    </TableRow>
```

```
<TableRow
    android:layout_width="match_parent"
    android:layout_height="match_parent"
    android:gravity="center"
    android:minHeight="80dp"
    android:orientation="horizontal">

    <Button
        android:id="@+id/button3"
        android:layout_width="wrap_content"
        android:layout_height="wrap_content"
        android:tag="1,0"
        android:onClick="onButtonClick"
        android:text=" " />

    <Button
        android:id="@+id/button4"
        android:layout_width="wrap_content"
        android:layout_height="wrap_content"
        android:tag="1,1"
        android:onClick="onButtonClick"
        android:text=" " />

    <Button
        android:id="@+id/button5"
        android:layout_width="wrap_content"
        android:layout_height="wrap_content"
        android:tag="1,2"
        android:onClick="onButtonClick"
        android:text=" " />
</TableRow>

<TableRow
    android:layout_width="match_parent"
    android:layout_height="match_parent"
    android:gravity="center"
    android:minHeight="80dp"
    android:orientation="horizontal">
```

```
<Button
    android:id="@+id/button6"
    android:layout_width="wrap_content"
    android:layout_height="wrap_content"
    android:tag="2,0"
    android:onClick="onButtonClick"
    android:text=" " />

<Button
    android:id="@+id/button7"
    android:layout_width="wrap_content"
    android:layout_height="wrap_content"
    android:tag="2,1"
    android:onClick="onButtonClick"
    android:text=" " />

<Button
    android:id="@+id/button8"
    android:layout_width="wrap_content"
    android:layout_height="wrap_content"
    android:tag="2,2"
    android:onClick="onButtonClick"
    android:text=" " />
        </TableRow>
    </TableLayout>

<Button
    android:id="@+id/restartButton"
    android:layout_width="match_parent"
    android:layout_height="wrap_content"
    android:text="Restart"
    android:onClick="onRestartButtonClick"
    android:textSize="30dp" />

</LinearLayout>
```

Running the Game

When the game is run on an AVD emulator the display presented to the user is shown below:

The human user can click on any one of the buttons in the three by three grid. The application will register this and display the users counter on the button. The application will then generate a computer player move. The result is that the user will see a display similar to:

The user and the computer will continue to play the game until either a tie occurs or a player has won, at this point the Restart button will be enlaced:

Printed in the United States
by Baker & Taylor Publisher Services